Business Forecasting

Business Forecasting
Second Edition

Charles W. Gross
Illinois Institute of Technology

Robin T. Peterson
New Mexico State University

HOUGHTON MIFFLIN COMPANY BOSTON
Dallas Geneva, Illinois Hopewell, New Jersey Palo Alto London

Cover design by Jill Haber.

Printed in the U.S.A.

Library of Congress Catalog Card Number: 82-81109

ISBN: 0-395-31762-2

To Dorine and Marge

Contents

Preface

Forecasting is a topic of growing importance in business. Literature is full of indications that Western industrialized nations face a future of limited growth. Accordingly, successful business executives of the future will not only need the critical ability to manage well, but will also be required to interpret the future more accurately than ever before. This importance of forecasting is recognized by the Securities and Exchange Commission (SEC), which has ruled that forecasts may be filed along with audited financial statements. Sound interpretations of forecasts and the development of appropriate plans will be the mark of successful managers. Therefore, managers require a basic understanding of the forecasting process and an exposure to fundamental techniques.

The 1970s and early 1980s witnessed an increase in the importance of sales forecasting to business concerns. During this time, inflationary cost spirals weakened profits, which were further constricted as the recession held demand at a relatively low level and competition within this country and from abroad intensified. Finally, interest rate increases made inventory holdings expensive, augmenting the need for reliable sales forecasts.

This text is designed as an introduction to business forecasting for current and future managers. Our emphasis is on forecasting at the firm and industry level rather than aggregate economic forecasting. Historically, techniques useful to firms have been scattered throughout diverse literature as statistics, marketing research, management science, and economics. We have gathered these techniques into one volume. Further, we have substantially upgraded the material in the first edition in both sophistication and coverage in order to provide readers with a comprehensive set of methods that we have found useful in a wide spectrum of settings. Although the techniques are advanced, the discussion is oriented toward the user of forecasts, the manager, rather than the technician.

The text is written for upper-division courses. As prerequisites, we assume that readers have had previous exposure to introductory statistics, computer science, and high school algebra. In addition, prior exposure to introductory marketing, accounting, and management is suggested. This background is necessary in order to fully grasp each technique and to appreciate the role of the manager in the forecasting process.

For more advanced and more comprehensive courses, additional reference material is suggested. For such courses, we have found that assigning problems for computer solutions is beneficial. Familiarity with canned statistical packages and their use is thus obtained.

In addition to courses in forecasting as such, we suggest that this book be considered for more advanced courses in marketing strategy, marketing research, accounting, and managerial economics. Each of these areas increasingly depends on forecasting.

Our approach in *Business Forecasting* centers on two basic types of methodology. First, the major portion of the materials focuses on the direct approach to forecasting for a firm. Second, indirect analysis presents the splitting of aggregate economic forecasts down to industry and finally firm levels. Sources of aggregate forecasts are presented, but techniques used for overall economic forecasting are not extensively treated. Aggregate forecasts of the economy are more the subject matter of economics and econometrics, even though many of the techniques are the same.

Direct methods are covered thoroughly in this text through an analysis of judgmental, projection, and model building and simulation techniques. Judgmental methods recognize that experts, because of their knowledge and experience, often have valid "gut feelings" which should be considered when establishing forecasts. Judgmental methods emphasize the "qualitative" aspects of forecasting. A greater emphasis is placed on the "quantitative" aspects when using the projection and model building and simulation methods. The projection methods employ techniques of trend analysis, correlation, regression, time series, and surveys. Model building and simulation are among the more exotic of the quantitative methods. This discussion is broken down into models based on learned behavior and simulation of the business throughput system with both hard and partially soft data. The reader is cautioned that the distinction by categories should not be considered fixed. Most techniques are equally applicable to both direct and indirect methods of forecasting.

Throughout the discussion of each technique, hypothetical and real examples are used to set the stage for applications of technique. Emphasis is placed on the essential components of each technique and their relative advantages and disadvantages. We also emphasize the role of forecasting in the overall planning process and the need to use sound judgment throughout the forecasting function.

We strongly recommend that the questions and problems provided at the end of each chapter be used as learning tools. Reading the text provides the background for a solid knowledge of forecasting, but practical usage of the subject matter is also required to convert the background into a foundation of knowdedge and ability. Selected references are provided at the end of each chapter for further study of specific techniques.

Numerous people have helped in preparing this text. The dedicated efforts of all those who have given advisory, editorial, and typing support is greatly appreciated. We are especially indebted to reviewers at other universities who spent many hours examining these materials and offering useful suggestions: Professors Cedric V. Fricke (University of Michigan at Dearborne); Robert C. Hutchins (California State University—San Diego); Thomas M. Kelly (Baylor University); Howard J. McBride (University of Cincinnati); and M. J. Riley (Kansas State University), who reviewed the first edition; and Dr. Milton H. Grannatt, 3rd (L.E.X. Service Incorporated) and Professors Algin B. King (Christopher Newport College) and Anthony Petto (DePaul University), who reviewed the second edition. We also greatly appreciate the assistance given us by users of the first edition: Dr. Grannatt and Professor King, and also Professors Philip Cateora (University of Colorado); Patrick Decker (Arizona State University); Kenneth Dunning (University of Akron); Marcel Fulop (Kean College); Robert C. Hutchins (California State University); Thomas Kelly (Hankamer School of Business); and Barbara Price (Wayne State University). We are grateful to the Literary Executor of the late Sir Ronald A. Fisher, F.R.S., to Dr. Frank Yates, F.R.S., and to Longman Group Ltd., London, for permission to reprint the Table of Critical Values of *t* from their book *Statistical Tables for Biological, Agricultural and Medical Research* (6th edition, 1974).

We remain even more indebted to our wives, Dorine and Marge. To our fortune and delight, both were unable to forecast what they were getting into.

C.W.G.

R.T.P.

Business Forecasting

Chapter 1
Introduction to Forecasting

INTRODUCTION

During the decade of the 1970s and into the 1980s, business executives have been confronted with continual change in all facets of the economic, cultural, and physical environments. Corporate bankruptcy filings reached a record of 39,800 in fiscal year 1981.[1] The rule of thumb in new product development is that eight out of ten new product attempts fail.[2] All indications are that these patterns will continue and may even accelerate. This has led to efforts to find means of anticipating and preparing for future changes. One means of preparation is forecasting—the subject of this book.

This chapter provides an introduction to forecasting. It defines the field, indicates what variables are forecast, discusses the need for forecasting, the parties that are involved in this function, types of forecasts, the nature of the forecasting function, and information systems.

WHAT IS FORECASTING?

"Forecasting is an attempt to foresee the future by examining the past."[3] It consists of generating unbiased estimates of the future magnitude of some variable, such as sales, on the basis of past and present knowledge and experience. Indeed, the essence of forecasting is estimating future events according to past patterns and applying judgment to projections of those patterns. Mere extensions of past sales tendencies into the future do not constitute forecasting. Projections are mechanical functions; forecasts require judgment.

Most estimates obtained in quality forecasting are derived in an objective and systematic fashion and do not depend solely on subjective

---

1. "Economic Diary," *Business Week*, November 3, 1980, p. 23.
2. "New Product Failures: Not Just a Marketing Problem," *Business*, 29 (September–October 1979), 2.
3. Wroe Alderson and Paul E. Green, *Planning and Problem Solving in Marketing* (Homewood, Ill.: Richard D. Irwin, 1964), p. 420.

1

guesses and hunches of the analyst. An analyst carefully selects a fore-casting tool, such as an equation, and applies it to quantitative data. The result is a forecast.

For example, the Andax Corporation prepares annual forecasts of sales of its Model 23 portable electronic calculator. Table 1.1 shows sales for the past five years.

A glance at the past sales data indicates that this variable behaves in a linear fashion, that is, it is best described graphically by a straight line. Hence, the analyst probably would conclude that this pattern will hold for the future (assuming that experience and familiarity with the sale of calculators do not indicate otherwise) and would forecast 1983 sales at a level of $500,000.

The Andax case exemplifies the forecasting process—applying an analytic tool to quantitative data. Actual applications, of course, are more complex than the situation typified by Andax. The choice of the analytic tool, the mathematical computations, and the number of variables are usually much more complicated. However, the principles demonstrated by such simple examples still apply to complex situations.

Forecasts are not to be confused with guesses. Guesses are estimates of future happenings, but they are not necessarily unbiased or objec-tively calculated. Through intuition, some self-styled prophets envision devastating earthquakes in San Francisco or the imminent demise of humanity through various natural catastrophes. In business, executives often predict that a union will strike or that competitors will not retaliate when the firm introduces a new product. Many of these opinions are based on guesses or hunches that do not require objective methods of prediction and formulation. Thus, they can reflect an exec-utive's lack of knowledge or inaccurate frames of reference regarding the behavior of the variables estimated. These factors, in turn, are not generally conducive to accurate and reliable forecasts.

In the business world, forecasting is not devoid of managerial judg-ment, although it is perhaps more an art than a science. Judgment is needed in selecting or constructing a particular forecasting tool. The analysts state their assumptions in explicit form. The executive, in turn,

Table 1.1 Sales of Model 23 Calculators

Year	Sales (in Thousands of Dollars)
1978	250
1979	300
1980	350
1981	400
1982	450

may question the assumptions or may propose new ones. Judgment is also required in interpreting the results of mathematical computations. Rarely do executives accept at face value forecasts that are the result of mathematical manipulations alone. Rather, they examine these variables and subject them to such judgmental tests as, "Is this forecast really reasonable in light of past experiences with customers and competitors?" or, "Now that we know that our closest rival probably will introduce a new product, is this forecast still valid?" The questioning of assumptions, however, does not disqualify the approach from being an objective forecasting method. Instead, this questioning strengthens the objectivity by providing the formal means of stating and examining problem parameters.

WHICH VARIABLES ARE ESTIMATED?

Business managers, academics, government employees, and others forecast a wide variety of variables, including income, employment, production, family sizes, crime rates, costs of living, wage levels, sales, and a host of others. Virtually every characteristic for which historical data are available is projected into the future in order to anticipate events. What is significant to one firm may be of no interest to others. Executives at the Chrysler Corporation are deeply concerned with projections of sales, whereas those at the Bank of Chicago focus on expected future deposit variables like anticipated stock levels, and stock brokers fix their attention on prices and dividend rates.

This book stresses sales forecasting, because this function is vital to executives and exerts a strong influence on the profitability of business enterprises. However, the techniques discussed are applicable also to forecasting other variables, such as employment, stock yields, and productivity. We examine the *magnitude* of the variable in question rather than the variables themselves. The latter are usually generated from experience and familiarity with the specific forecasting problem.

FORECASTING'S ROLE IN PLANNING

"Forecasting plays an important role in every major functional area of business management."[4] It is necessary because if change occurs when not anticipated, the results can be disastrous. An enterprise prepares for change by planning, which, in turn, requires making the forecasts, establishing goals based on the forecasts, and determining how these goals are to be reached. In short, forecasting is an integral part of the

4. Spyros Makridakis and Steven C. Wheelwright, "Forecasting: Issues and Challenges for Marketing Management," *Journal of Marketing*, 41 (October 1977), 24.

planning process. Further, forecasts directly relate to corporate
strategies. A forecast of declining sales, for instance, prompted executives of the Best Products Company to cut back expansion plans for
their catalog showrooms to nine units per year in 1981.[5]

The experience of the Mesa Corporation, a contract construction firm
in the American Southwest, further typifies this process. The firm's
sales forecast for the oncoming year has been pessimistic, suggesting a
10% decline from the current year. Management has reviewed these data
and has decided that two courses of action are possible.

1. Prepare for the expected decline in sales. This involves adjusting the
    concern's budgets—those involving sales, cash, sales expense, adver-
    tising and promotion, production, cost of goods sold, administrative
    expense, balance sheet, and sources and uses of funds—to reflect the
    expected decline in sales. The precise form of reacting to the sales
    forecast would depend on the objectives, philosophies, and resources
    of the managers involved. Some, for instance, might call for a 10%
    reduction in all budgets. Others could favor large reductions in
    particular budgets, such as administrative expense and cost of goods
    sold, and smaller decreases in others.
2. Attempt to offset the expected decline in sales. This course of action
    would be taken should management decide that such a reduction in
    revenue is unacceptable and should be prevented through increased
    advertising, more forceful personal selling, or decreases in prices. In
    this case, management has decided that the outcome of existing
    plans is unacceptable, thus calling for new plans. The formulation of
    new plans, of course, necessitates the construction of a new sales
    forecast.

Figure 1.1 depicts the series of steps required for each course of
action. In many organizations, more than two alternatives are available,
of course. Mesa, however, was able to reduce the options to two.

The discussion to this point illustrates an important concept that the
student of forecasting frequently does not comprehend: the forecast
can be prepared only after the marketing strategies of the firm are
known. Some students develop the impression that the reverse is true,
and that the marketing department plans its upcoming strategies after
reviewing the sales forecast. This approach cannot be realistic, because
the expected future level of sales depends on the marketing strategy.
Changes such as price decreases and alterations in the advertising budget
can be expected to influence sales and, as a corollary, should be
considered by the sales forecaster. Should the forecaster neglect to take
account of such variables, the analysis can be very unrealistic.

5. "No Christmas Cheer for Catalog Showrooms," *Business Week*, November 24,
    1980, p. 137

Figure 1.1 Alternative Reactions to Expected Sales Decline

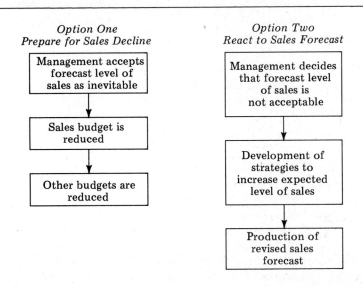

In practice, the sales forecast serves as a planning tool in all departments within the enterprise. Almost all internal forecasting and budgeting begin with the sales forecast. Executives study the forecast to determine the size of the labor force, advertising expenditure levels, the magnitude of production runs, working capital needs, and many other variables. The effect of considering expected levels of sales in making such decisions is to reduce uncertainty and lower costs.

In some concerns, forecasting is used in a manner that tends to reduce the need for planning. One source indicates that:

> In most companies, forecasting is undertaken first and may be carried to a fairly advanced stage before formal planning procedures are adopted. For some period in the history of a firm, forecasting may serve as a partial substitute for central planning. A sales goal based on the forecast is accepted as feasible by the various divisions or operating units of the company. Each unit is then expected to conform its individual activities in such a way as to make the maximum contribution to the stated goals.[6]

To use the forecast as a substitute for planning is, of course, a dangerous process. It removes much of the resourcefulness, vitality, and ingenuity from managerial decision making and forces the firm into a

6. Alderson and Green, *Planning and Problem Solving*, p. 420.

position where management tends to react to its environment instead of developing creative strategies. The optimum procedure is to consider planning and forecasting as complementary and not to use one as a substitute for the other. The actions of Consolidated Freightways Corporation in 1980 provide an example of this complementary use process. The firm produced a very optimistic five-year sales forecast and, as a result, decided to spend $136 million in capital investments as well as $32.5 million in expanding freight terminals.[7]

Thus far, forecasts have been emphasized as adjuncts to planning. They are also useful for the development of control mechanisms by management.[8] The control process requires formulating standards or criteria of performance and comparing actual performance with these criteria. For instance, supervisors in the production department may be assigned weekly or monthly output quotas (criteria), and their actual output compared to the quota level on a periodic basis. In cases where actual output falls significantly below the quota, management is informed and is in a position to act; for example, it can search for the causes of the below-standard performance.

Budgets are used as control mechanisms. Each budget sets forth a pattern of expected receipts and disbursements over a period of time, such as a year. The sales forecast, in turn, forms the base for all budgets used by the concern. In the sales budget, expected sales by product, territory, type of customer, or some other classification are listed. Should sales of a given product fall short of projected sales, management is informed that a problem exists and is in a position to determine why the disparity between actual and estimated performance took place. Similarly, the cash budget sets forth planned levels of cash receipts and expenditures. Comparison of budget with actual receipts and expenditures enables management to assess the cash-flow performance of the company and to detect problem areas before they become severe.

WHO FORECASTS?

Virtually all types of enterprises and institutions—business, governmental, religious, and social—engage in forecasting of some kind. Basically, their goal is to improve planning and control. Churches attempt to predict impending revenues from contributions of members in order to permit the construction of reasonable budget estimates. School administrators use enrollment forecasts to determine faculty

7. Michael Kolbenschlag, "Recession Be Damned," *Forbes*, April 28, 1980, pp. 34–40.
8. See, for example, James M. Halbert and Norman E. Troy, "A Strategic Framework for Marketing Control," *Journal of Marketing*, 41 (April 1977), 12–14.

size, supplies, and classroom requirements. Table 1.2 is an example of a master budget used by some schools, churches, and nonprofit institutions. It sets forth past-year revenues and expenditures and current-year projected revenues, budget figures, and expenditures to date. This budget provides administrators with a running account of the status of each item and permits remedial action where required, such as correcting the current year's deficit.

A budget of this type can be of considerable value to administrators. The budgeted revenue for the year is the forecast magnitude, which in turn is the basis for developing the budgeted expenditures in the various categories. In practice, the master budget is likely to embody more expense categories than are presented in the hypothetical case depicted in Table 1.2.

The monthly "last year," "this year," and "budgeted" expense classifications enable management to maintain control over each cost factor. In the example, total costs have advanced beyond last-year and budgeted levels, indicating the need for some form of action to avoid a continuing deficit. Both salaries and utilities are higher than in the preceding year. Many of the expense items are at an acceptable level, but repairs are responsible for the bulk of the excess of actual over expected costs, and should be brought in line with budgeted figures. The excessive repair expenses may require that other budget items be reduced in the future in order that the organization might avoid using up reserves or, if none exists, remain solvent.

In addition to nonprofit and government institutions, most business firms engage in some form of forecasting; those who do not are rare. Enterprises differ in placement of emphasis and methodologies employed, but those who do not forecast are uncommon. Generally, firms in industries where levels of demand, share of market, and prices are subject to abrupt and considerable variation place more emphasis on forecasting. For example, the cigarette industry experiences all three of these fluctuations. Failure to react in a timely manner could cause any firm to experience a considerable loss, hence the importance of well-conceived forecasting tools.

ORGANIZATION OF THE FORECASTING FUNCTION

Within an enterprise the forecasting function may be performed by any one of a number of departments. Some firms, especially those that are large and are in volatile industries, have a separate forecasting department. The head of this unit may report to the president, to an assistant, to a vice president, or to a departmental-level executive in marketing, finance, or production.

Usually, however, no department is designed exclusively for forecasting. Instead, this function may be the responsibility of marketing,

Table 1.2 Monthly Master Budget, Nonprofit Organization

	At This Date Last Year		At This Date This Year		Total Budget for the Year	
	Actual	Budgeted	Actual	Budgeted	Last Year	This Year
Revenue	$57,100	$60,200	$82,800	$72,100	$197,200	$219,400
Expenses						
Salaries	$41,400	$43,600	$48,500	$47,500	$142,000	$158,000
Debt retirement	12,700	12,700	12,700	12,700	50,800	50,800
Utilities	500	550	800	700	1,750	2,600
Repairs	900	1,000	19,500	9,200	1,300	6,400
Insurance	500	500	900	900	650	800
Tax	300	320	500	500	700	800
Total	56,300	58,670	82,900	71,500	197,200	219,400
Surplus/(deficit)	$800	$1,530	($100)	$600	$0	$0

marketing planning, marketing research, finance, production, corporate planning, or management information systems. The assignment of this responsibility is primarily a function of organizational emphasis on forecasting and on the resources of the various departments. Thus, in firms where the marketing department uses sales forecasts extensively, and where this unit possesses the needed personnel and data processing facilities, forecasting is likely to be assigned to that unit. Also, several departments may engage in the forecasting of those variables central to their operations.

Firms differ in the degree to which the forecasting function is centralized. These differences reflect the needs of the enterprises. Centralization has both strong advantages and disadvantages. In general, centralization avoids duplication of facilities and personnel, permits the use of highly qualified specialists, promotes coordination between forecasts of different product groups, territories, and classes of customers, and may be less costly and time-consuming than if separate forecasts are prepared by management of separate divisions, territories, or product lines. On the other hand, decentralized analysis may be more realistic when the forecasters are specialists in analyzing sales and understanding the particular elements of the firm's operation, or are intimately familiar with the environmental factors influencing sales. Very large firms with separate customer groupings, geographic territories, and product groups are most likely to decentralize the functions. Usually, centralized forecasting is the best arrangement for most firms.

DIMENSIONS OF FORECASTS

Forecasts vary according to whether they apply to a large aggregate (such as the economy) or to a component of this aggregate (such as an individual company). They differ according to the future time span they encompass, the products considered, means of measurement, consumer categories, and area. This section discusses some of these differences.

Macro and Micro

Some forecasts are *macro* in nature, in that they apply to some aggregate measure, such as the output of an entire economy, region, or industry. Examples are estimates of gross national product, national income, sales of the food-processing industry, and sales of microwave ovens.

Other forecasts are *micro* in nature. They are situationally defined and, as such, relate to only one firm. Thus, the projection of calculator sales of the Andax Corporation is a micro forecast.

This book emphasizes micro forecasts, since its intent is to serve prospective and current business executives. This does not mean that macro forecasts are of little importance to an organization; indeed, they are needed for using many of the micro methods. To a large degree, however, macro forecasts are made and distributed to the public by a variety of organizations (governments, universities, foundations, trade associations, and financial institutions). Many of these forecasts are the results of applied econometrics, which is an area of economics that practices the application of mathematical techniques to economic theory. Given the widespread availability of macro forecasts, the prime forecasting skills needed by business executives are in the micro realm.

Within the micro category, further subdivisions can be made, depending on the budgeting needs of the enterprise. Sales forecasts may be constructed for the company as a whole, for particular products or groups of products, for specific geographic regions or sales territories, for particular customers, or for some combination of these. Concerns that sell a wide variety of products or brands often find that the cost and effort required to forecast sales of each would be unduly burdensome. An alternative is to group together products and brands with similar demand characteristics (such as French fries and hamburgers for a franchisor like Burger King or McDonald's) and to prepare forecasts of their combined sales.

Budgets

Each enterprise has a hierarchy of forecasts, and there is usually a corresponding budget for each level, which is then used as a control device. Normally, all such budgets emanate from the sales forecast. This section describes, in brief, the format and the use of the various budgets that are common in most organizations.

The Sales Budget

One of the outcomes of the sales forecast is a sales budget. This specifies expected sales, sometimes by geographic area, channel of distribution, product group, and buyer group. Unit volume and price data may be included. Table 1.3 is an example of a relatively uncomplicated sales budget. Obviously, the budget becomes more complicated as the number of products, buyer groups, and other subdivisions increases.

Table 1.3 Hypothetical Annual Sales Budget

Product	Unit Forecast	Price	Sales Forecast ($000,000)
Inexpensive calculator	100,000	30	3
Expensive calculator	20,000	300	6
			9

Table 1.4 Hypothetical Annual Production Budget

	Products (in Units)	
	Inexpensive	Expensive
Sales volume forecast	100,000	20,000
Planned end-of-period finished-goods inventory	4,500	1,000
Requirement totals	104,500	21,000
Minus beginning-of-period finished-goods inventory	1,000	400
Production requirements	103,500	20,600

The Production Budget

Once the sales budget has been prepared, the production budget can be generated. Its function is to indicate the number of units that must be produced during the time period under consideration to meet forecast sales needs. Inventory policies of the firm have an impact on production. The latter increases as a result of planned end-of-period finished-goods inventory and decreases as a result of beginning-of-period finished-goods inventory. Table 1.4 illustrates the format of the production budget, using the calculations of Table 1.3. From the production budget, the manager prepares the direct-labor budget and the direct-material budget.

The Direct-Material Budget

The direct-material budget indicates the number and cost of the direct materials needed to fulfill expected production requirements. Some or all of the direct materials used may be produced by the firm, or they may be purchased from suppliers. The latter case is assumed here. Basically, direct-material needs are a function of planned end-of-period inventory, production requirements, beginning-of-period inventory, and cost per unit. Table 1.5 illustrates this budget.

The Direct-Labor Budget

Like the direct-material budget, the direct-labor budget is based on levels of output set forth in the production budget. In addition, the direct-labor budget is influenced by wage scales and by the manufacturing process, as reflected in the number of labor hours needed for each unit of finished product. The output of the direct-labor budget is a statement of the total costs expected for labor in producing each product as well as total direct-labor costs. Other labor costs, those that cannot be assigned to particular products, appear in the factory-overhead budget. These are termed *indirect-labor costs*. Table 1.6 illustrates a direct-labor budget.

Table 1.5 Hypothetical Annual Direct-Material Budget

	Material X	Material Y
Planned end-of-period direct-material inventory (in units)	2,000	3,000
Production needs[a]	30,000	40,000
Total requirements	32,000	43,000
Minus beginning-of-period direct-material inventory (in units)	2,000	2,000
Number of units to purchase or produce	30,000	41,000
Cost per unit	$1.20	$4.00
Total cost	$36,000	$164,000

[a] The production needs are the direct materials required to produce both products. These are determined by multiplying the production requirements of each product (from Table 1.4) by the number of units of each material needed to generate a finished product.

Table 1.6 Hypothetical Annual Direct-Labor Budget

	Production Requirements	Direct-Labor Hours per Unit of Finished Goods	Total Hours	Total Budget at $3 per Hour
Inexpensive product (units)	103,500	7	724,500	$2,173,500
Expensive product (units)	20,600	20	412,000	$1,236,000

The Factory-Overhead Budget

Another useful document is the factory-overhead budget (see Table 1.7). The expenses listed here are based on the level of factory capacity use dictated by the production requirements (Table 1.4). Some expenses, such as supplies, can be expected to increase as production levels increase. Others, such as depreciation, are not affected by changes in the level of production. The net output of the factory-overhead budget is an accounting of indirect costs. These are expenses that cannot be assigned to particular products.

The Cost-of-Goods-Sold Budget

A frequently employed tool is the cost-of-goods-sold budget (see Table 1.8). It is based primarily on data appearing in previously mentioned budgets, and it details anticipated costs of units to be sold as well as beginning and ending inventories.

The Sales and Administration Budget

Business concerns differ as to the specific way in which they budget such functions as selling and advertising. In many cases, individual budgets are prepared for each function. Another practice is to merge selling and advertising costs with others, such as administration, into composite budgets. That practice is exemplified in Table 1.9.

Table 1.7 Hypothetical Annual Factory-Overhead Budget

Depreciation	$15,000
Taxes	2,000
Insurance	500
Maintenance	3,000
Supplies	20,000
Indirect labor	14,000
Power	9,000
Total budget	$63,500

Table 1.8 Hypothetical Annual Cost-of-Goods-Sold Budget (Total)

Direct material (Table 1.5)	$ 200,000
Direct labor (from Table 1.6)	3,409,500
Factory overhead (from Table 1.7)	63,500
Total production costs	$3,673,000
Plus finished-goods inventory, beginning of period (costs per unit of inventory determined by accounting department)	100,000
	$3,773,000
Minus finished-goods inventory, end of period (costs per unit of inventory determined by accounting department)	320,000
Cost of goods sold	$3,453,000

Table 1.9 Hypothetical Annual Sales and Administrative-Expense Budget (Total)

Advertising	$ 30,000	
Sales force compensation	200,000	
Travel	60,000	
Sales promotion	10,000	
Total promotion costs		$300,000
Executive compensation	$200,000	
Clerical compensation	80,000	
Supplies	10,000	
Miscellaneous	5,000	
Total administrative expenses		295,000
Total promotion and administrative expenses		$595,000

The Budgeted Profit-and-Loss Statement

At this point, the organization is in a position to construct a budgeted profit-and-loss statement. This indicates the expected profitability of the firm in the upcoming year. Table 1.10 illustrates the process.

Table 1.10 Hypothetical Annual Budgeted Profit-and-Loss Statement (Total)

Sales (from sales budget)	$9,000,000	
Cost of goods sold (from cost-of goods-sold budget)	3,453,000	
Gross margin		$5,547,000
Sales and administrative expense (from sales and administrative-expense budget)	595,000	
Interest expense (given)	30,000	
Administrative expenses		625,000
Net income before income tax		4,922,000
Income tax (assumed)		1,300,000
Net income after income tax		$3,622,000

Other Budgets

Many firms prepare cash budgets showing the impact on cash position of the various activities given in Tables 1.3–1.10. The cash budget is useful to management in predicting possible shortages of funds and idle funds. It specifies the beginning-of-period cash balance, expected cash disbursements, expected financing requirements, and expected end-of-period cash balance.

It is common for enterprises to prepare budgeted balance sheets. These indicate expected levels of assets, liability, and capital items in light of the developments predicted by the other budgets. From the budgeted balance sheet, management visualizes the probable status of each account at the end of the period under consideration.

So far we have emphasized company-wide budgeting. That is, each of the budgets described encompassed the entire firm, including its various divisions, departments, offices, branches, and other subdivisions. It is important to recognize, however, that firms often develop budgets for their individual subdivisions. A common process is to develop the individual budgets and then sum them into composite company-wide budgets (buildup method). Another approach is to generate the composite budgets first and then allocate these to individual subdivisions (breakdown method). Both methods require considerable skill and diligence, but they produce documents that are essential for effective management of the total company and its subdivisions.

This section has emphasized budgets—basic tools for planning and controlling the activities of the enterprise. The process involves developing a sales forecast and, based on its magnitude, generating those budgets needed by the particular firm. Once developed, this system provides operating managers with a means of coordinating their efforts with other managers, of operating in accordance with the overall company plan, and of monitoring actual performance and comparing it to budget objectives. The role of forecasting in relation to budgeting (and planning) is summarized in Figure 1.2.

Figure 1.2 Summary of the Relation of Forecasting Among Budgets

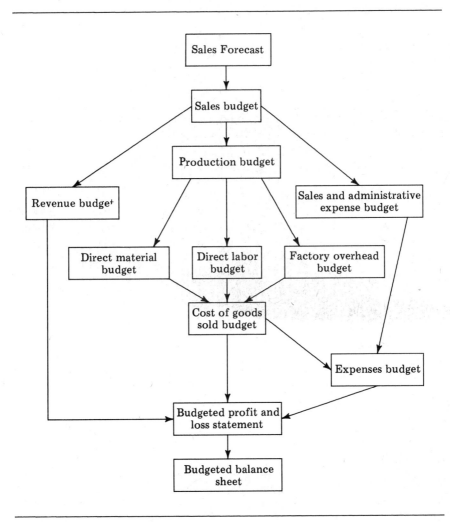

Long- and Short-Run Forecasts and Decision Making

Some forecasts cover only the immediate future, such as one month or one year. These are called *short-run* forecasts and normally cover time periods not exceeding five years. They often refer to periods of one year or less. Those that do exceed five years are termed *long-run* forecasts.

As logic would suggest, short-run forecasts are employed to aid decisions that must be made in the near future, such as determining needed levels of inventory, numbers of employees to be hired, working capital to be acquired, and supplies to be secured. These decisions arise frequently and are based on a series of short-run forecasts.

Conversely, in decision-making situations where the impact of the chosen alternative will influence the financial position of the firm over a period of years, long-run forecasts are required. Thus, management needs these estimates to resolve such questions as whether or not to construct a new plant, which foreign markets to enter, and whether or not to modernize production facilities. These are major decisions, and their impact over the long run must be estimated so that management might select the most profitable alternative.

Consider a case where the management of a company is considering the introduction of one of two proposed new products (A and B). Forecast sales for the two are as follows:

Year	Product A	Product B
1	$117,400	$ 89,200
2	174,800	102,900
3	198,700	120,500
4	208,800	150,900
5	227,200	179,500
6		204,400
7		248,100
Totals	$926,900	$1,095,500

Note that the product life cycle for product A is only five years, whereas that for product B is seven years. The total sales for the second product are expected to be larger. A valid comparison of the two, however, must allow for the value of money at various time periods—we cannot conclude that product B is superior just because it is expected to produce the larger volume of total sales. Following is a calculation of the present value of these sales—a calculation that reflects the time value of money. (A 15% interest rate is assumed.)

	Discount Rate*	Product A		Product B	
Year		Forecast Sales	Discounted Sales	Forecast Sales	Discounted Sales
1	0.8696	$117,400	$102,091	$ 89,200	$ 77,568
2	0.7561	174,800	132,690	102,900	77,803
3	0.6575	198,700	130,645	120,500	79,229
4	0.5718	208,800	119,392	150,900	86,285
5	0.4972	227,200	112,964	179,500	89,247
6	0.4323			204,400	88,362
7	0.3759			248,100	93,261
Total discounted sales			$597,782		$591,755

*Source: James E. Howell and Daniel Teichroew, *Mathematical Analysis for Business Decisions* (Homewood, Ill.: Richard D. Irwin, 1971), p. 392.

The calculations reveal that, when the present value is considered, product A is expected to contribute more to revenues than is product B. This example suggests how operating executives can use forecasting to enhance their decision making.

Most concerns need both long- and short-run forecasts, because the two types provide input for different kinds of decisions. Short-run estimates are particularly needed in volatile industries, where levels of sales change suddenly and in considerable magnitude; in extremely competitive industries, where management must make frequent strategy changes in response to the actions of rivals; and in industries with high variable costs. Examples of industries having these characteristics are home detergents, toys, cosmetics, and packaged foods. Failure on the part of firms in these sectors to act on the basis of well-formulated forecasts can lead to very damaging losses in share of market. On the other hand, long-run forecasts are needed by firms contemplating major actions, such as additions to plant capacity, which will have a long-run impact on the firm. In addition, they are needed by those with high fixed costs, which may impose financial strain should facilities be operated substantially below capacity. Examples are the aerospace and machine-tool sectors.

OTHER FORECASTING CONSIDERATIONS

Micro forecasts are geared toward estimating sales. This may more accurately be accomplished by taking into consideration product homogeneity, means of measurement, type of buyer, and geographic boundaries.

Products

Some forecasts are prepared for individual products. An industrial goods manufacturer headquartered in a Rocky Mountain state, for instance, prepares separate estimates for phosphate fertilizer and processed potatoes. This is logical, since the products' historical sales patterns have not been closely correlated, and this pattern is expected to continue in the future. There is no strong reason for believing that sales fluctuations for the two products will be similar, since the products are purchased by different customers, and the uses of the two are dissimilar.

Conversely, there are cases in which forecasts for groups of products are logical. When the manufacturer produces a large variety of items, the cost and time required to prepare separate forecasts for each one may be prohibitive. Under these circumstances, it is logical to group individual products into categories that are relatively homogeneous with respect to demand patterns. Thus, a producer of shoes for adults might prepare separate forecasts for (1) men's casual wear, (2) men's dress wear, (3) women's working shoes, and (4) women's dress wear. If this categorization does not produce sufficiently detailed information needed for managerial decision making, further subcategorization can be provided, of course. This, however, increases the costs of the forecasting process. Thus, a decision must be made as to the degree of detail that managers require and the extent to which this detail provides information that justifies the additional forecasting costs incurred.

Units or Dollar Volume?

The analyst may choose to prepare estimates of future dollar sales volume, unit sales volume, or a combination of these. Thus, a producer of electronic hand calculators may produce estimates of next year's expected sales at a level of $12,000,000 or 120,000 units (where the unit price is $100). Unit measures, of course, are likely to be confusing where the product mix is not homogeneous. If, for instance, the calculator producer expects to sell 100,000 inexpensive calculators at $30 each, and 20,000 higher-quality items at $300 each, a volume measure of 120,000 distorts the importance of the higher-priced line. In this case a dollar forecast of $9,000,000 ($3,000,000 low-priced and $6,000,000 high-priced) is appropriate. The major reason for using unit forecasts is that, when the product mix is homogeneous, the estimates are not affected by inflation and deflation. On the other hand, dollar measures can be adjusted for expected variations in the buying power of the dollar through the application of price change estimates, thus achieving the same end. If, for instance, the sales forecast is $9,000,000, and the purchasing power of the dollar is expected to decline by 7%, an adjusted sales forecast of $8,370,000 ($9,000,000 minus $630,000) can be used to measure true changes in sales volume from one year to the next. However, many executives prefer unit measures to adjusted-sales-volume measures, as the latter seems to be a rather artificial gauge of change.

Buyer Categories

Sales forecasts can be prepared either for specific categories of buyers or for the entire market. In some firms, management desires estimates for separate buyer categories. This is especially likely to be the case where the firm is pursuing a market segmentation policy. Here distinctive marketing programs are designed for the various classes of buyers to whom the enterprise is attempting to appeal.

The Control Data Corporation, for instance, focuses its computer sales on two segments: large and small firms. A vitamin manufacturer might detect two important market segments: those who want an inexpensive multiple vitamin that covers family nutritional needs and those who want tablets containing particular vitamins to prevent or correct health problems. Assuming research indicates that those in the first segment tend to purchase vitamins in supermarkets and those in the second segment in pharmacies, it then appears logical for the company to divide the market by type of retail outlet and to design separate products, promotion materials, distribution strategies, and pricing schemes for the two categories of outlets.

In line with market segmentation is a subdivision of sales forecast estimates by type of retail outlet. This enables management to develop strategies and tactics needed in light of expected sales in each buyer group. If, for instance, large sales increases to supermarkets are anticipated, management may wish to make arrangements for transportation and warehousing in advance so that undesirable effects, such as out-of-stocks, do not take place at a later date. Conversely, if sales in supermarkets are expected to decline radically, management may choose to investigate the possibility of dropping these outlets.

Area

Finally, sales forecasts for different geographic regions may be developed by firms, such as Hilton Hotels, Inc., who serve numerous states and countries. In addition to an overall estimate, management sometimes requests forecasts by country, state, county, city, market area, or some other designation. This enables management to generate plans and policies attuned to the needs of each area. If, for instance, substantial sales increases are expected in a particular region, steps can be taken to anticipate this, such as arranging for public warehousing and contacting transportation carriers in the region.

THE NATURE OF FORECASTING

This section sets forth the essence of the forecasting process. The steps described are normally accomplished in the order listed, although some overlap invariably occurs. Basically, forecasting involves

1. Determining the objective
2. Developing the model
3. Testing the model
4. Applying the model
5. Revising and evaluating the forecast
6. Considering the constraints

Determining the Objective

know these 9/8/89

The first stage consists of determining the kind of estimate desired. This objective, in turn, depends on the information needs of managers. The analyst confers with decision makers to learn just what their needs are, and to determine

1. What variables are to be estimated
2. Who will use the forecasts
3. The purposes for which they will be used
4. Whether long- or short-run estimates are desired
5. Desired accuracy of the estimates
6. When the estimates are needed
7. Desired forecast subdivisions, such as buyer groups, product groups, or geographical areas

Information needs vary from one company to another or, within the same company, from one time period to another. A firm with very stringent budgetary controls, for instance, may require highly accurate sales forecasts. On the other hand, an enterprise that is using forecasts to determine what new product to introduce may be content with only rough estimates of anticipated sales of several new-product additions.

Developing the Model

Once objectives have been specified, the analyst is in a position to develop a model. This consists of a simplified representation of the system under study. In forecasting, the model is an analytic framework which, when supplied with input data, produces estimates of future sales (or whatever variable is to be forecast). Analysts attempt to choose a model that realistically describes the behavior of the variable under consideration. Thus, if they are attempting to forecast sales, and the latter is expected to behave in a linear fashion, they might choose the model of sales $= A + BX$, where X represents units of time, and A and B are parameters describing the position and slope of the line on a graph.

The choice of an appropriate model is crucial. Each model has assumptions that must be met as a prerequisite to its use. The validity and reliability of estimates are highly dependent on the model employed.

Testing the Model

Before it is applied, the model usually is tested to determine its expected accuracy, validity, and reliability. This frequently involves applying it to historical data and preparing estimates for the current or recent years for which actual data are available. The worth of the model is determined by the degree to which its estimates diverge from actual figures. Other means of testing the model are to compare its output with those of other models and to scrutinize it from the standpoint of whether or not it has logical predictive power (face validity).

Applying the Model

After testing, the analysts apply the model. In this phase they introduce historical data to the model to produce a forecast. In the case of the sales = $A + BX$ model, they apply mathematical techniques (discussed in subsequent chapters) in order to produce the A and B statistics. Thus, they might, after performing the necessary computations, arrive at the formula, sales = \$500,000 + \$200X. The symbol X, in this case, refers to the year in question. If it is the thirtieth year (year one is the first year for which historical data are available), the predicted level of sales is \$506,000 [\$500,000 + \$200(30)].

Revision and Evaluation

Forecasts, once made, are not to be treated as sacred or even static in nature. Rather, they should often be revised and evaluated. Revision consists of altering a forecast in light of changes taking place within the firm or its environment. In addition, alterations of the methodology employed should be made in accordance with previous forecasting successes.

   The need for revision may be occasioned by changes in such elements as company price levels and discounts, product characteristics, advertising expenditures, and methods of distribution as well as marketing activities of rivals, levels of governmental spending, taxation, and monetary policy. Thus, forecasts may be extended upward if, after their development, management decides to increase advertising expenditures or competitors increase prices of their offerings. Downward revisions may be undertaken should product style produce some consumer dissatisfaction, if taxes are expected to increase, or if inflation reduces consumer propensity to spend.

   Evaluation requires comparing forecasts with actual results in order to assess the worth of the methodology producing the former. This is a control process and is a necessary step in maintaining quality estimates in the future. When evaluators discover that a forecast has missed the mark by a wide margin, they seek to find out why. It may be that the methodology was poorly chosen, that the calculations were imprecise, or that the data were incorrect. These deficiencies, once uncovered, can be eliminated in subsequent forecasting endeavors.

Considering the Constraints

Finally, forecasters must take into account constraints that will not allow their firms to achieve sales levels that would prevail in the absence of the constraints. Some examples are

1. Lack of plant capacity to fulfill demands for the product.
2. Inability to secure raw materials needed for production.
3. Managerial limitations. Management may not have the "know-how" required to sell new products or in new regions (such as new countries) or to new types of customers.
4. Management goals. Management may want to keep the company small and thus restrict sales. One motive for keeping the company small is to maintain private ownership (not going into the stock market or taking on partners).
5. Limited labor supply. The firm may not have or be able to secure adequate numbers of workers with needed skills.
6. Labor disputes and strikes that shut down or slow up production.
7. Laws. Some examples are antitrust law, mine safety legislation, and consumer legislation.[9]
8. Acts of God and other catastrophes—earthquakes, floods, fires, hurricanes—that disrupt production, transportation, and sale of goods and services.
9. Economic constraints, such as tightening interest rates, declines in employment, and so on.
10. Competitive actions, such as the introduction of new and improved products, intensive promotional campaigns, and so on.

Certainly, it is difficult to forecast the incidence of many of the constraints, for example, acts of God and labor union strikes, but an attempt should be made to make the best estimate possible. Otherwise, the demand-originated future sales estimates may be in serious error.

SOURCES OF DATA INPUT

Forecasts, of course, will be in error if the historical data fed into the model are incorrect, imprecise, or not in a proper form. Thus, the analyst should be familiar with sources and uses of data.

Much data are available within the firm. Some appear in records and reports, such as annual statements, shipping documents, invoices, employment records, and production reports. The concern may have a management information system that is charged with responsibility for

9. See "When Lawyers Dictate the Limits of the Market," *Business Week*, July 14, 1980, pp. 76, 80.

gathering and processing relevant information and transmitting it to the proper executives. Some of this information may be contained in reports, whereas other portions remain in the memory banks of computers. If there is no management information system, the analyst may have to seek data from a variety of sources, perhaps departmental records, accounting documents, and scattered reports.

Conversely, valuable data are available from sources outside the firm. These include publications of government units, universities, foundations, trade associations, and professional research firms. Government sources are particularly useful because federal agencies acquire a tremendous volume of data in a variety of fields and publish the results in an easily available and inexpensive form.

Analysts should strive to ensure that data obtained from others are accurate and relevant. They should be especially careful to determine that the diligence and degree of care exercised by the source were adequate. They may have to examine the definitions of variables used by others because these may not agree with their own. Finally, analysts should attempt to uncover evidence of purposeful distortion of the data by others in light of their special interests.

SUMMARY

This chapter has provided an introduction to the field of forecasting, which is the generating of unbiased estimates of the future magnitude of some variable. This is in contrast to guesses that are not necessarily objective or carefully calculated. Forecasting probably is more an art than a science, for some degree of judgment is required.

Analysts prepare forecasts of a wide variety of social, economic, and physical variables. The focus of this book is upon *sales* forecasting—the basic forecast of the business firm. However, most of the techniques presented can be applied to estimate other variables.

The purpose of forecasting is to help in managerial planning and control processes. Forecasts aid planning by signaling objectives and by indicating what forms the business strategy should take. They enhance control by providing standards of performance.

Most organizations engage in forecasting, particularly business concerns, most of which are involved in the process. Responsibility for the function may be housed in a special department or in any one of many other units. Forecasting may be oriented to the organization at large, or to separate divisions, territories, or product lines.

Forecasts can be either macro (applying to an aggregate unit, such as the national economy) or micro (applying to a smaller unit, such as the firm). This book is oriented to the latter. There are also long-run forecasts (input into long-run decisions) and short-run forecasts (input into decisions whose impact is of short duration). Finally, forecasts differ in regard to the products considered, means of measurement used, buyer categories encompassed, and geographic areas covered.

A standard decision-making process for a firm is to generate a sales budget from the sales forecast. This budget in turn is the basis for all other budgets, including the production, direct-material, direct-labor, factory-overhead, cost-of-goods-sold, and sales and administration budgets, as well as the profit-and-loss statement.

The forecasting process involves the following steps: determining the objective, developing the model, testing the model, applying the model, determining constraints, and revision and evaluation.

Forecasts are dependent on the receipt of valid input data. Thus, the forecaster must be familiar with sources and their uses. Valuable sources exist both inside and outside the firm.

DISCUSSION QUESTIONS

1. Define the term *forecasting*. Differentiate between forecasting and making subjective guesses.
2. "Judgment is needed in the forecasting process." Explain what is meant by this statement.
3. Why is the sales forecast more important to managers than most other forecasts?
4. Why are forecasts used by business firms?
5. Indicate how the following companies might benefit through the use of sales forecasts:
   a. The Chrysler Corporation
   b. Safeway, Inc.
   c. Kentucky Fried Chicken
   d. Holiday Inns, Inc.
   e. IBM
6. "Forecasting reduces the need for planning." Discuss this statement.
7. Identify some types of organizations, other than businesses, that utilize forecasting. Why do these organizations forecast?
8. Should forecasting be centralized or decentralized? Why?
9. Distinguish between each of the following pairs of types of forecasts:
   a. Macro and micro
   b. Long- and short-run
   c. Unit and dollar
   d. Segments and total
10. Discuss how budgets are used for planning purposes.

11. What is the function of each of the following budgets?
    a. Sales
    b. Production
    c. Direct-material
    d. Direct-labor
    e. Factory-overhead
    f. Cost-of-goods-sold
    g. Sales and sdministrative-expense
    h. Pro-forma profit-and-loss statement
    i. Cash
    j. Pro-forma balance sheet
12. Why would a company produce separate forecasts for different sets of buyer categories? Illustrate your answer with an example.
13. Provide an example of a company that probably would benefit by having separate sales forecasts for different geographical areas.
14. What is meant by each of the following components of the forecasting process?
    a. Determining the objective
    b. Developing a model
    c. Assessing the model
    d. Applying the model
    e. Considering the constraints
    f. Evaluating and revising the model
15. What are some major sources of input data for the forecaster?
16. What is the difference between budgeting and planning? How does forecasting support each? Discuss.

RECOMMENDED READINGS

Abell, Derel F. "Strategic Windows." *Journal of Marketing*, 42 (April 1977), 21–26.

Berry, Leonard Eugene, and Gordon B. Harwood. "Controlling the Growing Firm with Responsibility Accounting." *Business*, 29 (September–October 1979), 30–34.

"The Big Deal McDonnell Douglas Turned Down." *Business Week*, December 1, 1980, pp. 81–82.

Bridge, J., and J. C. Dodds. *Managerial Decision Making*. New York: John Wiley and Sons, 1975, Chapter 1.

Day, George S. "Diagnosing the Product Portfolio." *Journal of Marketing*, 42 (April 1977), 29–38.

"Detroit's High-Price Strategy Could Backfire." *Business Week*, November 24, 1980, pp. 109, 111.

Hussey, D. *Corporate Planning: Theory and Practice*. New York: Pergamon Press, 1974.

Koontz, Harold. *Essentials of Management*. New York: McGraw-Hill Book Company, 1978, Chapter 3.

McCarthy, Daniel J., Robert J. Minichiello, and Joseph P. Curran. *Business Policy and Strategy*. Englewood Cliffs, N.J.: Prentice-Hall, 1979, Chapter 6.

Nakalishi, Masao. "A New Technique for Forecasting New Store Sales." In *1976 Proceedings, American Marketing Association Educators' Conference*. Chicago: American Marketing Association, 1977, pp. 224–229.

"1980: The Year the Forecasters Really Blew It." *Business Week*, July 14, 1980, pp. 88–89.

Petralia, J. W. "Effective Use of Econometrics in Corporate Planning." *Business Economics*, 16 (May 1981), 59–61.

Robinson, Richard. "Forecasting and Small Business: A Study of the Strategic Planning Process." *Journal of Small Business Management*, 17 (July 1974), 19–27.

St. John, Harry M. "The Energy Market for High Technology Companies." *Journal of Marketing*, 42 (October 1978), 46–53.

Thompson, Arthur H., and A. J. Strickland. *Strategy Formulation and Implementation*. Dallas: Business Publications, Inc., 1980.

"The Unexpected Slows the Worldwide Upturn—Inflation, Revolutions, and Political Upheavals Are Disrupting World Trade and Investment." *Business Week*, March 29, 1976, pp. 28–31.

Wind, Yoram, John F. Grashof, and Joel Goldhar. "Market-Based Guideline for Design of Industrial Products." *Journal of Marketing*, 42 (July 1978), 27–37.

CASE 1: CARTIGAN'S MOBILE HOME PARK AND GROCERY

Cliff and Marie Cartigan own and operate a mobile home park and a small grocery store on a five-acre plot of land. They are situated just off a major highway several miles from a southwestern city with a population of about 50,000. The couple inherited the business from Marie's father in 1979. Shortly afterward, Bill quit his job as a plumber in order to devote all his efforts to managing the firm's affairs.

The mobile home park tends to attract persons who wish to remain in the city for at least three months and sometimes one or more years; it does not cater to transients who plan to stay in the city only a few days. Many of the customers are retirees who live in northern climates during the summer and live in the southwest during the winter. Cartigan's offers large and attractive sites, water and electricity hookups, shower and toilet facilities, a swimming pool, and a small park equipped with swings, slides, and picnic tables. In addition, a small grocery store is on the property, situated near the park office and the Cartigans' mobile home. This store offers mostly staple goods—its merchandise mix resembles that of a convenience store. The grocery outlet serves both residents of the mobile home park and others whose homes are located nearby.

In 1982 the park was about 95% full, on the average, during the winter months of the year. During the summer months, the occupancy rate was 75%. Revenues from the park and from the grocery outlet provide the family with what they regard as an adequate standard of living, but they would like to improve the profitability of the enterprise. Specifically, they would like to expand the size of the park facility (which occupies only one-tenth of their total acreage). This would require grading, landscaping, and installing additional water and electrical hookups. In addition, the couple would like to erect a larger roadside sign, to improve the landscaping around the pool area (which is currently not very attractive), and to expand the size of the grocery store building. In order to accomplish these improvements, a loan from a bank or some other financial institution is needed.

The Cartigans' bookkeeping system is a basic one: each day Marie enters expenses and revenues into a ledger, which, at the end of the month, shows how much money was received and how much was taken out. This system enables them to determine, on a monthly basis, if more money came in than was paid out and vice versa. It also provides the data their accountant uses to prepare sales tax, income tax, and other tax forms. No other financial records are kept, other than their checking-account stubs from the bank.

Currently the Cartigans are attempting to resolve several questions. Should they

1. Expand the size of the park?
2. Erect the larger sign?
3. Improve the landscaping around the pool area?
4. Expand the size of the grocery building?
5. Purchase industrial clothes washers and dryers for customer use (in effect, going into the laundromat business on a small scale)?
6. Place pinball machines in the grocery store?

The Cartigans have never worried much about budgeting and forecasting. In their opinion, "These are only for big business. We are too busy with operating our firm to spend time on these activities." On the other hand, their niece, who is currently taking a forecasting course at a local state university, has urged the couple to set up a sales budget, a cash-flow budget, and a sales forecast for each year. The niece has argued that these will be useful for both planning and control purposes, and will be of value in obtaining a loan.

1. Would you recommend that this firm begin preparing and using the three documents suggested by the niece? Why or why not?
2. Of what use would the budgets and forecast be to the Cartigans?
3. What breakdowns of data should the sales budget include?
4. What components should the sales budget include?
5. Would a long-run sales forecast be of value to this company? Why or why not?
6. In your opinion, is budgeting and forecasting primarily for big business, or is there a need for these processes in a small company like this one?

Chapter 2
Judgmental Methods

INTRODUCTION

Many of the forecasting techniques presented in this book are highly structured, with little provision for the subjective opinions of those with practical experience. However, other techniques incorporate within their framework the subjective judgments of "experts." This chapter discusses these judgmental methods.

Certainly, subjective judgment has its place in forecasting. Relying on objective methods that are not capable of incorporating judgmental inputs can produce estimates that are incomplete reflections of reality.[1] Extension of past trends, for instance, can produce long-run estimates that either overestimate or underestimate future trends (indicating that past patterns are not always indicative of the future). Figure 2.1 illustrates this. Here extension of past sales data produces what is probably

Figure 2.1 Extension of Past Trend to 1990—High Estimate

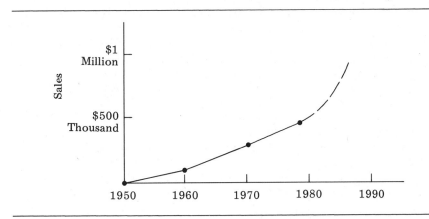

1. Spyros Makridokis and Steven C. Wheelwright, "Forecasting Issues and Challenges for Marketing Management," *Journal of Marketing*, 41 (October 1977), 31–32.

an unrealistically high forecast for 1990. Figure 2.2 illustrates the opposite condition, wherein extension of past tendencies results in what may be an unrealistically low estimate.

WHO ARE THE EXPERTS?

Virtually anyone may possess knowledge or insight that can be useful in formulating good estimates. However, the best sources of business forecasts are economists, executives, salespeople, customers, and a heterogeneous category of "experts" in various fields that includes county agents, officers of trade associations, and medical researchers. The specific experts who might be in a position to provide needed estimates vary considerably from one firm to another, depending on the firm's industry and the nature of the forecasting information needed.

Executives

Frequently, executives provide useful forecasting inputs. This is especially true of those managers who have long experience within the industry or within one that is similar. A seasoned executive in the textbook publishing industry, for instance, might be in a position to generate valid forecasts of sales of visual aids to instructors. Experience indicates that executives in production, sales, marketing, and upper-level management are particularly good sources. These individuals often have a working familiarity with the variables that determine sales levels. An example of an executive forecast is provided by George Warde,

Figure 2.2 Extension of Past Trend to 1990—Low Estimate

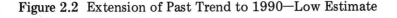
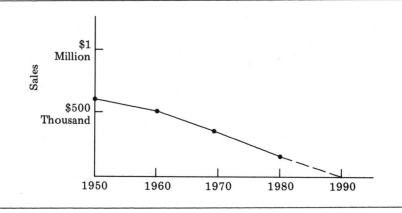

marketing director for Airbus Industries, who estimated that his firm will sell 960 aircraft to current customers over the next decade.[2] Another example: in 1980, the Hitachi Medical Corporation's officers forecasted a 20% sales increase in their firm's medical equipment for the year 1981.[3]

Salespeople

Another good source can be the sales force. Members of this group are in frequent contact with customers and are in a position to predict their buying plans, attitudes, and needs. Salespeople may also be able to provide accurate information regarding the current and expected future tactics of competitors.

In general, those salespeople who call on only a limited number of prospects are better sources of forecasts than those who call on an extensive number. This is because they spend more time with each prospect and are more likely to be intimately acquainted with his or her plans and needs.

However, care must be taken when weighing the inputs of salespeople. Some tend to be too optimistic, especially about new products. A salesman turned entrepreneur, for example, succeeded through his sales forecasts in selling several investors over half a million dollars worth of stock in his new company. The firm, located in Hartford, made concentrating solar collectors shaped as parabolic troughs for heating swimming pools. His forecasts were for sales of over 5,000 units a year, but the company went bankrupt in its second year, having sold only slightly over 300 units. As it turned out, 5,000 units would have represented over 400% of the entire solar collector market for the heating of swimming pools.

On the other hand, salespeople can be quite pessimistic sometimes. Sales forecasts are often turned into quotas, which in turn can become the basis for evaluating performance and compensating. The natural tendency, of course, is to try to keep forecasts low so as to improve future wages and evaluations.

These cautions do not mean that salespeople are necessarily poor sources of information. Experience in working with individual salespeople helps forecasters to recognize over- and underoptimism. Further, salespeople tend to be the best source of certain kinds of information, such as changes in the distribution system, new-product entries, changing needs among customers, new marketing thrusts of competitors,

2. Robert Ball, "Who's That Chasing After Boeing?" *Fortune*, April 21, 1980, pp. 72–74.
3. "Healthy Industry," *Asian Wall Street Journal Weekly*, September 14, 1980, p. 15.

changes in local economic conditions, and so on. This information can be vital for increasing forecast accuracy.

Table 2.1 shows a questionnaire that one firm asks salespeople to complete. The document provides past sales information for the purpose of inducing salespeople to use the past data in developing forecasts. Perhaps more important, it asks the sales force to spell out changes that have occurred in each territory that will affect future sales. This information is vital to forecasters and managers alike in preparing final forecasts. For example, it may be learned that a competitor has recently introduced a new improved product that looks like it will cut deeply into a company's sales. Or it may be learned that the local economy is expected to boom because of the recent announcement of a new plant opening. Because they are in the field, salespeople can be the best source of such information.

Table 2.1 Sales Forecasting Questionnaire

Date _____

Name of Salesperson _____

Territory Number _____

Directions: This form contains data on dollar sales in your territory for the last two years, and expected sales for this year. You are asked to estimate sales for next year. Please submit this questionnaire to the home office within thirty days.

1. Dollar sales in your territory two years ago _____ (to be provided by the home office)
2. Dollar sales in your territory last year _____ (to be provided by the home office)
3. Expected dollar sales in your territory this year _____ (to be provided by the home office)
4. Taking into account the status of your customers, the company's promotion and pricing efforts, and anticipated actions of competitors, what is your best estimate of dollar sales in your territory next year? _____
5. What changes have occurred in your territory that will affect sales? (Use a separate sheet if necessary.)_____
   _____
   _____
   _____
   _____
   _____

Customers

Those who purchase the output of an enterprise sometimes are willing to and can extend estimates of their impending buying plans. Indeed, some firms selling to industrial markets, such as purchasers of turbine generators, place great importance on this kind of feedback. Customers may give this information in person to salespeople and executives, or through response to mail, telephone, or personal-interview surveys.

Some customers, especially those in wholesaling and retailing, find it difficult to estimate their future needs accurately, because needs are highly dependent on factors beyond their control, such as actions of competitors, customers, government agencies, labor unions, financial agencies, transportation carriers, and so on. Nevertheless, executives and procurement personnel in these concerns are often in possession of information, such as future warehouse or market expansion programs, that is vital to the preparation of accurate forecasts and is not available from other sources. Similarly, consumer purchase intentions are often possible to gauge through surveys. This is especially true for major durables. Appliance companies like General Electric, for example, frequently survey consumers about their buying intentions.

Others

In some instances, specialists in a variety of occupations supply valuable judgments. Following is a partial list of various specialists and some types of enterprises they are able to serve.

Specialists	Enterprises That Can Use Judgment
1. County agents	Producers and distributors of seeds, fertilizers, and feed
2. Trade association officers	The industry within which the firm operates
3. Medical researchers	Producers of ingredients of prescription and proprietary drugs
4. Public school administrators	Textbook suppliers
5. Physicians	Pharmaceutical houses
6. Architects	Producers and distributors of building materials

continued

7.	Construction engineers	Producers and distributors of building materials
8.	Book reviewers	Publishing houses
9.	Home economists	Food processors
10.	Management consultants	Any industry
11.	Retail store buyers	Producers of apparel, durable goods, etc.
12.	Economists	Any industry

In some instances, analysts rely on judgments from only one or several noted specialists in a field. More commonly, they solicit information from a number of experts and use mean or median estimates.

TECHNIQUES FOR ELICITING EXPERTS' OPINIONS

One means of obtaining a subjectively based judgmental forecast is simply to ask, "What is your estimate of next year's sales?" This straightforward approach may elicit meaningful estimates; however, the subjective basis of the estimate is difficult to learn. If nothing else, the individual making the forecast and those receiving it feel uncomfortable with the uncertainty surrounding the judgmental basis of these estimates. This section outlines a number of techniques designed to help the analyst deal with the uncertainties associated with subjectively based estimates.

PERT-Derived Method

One method of producing estimates emanates from PERT (Program Evaluation and Review Technique). This method was originally designed to develop estimates of the time required to complete various phases of major projects (such as installing a new machinery complex). However, subsequent applications in generating other types of estimates (including forecasts) have been fruitful.[4]

The PERT method requires that the forecaster make three estimates: (1) optimistic, (2) pessimistic, and (3) the most likely. Experience indicates that these estimates combine to form an expected value, or forecast, which is:[5]

---

4. See, for instance, William R. Darden, "An Operational Approach to Product Pricing," *Journal of Marketing*, 32 (April 1968), 29–33.
5. The 1, 4, and 1 weights have been derived from applications of the technique in a wide variety of industrial settings.

what if?

$$EV = \frac{A + 4B + C}{6}$$

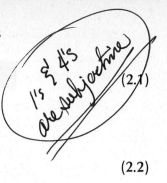

4's & 1's are subjective

(2.1)

with a standard deviation of

$$S = \frac{C - A}{6}$$

(2.2)

where EV = expected value (mean) of the forecast variable
A = pessimistic estimate
B = most likely estimate
C = optimistic estimate
S = standard deviation of the forecast variable

For example, assume that the forecasting committee of an oilfield-equipment producer believes that, if the firm is very successful, next year's sales will be $250,000,000 and if very unsuccessful, $200,000,000. The "most likely" estimate is $240,000,000. The PERT technique generates an expected value of sales as follows:

$$EV = \frac{\$200 \text{ MM} + 4(\$240 \text{ MM}) + \$250 \text{ MM}}{6} = \$235 \text{ MM}$$

with a standard deviation of

$$S = \frac{\$250 \text{ MM} - \$200 \text{ MM}}{6} = \$8.33 \text{ MM}$$

As the illustration indicates, this technique makes possible the conversion of experts' conceptions of extremes and most likely values into measures of central tendency and dispersion (mean and standard deviation). It is often easier for experts to conceive of optimistic, pessimistic, and most likely values than of a specific forecast value, as they must when asked to estimate next year's sales volume. A further advantage of PERT is that it includes a measure of dispersion (the standard deviation), which makes it possible to set forth probabilistic statements regarding future behavior of the dependent variable. In the foregoing illustration, the analyst can state that the approximate probability is 0.95 that the true value of estimated sales lies between plus or minus two standard deviations from the mean ($235,000,000). That is, the true value can be expected to be between $218,340,000 and $251,660,000.

PERT, like any model, has limitations. It assumes that the expert is capable of producing realistic, optimistic, pessimistic, and most likely estimates, but this may not be the case. Furthermore, it assumes that the distribution of pessimistic, optimistic, and most likely estimates is approximately normal. Since specialists' opinions may be biased (either toward the positive or toward the negative), a normal curve may not be appropriate. Finally, the formula used for computing standard deviation considers only the range between the optimistic and pessimistic estimates rather than a full distribution. As such, it is only an approximation.

Despite these limitations, PERT estimates can be of value, as indicated earlier. The principal application of the model is in situations where the analyst feels that experts' opinions should be taken into account and sufficient time or data for more lengthy objective methods is not available. Since PERT estimates can be made quickly, their figures are often used as controls to be compared with estimates produced by other methods as a means of assessing the worth of the latter.

Utility Theory

Utility theory primarily deals with algebraic structures of the preferences and satisfactions of individuals. The term *utility* refers to the ability of some object, service, or concept to satisfy a need or want. When utility is measured in money, it is termed *value*. Thus, for most individuals, new automobiles have greater utility than used automobiles and, as a corollary, a higher value.

The objective of utility theory in forecasting is to attach probabilities to various possible future levels of sales.[6] As a preliminary, the analyst develops a limited number of candidate estimates, often in corroboration with one or more experts. Then, the expert's feeling about the resulting probability of each estimate is established through a trade-off process. This requires determining what the expert is willing to exchange for a fixed and certain result.

The Colbo Industries Corporation produces the Gemini electric mixer, which enjoys a very favorable reputation among consumers. A sales forecaster consults with an expert (the sales manager), and the two decide that the four most likely levels of sales for the oncoming year are $38,500,000, $36,000,000, $34,000,000, and $28,000,000. These four levels were developed in light of assumptions regarding consumer acceptance of the brand, actions of competitors, per capita consumption of baked pastries, retailer merchandising and promotion efforts, and prices of raw materials and labor. Further, a minimum reasonable level of sales has been established. This is the magnitude that would be achieved if virtually all of the factors

6. Technically, the objective is to accommodate the nonlinearity of a decision maker's utility function.

determining sales—consumer desires and incomes, competitive activities, and so forth—operated adversely but within reason. For Gemini this level is assumed to be $10,000,000.

The analyst subjects each of the four candidates to the utility test. The $38,500,000 level is exemplified here. The following instructions are related by the analyst to the expert:

Assume that your continued employment by the firm depends on your ability to forecast accurately next year's sales. We have decided that the absolute minimum level of sales is $10,000,000. Assume that you have two choices: (1) being 100% certain of achieving this level, and (2) being 1% certain of achieving $38,500,000 and 99% certain of achieving nothing. Which of these two forecasts would you select, $10,000,000 or $38,500,000?

If the expert chooses the first value, it is determined that the person has a very small belief in the occurrence of a sales level of $38,500,000, and the testing of this alternative stops. If the expert takes the second choice (1% and 99%), the question is then asked, "Assume now that your choices are (1) being 100% certain of achieving the $10,000,000 level and (2) being 2% certain of achieving $38,500,000 and 98% certain of achieving nothing. Which of the two would you choose now?" The question is repeated by using successively higher probabilities of achieving $38,500,000 until a level is reached where the expert chooses the first level (100% choice of $10,000,000). It is assumed that the probability associated with this level represents the expert's degree of belief in the outcome ($38,500,000). Thus, if the question was repeated 40 times before the expert selected the $10,000,000 outcome, it is assumed that the degree of belief in the $38,500,000 outcome is 40%.

Each of the four candidate sales levels is subjected to the process outlined above. This generates four probabilities. The outcome with the highest probability is assumed to be the most valid. Thus in the Gemini case, the degrees of belief in the candidate outcomes might be as follows:

Candidate, $	Degree of Belief, %
38,500,000	40
36,000,000	20
34,000,000	70
28,000,000	10

It appears that the executive has a strong feeling that the $34,000,000 level is to be expected. At the other extreme, the $28,000,000 is not expected with a high degree of certainty. Thus, the best estimate is $34,000,000.[7]

Some disadvantages of this method are evident. As the foregoing example illustrates, employment of utility theory can be very time-consuming for the analyst and the expert. It also demands considerable patience on the part of the latter because of the repetitive nature of the questioning. The number of questions can be reduced, however, by increasing the interval by which the degrees of belief are increased (in the example, they might advance by 10% instead of 1% intervals, for instance). Finally, some executives object to "playing guessing games." This attitude may be taken by executives who are not convinced of the value of using this technique.

Utility theory is most applicable to situations where experts have produced several candidate sales forecasts but have experienced difficulty in evaluating their relative probabilities. It is used primarily by firms whose management is very highly concerned with producing an accurate forecast and is willing to have their executives spend the time necessary for the questioning process. This necessity has limited the use of the technique.

Judgment from the Extremes

A method that bears some resemblance to utility theory is judgment from the extremes. This is most useful when experts feel very incapable of producing a valid forecast, as in the case of estimating sales of a new product. This simple method involves asking experts whether or not they believe that the level of sales might lie at an extremely high or low point. If they do not believe this to be the case, the range between extremes is reduced until it is sufficiently small to produce an approximation of expected sales. The technique requires only yes or no answers —eliminating a need for experts to produce specific estimates of uncertain future behavior of sales—a task of which they may feel themselves to be incapable.

The sales forecaster for the Sexton Manufacturing Company (a producer of automobile accessories) is faced with the responsibility of estimating next year's sales of a new product, Prolir—a liquid which, when added to an automobile gas tank, increases gasoline mileage by as much as 5%. The analyst believes that maximum sales (full penetration

7. The process outlined above is an approach to the standard gamble technique. Another approach is to hold probabilities constant and vary the amounts involved in the lottery. There is conflict in the academic community as to which of the two approaches is superior.

of the fuel additive market) might be as high as $15,000,000. Conversely, if the product is a failure, sales might be as low as $50,000. The analyst might ask the executive, "Knowing next year's marketing strategy, do you think that next year's sales of Prolir could be as high as $15,000,000?" The answer to this question probably will be "No." The analyst then asks, "Could sales be as low as $50,000?" Again, the response probably will be "No." At this point the range is reduced. The next query might be "Could sales be as high as $14,000,000? Could they be as low as $70,000?" By asking a series of such questions, and successively reducing the range, the analyst can finally arrive at an estimated reasonable range. Thus, it may be that the expert is willing to speculate that sales might go as high as $3,000,000 and as low as $2,000,000. Figure 2.3 illustrates the range-reduction process. The technique has not produced a specific forecast level, but has considerably reduced uncertainty by bringing together the extremes.

As previously mentioned, the judgment-from-the-extremes method provides a range rather than a unique forecast and is consequently less precise than some other techniques. However, it is useful in situations where experts feel incapable of generating unique estimates.

Figure 2.3 Illustration of Reduction Range

$15,000,000

$50,000
Initial range

$14,000,000

$70,000
Second range

$3,000,000

$2,000,000
Final range

Decision Theory

Decision theory, emanating from the management science field of study, is most commonly used to suggest optimum strategies to management.[8] On the other hand, it contains some elements useful to the forecaster. Foremost among these is the expected-value concept.

A problem for analysts is that, once they have formulated a forecast, conditions may change. For example, competitors may launch a new promotion campaign, the firm's source of raw materials may be interrupted by a railroad strike, or advances in prices of packaging ingredients may necessitate a price increase that reduces customer purchases. Computations of expected value can take into account these changes in the environment. The expected value is a weighted mean that takes into account the impact of environmental states on the forecast along with the subjective probability estimate of the occurrence of each state.

The definitional formula of expected value is

$$EV = \sum_{i=1}^{n} P(S_i)O_i \qquad (2.3)$$

where EV = expected value
$P(S_i)$ = probability of occurrence of state of nature i
O_i = outcome under the ith state of nature
n = total number of outcomes under consideration

Wilhelm Schelenberg, owner and manager of Schelenberg's Supermarket located in a small midwestern city, wants to forecast sales for the forthcoming year. He thinks that his sales are primarily determined by personal income levels in the city. In decision-theory terms, the various income levels are states of nature. The latter are environmental conditions affecting sales levels. Schelenberg believes that four states of nature are possible: (1) incomes will decrease by 2%, (2) incomes will not change, (3) incomes will rise by 3%, and (4) incomes will rise by 8%. He estimates the probabilities of these as 0.10, 0.30, 0.50, and 0.10, respectively. Finally, he estimates that the outcomes (sales levels for next year for the four states of nature are $100,000, $130,000, $190,000, and $250,000 respectively. Table 2.2 sets forth these estimates in expected-value form.

Application of Equation 2.3 produces the following expected value:

$$EV = 0.10(\$100,000) + 0.30(\$130,000) + 0.50(\$190,000)$$
$$+ 0.10(\$250,000) = \$169,000$$

8. Robert C. Blattberg, "The Design of Advertising Experiments: Using Statistical Decision Theory," *Journal of Marketing Research*, 16 (Spring 1979), 191-202.

Table 2.2 Expected-Value Computation, Schelenberg's Supermarket

	States of Nature			
	Incomes Decrease by 2%	Incomes Do Not Change	Incomes Increase by 3%	Incomes Increase by 8%
Probabilities of states of nature	0.10	0.30	0.50	0.10
Outcomes of states of nature	$100,000	$130,000	$190,000	$250,000

The expected sales level is $169,000. This figure is based upon Schelenberg's estimates of the probabilities and the outcomes of each state of nature, so it is a judgment-type forecast. Employment of the expected-value formula ensures that each estimated outcome is weighted by its appropriate probability and that each state of nature identified is recognized. This is of great importance where the numbers of states of nature are substantial.

Effective use of the expected-value formula for forecasting requires that the executive be capable of identifying relevant states of nature and of supplying probability and outcome values for each. Many executives attempt to do this implicitly when they provide informed opinions of future years' sales. The expected-value formula transforms these opinions into quantitative forecasts. In other words, it enables the analyst to transform subjective opinions into data and to manipulate these in an objective manner. Thus, this formula takes into account the valuable judgment of management and still avoids producing estimates of future sales that are largely guesses.

Bayesian Decision Theory

Closely related to expected-value analysis is the Bayesian decision theory. This procedure combines subjective and objective probabilities with revised probabilities. The latter result from updated information, such as that obtained through research, from suppliers, salespeople, or other parties, that has a bearing on the forecast. In other words, the forecast is revised on the basis of new relevant information.

The marketing director of Edwards Industries, Inc., has asked for assistance in forecasting sales of a new product—the Duro snowmobile— that the company is contemplating introducing. The results of the forecast will decide whether or not the Duro snowmobile will be introduced.

After questioning the marketing director and obtaining a feel for the market, it is decided that the market may either be good, fair, or bad, depending on such factors as fuel availability and prices, economic conditions, snowfall, and so on. The marketing manager and other experts in the snowmobile field, including executives of the firm, do not feel that each possible event has an equal probability of occurrence. Instead, the following subjective probabilities are agreed upon as representing the likelihood of occurrence of each of these events:

Event	Probability
Good market	0.2
Fair market	0.7
Bad market	0.1
	1.0

Furthermore, resulting profit conditions caused by each of these events are understandably expected to be different. Obviously in a good market a greater profit may be expected than in a fair or bad market. The Edwards marketing department, after consulting with the controller, has made calculations to estimate the likely profit obtainable by the introduction of the Duro snowmobile under the various market conditions. Specifically, it is calculated that the profit likely to be earned under the various market conditions is as follows:[9]

Market Condition	Obtainable Profit/(Loss)
Good	$80,000,000
Fair	2,000,000
Bad	(40,000,000)

9. Note that in this example, Bayesian decision theory is employed to forecast profits rather than sales. The same forecasting procedure is followed, regardless of the forecast variable, however.

Equation 2.3 may be used to calculate the expected value of this potential market. This is calculated to be:

$$EV = 0.2(\$80,000,000) + 0.7(\$2,000,000) + 0.1(\$40,000,000)$$
$$= \$13,400,000$$

The expected value of $13,400,000 indicates that Edwards should introduce the Duro, based on the subjective probabilities and estimates of obtainable profit under the various market conditions. The $13,400,000 expected value of introducing the product is greater than the $0 expected profit of abandoning the project.

Thus far, the problem faced by Edwards Industries is simply that of expected-value analysis. This forecasting procedure is jointly associated with decision making, in that the expected value of one course of action serves as both the indicator of the attractiveness of each alternative as well as the forecast of value if one alternative is selected. For Edwards, the expected value of $13,400,000 is considered to be more attractive than that associated with the alternative of dropping the project, and also serves as the forecast of profit on the condition that the Duro is introduced.

Unfortunately, most decisions and forecasts are not so simply derived. Most are much more complex. Often, several alternatives are available which complicates analysis. Bayesian analysis is designed to accommodate expanded problems by using expected-value concepts as a base.

Expanded Problem

To illustrate, the marketing managers at Edwards Industries may have additional options available to them. Of course, they may investigate other opportunities that have greater associated expected values. This process essentially involves evaluating the desirability of each of the alternatives. In addition, the marketing directors may wish to obtain more information about the market for snowmobiles. One way to accomplish this is to conduct a research study that will attempt to evaluate the market and enable preparation of a forecast on the basis of the research information. At that time, the decision will be made as to whether or not to enter the market. Forecasting can aid the marketing managers by predicting the market potential after the receipt of the research information and by indicating whether or not the additional information will be worth its cost of obtainment.

After discussion with the Edwards marketing research managers, it is learned that two research plans are desirable. Other methods of collecting data are available, but they are not thought to be as feasible as the two that must be considered. The plans are these.

Research Plan A   Conduct a quick two-month study of 25% of the potential dealers and a survey of all customers of ten snowmobile outlets over a one-month period. Customers will be asked to complete a short questionnaire geared toward obtaining information about characteristics they seek in a snowmobile as well as their buying intentions. Dealers will be asked their opinion about the market possibilities for the Duro.

Students of the marketing research class at the state college have agreed to do the research as part of their class project, so the costs associated with this research are only out-of-pocket costs estimated to be $5,000. However, because surveying the market will cause a delay in the introduction of the Duro, the obtainable profit figures are estimated to be 5% lower than they would be if introduction were immediate; that is, competitive efforts and other market forces are estimated to reduce the potential market by 5% if introduction is delayed by two months.

On the other hand, accuracy of prediction will be increased by having the survey data. If introduction takes place immediately, there is no actual objective information available indicating whether a good, bad, or fair market exists. With sample information, however, more "real" data may be used in making the forecast. After survey data are available, a forecast of either a good, fair, or bad market can be made and accordingly affect the decision to introduce the Duro. Based on past experience with survey data, it is estimated that the resulting forecast has an 80% chance of being correct. The 20% chance that the forecast is wrong is assumed to be equally divided (0.10 each) to the other two categories of market condition. For example, assume that the final forecast after the survey is complete is that there is a fair market forecast. There is an 80% chance that this will be accurate, but there is also a 10% chance that the market will actually be good and a 10% chance that the market will be bad.

Research Plan B   The marketing manager may also adopt a more lengthy and, consequently, more reliable survey. This would cover a period of three months, but would include 30% of the potential dealers and a survey of all customers of 20 randomly selected outlets over a one-month period.

This study would be similar to plan A, except that it would be both longer and more expensive, and professional survey help would be needed to supervise and help the students. The cost of this plan is estimated to be $40,000, and the market is anticipated to be 10% worse than if introduction were to take place immediately.

The level of accuracy obtainable by this research plan is estimated to be substantially greater than that expected of plan A. In this case, it is estimated that the resulting forecast has a 90% chance of being correct. The 10% error factor is assumed to be equally divided between the two remaining categories of market condition.

Analysis of Plan A

Research plan A is evaluated first. The first step is to calculate the obtainable profit or loss available under each of the three possible market conditions. With the market anticipated to be 5% worse if the decision to survey is initiated, the anticipated market potentials are as follows:

Market Condition	Probability of Occurrence	Obtainable Profit/(Loss)
Good (CE_1)	0.2	$76,000,000
Fair (CE_2)	0.7	1,900,000
Bad (CE_3)	0.1	(42,000,000)
	1.0	

The next step in the analysis is to analyze each possibility after assuming one of the market conditions to be actually true; that is, the analysis assumes this event to be true, at least temporarily. The first conditional event to be analyzed is that of a good market (CE_1).

If CE_1 can be assumed to be true, the survey to be conducted has an 80% chance of its prediction; that is, there is an 80% chance that the survey results will warrant a forecast of $76,000,000 profit. Of course, if the results of the survey reflect a $76,000,000 profit, the decision to introduce the Duro shall, in fact, be made. There is an 80% chance of being right. However, the survey may reflect only a $1,900,000 market. In this case, Edwards would nevertheless introduce the Duro, because a $1,900,000 anticipated profit is certainly better than a $0 profit resulting from not introducing the product.[10] Nevertheless, after introduction, Edwards would realize a $76,000,000 profit—not a $1,900,000 profit— because the forecast was wrong. If the market is good (conditional event), Edwards will realize the full profit of this condition.[11] In fact, assuming CE_1, full profits will not be realized only if the survey is wrong and predicts a bad market. If the survey forecasts a bad market, the Duro project will be dropped and $0 profit will be realized. There is a 10% chance of this occurring.

10. The problem and analysis may be expanded to reflect other alternatives.
11. This may be modified to reflect production capacities and the like.

Expected Value of a Conditional Event   The foregoing analysis may be expanded to calculate what is termed an *expected value of a conditional event (EVCE)*. This concept is simply an extension of that of expected value. $EVCE_1$ refers to the expected value of CE_1, of course, assuming CE_1 to be the actual market condition. Table 2.3 represents the calculation of $EVCE_1$. Therefore, the $EVCE_1$ is $68,400,000. However, this value assumes a good market to be true. The two other market conditions could also be true and must also be evaluated.

If CE_2 is assumed to be true, there may again be three possible forecast results from the survey. The first forecast possibility is that there is a predicted good market. However, even though it is forecasted and the Duro is introduced, a $76,000,000 profit will not be realized. It must be remembered that CE_2 (fair market) is assumed to be the true condition. Therefore, only a $1,900,000 profit will be realized. There is a 10% chance that this forecast situation will exist. Furthermore, it is 80% likely that, if CE_2 is true, it will be predicted on the basis of the survey. In this case, the decision will have been made to introduce the Duro, and the $1,900,000 profit will be realized. Only when the survey results in a forecast of a bad market (10% chance) will the project be abandoned and a profit of $0 be earned. Table 2.4 summarizes CE_2. Therefore, the $EVCE_2$ is $1,710,000; that is, if CE_2 is true, a $1,710,000 profit may be expected.

The final conditional event to be analyzed is that of CE_3. Even if a bad market actually exists, there are, nevertheless, three possibilities of forecasted market condition. First, a good market may be predicted. If this is the case (resulting in Duro's introduction) but a bad market actually materializes, a $42,000,000 loss will be realized. Similarly, if a fair market is forecasted and the Duro is introduced, a $42,000,000 loss will also occur. Each of these two possibilities has a 10% chance of occurrence. Only a bad-market forecast will prevent the introduction of the Duro and the resulting loss. If CE_3 is, in fact, true, there is an 80% chance that the forecast will result in the loss-avoidance category. Table 2.5 summarizes the possibilities for CE_3. Therefore, if CE_3 is, in fact, true, Edwards may expect to lose $8,400,000 after sampling.

The foregoing calculations of the expected values of each conditional event have as a major underpinning the assumption that the event being analyzed is, in fact, true. However, each of the events cannot all be true at the same time. If the events being considered were properly determined, they must be mutually exclusive. Instead, each of the events has a probability of occurrence. If the event occurs, the related *EVCE* represents the expected profit. The entire forecast for the survey action is determined by weighting each of the *EVCE*s by its probability of occurring. Essentially, the forecast of profit for the alternative of conducting the short survey is obtained by calculating the expected value of the *EVCE*s. Table 2.6 presents the forecast calculation for the short-survey alternative.

Table 2.3 Expected Value of CE_1

Survey Forecast	Resulting Action	Probability of Forecast	Conditional Profit Resulting from Action, $	$EVCE_1$ Calculation, $
Good	Introduction	0.8	76,000,000	60,800,000
Fair	Introduction	0.1	76,000,000	7,600,000
Bad	Abandonment	0.1	0	0
		1.0		68,400,000

Table 2.4 Expected Value of CE_2

Survey Forecast	Resulting Action	Probability of Forecast	Conditional Profit Resulting from Action, $	$EVCE_2$ Calculation, $
Good	Introduction	0.1	1,900,000	190,000
Fair	Introduction	0.8	1,900,000	1,520,000
Bad	Abandonment	0.1	0	0
		1.0		1,710,000

Table 2.5 Expected Value of CE_3

Survey Forecast	Resulting Action	Probability of Forecast	Conditional Profit Resulting from Action, $	$EVCE_3$ Calculation, $
Good	Introduction	0.1	(42,000,000)	(4,200,000)
Fair	Introduction	0.1	(42,000,000)	(4,200,000)
Bad	Abandonment	0.8	0	0
		1.0		(8,400,000)

Table 2.6 Forecast of Profit for Research Plan A

Conditional Event	$EVCE$, $	Probability of CE's Occurrence	Forecast Calculation (Expected Value), $
Good (CE_1)	68,400,000	0.2	13,680,000
Fair (CE_2)	1,710,000	0.7	1,197,000
Bad (CE_3)	(8,400,000)	0.1	(840,000)
		1.0	14,037,000

One additional adjustment must be made to the expected-value calculation to establish the forecast of profit for research plan A. The cost of obtaining the added information must be deducted from the $14,037,000 figure. Costs for the short survey were estimated to be $5,000. Therefore, the forecast of profit resulting from the adoption of plan A is calculated to be $14,032,000 ($14,037,000 – $5,000).

The forecast of $14,032,000 compares favorably with that of $13,400,000 relating to the alternative of immediate introduction with no additional research whatsoever. This means that conducting the two months of research may increase expected profits.

Decision Trees   Figure 2.4 portrays the elements of research plan A in a graphic form known as a decision tree. A decision tree is a network of lines depicting results of each possible event of an alternative, as well as

Figure 2.4 Decision Tree for Duro Research Plan A

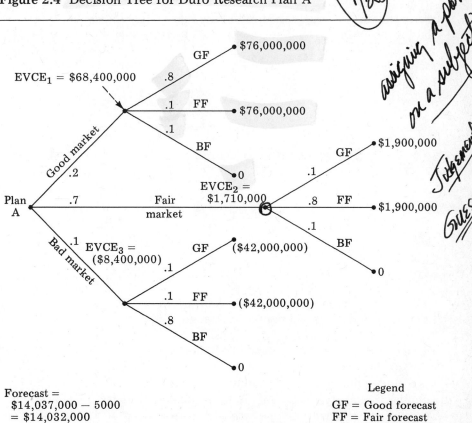

Forecast =
$14,037,000 – 5000
= $14,032,000

Legend

GF = Good forecast
FF = Fair forecast
BF = Bad forecast

the expected relevant values and probabilities. The analyst structures a decision tree in a left-to-right direction by breaking major events into their components. Once it is structured, the analyst proceeds backward, in a right-to-left direction, in order to calculate expected values of the various conditional events.

Figure 2.4 is only a partial representation of the problem, in that research plan A is the only portion being analyzed. In addition, the alternatives of immediate introduction and of research plan B must be included for the decision tree to be considered complete. Before we look at the entire decision tree, however, we will analyze research plan B.

Analysis of Plan B

Like plan A, the analysis of plan B begins with the determination of obtainable profit or loss results under each of the possible conditional events. In each of the possible events, the market is expected to be 10% worse than if introduction were to take place immediately because of the three-month delay. However, it must be remembered that this plan, because of its stronger sample, is expected to result in a forecast of market condition that has a 90% chance of being correct. The anticipated potentials are as follows:

Market Condition	Probability of Occurrence	Obtainable Profit/(Loss)
Good (CE_1)	0.2	$72,000,000
Fair (CE_2)	0.7	1,800,000
Bad (CE_3)	0.1	(44,000,000)
	1.0	

Table 2.7 presents calculations necessary to compute $EVCE_1$. The expected conditional value of an actual good market is $68,400,000. As with the evaluation of plan A, it must be remembered that the cost of the survey for plan B must be deducted. However, because this $40,000 cost is incurred once the decision to survey the market is made, it will result in a reduction in profit regardless of the event. Therefore, for simplicity of analysis, the $40,000 may be deducted from the expected value of the entire alternative rather than from each of the events.

Table 2.8 presents calculations necessary to compute $EVCE_2$ and Table 2.9 refers to those calculations relating to $EVCE_3$. The reader is encouraged to verify the calculations.

Table 2.7 Expected Value of CE_1

Survey Forecast	Resulting Action	Probability of Forecast	Conditional Profit Resulting from Action, $	$EVCE_1$ Calculation, $
Good	Introduction	0.90	72,000,000	64,800,000
Fair	Introduction	0.05	72.000,000	3,600,000
Bad	Abandonment	0.05	0	0
		1.00		68,400,000

Table 2.8 Expected Value of CE_2

Survey Forecast	Resulting Action	Probability of Forecast	Conditional Profit Resulting from Action, $	$EVCE_2$ Calculation, $
Good	Introduction	0.05	1,800,000	90,000
Fair	Introduction	0.90	1,800,000	1,620,000
Bad	Abandonment	0.05	0	0
		1.00		1,710,000

Table 2.9 Expected Value of CE_3

Survey Forecast	Resulting Action	Probability of Forecast	Conditional Profit Resulting from Action, $	$EVCE_3$ Calculation, $
Good	Introduction	0.05	(44,000,000)	(2,200,000)
Fair	Introduction	0.05	(44,000,000)	(2,200,000)
Bad	Abandonment	0.90	0	0
		1.00		(4,400,000)

Table 2.10 Forecast of Profit for Research Plan B

Conditional Event	$EVCE$, $	Probability of CE's Occurrence	Forecast Calculation (Expected Value), $
Good (CE_1)	68,400,000	0.2	13,680,000
Fair (CE_2)	1,710,000	0.7	1,197,000
Bad (CE_3)	(4,400,000)	0.1	(440,000)
		1.0	14,437,000

Finally, it remains necessary to compute the forecast of profit for plan B. Table 2.10 presents this forecast calculation as determined by the expected value of the *EVCE*s related to this alternative.

As for plan A, one additional adjustment is necessary to establish the forecast of profit for plan B. The cost of the research must be deducted from the profits. Costs for the longer survey were estimated to be $40,000. Therefore, the forecast of profit for plan B is $14,397,000.

Through the use of Bayesian analysis, objective and subjective estimates of probabilities are combined to forecast the expected values of various alternatives. The forecasts are prepared to assist the manager in decision making. The following is a summary of the forecast of profit for each alternative.

Alternative	Expected Profit
Abandon immediately	$ 0
Introduce immediately	13,400,000
Initiate research plan A and then decide	14,032,000
Initiate research plan B and then decide	14,397,000

From the foregoing, it appears that plan B is the best alternative and that the longer of the two surveys is the preferable choice. Of course, the forecast itself serves only as a guide to the decision maker. Other criteria may also enter the analysis of alternatives. The company's financial position, for example, may be such that a wrong decision could be catastrophic. This condition could result in selection of the alternative that has the least likelihood of failure rather than the greatest expected value. Or management may decide that the $997,000 greater expected value of research plan B over immediate introduction is not sufficient to warrant the three-month wait. Several conditions may serve to influence decision making in a direction other than that suggested by expected-value computations. Nevertheless, whichever alternative is selected, the related expected value is to be used as the forecast.

A decision tree for the entire question of whether or not to introduce the Duro is presented in Figure 2.5.

Value of Additional Research

Management is, of course, concerned with an additional evaluation of the market, namely, "Is it worthwhile?" Bayesian analysis provides an

Figure 2.5 Decision Tree for Duro Snowmobiles

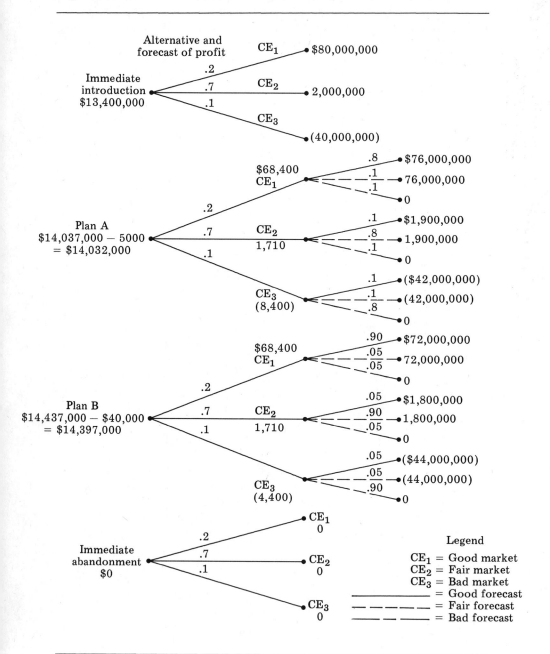

answer to this question. The expected value of additional research is simply the total expected profit of the research alternative minus that forecast without additional research. In the Duro example, the extensive-forecast alternative (plan B) has an expected value of

$14,397,000 = expected profit of plan B
13,400,000 = expected profit of no research
_____
$ 997,000 = value of research

The computation of expected profit of added research and its effects on refining the final forecast involve a rather high degree of subjectivity, of course. However, the judgment of the analyst and the manager is often surprisingly accurate in predicting anticipated costs and benefits of this activity.

JUDGMENT OF GROUPS

Frequently the analyst feels that more than one specialist should participate in judgmental forecasting. Thus, production, finance, distribution, and sales executives may be asked to participate in joint development of a sales forecast. Most frequently, members of the team are asked to meet as a group and to develop estimates through consensus. This has the advantage of ensuring that points of view from divergent functions are taken into account. Furthermore, the moderating effect of the group tends to lessen the probability of biased judgments, which can easily come from one individual.

Unfortunately, consensus methods have several drawbacks. Sometimes one or several high-ranking executives tend to dominate group decisions; or the group members may compromise to the degree that forecasts are unduly conservative; or some members may take unyielding positions, leading to unproductive argumentation and bickering. Finally, since responsibility is assigned not to individuals but to the group, members may not devote sufficient time and effort to the group task. Rather, they may concentrate on activities for which they are individually responsible and on which they are evaluated by superiors.

Delphi Technique

Some of the drawbacks inherent in group opinions can be overcome through the Delphi process.[12] The group members are asked to provide

12. Named after the famed Oracle of Delphi in ancient Greece. According to Greek mythology, the oracle was capable of predicting the future of those who sought counsel.

a sequence of forecasts through response to questionnaires. In turn, before each step in the sequence, these individuals are informed as to median, fiftieth, or seventy-fifth percentile forecast levels on the last measurement. Since response is by questionnaire rather than by group discussion, domination by a few individuals, undue conservatism, and argumentation are avoided. In addition, informing group members as to the median- or high-percentile response on the last forecast provides them with insights emanating from the expertise of other members.

The Delphi process assumes that, as repeated forecasts are conducted, the range of responses will diminish and the median will move to a position representing the most valid consensus value. The median rather than the mean is the measure of central tendency, since it is unaffected by extreme values.

Delphi questionnaires vary, but a typical initial first-round questionnaire is likely to contain the following example:

Indicate your estimate of the probability of each of the following levels of sales for 1976:

Level of Sales, $	Probability
100,000–139,999	_____
140,000–179,999	_____
180,000–219,999	_____
220,000–259,999	_____
260,000–299,999	_____
300,000–339,999	_____
340,000–379,999	_____
380,000–419,999	_____
420,000–459,999	_____

A second questionnaire is similar to the first, except that it indicates the medians and/or fiftieth- or seventy-fifth-percentile scores for the previous round. The percentile adopted by analysts reflects their feelings regarding the degree of consensus that must be obtained. Reports on the outcome of the first questionnaire furnish the feedback required by the Delphi assumptions. Third, fourth, and further rounds follow. The process terminates when the median and percentile scores stabilize, that is, when further rounds do not greatly change the results of those that preceded.

The Delphi process has been employed for a number of estimation tasks.[13] It has substantial potential for forecasting purposes because it removes much of the weakness found in other consensus methods. The available evidence suggests that it is a valid and reliable technique.[14]

SUMMARY

This chapter has discussed subjective judgmental forecasts made by experienced and insightful experts or specialists, such as executives, sales representatives, customers, and other specialists. Each may have particular insights that may be highly predictive of future sales levels. Their estimations, however, are sometimes subject to bias—a force that the forecaster must recognize and account for.

There are a number of techniques for eliciting experts' judgments. One is PERT, which involves applying a formula to optimistic, pessimistic, and most likely estimates. This method produces measures of central tendency and of dispersion. It is useful when sufficient time and data for more lengthy objective methods are not available.

Utility theory is another source of judgmental forecasts. Here, specialists indicate what trade-offs in probabilities they are willing to make between the forecast and another variable with a known probability. This method is useful when experts have produced several possible forecasts but find it difficult to evaluate their relative probabilities.

Judgment from the extremes is a means of arriving at ranges of forecasts. Here, the analyst begins with extremes with a high range and, through a series of yes–no questions to the specialist, attempts to reduce the range. This is a good method to use when experts experience difficulty in producing sales forecasts.

Another method, emanating from decision theory, is the expected-value technique. Here, the forecast is the magnitude that is expected in light of various states of nature in the firm's environment. Thus, changes in the environment can be accommodated. Essentially, the expected value is a weighted mean that provides for the magnitude of environmental states and the subjective probability estimate of each state.

Bayesian decision theory also employs computations of expected value. In addition, it relates judgments to outside information (such as that derived from research). Here, subjective and objective probabilities

13. For an example, see Mark P. McElreath, *Priority Research Questions in Public Relations, Key Results from a Delphi Survey* (Lawrence, Dan.: Association for Education in Journalism, 1980).
14. Marvin A. Jolson and Gerald L. Rossow, "The Delphi Process in Marketing Decision Making," *Journal of Marketing Research*, 8 (November 1971), 443–448.

are combined to produce revised probabilities. The dependent variable in this case is the expected value of a conditional event. Sometimes decision trees are used to help managers and researchers visualize the Bayesian forecasts. Finally, the Bayesian approach yields estimates of the value of additional research.

Group methods involve assembling panels of experts and then trying to discern their consensus regarding forecast values. There are potential weaknesses in group methods, however, including domination of a group by high-ranking executives, unduly conservative forecasts, unyielding positions on the part of some group members, and individual failure to assume responsibility for group decisions. In order to overcome these weaknesses at least partly, the Delphi technique is sometimes used. A consensus method, it employs questionnaires, repeated measurements, and feedback to the panel on each round of forecasting.

DISCUSSION QUESTIONS

1. "Forecasting is a science that has no need for judgments." Comment.
2. Identify the individuals who are most likely to constitute "expert" sources of forecasts for the following concerns:
   a. A manufacturer of automatic clothes washers and dryers, such as GE
   b. A small toy store, recently opened and located in a large shopping mall
   c. A manufacturer and national distributor of pesticides for farmers
   d. A producer of aircraft sold to the United States and foreign air forces
   e. A mail-order retailer of expensive Bibles
3. What characteristics of executives might make them especially effective as providers of forecasting judgments?
4. What are the advantages and disadvantages of using sales representatives to provide estimates of future sales? In your opinion, would those who sell magazines on a door-to-door basis be effective forecasters? Why or why not?
5. Explain why customers of the firm might find it difficult to estimate their future purchases.
6. Design several questions that could be included in a questionnaire to be distributed to heads of household and intended to estimate their future purchases of Buick Skylarks.
7. Using the PERT-derived technique, compute expected value and standard deviation with the following data:
   a. Pessimistic estimate $110,000
   b. Optimistic estimate $206,000
   c. Most likely estimate $172,000

8. Following are four possible sales forecasts and four associated degrees of belief in each. Which forecast would the firm utilize?

Forecast Level	Degree of Belief
$34,570,000	0.35
$36,350,000	0.80
$38,890,000	0.50
$40,650,000	0.20

9. Describe how the judgment-from-the-extremes technique could be used to forecast sales of a restaurant that has been in business for over three decades.

10. An exporter of ladies' quartz watches uses expected values as estimates of future sales. In this case, the levels of personal income in the foreign markets are the states of nature. The states of nature and associated probabilities and sales levels appear below. Compute the sales forecast.

State of Nature	Probability	Sales
High income	0.30	$52 million
Medium income	0.50	$47 million
Low income	0.20	$37 million

11. Assume that a survey costing $500,000 could be conducted for Question 10 which has an 85% chance of being right. Because of the delay, however, the market is expected to worsen by 10%. Would the survey be worthwhile?

12. Cite the advantages and disadvantages of obtaining judgmental forecasts from groups rather than from individuals.

13. Describe the Delphi technique. What advantages does it have over other group methods?

14. Would you recommend the Delphi technique for a business that is owned and managed by a single family?

15. How are forecasts constructed with the use of Bayesian decision theory?

16. Define each of the following:
   a. Subjective probabilities
   b. Conditional event

     c. Expected value of a conditional event

     d. Decision tree

     e. Value of additional research

17. Set forth the various steps required to generate a utility-theory sales forecast. What are the advantages and disadvantages of this approach?

RECOMMENDED READINGS

Anderson, Earl H. "Probabilistic Forecasting for New Small Business." *Journal of Small Business Management*, 17 (July 1979), 8–13.

Brown, Bernice B. *Delphi Process: A Methodology Used for the Elicitation of Opinions of Experts*. Santa Monica, Calif.: Rand Corporation, 1968.

Carr, Richard P., Jr. "Identifying Trade Areas for Consumer Goods in Foreign Markets." *Journal of Marketing*, 42 (October 1978), 76–80.

Edwards, W. "The Theory of Decision Making." *Psychological Bulletin*, 54 (1954), 380–417.

Enis, Ben M., and Charles L. Broome. *Marketing Decisions: A Bayesian Approach.* Scranton, Pa.: Intext Educational Publishers, 1971.

"Lifting the Haze from the Future." *Business Week*, December 17, 1966, pp. 100–102.

Loye, D. *The Knowledgeable Future: A Psychology of Forecasting and Prophecy.* New York: John Wiley and Sons, 1978.

Mason, Robert. *Statistical Techniques in Business and Economics*. Homewood, Ill.: Richard D. Irwin, 1978, Chapter 20.

Moore, Franklin, and Thomas Hendrick. *Production Operations Management.* Homewood, Ill.: Richard D. Irwin, 1980, Chapter 25.

Meade, N. *Short and Medium Term Forecasting.* New York: Pergamon Press, 1980, Chapter 4.

Schlaifer, Robert. *Probability and Statistics in Business Decisions.* New York: McGraw-Hill Book Company, Inc., 1959, pp. 544–570.

Shoemaker, Robert W. "An Analysis of the Purchase Quantity Decision." *1976 Proceedings, American Marketing Association Educators' Conference.* Chicago: American Marketing Association, 1977, pp. 179–184.

Timmins, Sherman A., Martha C. Fraker, and James Brown. "Large-Firm Forecasting Techniques *Can* Improve Small Business Decision Making." *Journal of Small Business Management*, 17 (July 1979), 14–18.

Vatter, Paul, Stephen P. Bradley, Charles Sherwood, Charles Frey, and Barbara Bund Jackson. *Quantitative Methods in Management: Text and Cases.* Homewood, Ill.: Richard D. Irwin, 1978, Chapters 3, 4.

Weinwerm, E. H. "Limitations of the Scientific Method in Management Science." *Management Science*, 3 (April 1957), 225–233.

Woodlock, Joseph, and Louis Fourt. "Prediction Model for New Products." *Bulletin of the Operations Research Society of America*, 8 (May 1960), 13–15.

CASE 2:   EVANSTON COMMUNICATIONS, INC.

Executives of Evanston Communications, Inc., are considering whether or not to expand the company's operations. Evanston provided cable

television service to Evanston, Illinois, one of Chicago's near-north
suburbs.

Evanston's operations have been quite successful. Revenues grew from
nothing, at the company's inception in 1978, to $1.4 million at year
end, 1981. Net income for 1981 was $290,000. Executives feel that this
performance was excellent, considering especially that net investment
stood at $526,000.

"However, the only way for us to grow is to develop a new market,"
said Hiram Walther, Evanston's president. With 53,200 subscribers, the
company holds a 56% penetration rate in the Evanston market. Much
further penetration is not considered likely.

This poses a problem. Because each community grants licenses and
permits to only one cable company, Evanston faces no direct competitors in its primary market. The problem is that all the other com-
munities with high population densities, like Evanston, have already
granted licenses to other companies.

Walther is confident that Evanston can acquire the licensing for
Barrington, Illinois, for a $10,000 yearly fee, but he is not as confident
that the operation will prove profitable. "Our biggest initial difficulty in
Evanston was to get the licenses and permits," said Walther. "We knew
that our operations would be successful because of the high population
density. Barrington, on the other hand, is a different matter."

Evanston's population is bounded in a 15-square-mile area. Although
many single-family homes are generally spaced relatively close together,
about half the population resides in apartments. The community can be
characterized as middle class, with houses valued between $75,000 and
$150,000. Because of Northwestern University's presence, many
residents are considered "intellectuals."

In contrast, Barrington is known for its spaciousness. A distant northwest suburb of Chicago, the community encompasses an area of over
200 square miles with a population just under 30,000. The community
can be labeled upper-middle and lower-upper class. Most residences
range in value between $150,000 to $350,000, with several being worth
over $2 million. Because of restrictive zoning, almost all the properties
are larger than 1½ acres, and several are over 20 acres. The community
is known as "horse country," and it attracts many of Chicago's top
business executives.

Almost all national cable television companies serving areas similar to
Evanston have been profitable. However, the performances of companies
serving areas like Barrington have been mixed. Spaciousness means added
operating costs for cable, repair crews, and the like. Low population
densities require unusually high subscription rates for success. Evanston's
management has compiled the following summary of companies serving
areas similar to Barrington:

Category (Excludes Licensing Fees)		Number of Companies
Average operating loss of	$200,000	2
Average operating loss of	50,000	18
Average operating profit of	100,000	20
Average operating profit of	300,000	10
Total		50

Conducting a market research study is an option open to Evanston. A reading of Barrington's demand for cable television would be of obvious benefit to Walther. Such a study would cost $15,000 and would be about 85% accurate, according to industry estimates.

One problem with doing such a study, however, is that results would not be known for three months. Walther is afraid that the delay, as well as the "stirring-up of attention" by conducting a study, might trigger interest among other companies to serve Barrington. This could lead to a bidding war and a larger licensing fee. If so, Walther is nevertheless confident that Evanston can get the license for $20,000. He feels that there is a 50% chance that such a war would ensue.

What should Walther do?

Chapter 3
Time-Series Analysis: Informal Methods and Smoothing

INTRODUCTION

In the case of some products and companies, sales seem to depend very heavily upon the passage of time. Thus, greeting cards, Easter baskets, fireworks, and turkeys are sold in greater volumes at certain times of the year than at others. Similarly, some durable goods, such as homes and automobiles, are purchased in much greater quantities during some years than they are in others. Finally, some sales patterns follow a clear trend, as when they increase arithmetically, as illustrated in Figure 3.1. Business firms are not unaware of such patterns. Sears, Roebuck, and Company, for instance, utilizes a "strategic trend information system," whereby groups of high-level executives are provided with extensive information and are asked to formulate predictions of trends that they expect to materialize in the future.[1]

Time-series analysis, the subject of this chapter, involves a systematic examination of historical values of a variable, such as the revenues of a firm or one of its products. The intention is to identify orderly periodic patterns that may be used to generate projections into the future. To illustrate, consider the following historical series relating unit sales with successive intervals of time, say months, denoted by the variable t:

$$t = \quad 1 \qquad 2 \qquad 3 \qquad 4 \qquad 5$$
$$\text{Sales} = 100 \quad 105 \quad 110 \quad 115 \quad 120$$

Even a casual examination reveals that unit sales have increased by 5 units each month. Thus, there has been a linear relationship between sales and the passing of time. It would appear that this information can be used in forecasting into the future. Thus, sales of 125 units would be forecast for $t = 6$. Herein lies the simple logic of time series—what has happened in the past forms the basis for estimating what will happen during future periods.

---

1. "Info System Identifies Company Opportunities," *Marketing News*, 8 (May 30, 1980), 14.

Figure 3.1 Illustration of Arithmetical Sales Increase Over Time

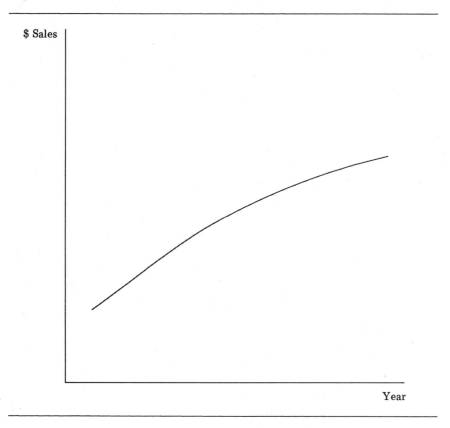

There are various types of time-series models, each of which has a slightly different purpose. Some, for example, are especially suited for situations in which there is a significant long-term trend—as with solar hot-water heating units—of sales growing steadily at a fairly even rate. Others are useful when regular seasonal patterns are evident, as typified by revenues of sellers of air conditioners, skis, and lawn fertilizer. Certainly, some of the techniques are very simple to conceptualize and to use, whereas others are quite complicated.

This chapter provides an exposition of the most widely used of the time-series techniques, namely informal methods and smoothing. Chapter 5 will cover a more intricate method, decomposition. Before proceeding with either set of techniques, however, we must first consider two concepts: scatter diagrams and measuring forecast error.

SCATTER DIAGRAMS

The first step in attempting to analyze sales behavior over time is to construct a scatter diagram. In such a diagram, historical values of sales are plotted (graphed) so that they schematically picture any relationship with time. This procedure is really quite simple, especially with the widespread use of computers and terminals with software capable of producing the graphs automatically. And the diagrams yield tremendously useful information in helping to identify order within the time series.

Table 3.1 sets forth sales of brass screws over the past ten years for Precision Screw Products, Inc. Note that it is difficult to deduce much about the sales/time relationship from the raw data. It is evident that the sales trend is upward, but not much beyond this observation is clear.

Figure 3.2 is a scatter diagram of Precision's brass screw sales. The graph confirms that, despite a drop in 1981, there has been a general upward trend in sales over the past ten years. In addition, the trend appears to be linear in nature, in that the sales/time relationship follows the pattern of a straight line. Also, it is likely that a straight-line extension of past fluctuations would be a good predictor of the future with only minimal error, since it appears that all the dots are close to being on some positively sloped line.

Observations from a scatter diagram like this can be very significant, as they indicate the method that is appropriate for analyzing a particular time series. On the other hand, the observations may indicate that certain methods (such as those assuming a curvilinear behavior of sales over time) should be avoided when a linear trend is present. More will

Table 3.1 Precision Screw Products' Sales of Brass Screws

Year	Sales, $
1973	504,063
1974	507,205
1975	516,832
1976	527,310
1977	530,090
1978	535,870
1979	548,925
1980	574,412
1981	556,770
1982	568,830

Figure 3.2 Precision Screw Products' Sales of Brass Screws

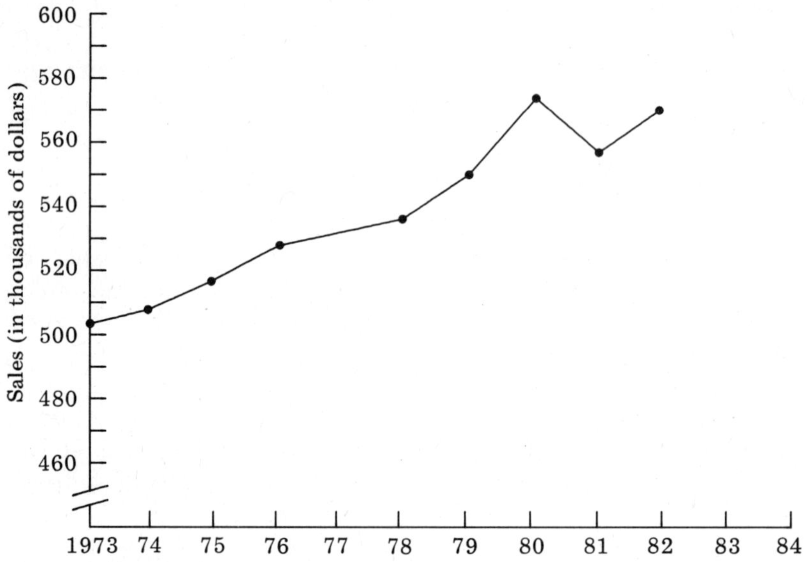

be said about choosing the correct technique later. For now, it is enough to see how a scatter diagram is of value in visualizing a time-series relationship.

MEASURING FORECAST ERROR

The Need

In the case of time series or, for that matter, any other forecasting technique, it is essential that we have some means of determining the expected difference between forecasted and actual values. This measure will allow us to determine which of one or more forecasting methods is to be employed. Let us now, then, examine a means of evaluating the expected accuracy of various forecasting techniques. We will use this tool repeatedly in subsequent chapters, so it is important to master it at this point.

The Issues

The "proof of the pudding is in its taste" goes the old adage. And the same is true of forecasts, except that "taste" refers to how well some specific technique performs. Two basic issues are relevant here. The first involves a comparison of how close a forecast comes to the actual value. After a period of time has elapsed and the information is known, one is in a position to make this comparison. Many useful insights can be gained about the forecasting accuracy of the procedure in question and whether a different procedure should be used for producing the next forecast. Not unlike other analysts, forecasters are in a position to employ past experience as a learning device and therefore to improve their performance in the future.

The second issue concerns assessing how accurate a particular method is likely to be when the technique is first chosen. This requires "pretending" that forecasts were made to estimate sales over a past time period and comparing the values that would have been forecasted through the method in question with actual sales values. Comparing the "forecasts" with the historical actual values can help assess how a model fits the history.

To illustrate, consider a naive means of forecasting, one whereby the most recent actual value is used as a forecast of the next value. Some managers actually use such a method. Table 3.2 presents such a forecasting system for the Precision data from Table 3.1.

Table 3.2 Naive Forecast of Precision's Sales of Brass Screws

(1) Year	(2) Actual Sales, $	(3) Forecast, $	(4) Error, $	(5) Squared Error, $
1973	504,063			
1974	507,205	504,063	3,142	9,872,164
1975	516,832	507,205	9,627	92,679,129
1976	527,310	516,832	10,478	109,788,484
1977	530,090	527,310	2,780	7,728,400
1978	535,870	530,090	5,780	33,408,400
1979	548,925	535,870	13,055	170,433,035
1980	574,412	548,925	25,487	649,587,179
1981	556,770	574,412	(17,642)	311,240,164
1982	568,830	556,770	12,060	145,443,600
1983		568,830		

Summary: MSE = $170,020,060

Square Root of MSE = $13,039

Mean Squared Error

There are several ways of evaluating how well a forecasting method would have worked over a historical period of time. All of them begin with first calculating the size of the *error* (difference between actual and forecasted value) for each of the time periods under examination. Note that column 4 of Table 3.2 provides this information, which was determined by subtracting the entry in column 3 from that in column 2. Some analysts then calculate the percentage that each error is of its corresponding actual value and then average all the percentages to determine how well the method fits the time series. But the most common method—and the one employed in this book—is to calculate the mean squared error (MSE), which is the average of the errors squared. For example:

$$\text{MSE} = \frac{\$9,872,164 + \$92,679,129 + \cdots + \$145,443,600}{9} \quad (3.1)$$

$$= \$170,020,060$$

MSE can be interpreted as being analogous to the variance statistic. The closer the forecasts are to the actual values, the smaller the MSE will be. Further, a model that results in a lower MSE for a given time series is considered to be a better choice than a model that has a higher MSE. Thus, one can use MSE calculations from two or more models as one guide in picking the appropriate one to utilize.

The square root of a calculated MSE can often yield additional insight into how well the method can be expected to perform. (Such a square root, of course, generates a measure that is analogous to the standard deviation statistic.) Continuing with the example, the naive model results in the following:

$$\sqrt{\text{MSE}} = \sqrt{\$170,020,060} = \$13,039$$

This now puts the mean error calculation in the same unit of measurement as the original data. More will be said later about using the square root of an MSE. For now, it is important to see only that using MSE provides a measure of how well a forecasting method fits a time series and that such measures can be used to compare the value of two or more forecasting techniques for a particular series.

Major Components

Every real-world time series has at least two components. The first is some functional relationship between the forecast variable (Y) and time (t). This can be expressed as $Y = f(t)$. There is also a second component, one that represents random fluctuation, termed *error* (e). Though difficult, it would be possible to calculate the exact complex mathematical function that precisely matches every observation of a time series. This would be the same as exactly connecting every dot of the related scatter plot and would force $e = 0$ in the forecasting model.

But such a procedure is inappropriate in forecasting. Some random fluctuation is natural and should be allowed. Further, the resulting equation from exactly matching every observation would be very complex (an nth-order polynomial), so that employing it to project into the future would yield highly unreliable results. By analogy, it would be similar to turning on a fire hose without anchoring its nozzle.

Consequently, all time-series methods have a general equation as $Y = f(t) + e$. The particular model to be used should be the one that results in the smallest MSE, provided that the general nature of the model fits the nature of the situation. More will be said about this later.

INFORMAL METHODS

The first set of time-series techniques can be labeled informal. This nomenclature is a result of their simplistic mathematical bases. Despite this characteristic, they are often used by managers and can provide very useful information. Freehand smoothing, percentage change, weighted average, moving average, and double moving average are the most frequently encountered informal methods, in addition to some versions of the naive method already considered (Table 3.2).

Freehand Smoothing

Freehand smoothing is one way of attempting to identify any long-term trend in a time series. We will continue with an analysis of Precision's sales of brass screws (Figure 3.2). As was previously indicated, there does appear to be an upward linear trend in sales. The task now is to identify the linear function so that a forecast can be made.

We can create visual representation of a linear function that appears to minimize the vertical distances between that line and all the points in the scatter diagram. (A mathematical procedure termed *least squares*, which actually defines the best linear function, appears in Chapter 4's discussion of regression.) Figure 3.3 presents such a function for the example. Note that, for convenience, the annual time periods are converted to a unit scale (1973 = 1, 1974 = 2, and so on) and that sales are stated in thousands of dollars.

In order to generate a forecast for $t = 10$ (1983), one could extend the $Y = a + bt$ function and read the forecast off the graph. For the

Figure 3.3 Algebraic Calculation from Freehand Smoothed Function Between Brass Screws Sales and Time

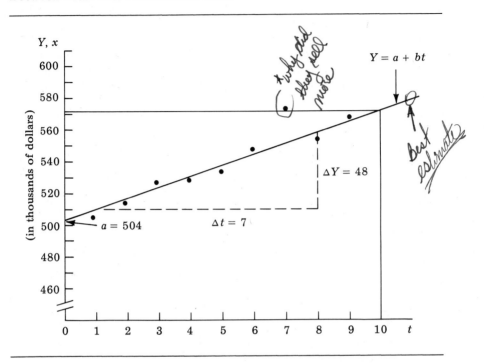

example it would be $572,000. Another way is to estimate the algebraic equation for the straight line:

$$Y_t = a + bt \qquad (3.2)$$

where Y_t = the forecast of x at time t
x_t = the actual value of the forecast variable (brass screw sales) at time t
a = the Y intercept, which is the value of Y when $t = 0$
b = the slope of the line
t = the time period

For the Precision example, $a = \$504,000$ (examine Figure 3.3 and see where the line intersects the Y axis—this point is $504,000). In turn, the slope coefficient is calculated as follows:

$$b = \frac{\Delta Y}{\Delta t} \qquad (3.3)$$

where ΔY = the change in the value of Y corresponding to a particular change in the value of t
Δt = the particular change in t

For the example, two arbitrary but convenient points along the
linear function were selected and are depicted in Figure 3.3. From the
graph and Equation 3.3, one can see that the functional relationship is
estimated to be

$$Y = \$504{,}000 + \$6{,}857t \tag{3.4}$$

And using this equation, the forecast of sales for 1983 is $572,570.
Forecasts for years beyond 1983 are calculated simply by adding the
slope value for each additional year to $572,570. Thus, the forecast
for 1984 is $572,570 + $6,857 = $579,327, and for 1985 it is
$572,570 + 2($6,857) = $586,084, and so on.
    Equation 3.4 is now used to assess how well the model fits the
historical series through a computation of MSE. The data appear in
Table 3.3. Notice that considerable improvement has been made over
the naive model set forth in Table 3.2. In fact, there is a ($13,039 −
$7,888)/$13,039 = 39.5% reduction in the $\sqrt{\text{MSE}}$. It is evident, then,

Table 3.3 Freehand-Smoothed Forecast of Precision's Sales of Brass
Screws

(1) T	(2) Actual, $	(3) Y, $	(4) Error, $	(5) Squared Error, $
0	504,063	504,000	63	3,969
1	507,205	510,857	(3,652)	13,337,104
2	516,832	517,714	(882)	777,924
3	527,310	524,571	2,739	7,502,121
4	530,090	531,428	(1,338)	1,790,244
5	535,870	538,285	(2,415)	5,832,225
6	548,925	545,142	3,783	14,311,089
7	574,412	551,999	22,413	502,342,570
8	556,770	558,856	(2,086)	4,351,396
9	568,830	565,713	3,117	9,715,689
10		572,570		

Summary: MSE = $62,218,259
Square Root of MSE = $7,888

that this model is much better than the naive one. The model explicitly considers the linear trend visible in the scatter diagram, and it has a much lower MSE.

Another important observation can be made from Table 3.3. Follow the values in the error column—they do not appear to follow a consistent pattern over the time series. That is, they are randomly distributed around the value of zero. This means that the model is appropriate for the time series, in that the assumptions of the model fit the circumstances of the historical data. Contrast this with Table 3.2, where there is clearly a pattern in the errors—all but one are positive. Of the two models, therefore, the freehand-smoothing one is the better, and a forecast of $572,570 would be made for 1983.

The major limitation of the freehand-smoothing method, however, is that it depends on a visual estimation of the linear function. Although the resulting function may approximate the true pattern, it is likely that it is not the best one because of possible judgmental error. A computationally more accurate method, termed *least squares*, should be employed instead. Chapter 4 provides a discussion of this technique.

Percentage-Change Method

One of the least complex forecasting techniques is the percentage-change method. In essence, this method attempts to evaluate the percentage change in the forecast variable between successive periods of time. Table 3.4 presents sales of the Maycrest Corporation along with the percentage change from one year to the next. After calculation, the percentage changes are examined to determine if a regular pattern is evident.

The data in Table 3.4 suggest that a general trend exists for increasing sales of the Maycrest Corporation. Several methods are available for determining the appropriate percentage change in sales to be used in forecasting for next year's level. One is to calculate the average of all period changes. This is calculated to be 2.038%. The resulting forecast for 1983 is $90,365,000 obtained as follows:

$$\$88,560,000 \times 1.02038 = \$90,365,000$$

Major Limitations

There are several problems with the use of the percentage-change method for forecasting. The first, and perhaps most important, is that a long-term trend may easily be overlooked. To illustrate, the following values were calculated with the straight-line equation $Y = 10 + 5t$:

Table 3.4 Maycrest Corporation, Forecast of Sales Using the
Percentage-Change Method

T Year	Sales (in $000)	% Increase/ (Decrease)	Forecast $Y(t+1) =$ $1.02038*T_t$	Error (in $000)	Squared Error (in $000,000)
1973	73,964	—	—	—	—
1974	75,847	2.55	75,471	376	141,376
1975	77,398	2.04	77,393	5	25
1976	76,537	(1.11)	78,975	(2,438)	5,943,844
1977	79,320	3.64	78,097	1,223	1,495,729
1978	81,542	2.80	80,937	605	366,025
1979	80,735	(0.99)	83,204	(2,469)	6,095,961
1980	84,386	4.52	82,380	2,006	4,024,036
1981	86,021	1.94	86,106	(85)	7,225
1982	88,560	2.95	87,774	786	617,796
1983	—	—	90,365	—	—

Summary: Average % change = (2.55 + 2.04 . . . + 2.95)/9
= 2.038

MSE = $2,076,891E 06   (See Note)

Square root of MSE = $1,441,142

Note: Read $2,076,891 times 10 to the 6th power.

$\dfrac{t}{x}$	Y	Percentage Increase, %
0	10	—
1	15	50.0
2	20	33.3
3	25	25.0
4	30	20.0
5	35	16.7

In this example, the simple average of the percentage increases is 29%.
As a result, a forecast using this procedure would be (35 × 1.29) =
45.15. However, linear analysis reveals that the forecast should be 40.
Simply computing the average percentage change produces a forecast

that is greater than warranted. In practice, similar results will often be obtained whenever a long-term trend is evident in the data. If the long-term trend is positive, the percentage-change method will tend to over-estimate the forecast. Conversely, when a long-term trend is negative, the percentage-change method will tend to underestimate the forecast.

A second limitation is that recent changes may be more indicative of the future than older data. Recent changes may reflect more accurately that which may be expected in the future because of such factors as competitive conditions, operating strategies, and so on. To combat this problem, the forecaster may weight the percentage changes for recent data, as discussed later in this chapter.

Using the Percentage-Change Method

The percentage-change procedure is often used by accountants as well as businesspeople, usually in conjunction with the preparation of financial statements for analysis. The intent is often not to construct a forecast of a single variable's level. Instead, the intention is often to isolate problem areas and to make general inferences about an operation's possible performance in certain key areas. To illustrate, Table 3.5 presents key elements of the Maycrest Corporation's income statements for the past three years.

Table 3.5 indicates that attention should at least be directed toward expenses for utilities, hourly wages and benefits, and miscellaneous expenses. These expenses increased at a much faster rate than sales in both years. Used in this manner, the percentage-change method may be quite useful in the forecasting of problem areas toward which management attention should be directed.

The percentage-change method used to forecast potential problem areas from financial statements is consistent with the principle of *management by exception*, which is to direct attention primarily to problems rather than to all areas. It helps the decision makers focus on forecast problem areas so that they might act to correct the problem before it is too late. An additional advantage is that numerous time periods are not required for analysis. In situations where only a few periods of historical information are available or where significant recent changes in the environment are suspected, this method may lead to more accurate results than procedures based on a statistical analysis of historical data.

Weighting for Recent Data

Certainly, a fundamental question to be answered by the users of time-series techniques is whether recent history is more reflective of the

Table 3.5 Comparative Income Statements of the Maycrest Corporation (Amounts in Thousands)

	1980	1981		1982	
	Amount, $	Amount, $	Percent Change, %	Amount, $	Percent Change, %
Sales	84,386	86,021	1.94	88,560	2.95
Cost of goods sold	37,043	39,405	6.38	40,372	2.45
Gross margin	47,343	46,616	(1.54)	48,188	3.37
Depreciation	10,000	10,000	0	10,000	0
Utilities	837	904	8.00	1,292	42.92
Hourly wages and benefits	15,842	16,537	4.39	17,393	5.18
Salaries and benefits	12,500	12,900	3.20	13,000	0.78
Misc. expenses	2,500	2,850	14.00	3,000	5.26
Total expenses	41,679	43,191	3.63	44,685	3.46
Net income	5,664	3,425	(39.53)	3,503	2.28

future than distant history. Changes in underlying factors may have occurred over time, such as alterations in fashions, economic conditions, and tastes, which would cause historical relationships to differ from more recent ones. Consequently, recent history may need to be granted heavier consideration when preparing a forecast.

The weighting of time-series data by the time-of-occurrence problem introduces two issues. The first concerns whether or not all of an available history should be *used*. The second deals with whether or not all the time-series values used should be given *equal weight* in affecting the forecast. Moving- and weighted moving-average techniques address these issues.

Moving Average

One way to treat recent history when analyzing a time series is to utilize a moving average, which is simply a mean value—one that is recalculated as time elapses. As the name implies, the technique takes into account only a specific number of historical periods in calculating a forecast. Each time another period is experienced, the oldest period is dropped from consideration and the most recent is added to the moving-average base. The moving average itself represents the forecast for the upcoming period. This method may be expressed as follows:

$$Y_{t+1} = \frac{X_t + X_{t-1} + \cdots + X_{t-N+1}}{N} \qquad (3.5)$$

where Y_{t+1} = the forecast for time $t+1$

X_t = the actual value at time t, and

N = the number of values included in the average

Table 3.6 presents Harrington Computer Corporation's monthly unit sales of its PLP model computer over the past two years, beginning with January 1981 ($t=1$). Also presented is a comparison of results of a three- and a five-month model.[2]

Generally, management used judgment when determining how many months to include in the average. Obviously, the greater the number, the less weight is given to more recent periods. Conversely, the lower the number, the more weight is given to recent history. A large number is most desirable when there are wide sporadic fluctuations in the time

2. When an even number of periods are used, the moving average is often centered, that is, presented next to the series midpoint. A discussion of centering appears in Chapter 5.

Table 3.6 Harrington Computer Corporation's Monthly Unit Sales of PLP Computers, Moving Average

(1) Time Period	(2) Unit Sales	(3) Three-Month Moving Forecast	(4) Error	(5) Average Squared Error	(6) Five-Month Moving Forecast	(7) Error	(8) Average Squared Error
1	256	—	—	—	—	—	—
2	263	—	—	—	—	—	—
3	270	—	—	—	—	—	—
4	275	263	12	144	—	—	—
5	277	269	8	64	—	—	—
6	277	274	3	9	268	9	81
7	281	276	5	25	272	9	81
8	285	278	7	49	276	9	81
9	294	281	13	169	279	15	225
10	297	287	10	100	283	14	196
11	294	292	2	4	287	7	49
12	298	295	3	9	290	8	64
13	301	296	5	25	294	7	49
14	305	298	7	49	297	8	64
15	308	301	7	49	299	9	81
16	306	305	1	1	301	5	25
17	310	306	4	16	304	6	36
18	312	308	4	16	306	6	36

continued

Table 3.6 Harrington Computer Corporation's Monthly Unit Sales of PLP Computers, Moving Average *continued*

(1) Time Period	(2) Unit Sales	(3) Three-Month Moving Forecast	(4) Error	(5) Average Squared Error	(6) Five-Month Moving Forecast	(7) Error	(8) Average Squared Error
19	315	309	6	36	308	7	49
20	313	312	1	1	310	3	9
21	316	313	3	9	311	5	25
22	321	315	6	36	313	8	64
23	328	317	11	121	315	13	169
24	330	322	8	64	319	11	121
25	—	326	—	—	322	—	—

Summary: Three-month model MSE = 47.43 units

Square root of MSE = 6.89 units

Five-month model MSE = 79.21 units

Square root of MSE = 8.90 units

series. On the other hand, a small number is desirable when there are sudden shifts in the level of the series. For example, a small number of periods would be sought in forecasting the following hypothetical series: 5, 5, 5, 10, 10, 10, 10, 10, 7, 7, 7, 7. Heavy weight on recent history will enable the forecasts to catch up more rapidly to the relevant level.

In our example, the three-month moving-average method is the better of the two illustrated, since its related mean square error is the smallest. Accordingly, the forecast for January 1983, period $t = 25$, is

$$\frac{321 + 328 + 330}{3} = 326$$

The same amount, 326 units, is also the current forecast for period $t = 26$ and beyond. Note that an assumption of the moving average is that there is *no* trend inherent in the time series. Only when a new actual value is learned and a new moving average is computed may the forecast change. Even a casual observation of Harrington's data indicates that there is in fact a positive trend. And look at what it causes. Every entry in the error columns is positive, signifying that the forecasts do not catch up to the trend—they are always behind. This observation suggests that we introduce the double moving-average and the moving percentage-change methods.

Double Moving Average

One way of dealing with time-series data that have a linear trend is through the double moving-average technique. As the name implies, the method begins with a calculation of one set of moving averages and then another. The first set is computed in a manner identical to that of the previously discussed method, and the second set is a moving average of the first set. Table 3.7 illustrates the calculations with the Harrington data. Column 3 contains the same values as the forecasts of Table 3.6, only now the moving averages relate to one previous period. Column 4 contains the three-month moving averages of column 3.

Figure 3.4 depicts graphically actual sales and both sets of moving averages. Notice how the first set lags behind the actual values for comparable periods. Of more importance, note that the second set of moving averages lags behind the first set on average about as much as the first set lags behind the actuals. This is the essential concept of the double moving average. The difference between the averages is used in calculating the forecast. That is, the difference between the averages is added to the first average to estimate the actual.

In concept, this is exactly how double moving averages work. These are the *a* values in column 5 of Table 3.7. However, a final refinement

Table 3.7 Harrington Computer Corporation's Monthly Unit Sales of PLP Computers, Double Moving Average

(1) Time Period	(2) Unit Sales	(3) Y' Three-Month Moving Average of (2)	(4) Y'' Three-Month Moving Average of (3)	(5) Value of a	(6) Value of b	(7) Y Forecast $(a + bm)$ When $m = 1$	(8) Error	(9) Squared Error
1	256	—	—	—	—	—	—	—
2	263	—	—	—	—	—	—	—
3	270	263	—	—	—	—	—	—
4	275	269	—	—	—	—	—	—
5	277	274	269	279	5	—	—	—
6	277	276	273	279	3	284	(7)	49
7	281	278	276	280	2	282	(1)	1
8	285	281	278	284	3	282	3	9
9	294	287	282	292	5	287	7	49
10	297	292	287	297	5	297	0	0
11	294	295	291	299	4	302	(8)	64
12	298	296	294	298	2	303	(5)	25
13	301	298	296	300	2	300	1	1
14	305	301	298	304	3	302	3	9
15	308	305	301	309	4	307	1	1
16	306	306	304	308	2	313	(7)	49
17	310	308	306	310	2	310	0	0
18	312	309	308	310	1	312	0	0

continued

Table 3.7 Harrington Computer Corporation's Monthly Unit Sales of PLP Computers, Double Moving Average *continued*

(1) Time Period	(2) Unit Sales	(3) Y' Three-Month Moving Average of (2)	(4) Y'' Three-Month Moving Average of (3)	(5) Value of a	(6) Value of b	(7) Y Forecast $(a + bm$ When $m = 1)$	(8) Error	(9) Squared Error
19	315	312	310	314	2	311	4	16
20	313	313	311	315	2	316	(3)	9
21	316	315	313	317	2	317	(1)	1
22	321	317	315	319	2	319	2	4
23	328	322	318	326	4	321	7	49
24	330	326	322	330	4	330	0	0
25	—	—	—	—	—	334	—	—

Summary: MSE = 17.68

Square root of MSE = 4.21

Figure 3.4 Double Moving Averages, Harrington Data. Actual Sales = ____ . First Three-Month Moving Average = ____ . Second Three-Month Moving Average = ____ .

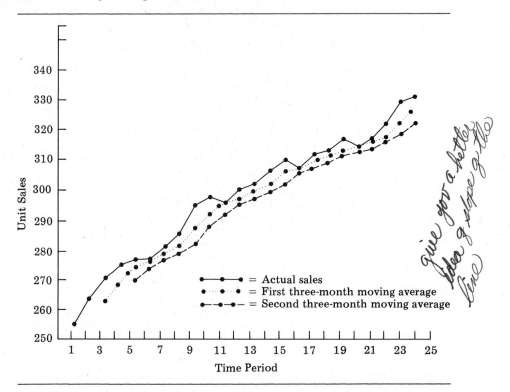

is required. Researchers over the years have learned that more accurate results are made possible by an additional adjustment factor, which is roughly analogous to a slope measure that can change over the series.

The forecasting method can be summarized mathematically as follows:

$$\text{Column 3:} \quad Y'_t = \frac{x_t + x_{t-1} + \cdots + x_{t-N+1}}{N} \tag{3.6}$$

$$\text{Column 4:} \quad Y''_t = \frac{Y'_t + Y'_{t-1} + \cdots + Y'_{t-N+1}}{N} \tag{3.7}$$

$$\text{Column 5:} \quad a_t = 2Y'_t - Y''_t \tag{3.8}$$

$$\text{Column 6:} \quad b_t = \frac{2}{N-1}(Y'_t - Y''_t) \tag{3.9}$$

$$\text{Column 7:} \quad Y_{t+m} = a_t + b_t m \qquad (3.10)$$

where N = the number of periods in the moving average (3 for the example)

   m = the number of periods ahead one wishes to forecast (1 for the example)

   x_t = the actual value at time period t

Given that we are at time period 24, the forecast for period 25, therefore, is $Y_{24+1} = 330 + 4 = 334$. The forecast for period 26 would be $Y_{24+2} = 330 + 2(4) = 338$.

This model is much more accurate than is the regular moving-average method. Nearly a 40% reduction in MSE was attained simply because the model allows for trend. Further, the error factors appear random around zero, suggesting that the model is appropriate. The major drawback of the model, however, is that it is rather complicated, requiring many calculations.

Moving Percentage Change

A method that we have found in practice to be as accurate as, and sometimes more accurate than, the double moving averages for time series containing trend is the moving percentage-change technique. Further, this method is distinguished by being much simpler to use. Table 3.8 illustrates the method, again employing Harrington's sales of PLP computers, permitting comparisons with the other methods.

For this technique, the percentage changes from period to period (column 3) are calculated in the same way as was the simple percentage-change technique (Table 3.4). This time, however, moving averages of the percentage changes are utilized (column 4) instead of an overall simple average. Three-month moving averages were used in the example for comparison with the other techniques. The method can be expressed mathematically as follows:

Column 4: $\hspace{9.5cm}$ (3.11)

$$MPC_t = \left(\frac{(x_t - x_{t-1})}{x_{t-1}} + \frac{(x_{t-1} - x_{t-2})}{x_{t-2}} + \cdots + \frac{(x_{t-N+1} - x_{t-N})}{x_{t-N}} \right) \div N$$

Column 5: $Y_{t+1} = x_t + (1.0 + MPC_t)$ $\hspace{5cm}$ (3.12)

where MPC = moving percentage change

   N = number of periods in the moving percentage change

Notice in the summary of Table 3.8 that this method results in a smaller MSE than does the double moving-average method, and also that the errors of column 6 appear rather randomly distributed around zero. It would appear, then, that the moving percentage-change method is a good candidate to be used to forecast Harrington's sales of PLP

Table 3.8 Harrington Computer Corporation's Monthly Unit Sales of PLP Computers, Moving Percentage Change

(1)	(2)	(3)	(4)	(5)	(6)	(7)
			Three-Month			
Time	Unit	Percent	Moving Average			Squared
Period	Sales	Change	Percent Change	Forecast	Error	Error
1	256	—	—	—	—	—
2	263	2.73	—	—	—	—
3	270	2.66	—	—	—	—
4	275	1.85	2.41	—	—	—
5	277	0.73	1.75	282	(5)	25
6	277	0	0.86	282	(5)	25
7	281	1.44	0.72	279	2	4
8	285	1.42	0.95	283	2	4
9	294	3.16	2.01	288	6	36
10	297	1.02	1.87	300	(3)	9
11	294	(1.01)	1.06	303	(9)	81
12	298	1.36	0.46	297	1	1
13	301	1.01	0.45	299	2	4
14	305	1.33	1.23	302	3	9
15	308	0.98	1.11	309	(1)	1
16	306	(0.65)	0.55	311	(5)	25
17	310	1.31	0.55	308	2	4
18	312	0.65	0.44	312	0	0
19	315	0.96	0.97	313	2	4
20	313	(0.63)	0.33	318	(5)	25
21	316	0.96	0.43	314	2	4
22	321	1.58	0.64	317	4	16
23	328	2.18	1.57	323	5	25
24	330	0.61	1.46	333	(3)	9
25	—	—	—	335	—	—

Summary: MSE = 15.55 units

Square root of MSE = 3.94 units

computers. Forecasts for subsequent periods to $t = 25$ are obtained as follows:

$$Y_{k+m} = (MPC_k)(m)(x_k) + x_k \qquad (3.13)$$

where MPC_k = moving percentage change at period k
$\quad\quad k$ = the last actual period in the time series
$\quad\quad m$ = the number of future periods for which a forecast is required

To illustrate with the example, the forecast for $t = 26$ is Y_{24+2} = $(1.46\%)(2)(330) + 330 = 340$ units.

Weighted Average

The final informal method that we will consider uses weighted averages. This technique begins with the assignment of weights to each of the historical observations of a time series according to its relative chronological age. The intention is to grant greater weight to recent history than to the past so that more consideration is given to emerging changes in underlying relationships.

Management subjectively determines the weights that are to be employed—a judgmental process. One scheme often used is to weight each time period according to its respective proportional chronological age. Here the oldest receives an initial weight of 1.0, the next oldest a weight of 2.0, and so on. Then each of these initial weights is divided by the sum of all the weights to arrive at the final weight set. In short, this is a weighted mean computation. The method may use actual historical values, weighted moving averages, or weighted moving-percentage changes.

Table 3.9 illustrates the weighted moving percentage-change procedure, again using the Harrington Computer Corporation's data from previous examples. A three-month weighted moving percentage-change scheme was used to permit comparison with the previous techniques. Notice that the entries in column 4 differ from those in the same column of Table 3.8. This is because each entry in column 3 of Table 3.8 received an equal weight in calculating column 4. In Table 3.9, however, column 3's percentage changes were weighted as follows:

Column 4: $WMPC_t = \frac{1}{6}(PC_{t-2}) + \frac{2}{6}(PC_{t-1}) + \frac{3}{6}(PC_t)$ $\qquad (3.14)$

where $WMPC_t$ = weighted moving percentage change at time period t
$\quad\quad PC$ = percent change (column 3)

The result is that there is a modest improvement in the MSE over the moving average percent-change method. And again, the errors of column 6 appear randomly distributed around zero. Therefore, this model seems to be the most accurate of the informal methods employed for this example and shall be used to forecast unit sales of PLP computers.

Table 3.9 Harrington Computer Corporation's Monthly Unit Sales of PLP Computers, Weighted Moving-Percentage Change

(1)	(2)	(3)	(4)	(5)	(6)	(7)
			Three-Month Weighted			
Time Period	Unit Sales	Percent Change	Moving Percent Change	Forecast	Error	Squared Error
1	256	—	—	—	—	—
2	263	2.73	—	—	—	—
3	270	2.66	—	—	—	—
4	275	1.85	2.27	—	—	—
5	277	0.73	1.43	281	(4)	16
6	277	0	0.55	281	(4)	16
7	281	1.44	0.84	279	2	4
8	285	1.42	1.19	283	2	4
9	294	3.16	2.29	288	6	36
10	297	1.02	1.80	301	(4)	16
11	294	(1.01)	0.36	302	(8)	64
12	298	1.36	0.51	295	3	9
13	301	1.01	0.79	300	1	1
14	305	1.33	1.23	303	2	4
15	308	0.98	1.10	309	(1)	1
16	306	(0.65)	0.22	311	(5)	25
17	310	1.31	0.60	307	3	9
18	312	0.65	0.65	312	0	0
19	315	0.96	0.92	314	1	1
20	313	(0.63)	0.11	318	(5)	25
21	316	0.96	0.43	313	3	9
22	321	1.58	1.01	317	4	16
23	328	2.18	1.78	324	4	16
24	330	0.61	1.30	334	(4)	16
25	—	—	—	334	—	—

Summary: MSE = 14.40 units

Square root of MSE = 3.79 units

Forecasts for two or more periods into the future are obtained in the same manner as in the previous method, only now we substitute the final WPMC for the final MPC. The forecast for $t = 26$, to illustrate, is $Y_{24+2} = (1.30\%)(2)(330) + 330 = 339$ units.

Major Problem Areas

As might be expected, there are several problems with all the methods discussed so far. For one, there are many possible alternative models within any given technique. The four-month, five-month, or some other number used in the moving percentage-change method, for instance, could result in an even more accurate forecasting model than that presented in Table 3.9. Or some entirely different weighting scheme could be better. For that matter, one of the other techniques, such as double moving averages, could yield the best results if the right number of periods to be averaged were known. Far too many possibilities exist for all of them to be efficiently analyzed and compared. Consequently, judgment is often the major basis for picking an appropriate number of periods to use, which can easily lead to less accurate forecasts than are needed or desired.

Another problem relates to the extensive number of calculations required as well as the relatively large volume of data that must be stored in order to use the models depicted above. To illustrate, suppose six-month double moving averages are chosen as the forecasting model. Twelve historical observations, a forecast, plus the most recent actual data would, at the minimum, need to be stored, reanalyzed, and updated for every new period. The number of computations and the amount of data that must be stored and updated can easily become overwhelming, especially if forecasts are made for large numbers of products. To overcome these problems, more sophisticated forecasters rely on the formal methods discussed next. As the reader shall see, these correspond to several of those already discussed, but they are easier to use and generally yield more accurate results.

FORMAL METHODS

Formal methods differ from those already mentioned by their greater mathematical support and by the fact that they are generally easier to use. In addition, when properly employed, they can be expected to produce much more accurate results. The techniques discussed in this section are (1) single exponential smoothing, (2) double exponential smoothing, (3) quadratic smoothing, and (4) Winters's model.

Single Exponential Smoothing

The Model

As you will see, single exponential smoothing is very similar to the moving-average model. However, it does not require that all the historical data be stored and averages computed each time. Instead, exponential smoothing necessitates saving *only* the previous forecast and the actual value for the previous period, once the model is determined. When a forecast is prepared, it is necessary to retain only the new value and, of course, the mathematical model itself in memory. The remaining data need not be stored.

Essentially the technique involves calculating a new forecast on the basis of the old forecast *plus* a fraction of the amount by which the old forecast deviated from the actual value. More specifically, the forecast is constructed using the following equation:

$$Y_{t+1} = \alpha x_t + (1 - \alpha)Y_t \qquad\qquad (3.15)$$

where Y_{t+1} = the forecast for period $t + 1$
  x_t = the actual value for period t
  α = a smoothing constant, generally constrained to be between 0 and 1.0

Table 3.10 presents United Microcircuit Company's monthly unit sales of semiconductors. Also illustrated are three sets of forecasts derived from Equation 3.15, employing α values of 0.1, 0.9, and 0.4002, respectively. (Note: Some of the entries in this table vary slightly from those obtained by single sets of calculations due to rounding.) The forecast for time period 11, for instance, when $\alpha = 0.1$, is obtained as follows:

$$Y_{11} = \alpha x_{10} + (1 - \alpha)Y_{10} = (0.1)(386.44) + (0.9)(366.90) = 368.85$$

Despite the apparent simplicity, the exponential-smoothing technique is more complicated than it might first appear. Equation 3.15 indicates that only the forecast for time period t and the actual value for period t have an impact on the forecast for $t + 1$. At first glance, this may suggest that all other historical values are ignored. This is far from true. All historical values influence the forecast, and this influence occurs through the forecast for the previous period. To illustrate:

$$Y_{t+1} = \alpha x_t + (1 - \alpha)Y_t$$

But, $$Y_t = \alpha x_{t-1} + (1 - \alpha)Y_{t-1}$$

therefore $$Y_{t+1} = \alpha x_t + \alpha(1 - \alpha)x_{t-1} + (1 - \alpha)^2 Y_{t-1}$$

Table 3.10 United Microcircuit Company's Monthly Unit Sales of Semiconductors. Forecasting with Single Exponential Smoothing: Alpha = 0.1, 0.9, and 0.4002 (in Thousands of Units).

Time Period	Unit Sales	Alpha = 0.1			Alpha = 0.9			Alpha = 0.4002		
		Forecast	Error	Squared Error	Forecast	Error	Squared Error	Forecast	Error	Squared Error
1	358.97	358.97	0	0	358.97	0	0	358.97	0	0
2	368.12	358.97	9.15	83.72	358.97	9.15	83.72	358.97	9.15	83.72
3	372.25	359.89	12.37	152.89	367.21	5.05	25.45	362.63	9.62	92.51
4	361.17	361.12	0.45	0	371.75	(10.58)	111.84	366.48	(5.31)	28.21
5	352.61	361.13	(8.52)	72.53	362.23	(9.62)	92.50	364.36	(11.75)	137.96
6	383.45	360.27	23.18	537.09	353.57	29.88	892.71	359.65	(23.80)	566.20
7	378.12	362.59	15.53	241.11	380.46	(2.34)	5.49	369.18	8.94	79.96
8	366.72	364.15	2.57	6.63	378.35	(11.63)	135.36	372.76	(6.04)	36.44
9	389.35	364.40	24.95	622.38	367.88	21.47	460.81	370.34	19.01	361.36
10	386.44	366.90	19.54	381.92	387.20	(0.76)	0.58	377.95	8.49	72.11
11	375.57	368.85	6.72	45.14	386.52	(10.95)	119.82	381.35	(5.78)	33.37
12	390.16	369.52	20.64	425.87	376.66	13.50	182.12	379.03	11.13	123.77
13	383.42	371.59	11.83	140.02	388.81	(5.39)	29.06	383.49	(0.07)	0
14	387.66	372.77	14.89	221.70	383.96	3.70	13.70	383.46	4.20	17.64
15	367.76	374.26	(6.50)	42.24	387.29	(19.53)	381.42	385.14	(17.38)	302.10
16	372.02	373.61	(1.59)	2.53	369.71	2.31	5.32	378.19	(6.17)	38.01
17	365.83	373.45	(7.62)	58.07	371.79	(5.96)	35.51	375.72	(9.89)	97.77
18	374.27	372.69	1.58	2.50	366.43	7.84	61.53	371.76	2.51	6.30
19	382.12	372.85	9.27	86.00	373.49	8.63	74.55	372.76	9.36	87.52
20	379.52	373.77	5.75	33.02	381.26	(1.74)	3.02	376.51	3.01	9.07
21	—	374.35	—	—	379.69	—	—	377.71	—	—

Summary:

MSE = 157.79E 06 units
Square root of MSE = 12.56E 03 units

MSE = 135.73E 06 units
Square root of MSE = 11.65E 03 units

MSE = 108.70E 06 units
Square root of MSE = 10.43E 03 units

Note: E 06 read times 10 to the 6th power

The preceding equations indicate that the forecast Y_{t+1} depends upon x_t, x_{t-1}, and Y_{t-1}. This process could be continued by substituting for Y_{t-1} into the above equation. Thus, exponential smoothing does in fact take account of historical observations. This is because the most recent forecast is based, in part, on past forecasts. And past forecasts are, in turn, based in part on their predecessors. The weight assigned to each historic observation *decreases* exponentially with its age, which gives the technique its name.

Exponential smoothing can produce essentially the same forecast results as are obtained through a moving average. This is accomplished by selecting an α value that sets the average age of the exponential series to equal the average age obtained by the moving-average method. This relationship is expressed as follows:

$$\alpha = \frac{2}{N+1} \qquad (3.16)$$

where α = the smoothing constant
$\quad\quad\ N$ = the number of time periods employed in the moving average

Table 3.11 was constructed from Equation 3.16 to demonstrate the correspondence between several smoothing constants and the number of

Table 3.11 Some Corresponding Values of N, the Number of Time Periods, in a Moving Average and Alpha, the Constant, in an Exponential-Smoothing Model

Values of N	Corresponding Values of Alpha (Rounded)
100	0.020
75	0.026
50	0.039
24	0.080
12	0.154
6	0.286
5	0.333
4	0.400
3	0.500
2	0.667
1	1.000

periods in a moving average. The table furnishes a convenient vehicle for establishing appropriate α levels if the appropriate N values are known for moving averages, and vice versa. In addition, the table illustrates that the lower the α value, the less is the weight granted to the most recent observation and the more is the weight given to history. Conversely, the higher the α value, the more the opposite is true.

Selecting α Values

On many occasions, management employs a rather arbitrary decision in choosing an α level for exponential smoothing. For some reason, perhaps mere custom, magnitudes of 0.1 and 0.2 are common. But arbitrary choices should be avoided, as they may produce misleading results. For an illustration, re-examine Table 3.10 for $\alpha = 0.1$. The model does not appear to be a very good one, since almost all the errors are positive. On the other hand, forecasts made with $\alpha = 0.9$ look much better, but there still remains the fundamental question as to what specific level of α generates the optimal results.

 Appendix 3.A contains a computer program designed to calculate the optimal α magnitude. This value is defined as the one that minimizes the mean squared error between the historical actual values and forecasts of these values utilizing the model. Table 3.12 sets forth output of the

Table 3.12 Optimal Alpha Calculated for United Microcircuit

Routine for Optimal Alpha Level for Exponential Smoothing—Single Order	
Variance	At Alpha
358.26025	0.0
157.78828	0.1000
121.11371	0.2000
110.94112	0.3000
108.70152	0.4000
110.23619	0.5000
108.71825	0.4100
108.70186	0.4010
108.70123	0.4001
108.70091	0.4002
108.70155	0.4003

Optimum alpha calculated = 0.4002

Final forecast = 376.51

program for United Microcircuit. The entries in the "variance" column correspond exactly to measures of MSE.

This computer output and the optimal value of $\alpha = 0.4002$ can also be used to illustrate the best forecasting model for the example. Notice in Table 3.10 that the resulting MSE is considerably smaller than for the other weights. Accordingly, calculating the optimal α weight should always precede the making of forecasts.

Given the information that we have gathered to this point, the next time period forecast for the example is

$$Y_{21} = (0.4002)(379.52) + (0.5998)(376.51) = 377.71 \text{ thousand units}$$

Further, subsequent forecasts to $t = 21$ also equal 377.71 thousand units, provided that they are made $t = 20$. This is because single exponential smoothing assumes that a trend does not exist over time. Thus, $Y_{22} = 377.71$ thousand units. Only when a new actual is learned will the forecasts be updated.

Tracking Signals

It is a common practice to continue with the same α magnitude for many periods before attempting to determine if a revision is necessary. This is especially true for companies with many products and related forecasts, such as Motorola, Inc. Consider, for example, the United Microcircuit case, where the firm learns that actual $t = 21$ sales are 366.41. The company can forecast for $t = 22$ with only a minimal amount of calculations, provided that the model is not changed:

$$Y_{22} = (0.4002)(366.41) + (0.5998)(377.71) = 373.19 \text{ thousand units}$$

And future forecasts would continue to be generated in much the same way, once new actual values are learned. The simplicity and ease of calculation accompanying use of the same model are strong motivators for not making a change.

But at some point it is wise to update α. A change is merited when the model produces forecasts containing a great deal of error. In turn, a tracking system provides a very workable means of monitoring the need for change. Such a system contains a range of permissible variations of the forecast from actual values. So long as a forecast falls within this range, no change in α is necessary. However, if a forecast falls outside the range, the system signals a need to update the α value.

One practical way of determining such a range is to utilize the MSE (variance) found in establishing the optimal α magnitude. The computer output (Table 3.12) and Table 3.10 indicate that for $\alpha = 0.4002$, the MSE $= 108.70 \times 10^6$ units. The standard deviation of the forecast error ($\sqrt{\text{MSE}}$) equals 10.43×10^3 units.

If the exponential-smoothing technique is reasonably accurate, the forecast error should be normally distributed about zero. Under this condition, there is a 95.5% chance that the actual observation will fall within two standard deviations of the forecast.[3] For the example, therefore, the permissible variation is $\pm 2(\sqrt{\text{MSE}}) = \pm 2(10.43) = \pm 20.86$ thousand units. If at any future time period, therefore, the forecast error is greater than ± 20.86 thousand packages, there is reason to believe that a new optimal α should be calculated. The preceding discussion on tracking signals also applies directly to the smoothing methods yet to be discussed, but it will not be repeated, to avoid redundancy.

Double Exponential Smoothing

The Technique

Double exponential smoothing is to double moving averages as single exponential smoothing is to simple moving averages. Whenever a significant trend line exists, either positive or negative, single exponential smoothing will lag behind the time-series changes over time. To illustrate, Table 3.13 presents Eastern Electric Company's sales of 60-watt light bulbs; they provide nearly as much light as 75-watt lamps, but they use less energy. Consequently, sales have been consistently increasing.

Using the computer program set forth in Appendix 3.A, the optimal single exponential-smoothing α value is calculated to be 1.40. Figure 3.5 presents a graph of the related single exponential-smoothing forecasts compared to the actual values.

We can readily arrive at two important observations. First, forecasts based upon single exponential-smoothing models lag behind actual values whenever a significant long-run trend is present. This will always be the case, even if the α magnitude is allowed to be greater than 1.0 (and, hence, $1 - \alpha$ is negative). Second, in many cases, such a lag will not be detected by normal tracking procedures. An MSE of 44.68 thousand units was calculated for the example. Thus, the permissible range of variation is $\pm 2\sqrt{44.68} = \pm 13.37$ thousand units. In no instance did the forecast fluctuate from the actual by more than this amount. Therefore,

3. The setting of a 95.5 confidence interval for tracking systems is generally sufficient. To obtain other Z values, refer to any statistics textbook with appropriate tables. For example, see Paul G. Hoel and Raymond J. Jessen, *Basic Statistics for Business and Economics* (Santa Barbara, Calif.: Wiley/Hamilton, 1977).

whenever an optimal α is calculated to be greater than 1.0, using Appendix 3.A, it signals that a significant trend is present. This means that a higher order exponential-smoothing method should be used.

Table 3.13 Eastern Electric Company's Monthly Sales of 60-Watt Light Bulbs (in Thousands of Units)

Time Period	Unit Sales	Time Period	Unit Sales
1	308.03	11	381.81
2	312.87	12	383.07
3	323.56	13	394.81
4	328.48	14	401.20
5	334.43	15	409.44
6	345.34	16	415.52
7	353.17	17	417.86
8	356.63	18	429.23
9	366.93	19	432.75
10	372.26	20	443.91

Figure 3.5 Graph of Monthly Historical Actual and Calculated Forecast Sales of 60-Watt Light Bulbs. Single Exponential Smoothing ($\alpha = 1.40$, the optimal value), Actual Sales = ——, Forecast Sales = ——.

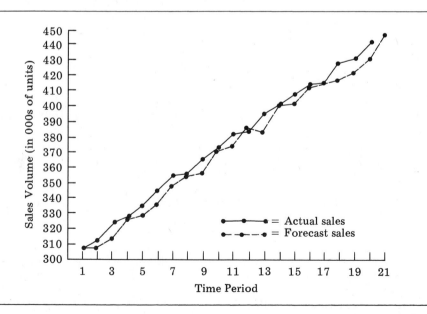

Like double moving averages, double exponential smoothing is a technique designed for situations where a linear trend is in existence. Further, the method includes two separate functions that are combined in a prescribed manner to produce forecasts. The basic concepts are analogous to those of double moving averages. Using the same type of mathematical notation, the steps in double exponential smoothing are summarized as follows (refer to Table 3.14):

$$\text{Column 3:} \quad Y'_t = \alpha x_t + (1 - \alpha) Y'_{t-1} \tag{3.17}$$

$$\text{Column 4:} \quad Y''_t = \alpha Y'_t + (1 - \alpha) Y''_{t-1} \tag{3.18}$$

$$\text{Column 5:} \quad a_t = 2Y' - Y''_t \tag{3.19}$$

$$\text{Column 6:} \quad b_t = \frac{\alpha}{1 - \alpha} (Y'_t - Y''_t) \tag{3.20}$$

$$\text{Column 7:} \quad Y_{t+p} = a_t + b_t p \tag{3.21}$$

where p = the number of periods ahead for which a forecast is being made

To illustrate, consider period 20:

$$Y'_{20} = 0.1251(443.91) + 0.8749(390.398) = 397.092$$

$$Y''_{20} = 0.1251(397.092) + 0.8749(355.744) = 360.917$$

$$a_{20} = 2(397.092) - 360.917 = 433.267$$

$$b_{20} = (0.1251/0.8749)(397.092 - 360.917) = 5.173$$

$$Y_{21} = 433.267 + 5.173(1) = 438.440$$

Forecasts for yet more future periods made at time period 20 are also calculated with Equation 3.21. Thus:

$$Y_{22} = 433.267 + 5.173(2) = 443.613$$

$$Y_{23} = 433.267 + 5.173(3) = 448.786$$

and so on.

Table 3.14 Eastern Electric's Monthly Sales of 60-Watt Light Bulbs. Double Exponential Smoothing with Naive Initializations. Alpha = 0.1251

(1) Time	(2) Actual	(3) Y'	(4) Y''	(5) a	(6) b	(7) Forecast	(8) Error	(9) Squared Error
1	308.030	308.030	308.030	308.030	0.000	308.030	0.000	0.000
2	312.870	308.635	308.106	309.165	0.076	308.030	4.840	23.426
3	323.560	310.502	308.405	312.599	0.300	309.241	14.319	205.036
4	328.480	312.751	308.949	316.554	0.544	312.899	15.581	242.764
5	334.430	315.463	309.764	321.163	0.815	317.097	17.333	300.423
6	345.340	319.201	310.944	327.457	1.181	321.978	23.362	545.803
7	353.170	323.450	312.509	334.392	1.564	328.638	24.532	601.836
8	356.630	327.601	314.397	340.805	1.888	335.956	20.674	427.410
9	366.930	332.521	316.664	348.378	2.267	342.693	24.237	587.426
10	372.260	337.492	319.269	355.715	2.606	350.645	21.615	467.200
11	381.810	343.036	322.243	363.830	2.973	358.320	23.490	551.757
12	383.070	348.044	325.470	370.618	3.228	366.803	16.267	264.610
13	394.810	353.895	329.026	378.763	3.556	373.846	20.964	439.484
14	401.200	359.812	332.878	386.747	3.851	382.319	18.881	356.491
15	409.440	366.021	337.024	395.018	4.146	390.599	18.841	354.993
16	415.520	372.213	341.426	403.000	4.402	399.164	16.356	267.517
17	417.860	377.923	345.992	409.855	4.566	407.402	10.458	109.362
18	429.230	384.342	350.789	417.894	4.798	414.421	14.809	219.311
19	432.750	390.398	355.744	425.051	4.955	422.692	10.058	101.167
20	443.910	397.092	360.917	433.267	5.173	430.006	13.904	193.321
21						438.440		

Summary: MSE = 312.97

Square root of MSE = 17.69

Initialization

The foregoing calculations illustrate the basic procedures for double exponential smoothing. But notice in Table 3.14 that the bulk of the calculated MSE is largely the result of error over the first two-thirds or so of the historical series. The reason for this is that naive estimates were made for the initial values of Y', Y'', a, and b.

The initial actual value of the series was used for Y'_1 and Y''_2. A similar procedure was employed in the single exponential-smoothing case. The problem is that the single smoothing model assumes that there is no trend present, and consequently the first value in a series is a good estimate of future ones. But a trend is assumed in the case of double smoothing. As a result, using the initial value in its raw form will *always* result in error. It will always underestimate a positive trend and overestimate a negative one. The problem is especially crucial in cases where very few historical observations exist. Here, the forecasts are simply unable to catch up with the trend. This is commonly experienced by users of smoothing who do not make adjustments to the initial values.

The beginning values should always be initialized to reflect an estimate of the trend's slope and intercept. One way of doing this is to estimate the trend using the first third of the historical data, as in Figure 3.6. It is not necessary to utilize all the data to obtain this initial estimate. For the example, $20/3 = 6.67$ or 6 observations are enough to acquire good initial value estimates.

Of course, one could employ freehand smoothing in order to acquire the estimates. The values $a = 299.84$ and $b = 7.3186t$, however, are the product of the least-squares procedure, which is explained in Chapter 4.[4] Note that the estimates are generated for the period $t = 0$. This is essential. Such estimates are needed so that the smoothing process can begin.

Initial values are established through the following set of equations:

$$Y'_0 = a_0 - \frac{1 - \alpha}{\alpha} b_0 \qquad (3.22)$$

$$Y''_0 = a_0 - 2\frac{1 - \alpha}{\alpha} b_0 \qquad (3.23)$$

$$Y_1 = a_0 + b_0 \qquad (3.24)$$

---

4. The least-squares procedure is simply a precise mathematical method for estimating the parameters of a trend line.

Figure 3.6 The First Six Months of Eastern Electric's Sales of 60-Watt Light Bulbs

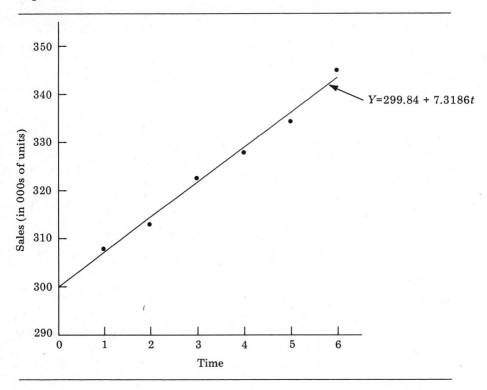

For the example:

$$Y_0' = 299.84 - \frac{0.8749}{0.1251}\,7.3186 = 248.66$$

$$Y_0'' = 299.84 - 2\frac{0.8749}{0.1251}\,7.3186 = 197.47$$

$$Y_1 = 299.84 + 7.3186 = 307.16$$

The smoothing then begins using these values. Accordingly,

$$Y_1' = (0.1251)(308.03) + (0.8749)(248.66) = 256.08 \text{ thousand}$$

$$Y_1'' = (0.1251)(256.08) + (0.8749)(197.47) = 204.80 \text{ thousand}$$

The remaining calculations are then performed as they were with Equations 3.17 through 3.21.

Appendix 3.B sets forth a computer program capable of calculating the optimal alpha weight for double exponential smoothing. The program automatically estimates initial values for Y' and Y'' in the manner depicted above. Table 3.15 presents the output of the program. The α of 0.1251 used in the naive initialization illustration was obtained from this output to demonstrate the reduction in MSE from 312.97×10^6 units to 5.129×10^6 units from the improved initialization. The $\sqrt{\text{MSE}}$ went from 17.69 thousand units to $\sqrt{5.1286} = 2.265$ thousand. Indeed, this is a drastic reduction. With the improved model, the forecast for period $t = 21$ is 450.10 thousand units, which is read directly from the output. Each subsequent forecast made at period $t = 20$ increases 7.14 thousand units. Thus, $Y_{22} = 450.10 + 7.14 = 457.24$ thousand, and so on.

Quadratic Exponential Smoothing

Exponential smoothing can be extended to estimate the coefficients in more complex polynomial models. Such models are useful when a trend is present, but it is nonlinear. Quadratic, or triple, exponential smoothing is the first of this type. The general model is

$$Y = a + bx + \frac{1}{2}cx^2 \qquad (3.25)$$

Figure 3.7 illustrates the scatter diagram of historical monthly sales of Eastern Electric's recently introduced 35-watt super-energy-saving light bulbs. Notice that a trend is clearly present. Consequently, one might be tempted to forecast sales for period $t = 19$ using double smoothing. But such a forecast would contain systematic error because the trend is clearly nonlinear. Fortunately, the logic of double exponential smoothing can be extended through adding a third function to be smoothed, the essence of quadratic smoothing, to capture the nonlinearity.

Appendix 3.C sets forth a computer program that calculates the optimal alpha level for quadratic smoothing. Table 3.16 presents the computer output for Eastern's 35-watt bulb example (explained below).

The basic smoothing procedure is accomplished with the following equations:

Column 3: $Y'_t = \alpha x_t + (1 - \alpha)Y'_{t-1}$ (3.26)

Column 4: $Y''_t = \alpha Y'_t + (1 - \alpha) Y''_{t-1}$ (3.27)

Column 5: $Y'''_t = \alpha Y''_t + (1 - \alpha) Y'''_{t-1}$ (3.28)

Column 6: $a_t = 3Y'_t - 3Y''_t + Y'''_t$ (3.29)

Table 3.15 Eastern Electric's Monthly Sales of 60-Watt Light Bulbs. Double Exponential Smoothing with Improved Initialization. Alpha = 0.1251

(1)	(2)	(3)	(4)	(5)	(6)	(7)	(8)	(9)
TIME	ACTUAL	Y1	Y2	A	B	FOREC.	ERROR	SQ.ER.
1	308.030	256.081	204.802	307.360	7.332	307.155	0.875	0.766
2	312.870	263.185	212.105	314.265	7.304	314.693	-1.823	3.322
3	323.560	270.738	219.440	322.036	7.335	321.569	1.991	3.965
4	328.480	277.961	226.761	329.162	7.321	329.371	-0.891	0.793
5	334.430	285.026	234.050	336.001	7.289	336.483	-2.053	4.213
6	345.340	292.571	241.371	343.771	7.321	343.290	2.050	4.202
7	353.170	300.152	248.724	351.579	7.353	351.092	2.078	4.320
8	356.630	307.217	256.042	358.392	7.317	358.932	-2.303	5.302
9	366.930	314.687	263.378	365.996	7.337	365.710	1.220	1.489
10	372.260	321.889	270.698	373.081	7.320	373.332	-1.072	1.150
11	381.810	329.385	278.040	380.731	7.342	380.400	1.410	1.987
12	383.070	336.101	285.303	386.899	7.263	388.073	-5.003	25.027
13	394.810	343.445	292.577	394.314	7.274	394.163	0.647	0.419
14	401.200	350.670	299.844	401.497	7.268	401.588	-0.388	0.150
15	409.440	358.022	307.122	408.923	7.278	408.764	0.676	0.457
16	415.520	365.215	314.389	416.041	7.267	416.201	-0.681	0.464
17	417.860	371.801	321.572	422.031	7.182	423.309	-5.449	29.687
18	429.230	378.985	328.754	429.217	7.182	429.213	0.017	0.000
19	432.750	385.711	335.879	435.543	7.125	436.399	-3.649	13.316
20	443.910	392.992	343.024	442.960	7.145	442.668	1.242	1.542

Table 3.15 Eastern Electric's Monthly Sales of 60-Watt Light Bulbs. Double Exponential Smoothing with Improved Initialization. Alpha = 0.1251 *continued*

```
ROUTINE FOR OPTIMAL ALPHA LEVEL FOR
DOUBLE EXPONENTIAL SMOOTHING
LEAST SQUARES INITIALIZATIONS
INITIAL INTERCEPT ESTIMATE = 299.836
INITIAL SLOPE ESTIMATE =      7.319
VARIANCE        AT ALPHA
6233.0273        0.0000
   5.1799        0.1000
   5.4232        0.2000
   6.6043        0.0100
   6.3107        0.0200
   6.0575        0.0300
   5.8434        0.0400
   5.6644        0.0500
   5.5161        0.0600
   5.3971        0.0700
   5.3022        0.0800
   5.2309        0.0900
   5.1799        0.1000
   5.1472        0.1100
   5.1312        0.1200
   5.1296        0.1300
   5.1414        0.1400
   5.1303        0.1210
   5.1297        0.1220
   5.1295        0.1230
   5.1289        0.1240
   5.1288        0.1250
   5.1285        0.1260
   5.1286        0.1270
   5.1285        0.1251
   5.1286        0.1252
OPTIMAL ALPHA CALCULATED =        0.1251
FINAL Y1 FUNCTION VALUE =     392.9917
FINAL Y2 FUNCTION VALUE =     343.0238
FINAL INTERCEPT VALUE =       442.9596
FINAL SLOPE VALUE =             7.1448
FINAL HISTORICAL FORECAST =   442.6684
NEXT PERIOD FORECAST =        450.1044
SUCCESSIVE PERIOD FORECASTS
INCREMENT BY:    7.1448
```

Figure 3.7 Scatter Diagram of Eastern Electric's 35-Watt Light Bulbs

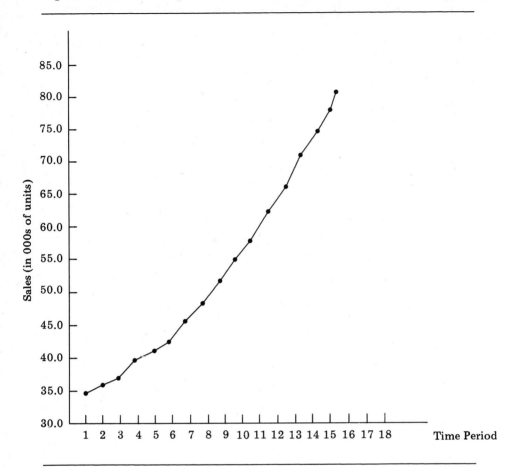

Table 3.16 Eastern Electric's Monthly Sales of 35-Watt Light Bulbs. Quadratic Exponential Smoothing. Least-Squares Initializations

```
ROUTINE FOR OPTIMAL ALPHA LEVEL FOR
QUADRATIC EXPONENTIAL SMOOTHING
VARIANCE        AT ALPHA
INITIAL INTERCEPT ESTIMATE =      33.7798
INITIAL SLOPE ESTIMATE     =       0.6888
INITIAL CHANGE RATE ESTIM. =       0.1285
VARIANCE        AT ALPHA
516.44788        0.0000
  7.66490        0.1000
  0.92645        0.2000
  0.23663        0.3000
  0.16173        0.4000
  0.18148        0.5000
  0.21899        0.3100
  0.20477        0.3200
  0.19338        0.3300
  0.18435        0.3400
  0.17726        0.3500
  0.17178        0.3600
  0.16768        0.3700
  0.16475        0.3800
  0.16282        0.3900
  0.16173        0.4000
  0.16141        0.4100
  0.16173        0.4200
  0.16166        0.4010
  0.16162        0.4020
  0.16155        0.4030
  0.16152        0.4040
  0.16149        0.4050
  0.16145        0.4060
  0.16143        0.4070
  0.16142        0.4080
  0.16141        0.4090
  0.16141        0.4100
  0.16140        0.4110
  0.16143        0.4120
  0.16141        0.4101
  0.16140        0.4102
  0.16141        0.4103
  0.16140        0.4102
```

Table 3.16 Eastern Electric's Monthly Sales of 35-Watt Light Bulbs. Quadratic Exponential Smoothing. Least-Squares Initializations   *continued*

```
OPTIMAL ALPHA CALCULATED =      0.4102
FINAL Y1 FUNCTION VALUE =      73.4321
FINAL Y2 FUNCTION VALUE =      67.3499
FINAL Y3 FUNCTION VALUE =      61.8805
FINAL A FUNCTION VALUE =       80.1273
FINAL B FUNCTION VALUE =        5.2310
FINAL C FUNCTION VALUE =        0.2965
NEXT PERIOD FORECAST =         85.5065
FUTURE FORECASTS ARE CALCULATED AS FOLLOWS:
Y(T+P)=  80.1273 +  5.2310P +  0.2965*0.5*P**2
```

TIME	ACTUAL	Y1	Y2	Y3	A	B	C	F CAST	ERROR	SQ.ER.
1	34.6000	33.7434	33.1759	32.8837	34.5862	0.8443	0.1332	34.5328	0.0672	0.0045
2	35.7000	34.5460	33.7379	33.2341	35.6584	1.0589	0.1472	35.4971	0.2029	0.0412
3	36.9000	35.5116	34.4654	33.7392	36.8776	1.2499	0.1547	36.7909	0.1091	0.0119
4	38.7000	36.8195	35.4311	34.4332	38.5984	1.6033	0.1889	38.2048	0.4951	0.2452
5	40.4000	38.2882	36.6031	35.3233	40.3787	1.8339	0.1961	40.2961	0.1039	0.0108
6	42.0000	39.8108	37.9188	36.3880	42.0637	1.9053	0.1746	42.3106	-0.3106	0.0965
7	45.1000	41.9804	39.5849	37.6993	44.8859	2.4987	0.2467	44.0564	1.0436	1.0891
8	47.8000	44.3676	41.5468	39.2775	47.7401	2.8626	0.2668	47.5079	0.2921	0.0853
9	50.9000	47.0472	43.8030	41.1339	50.8664	3.1952	0.2781	50.7360	0.1640	0.0269
10	54.3000	50.0223	46.3541	43.2752	54.2796	3.5132	0.2850	54.2006	0.0993	0.0099
11	57.5000	53.0896	49.1170	45.6715	57.5893	3.6236	0.2550	57.9353	-0.4353	0.1895
12	62.0000	56.7447	52.2459	48.3683	61.8647	4.1432	0.3005	61.3404	0.6596	0.4351
13	65.7000	60.4181	55.5981	51.1340	65.7940	4.2599	0.2689	66.1581	-0.4581	0.2099
14	70.2000	64.4306	59.2212	54.5693	70.1976	4.5334	0.2697	70.1883	0.0117	0.0001
15	74.9000	68.7251	63.1197	58.0767	74.8930	4.8168	0.2720	74.8659	0.0341	0.0012
16	80.2000	73.4321	67.3499	61.8805	80.1273	5.2310	0.2965	79.8458	0.3542	0.1254

Column 7:

$$b_t = \frac{\alpha}{2(1-\alpha)^2}[(6-5\alpha)Y_t' - 2(5-4\alpha)Y_t'' + (4-3\alpha)Y_t'''] \quad (3.30)$$

Column 8: $$c_t = \left(\frac{\alpha}{1-\alpha}\right)^2 [Y_t' - 2Y_t'' + Y_t'''] \quad (3.31)$$

Column 9: $$Y_{t+p} = a_t + b_t p + \frac{1}{2}c_t p^2 \quad (3.32)$$

where p = the number of periods ahead for which a forecast is being made

For the example at time period $t = 16$ and with the optimal $a =$ 0.4102:

$$Y_{16}' = (0.4102)(80.20) + (0.5898)(68.7251) = 73.43$$

$$Y_{16}'' = (0.4102)(73.43) + (0.5898)(63.1197) = 67.35$$

$$Y_{16}''' = (0.4102)(67.35) + (0.5898)(58.0767) = 61.88$$

$$a_{16} = (3)(73.43) - (3)(67.35) + 61.88 = 80.13$$

$$b_{16} = \frac{0.4102}{(2)(0.5898)^2} \times$$

$$[(3.949)(73.43) - (6.7184)(67.35) + (2.7694)(61.88)] = 5.23$$

$$c_{16} = \left(\frac{0.4102}{0.5898}\right)^2 [73.43 - (2)(67.35) + 61.88] = 0.297$$

Forecasts are as follows:

$$Y_{17} = 80.13 + 5.23(1) + (0.5)(0.297^2)(1) = 85.51$$

$$Y_{18} = 80.13 + 5.23(2) + (0.5)(0.297^2)(2) = 90.68$$

(Note: The above calculations yield values slightly different from those in the table because of rounding.)

Like double smoothing, the initial values used in quadratic smoothing are very critical in affecting the results. The computer program employs the least-squares procedure to generate initial values. Chapter 4 elaborates upon the concept of least squares, so the discussion is not expanded upon here. (Chapter 4's discussion involves the linear trend case only, but the concept is identical for a more complex model.) For interested readers, Appendix 3.D contains the methodology for arriving at the initial values. From Table 3.16, we see that the optimal alpha level, $\alpha = 0.4102$, results in a mean squared error of 0.16140 thousand light bulbs. This means, of course, that the model fits the historical data very well.

Even higher forms of smoothing are possible, but they should be avoided in most practical situations. This is because the models become so complex that one can have little confidence in the resulting forecasts. Wild gyrations are entirely likely if one attempts to use such models to generalize beyond limits of recorded history.

Winters's Exponential Smoothing

Many time series exhibit systematic periodic fluctuations that are due to seasonal influences. For instance, lawn-care products sell heavily in the spring and much more slowly in the fall. Toys sell most heavily before Christmas, gift watches before graduation dates, and so on. Figure 3.8 illustrates Hinze Manufacturing Company's quarterly sales of Model 593 barbecue grills over the past four years. Such a systematic seasonal pattern of fluctuation cannot be forecast very well with the techniques discussed so far.

Several methods have been proposed to handle such seasonal variations. Of these, decomposition (discussed in Chapter 5) and Winters's model are the most widely utilized.

Components of the Model

Winters's method assumes a time-series model as follows:

$$Y_t = (a + bt)c_t \qquad (3.33)$$

where
$a =$ an intercept component
$b =$ a linear trend component
$c_t =$ a seasonal factor for time t

Assuming that there are L seasons in one full cycle of seasons, the procedure for periodically revising estimates of the model's parameters and for forecasting is the following.[5] At the end of period t, after observing x_t:

5. P. R. Winters, "Forecasting Sales by Exponentially Weighted Moving Averages," *Management Science*, 6 (1960), 324–342.

Figure 3.8 Hinze Manufacturing Company Quarterly Sales of Model 593 Barbecue Grills

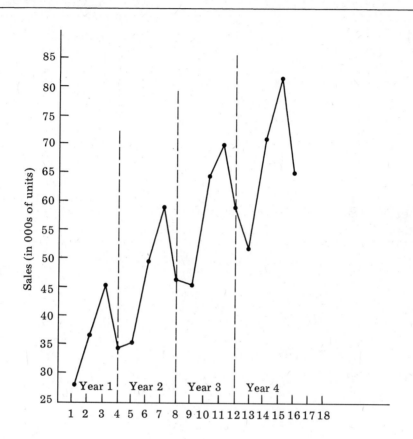

1. Revise the intercept component:

$$a_t = \alpha \left[\frac{x_t}{c_{t-L}} \right] + (1 - \alpha)(a_{t-1} + b_{t-1}) \qquad (3.34)$$

2. Revise the trend component:

$$b_t = \beta(a_t - a_{t-1}) + (1 - \beta)b_{t-1} \qquad (3.35)$$

3. Revise the seasonal factor for period t:

$$c_t = \gamma\left(\frac{x_t}{a_t}\right) + (1 - \gamma)c_{t-L} \qquad (3.36)$$

4. Forecast for any future period $t + \tau$ with

$$Y_{t+\tau} = (a_t + \tau b_t)c_{t+\tau-L} \qquad (3.37)$$

The preceding equations may look more complicated than they actually are. It is important to note that the subscripting relates to the time period in question. Thus, $c_{t+\tau-L}$, to illustrate, refers to the seasonal component associated with period $t + \tau$, which was estimated L periods (one full cycle of seasons) before that time.

Also notice that unlike the previously discussed smoothing methods, Winters's method involves three separate weights—one for each component. Each weight may have a different value, but each is constrained to be between 0 and 1.

Appendix 3.E presents a computer program that calculates the optimal alpha, beta, and gamma weights for Winters's exponential smoothing. Table 3.17 contains output of the program for the Hinze example. The following illustrates the calculations required for period $t = 16$ with $L = 4$:

$$a_{16} = \alpha\left(\frac{x_{16}}{c_{12}}\right) + (1 - \alpha)(a_{15} + b_{15})$$

$$= 0.1\left(\frac{64.7}{0.869}\right) + (0.9)(69.618 + 2.536) = 72.384$$

$$b_{16} = \beta(a_{16} - a_{15}) + (1 - \beta)b_{15}$$
$$= 0.3(72.384 - 69.618) + (0.7)(2.536) = 2.605$$

$$c_{16} = \gamma\left(\frac{x_{16}}{a_{16}}\right) + (1 - \gamma)c_{12}$$

$$= 0.1\left(\frac{64.7}{72.384}\right) + (0.9)(0.869) = 0.872$$

$$Y_{16+\tau} = (a_{16} + \tau b_{16})c_{16+\tau-4}$$

$$Y_{17} = [72.384 + 1(2.605)](0.843) = 63.23$$

$$Y_{18} = [72.384 + 2(2.605)](1.067) = 82.79$$

$$Y_{19} = [72.384 + 3(2.605)](1.202) = 96.38$$

$$Y_{20} = [72.384 + 4(2.605)](0.872) = 72.17$$

(Note: The above calculations yield results slightly different from those in the table because of rounding.)

Table 3.17 Hinze Manufacturing's Quarterly Sales of Model 593
Barbeque Grills

```
OPTIMAL WEIGHT ROUTINE FOR
WINTERS' EXPONENTIAL SMOOTHING
USES TWO TIMES THE SEASON LENGTH
TO INITIALIZE TREND AND SEASONALS

INITIAL SLOPE = 2.81875    AND INTERCEPT =28.82813
    VARIANCE AT OPTIMAL WEIGHTS =    3.27
    OPTIMAL INTERCEPT WEIGHT   =0.1
    OPTIMAL SLOPE WEIGHT       =0.3
    OPTIMAL SEASONAL WEIGHT    =0.1
    THE FOLLOWING ARE FINAL ESTIMATES
    INTERCEPT =    72.38
    SLOPE     =     2.60
    SEASONS AHEAD    INDEX
         1          0.84317
         2          1.06698
         3          1.20172
         4          0.87156
    FORECASTS FOR THE NEXT 4 SEASONS:
         1          63.228
         2          82.791
         3          96.376
         4          72.168
```

TIME	ACTUAL	A	B	C	FOREC.	ERROR	SQ.ER.
1	28.000	31.776	2.857	0.853	26.903	1.097	1.203
2	36.500	34.600	2.848	1.063	36.852	-0.352	0.124
3	45.000	37.425	2.841	1.208	45.271	-0.271	0.074
4	34.000	40.145	2.804	0.868	35.056	-1.056	1.114
5	35.000	42.757	2.747	0.850	36.645	-1.645	2.705
6	48.900	45.553	2.761	1.064	48.376	0.524	0.275
7	58.800	48.349	2.772	1.209	58.376	0.424	0.180
8	45.900	51.295	2.824	0.871	44.385	1.515	2.296
9	45.000	54.003	2.789	0.848	45.988	-0.988	0.976
10	63.500	57.081	2.876	1.069	60.437	3.063	9.381
11	69.600	59.717	2.804	1.205	72.490	-2.890	8.354
12	53.200	62.378	2.761	0.869	54.449	-1.249	1.560
13	51.700	64.721	2.636	0.843	55.244	-3.544	12.561
14	70.500	67.216	2.593	1.067	72.004	-1.504	2.262
15	81.800	69.618	2.536	1.202	84.099	-2.299	5.285
16	64.700	72.384	2.605	0.872	62.708	1.992	3.966

****ST

Utilizing appropriate initial-value estimates is equally important for Winters's method as for the other smoothing techniques. Now, however, the least-squares procedure does not yield good estimates because of the seasonal influence, which least squares does not estimate. Instead, an even simpler technique is useful. All the effects of seasonality should be felt during each full L (one full cycle of seasons). This means that an average of the second L of seasons can be compared with the average of the first L of seasons to obtain estimates of any trend's slope and intercept.

This can be expressed as follows:

$$b_0 = \left(\frac{\sum\limits_{i=L+1}^{2L} x_i}{L} - \frac{\sum\limits_{i=1}^{L} x_i}{L} \right) \div L \tag{3.38}$$

For the example:

$$\left(\frac{35.0 + \cdots + 45.9}{4} - \frac{28.0 + \cdots + 34.0}{4} \right) \div 4 = (47.15 - 35.875) \div 4$$

$$b_0 = 2.81875$$

From this, the initial intercept can be estimated. The average of the first two L seasons should also be void of seasonal influence. This average corresponds to the time midpoint between L and $L + 1$. One can estimate the intercept, therefore, by subtracting from this average the slope times $(L + L + 1) \div 2$. This is expressed as follows:

$$a_0 = \frac{\sum\limits_{i=1}^{2L} x_i}{2L} - b_0 \frac{2L + 1}{2} \tag{3.39}$$

For the example,

$$a_0 = \frac{28.0 + 36.5 + \cdots + 45.9}{8} - 2.81875\left(\frac{9}{2}\right) = 28.828$$

Finally, initial estimates of L seasonal factors are needed. The previously estimated slope and intercept are useful here. Actual values can be compared with values calculated with the slope and intercept for the corresponding time period to estimate the seasonals. Because random error should be excluded, an average of the corresponding seasonals within the first two L periods should be employed. This can be expressed as follows:

$$C(i)_j = \left(\frac{x_j}{a_0 + b_0 t_j} + \frac{x_{j+L}}{a_0 + b_0 t_{j+L}} \right) \div 2 \qquad (3.40)$$

where
$$j = \text{the } j\text{th index,}$$
$$\Sigma j = L, \text{ and}$$
$$i = \text{initial estimate}$$

For the example:

$$C(i)_1 = \left(\frac{x_1}{a_0 + b_0} + \frac{x_5}{a_0 + b_0(5)} \right) \div 2$$

$$= \left(\frac{28.0}{28.828 + 2.819} + \frac{35.0}{28.828 + (2.8188)(5)} \right) \div 2$$

$$= 0.85001$$

$$C(i)_2 = \left(\frac{x_2}{a_0 + b_0(2)} + \frac{x_6}{a_0 + b_0(6)} \right) \div 2$$

$$= \left(\frac{36.5}{28.828 + (2.819)(2)} + \frac{48.9}{28.828 + (2.819)(6)} \right) \div 2$$

$$= 1.0640$$

$$C(i)_3 = \left(\frac{x_3}{a_0 + b_0(3)} + \frac{x_7}{a_0 + b_0(7)} \right) \div 2$$

$$= 1.2089$$

$$C(i)_4 = \left(\frac{x_4}{a_0 + b_0(4)} + \frac{x_8}{a_0 + b_0(8)} \right) \div 2$$

$$= 0.8706$$

Smoothing then begins at period $t = 1$, with the above initial values and equations 3.34 through 3.37. Table 3.17 also indicates that with the optimal weighting factors, Winters's method of exponential smoothing results in a very close fit with the historical data. (Note that the above initialization procedure requires that there be at least $2L$ of historical observations for the method to be employed.)

In most instances, the seasons are selected so that L equals a full year. To illustrate, in the example, there were four quarters in L. With monthly data, of course, L would equal 12. But this does not have to be the case. L could be set equal to a year and a half of history, for example. This would permit the estimation of intermediate fluctuations of more than a year but less than long-run. Such fluctuations are termed *cyclical*. More will be said about cycles in Chapter 5.

SOME LIMITATIONS

Know This!

Time-series techniques are widely used, but they do have several weaknesses. Probably the most glaring of these is that the causes of the forecast variable's values are ignored or held constant. A host of forces, including economic factors, marketing efforts, competitive actions, and so on have an influence on sales. However, such variables are essentially ignored by the methods. Underlying historical relationships may suddenly change and time-series analysis would not detect such events. This results in increased forecast error.

Another weakness is that several of the techniques, especially the informal ones, often involve considerable guesswork. Still another limitation is that the methods typically require numerous repetitive calculations. The widespread availability of computers, though, has eliminated this problem for all but the smallest businesses.

Despite the limitations, however, many businesses employ time-series methods to forecast at the individual product level. Certainly, more complex models can yield greater accuracy, but time-series models are relatively simple to construct, especially with the aid of an interactive computer, and have been found to be very accurate, especially for short-run forecasts. Also they have the advantage of being relatively easy to maintain after the initial model is constructed. Subsequent calculations in future periods become very limited, provided that the forecasts do not exceed their tracking limits. Hence, the techniques are very useful when forecasts are needed for many products.

SUMMARY

Time-series analysis is the process of analyzing the historical relationships between the forecast variable and time. Essentially, the purpose is to identify any regular periodic relationships and to use them to formulate projections into the future. The concept of first developing a forecasting model and then evaluating how well it would have performed over history was introduced first. The mean squared error (MSE) calculation was described as a quantitative measure of such past performance. The chapter then furnished a discussion of both informal and formal techniques.

The first of the informal methods to be examined was freehand smoothing. This methodology requires attempting to visually estimate the slope and the intercept of the historical data over time. A major problem with this technique, however, is that the resulting estimates are bound to contain some degree of error because of inaccuracies in constructing the visual estimate of the function that minimizes the vertical deviations between the line and the historical data.

The next technique discussed involved percentage changes. This method is especially useful for evaluating and forecasting from financial statements potential problem areas on which management may then focus its attention. The method may also lead to very accurate results in situations where there are few historical observations or where recent significant changes in the environment are suspected.

Next, the discussion centered on schemes that weight historical data for their recency. First, the moving-average model was presented. This technique is most appropriate where there is no overall trend in evidence. Double moving average and moving percentage change are two methods expressly designed for cases where a long-run trend exists. Finally, a weighted-average procedure was discussed. This procedure involves weighting recent observations more heavily than older ones in an attempt to grant larger consideration to possible environmental changes affecting historical relationships.

A major problem with all the informal methods is that they are difficult to employ in real-world situations where forecasts must be constructed repeatedly. Morever, it is difficult to determine any semblance of optimal model configuration. For instance, are three periods better than two or four as a base in a moving average?

A discussion of formal models was provided. These require greater mathematical support, and they are actually simpler to employ than are the informal methods, especially with the widespread availability of computers. Single exponential smoothing is analogous to the moving-average method and is designed for situations where a long-term trend is not present. It has an advantage in that the optimal weighting factor can be readily determined. Further, like all the smoothing methods, once the model is specified, subsequent forecasts as history unfolds do not require a complete re-evaluation of the old data, that is, unless the forecasts miss their mark by an amount in excess of that described by a tracking signal.

Double exponential smoothing is designed for situations where a linear trend does exist. Because of the trend, however, one must take care to initialize the model properly. Quadratic exponential smoothing is designed for situations where there is a long-term trend, but it is a quadratic function instead of a linear one. It too requires careful initialization. Finally, Winters's exponential smoothing was examined. This methodology is intended for situations where seasonal influences are in existence. The intercept, trend, and seasonality are all separately smoothed through this method.

Certainly time-series techniques have their limitations. The most notable is that they presume that historical relationships will remain constant in the future. Despite this limitation, however, they are widely employed, largely because of their simplicity and frequent credibility. This makes them especially useful in situations where numerous forecasts must be formulated, such as at the individual product or departmental levels. Further, they provide reasonably accurate forecasts, especially for the short-run future.

DISCUSSION QUESTIONS

1. What criteria are most useful in determining which type of time-series technique is the most appropriate for a given situation? Under what conditions are each of the techniques presented in Chapter 3 the most appropriate?
2. Obtain a published financial statement of some company. (Annual reports are often available in college and public libraries.) Examine the income statements for two years with the percentage-change method and discuss your findings.

   The following are ACP Electric's sales of Model A-95L circuit assemblies over the past 16 months (in thousands of units):

Sept.	1981	58.0	May	1982	66.0
Oct.	1981	56.0	June	1982	56.0
Nov.	1981	63.0	July	1982	54.0
Dec.	1981	52.0	Aug.	1982	61.0
Jan.	1982	51.0	Sept.	1982	58.0
Feb.	1982	62.0	Oct.	1982	53.0
Mar.	1982	58.0	Nov.	1982	55.0
Apr.	1982	57.0	Dec.	1982	62.0

3. Use the moving-average technique to forecast sales of ACP's model A-95L for January 1983 (use a three-month base). What is the forecast for February 1983? Does the model appear to be appropriate? Why?
4. Employ the single exponential-smoothing technique to forecast sales of ACP's model A-95L for January 1983 (use $\alpha = 0.8$). Does the model seem to be appropriate? What is the forecast for February?
5. Utilize the single exponential-smoothing technique to forecast sales of ACP's model A-95L for January 1983 (use $\alpha = 0.1$). How do the results compare with those in question 4? Why is one better than another?
6. Determine the optimal α weight for forecasting ACP's model A-95L with single exponential smoothing. What is the forecast for February 1983 at the optimal α level?

The following are ACP Electric's sales of A-27C microcircuits over the past 16 months (in thousands of units):

Sept.	1981	53.0	May	1982	73.0
Oct.	1981	53.0	June	1982	76.0
Nov.	1981	59.0	July	1982	78.0
Dec.	1981	62.0	Aug.	1982	91.0
Jan.	1982	65.0	Sept.	1982	91.0
Feb.	1982	68.0	Oct.	1982	87.0
Mar.	1982	75.0	Nov.	1982	94.0
Apr.	1982	72.0	Dec.	1982	97.0

7. Forecast sales of ACP Electric's A-27C microcircuits for February 1983 with the double moving-average technique (use a three-period base).

8. Determine the initial values to utilize in forecasting sales of A-27C microcircuits with double exponential smoothing. Explain why such a calculation is important. Forecast sales for February 1983, using these initial values and an $\alpha = 0.3$.

9. What is optimal α level in forecasting sales of A-27C microcircuits? What is the resulting forecast for the next two months?

The following are weekly retail sales of a new fad item, a weight-control exercise kit, over the past 12 weeks:

t	Unit Sales	t	Unit Sales
1	10	7	65
2	13	8	79
3	18	9	100
4	26	10	121
5	37	11	144
6	48	12	171

10. Estimate the initial values to employ in forecasting sales of weight-control kits with quadratic exponential smoothing. Use these estimates and $\alpha = 0.3$ to forecast sales for the next four weeks.

11. What is the optimal α weight to utilize when forecasting sales of the weight-control kits with quadratic smoothing? What are the forecasts for the next two weeks?

12. What are some of the concerns that you envision relative to employing quadratic smoothing, especially for forecasting distant periods ahead?

The following are unit sales of imported microwave ovens by a leading competitor, by quarter (in thousands of units):

Date	Units	Date	Units
1979		1981	
Winter	1.86	Winter	2.07
Spring	2.11	Spring	2.55
Summer	2.63	Summer	3.30
Fall	3.01	Fall	3.47
1980		1982	
Winter	1.98	Winter	2.25
Spring	2.12	Spring	2.61
Summer	3.02	Summer	3.25
Fall	3.31	Fall	3.76

13. To help them in shaping strategy, management has asked you to forecast the competitor's sales for the next four quarters. What are the appropriate initial values to utilize in Winters's method? (Use $\alpha = 0.1$, $\beta = 0.2$, $\gamma = 0.3$.) Forecast unit sales.

14. What is the optimal set of weights to use for problem 13? What are the resulting forecasts?

15. Refer to question 5. Suppose it is now the end of January 1983 and sales are known for the month as 99.3 thousand units. What is the forecast for February 1983?

16. Refer to question 15. What would the sales forecast be for February 1983 if January's sales were 127.4 thousand units?

17. Forecast sales for the next period for the following. Identify the appropriate technique and prepare the forecast:

t	Sales	t	Sales
1	68.7	9	60.7
2	59.8	10	56.4
3	32.4	11	28.8
4	42.8	12	40.6
5	61.3	13	58.3
6	57.4	14	54.8
7	29.8	15	24.3
8	43.6	16	38.2

18. Forecast sales for the next period for the following. Identify the appropriate technique and prepare the forecast:

t	Sales	t	Sales
1	42.4	9	63.7
2	43.9	10	71.3
3	43.1	11	79.8
4	46.2	12	89.2
5	47.9	13	101.3
6	50.3	14	108.6
7	58.7	15	119.4
8	57.8	16	129.8

19. Refer to question 13. Suppose that January 1983's results have just become known: sales were 2.41 thousand units. Use this information in addition to that provided in question 13 to forecast sales for the next four quarters.

RECOMMENDED READINGS

Brown, R. G. *Smoothing, Forecasting and Prediction of Discrete Time Series.* Englewood Cliffs, N.J.: Prentice-Hall, 1963.

Brown, R. G. *Decision Rules for Inventory Management.* New York: Holt, Rinehart, and Winston, 1967.

Chou, W. M. "Adaptive Control of the Exponential Smoothing Constant." *Journal of Industrial Engineering*, 16 (1965), 314-317.

Johnson, James C., and Donald F. Wood. *Contemporary Physical Distribution.* Tulsa: Petroleum Publishing Co., 1977, pp. 211-236.

Johnson, L. A., and D. C. Montgomery. *Operations Research in Production Planning, Scheduling, and Inventory Control.* New York: John Wiley and Sons, 1974.

Montgomery, D. C. "Adaptive Control of Exponential Smoothing Parameters by Evolutionary Operation." *AIIE Transactions*, 2 (1970), 268-269.

Montgomery, D. C. "An Introduction to Short-Term Forecasting." *Journal of Industrial Engineering*, 19 (1968), 500-503.

Roberts, S. D., and R. Reed. "The Development of a Self Adaptive Forecasting Technique." *AIIE Transactions*, 1 (1969), 314-322.

Theil, Henry. "How to Worry About Increased Expenditures." *Accounting Review*, XLIV (January 1969), 27-37.

Winters, P. R. "Forecasting Sales by Exponentially Weighted Moving Averages." *Management Science*, 6 (1960), 324-342.

APPENDIX 3.A   COMPUTER PROGRAM TO COMPUTE OPTIMAL ALPHA LEVEL IN EXPONENTIAL SMOOTHING—SINGLE ORDER

```
C SINGLE ORDER EXPONENTIAL SMOOTHING PROGRAM
C SPECIFY NUMBER OF OBSERVATIONS AS FIRST ITEM IN DATA FILE
C PLACE MOST RECENT OBSERVATION LAST
      DIMENSION VALUE(100,3)
      WRITE(3,20)
      WRITE(3,21)
      WRITE(3,44)
      READ(6,1)ANUMB
      N=ANUMB
C READ DATA
      READ(6,1)(VALUE(1,1),1=1,N)
      FORMAT(F6.2)
      M=N-1
      A=0
      VALUE(1,2)=VALUE(1,1)
      VALUE(1,3)=VALUE(1,1)
      DO 5 J=2,N
      K=J-1
    5 VALUE(J,2)=VALUE(K,2)
      VAR=0
      DO 6 J=1,N
    6 VAR=VAR+((VALUE(J,1)-VALUE(J,2))**2)/ANUMB
      WRITE(3,99)VAR,A
      A2=0
C INCREMENT TEST ALPHA  -  TO NEAREST .0001
      DECINC=1.0
      DO 18 1=1,4
      DECINC=DECINC/10.0
      A2=A
    8 A2=A2+DECINC
      B=1.0-A2
      VAR2=0
C FORECAST
      DO 10 J=2,N
      K=J-1
   10 VALUE(J,3)=(VALUE(K,1)*A2)+(VALUE(K,3)*B)
      DO 12 J=1,N
C CALCULATE VARIANCE
   12 VAR2=VAR2+((VALUE(J,1)-VALUE(J,3))**2)/ANUMB
      WRITE(3,99)VAR2,A2
      IF(VAR2-VAR)14,18,18
   14 VAR=VAR2
      A=A2
C SAVE IMPROVEMENTS (REDUCED VARIANCE)
      DO 16 J=2,N
   16 VALUE(J,2)=VALUE(J,3)
      GO TO 8
   18 CONTINUE
      WRITE(3,22)A
      WRITE(3,24)VALUE(N,2)
   20 FORMAT(1H0,5X,'ROUTINE FOR OPTIMAL ALPHA LEVEL FOR')
   21 FORMAT(1H,5X,'EXPONENTIAL SMOOTHING - SINGLE ORDER')
   22 FORMAT(1H0,5X,'OPTIMUM ALPHA CALCULATED=',F8.4)
   24 FORMAT(1H,5X,'FINAL FORECAST =',F9.2)
   44 FORMAT(1H0,4X,'VARIANCE',7X,'AT ALPHA')
   99 FORMAT(1H ,F12.5,7X,F7.4)
      RETURN
      END
```

APPENDIX 3.B   COMPUTER PROGRAM A TO COMPUTE ORIGINAL OPTIMAL ALPHA LEVEL FOR DOUBLE EXPONENTIAL SMOOTHING, USING LEAST-SQUARES INITIALIZATIONS

```
C DOUBLE EXPONENTIAL SMOOTHING
C LEAST SQUARES INITIALIZATION BASED ON FIRST 3RD OF DATA
      DIMENSION VALUE(100,6),HOLD(6)
      WRITE(1,20)
      WRITE(1,21)
      WRITE(1,215)
      READ(5,1)ANUMB
      N=ANUMB
      READ(5,1)(VALUE(J,1),J=1,N)
    1 FORMAT(F6.2)
C THE FOLLOWING ARE FOR INITIALIZATION
      SXY=0.
      SX=0.
      SY=0.
      SX2=0.
      K=N/3
      AK=K
      DO 999 J=1,K
      A=J
      SXY=SXY+A*VALUE(J,1)
      SX=SX+A
      SY=SY+VALUE(J,1)
  999 SX2=SX2+A**2
      RSLOP=((AK*SXY)-(SX*SY))/((AK*SX2)-(SX**2))
      RINT=(SY/AK)-(RSLOP*(SX/AK))
      WRITE(1,650)RINT
      WRITE(1,660)RSLOP
      WRITE(1,44)
      VALUE(1,2)=VALUE(1,1)
      DO 5 J=2,N
      K=J-1
    5 VALUE(J,2)=VALUE(K,2)
      IKNOW=0
      A=0
      DO 555 J=1,6
  555 HOLD(J)=VALUE(1,1)
      VAR=0
      DO 6 J=1,N
    6 VAR=VAR+((VALUE(J,1)-VALUE(J,2))**2)/ANUMB
      WRITE(1,99)VAR,A
      A=0
      A1=0
```

Appendix 3.B, copyright © 1983 by Charles W. Gross.

```
          A2=0
          VAR1=VAR
          VAR2=0
          DECINC=1.0
          ICOUNT=0
          DO 18 I=1,4
          ICOUNT=ICOUNT+1
          DECINC=DECINC/10.
     8 A2=A2+DECINC
     9 CONTINUE
          B=1.0-A2
          VAR2=0
          VALUE(1,2)=A2*VALUE(1,1)+B*(RINT-B/A2*RSLOP)
          VALUE(1,3)=A2*VALUE(1,2)+B*(RINT-2.*B/A2*RSLOP)
          VALUE(1,4)=2.*VALUE(1,2)-VALUE(1,3)
          VALUE(1,5)=A2/B*(VALUE(1,2)-VALUE(1,3))
          VALUE(1,6)=RINT +RSLOP
          VALUE(2,6)=VALUE(1,4)+VALUE(1,5)
          DO 10 J=2,N
          K=J-1
    10 VALUE(J,2)=(VALUE(J,1)*A2)+(VALUE(K,2)*B)
          DO 12 J=2,N
          K=J-1
    12 VALUE(J,3)=(VALUE(J,2)*A2)+(VALUE(K,3)*B)
          DO 14 J=2,N
          K=J+1
          VALUE(J,4)=2.*VALUE(J,2)-VALUE(J,3)
          VALUE(J,5)=A2/B*(VALUE(J,2)-VALUE(J,3))
    14 VALUE(K,6)=VALUE(J,4)+VALUE(J,5)
          IF(IKNOW-1)1440,120,120
  1440 CONTINUE
          DO 15 J=1,N
    15 VAR2=VAR2+((VALUE(J,1)-VALUE(J,6))**2)/ANUMB
          WRITE(1,99)VAR2,A2
          IF(VAR2-VAR1)16,1650,1650
    16 A=A1
          VAR=VAR1
          A1=A2
          VAR1=VAR2
          DO 1601 J=1,5
          K=J+1
  1601 HOLD(J)=VALUE(N,K)
          K=N+1
          HOLD(6)=VALUE(K,6)
          GO TO 8
  1650 IF(ICOUNT-4)1660,18,18
  1660 A2=A
```

```
        VAR1=VAR
        A1=A
  18 CONTINUE
        IKNOW=IKNOW+1
        IF(IKNOW-1)100,100,120
 100 WRITE(1,22)A1
        WRITE(1,88)HOLD(1)
        WRITE(1,89)HOLD(2)
        WRITE(1,90)HOLD(3)
        WRITE(1,91)HOLD(4)
        WRITE(1,24)HOLD(5)
        WRITE(1,105)HOLD(6)
        WRITE(1,106)
        WRITE(1,107)HOLD(4)
 110 A2=A1
        GO TO 9
 120 CONTINUE
        WRITE(1,125)
        WRITE(1,125)
        WRITE(1,125)
 125 FORMAT(1H )
        WRITE(1,145)
 145 FORMAT(1H ,' TIME',4X,'ACTUAL',8X,'Y1',10X,'Y2',11X,'A',
    112X,'B',7X,'FOREC.',8X,'ERROR',8X,'SQ.ER.')
        DO 150 J=1,N
        DIF=VALUE(J,1)-VALUE(J,6)
        DIFSQ=DIF**2
 150 WRITE(1,160)J,(VALUE(J,K),K=1,6),DIF,DIFSQ
 160 FORMAT(1H ,2X,I2,7(4X,F8.3),5X,F8.3)
  20 FORMAT(1H ,5X,'ROUTINE FOR OPTIMAL ALPHA LEVEL FOR')
  21 FORMAT(1H ,5X,'DOUBLE EXPONENTIAL SMOOTHING')
  22 FORMAT(1H ,5X,'OPTIMAL ALPHA CALCULATED =',5X,F8.4)
 215 FORMAT(1H ,5X,'LEAST SQUARES INITIALIZATIONS')
  24 FORMAT(1H ,5X,'FINAL HISTORICAL FORECAST =',3X,F9.4)
  44 FORMAT(1H ,4X,'VARIANCE',7X,'AT ALPHA')
  88 FORMAT(1H ,5X,'FINAL Y1 FUNCTION VALUE =',2X,F12.4)
  89 FORMAT(1H ,5X,'FINAL Y2 FUNCTION VALUE =',2X,F12.4)
  90 FORMAT(1H ,5X,'FINAL INTERCEPT VALUE =',4X,F12.4)
  91 FORMAT(1H ,5X,'FINAL SLOPE VALUE =',8X,F12.4)
  99 FORMAT(1H ,F12.4,7X,F7.4)
 105 FORMAT(1H ,5X,'NEXT PERIOD FORECAST =',5X,F12.4)
 106 FORMAT(1H ,5X,'SUCCESSIVE PERIOD FORECASTS')
 107 FORMAT(1H ,5X,'INCREMENT BY: ',F9.4)
 650 FORMAT(1H ,5X,'INITIAL INTERCEPT ESTIMATE =',F8.3)
 660 FORMAT(1H ,5X,'INITIAL SLOPE ESTIMATE =      ',F8.3)
        STOP
        END
```

APPENDIX 3.C   COMPUTER PROGRAM TO COMPUTE OPTIMAL ALPHA LEVEL FOR QUADRATIC EXPONENTIAL SMOOTHING, USING LEAST-SQUARES INITIALIZATIONS

```
C QUADRATIC EXPONENTIAL SMOOTHING
C INCLUDES INITIALIZATIONS CALCULATED WITH SECOND ORDER POLYNOMIAL
C LEAST SQUARES ESTIMATES BASED ON FIRST THIRD OF DATA
      DIMENSION SIMEQ(4,4)
      DIMENSION VALUE(100,8),HOLD(8)
      WRITE(1,20)
      WRITE(1,21)
      WRITE(1,44)
      READ(5,1)ANUMB
      N=ANUMB
      READ(5,1)(VALUE(J,1),J=1,N)
    1 FORMAT(F7.3)
      LN=ANUMB/3.0
      DO 2200 I=1,4
      DO 2200 J=1,4
 2200 SIMEQ(I,J)=0
      DO 2205 J=1,LN
      I=J
      SIMEQ(1,2)=SIMEQ(1,2)+I
      SIMEQ(1,3)=SIMEQ(1,3)+I**2
      SIMEQ(1,4)=SIMEQ(1,4)+VALUE(I,1)
      SIMEQ(2,3)=SIMEQ(2,3)+I**3
      SIMEQ(2,4)=SIMEQ(2,4)+VALUE(I,1)*I
      SIMEQ(3,3)=SIMEQ(3,3)+I**4
 2205 SIMEQ(3,4)=SIMEQ(3,4)+I**2*VALUE(I,1)
      SIMEQ(1,1)=I
      SIMEQ(2,1)=SIMEQ(1,2)
      SIMEQ(2,2)=SIMEQ(1,3)
      SIMEQ(3,1)=SIMEQ(1,3)
      SIMEQ(3,2)=SIMEQ(2,3)
      DO 2220 I=1,3
      VAL=SIMEQ(I,1)
      DO 2220 J=1,4
 2220 SIMEQ(I,J)=SIMEQ(I,J)/VAL
      DO 2222 J=1,4
 2222 SIMEQ(4,J)=SIMEQ(3,J)
      DO 2225 I=2,3
      DO 2225 J=1,4
 2225 SIMEQ(I,J)=SIMEQ(I,J)-SIMEQ(1,J)
      DO 2230 I=2,3
      VAL=SIMEQ(I,2)
      DO 2230 J=1,4
 2230 SIMEQ(I,J)=SIMEQ(I,J)/VAL
      DO 2250 I=1,4
 2250 SIMEQ(3,I)=SIMEQ(3,I)-SIMEQ(2,I)
      CEST=SIMEQ(3,4)/SIMEQ(3,3)
      BEST=SIMEQ(2,4)-(SIMEQ(2,3)*CEST)
      AEST=SIMEQ(4,4)-((SIMEQ(4,2)*BEST)+(SIMEQ(4,3)*CEST))
      WRITE(1,2290)AEST
      WRITE(1,2291)BEST
```

```
      WRITE(1,2292)CEST
2290  FORMAT(1H ,5X,'INITIAL INTERCEPT ESTIMATE =',F12.4)
2291  FORMAT(1H ,5X,'INITIAL SLOPE ESTIMATE     =',F12.4)
2292  FORMAT(1H ,5X,'INITIAL CHANGE RATE ESTIM. =',F12.4)
      SIMEQ(1,4)=AEST
      SIMEQ(2,4)=BEST
      SIMEQ(3,4)=CEST
      WRITE(1,44)
      VAR=0
      A=0
      VALUE(1,2)=VALUE(1,1)
      DO 5 J=2,N
      K=J-1
      VALUE(J,2)=VALUE(K,2)
   5  VAR=VAR+((VALUE(J,2)-VALUE(J,1))**2)/ANUMB
      WRITE(1,99)VAR,A
      A1=0
      A2=0
      VAR1=VAR
      VAR2=0
      DECINC=1.0
      ICOUNT=0
      IKNOW=0
      DO 18 I=1,4
      DECINC=DECINC/10.
      ICOUNT=ICOUNT+1
   8  A2=A2+DECINC
   9  CONTINUE
      B=1.-A2
      VAR2=0
      VALUE(1,2)=A2*VALUE(1,1)+B*(AEST-(B/A2*BEST)+((B*(2-A2)/(2*A2**2))
     1*CEST))
      VALUE(1,3)=A2*VALUE(1,2)+B*(AEST-(2*B/A2*BEST)+(((2*B*(3-2*A2))/
     1(2*A2**2))*CEST))
      VALUE(1,4)=A2*VALUE(1,3)+B*(AEST-(3*B/A2*BEST)+(((3*B*(4-3*A2))/
     1(2*A2**2))*CEST))
      BCOF1=A2/(2.*B**2)
      BCOF2=6.-5.*A2
      BCOF3=2*(5.-4*A2)
      BCOF4=4-3*A2
      CCOF1=(A2/B)**2
      DO 10 J=2,N
      K=J-1
      VALUE(J,2)=(VALUE(J,1)*A2)+(VALUE(K,2)*B)
      VALUE(J,3)=(VALUE(J,2)*A2)+(VALUE(K,3)*B)
  10  VALUE(J,4)=(VALUE(J,3)*A2)+(VALUE(K,4)*B)
      DO 12 J=1,N
      VALUE(J,5)=3.0*VALUE(J,2)-3.0*VALUE(J,3)+VALUE(J,4)
      VALUE(J,6)=BCOF1*(BCOF2*VALUE(J,2)-BCOF3*VALUE(J,3)+
     1BCOF4*VALUE(J,4))
  12  VALUE(J,7)=CCOF1*(VALUE(J,2)-2*VALUE(J,3)+VALUE(J,4))
      VALUE(1,8)=AEST+BEST+0.5*CEST
      K=N-1
      DO 14 J=1,K
      L=J+1
  14  VALUE(L,8)=VALUE(J,5)+VALUE(J,6)+0.5*VALUE(J,7)
```

```
      DO 15 J=1,N
   15 VAR2=VAR2+((VALUE(J,1)-VALUE(J,8))**2)/ANUMB
      WRITE(1,99)VAR2,A2
      IF(VAR2-VAR1)16,1650,1650
   16 A=A1
      VAR=VAR1
      A1=A2
      VAR1=VAR2
      DO 1601 J=2,7
 1601 HOLD(J)=VALUE(N,J)
      GO TO 8
 1650 IF(ICOUNT-4)1660,18,18
 1660 A2=A
      VAR1=VAR
      A1=A
   18 CONTINUE
      IKNOW=IKNOW+1
      IF(IKNOW-1)100,100,110
  100 A2=A1
      GO TO 9
  110 CONTINUE
      WRITE(1,22)A1
      DO 300 I=1,3
      K=I+1
  300 WRITE(1,400)I,HOLD(K)
      WRITE(1,410)HOLD(5)
      WRITE(1,420)HOLD(6)
      WRITE(1,430)HOLD(7)
      FCAST=HOLD(5)+HOLD(6)+0.5*HOLD(7)
      WRITE(1,440)FCAST
      WRITE(1,445)
      WRITE(1,450)(HOLD(KK),KK=5,7)
      WRITE(1,920)
      WRITE(1,920)
      WRITE(1,925)
      DO 850 J=1,N
      DIF=VALUE(J,1)-VALUE(J,8)
      DIFSQ=DIF**2
  850 WRITE(1,930)J,(VALUE(J,K),K=1,8),DIF,DIFSQ
  920 FORMAT(1H )
  925 FORMAT(1H ,' TIME',3X,'ACTUAL',5X,'Y1',9X,'Y2',8X,'Y3',9X,'A',10X,
     1'B',9X,'C',5X,'F CAST',5X,'ERROR',5X,'SQ.ER.')
  930 FORMAT(1H ,2X,I2,10(2X,F8.4))
   20 FORMAT(1H ,5X,'ROUTINE FOR OPTIMAL ALPHA LEVEL FOR')
   21 FORMAT(1H ,5X,'QUADRATIC EXPONENTIAL SMOOTHING')
   44 FORMAT(1H ,5X,'VARIANCE',7X,'AT ALPHA')
   99 FORMAT(1H ,F12.5,8X,F7.4)
   22 FORMAT(1H ,5X,'OPTIMAL ALPHA CALCULATED =',5X,F8.4)
  400 FORMAT(1H ,5X,'FINAL Y',I1,' FUNCTION VALUE =',6X,F8.4)
  410 FORMAT(1H ,5X,'FINAL A FUNCTION VALUE =',7X,F8.4)
  420 FORMAT(1H ,5X,'FINAL B FUNCTION VALUE =',7X,F8.4)
  430 FORMAT(1H ,5X,'FINAL C FUNCTION VALUE =',7X,F8.4)
  440 FORMAT(1H ,5X,'NEXT PERIOD FORECAST =',9X,F8.4)
  445 FORMAT(1H ,5X,'FUTURE FORECASTS ARE CALCULATED AS FOLLOWS:')
  450 FORMAT(1H ,5X,'Y(T+P)= ',F8.4,' + ',F8.4,'P + ',F8.4,'*0.5*P**2')
      STOP
      END
```

APPENDIX 3.D   CALCULATIONS REQUIRED TO EMPLOY LEAST SQUARES IN ESTIMATING INITIAL VALUES FOR QUADRATIC EXPONENTIAL SMOOTHING, USING THE FIRST THIRD OF THE HISTORICAL SERIES

Step 1. Solve the following system of equations simultaneously:

$$an + b\Sigma t + c\Sigma t^2 = \Sigma x$$
$$a\Sigma t + b\Sigma t^2 + c\Sigma t^3 = \Sigma tx$$
$$a\Sigma t^2 + b\Sigma t^3 + c\Sigma t^4 = \Sigma t^2 x$$

where

a = intercept
b = slope
c = change in slope
n = number of data observations
t = time period
x = actual

For the example (Table 3.16) using one-third of history:

t	x	t^2	t^3	tx	t^4	$t^2 x$
1	34.6	1	1	34.6	1	34.6
2	35.7	4	8	71.4	16	142.8
3	36.9	9	27	110.7	81	332.1
4	38.7	16	64	154.8	256	619.2
5	40.4	25	125	202.0	625	1,010.0
15	186.3	55	225	573.5	979	2,138.7

Then:

$$5a + 15b + 55c = 186.3$$
$$15a + 55b + 225c = 573.5$$
$$55a + 225b + 979c = 2138.7$$

which equals (divide each equation by its respective a coefficient):

$$a + 3b + 11c = 37.26$$
$$a + 3.66667b + 15c = 38.233333$$
$$a + 4.09091b + 17.8c = 38.88546$$

Then, subtract the first equation from the second two:

$$0.66667b + 4c = 0.97333$$
$$1.09091b + 6.8c = 1.62546$$

which equals (divide each equation by its respective b coefficient):

$$b + 6.0c = 1.46$$
$$b + 6.23333c = 1.49$$

Then subtract the first from the second equation:

$$0.23333c = 0.03$$

which means

$$c = 0.12857$$

Next, insert c's value into one of the previous equations:

$$b + (6.23333)(0.12857) = 1.49$$

which means

$$b = 0.68858$$

Finally, insert a and b values into a previous equation:

$$a + (4.09091)(0.68858) + (17.8)(0.12857)$$
$$= 38.88546$$

which means

$$a = 33.7799$$

Step 2. Calculate estimates of Y', Y'', and Y''' at time period 0.

$$\text{Let } Y_t = \begin{bmatrix} Y'_t \\ Y''_t \\ Y'''_t \end{bmatrix} \qquad d = \begin{bmatrix} a_t \\ b_t \\ c_t \end{bmatrix}$$

$$\text{and } M = \begin{bmatrix} 1 & -\dfrac{\beta}{\alpha} & \dfrac{\beta(2-\alpha)}{2\alpha^2} \\[2ex] 1 & -\dfrac{2\beta}{\alpha} & \dfrac{2\beta(3-2\alpha)}{2\alpha^2} \\[2ex] 1 & -\dfrac{3\beta}{\alpha} & \dfrac{3\beta(4-3\alpha)}{2\alpha^2} \end{bmatrix}$$

where $\beta = 1 - \alpha$

Brown has shown that:[1]

$$Y_t = Md$$

For the example, at the optimal $\alpha = 0.4102$:

$$M = \begin{bmatrix} 1 & -\dfrac{0.5898}{0.4102} & \dfrac{0.5898(2-0.4102)}{(2)0.4102^2} \\[2ex] 1 & -\dfrac{(2)0.5898}{0.4201} & \dfrac{(2)(0.5898)[3-2(0.4102)]}{(2)0.4102^2} \\[2ex] 1 & -\dfrac{(3)0.5898}{0.4102} & \dfrac{(3)(0.5898)[4-3(0.4102)]}{(2)0.4102^2} \end{bmatrix}$$

$$\text{and } d = \begin{bmatrix} 33.7799 \\ 0.68858 \\ 0.12857 \end{bmatrix}$$

Thus:

$$M = \begin{bmatrix} 1 & -1.4378 & 2.7863 \\ 1 & -2.8757 & 7.6399 \\ 1 & -4.3135 & 14.5610 \end{bmatrix}$$

Therefore:

$$Y_0 = Md$$

$$Y_0 = \begin{bmatrix} 1 & -1.4378 & 2.7863 \\ 1 & -2.8757 & 7.6399 \\ 1 & -4.3135 & 14.5610 \end{bmatrix} \times \begin{bmatrix} 33.7799 \\ 0.68858 \\ 0.12857 \end{bmatrix} = \begin{bmatrix} 33.1481 \\ 32.7820 \\ 32.6818 \end{bmatrix}$$

1. R. G. Brown, *Smoothing, Forecasting, and Prediction of Discrete Time Series* (Englewood Cliffs, N.J.: Prentice-Hall, 1963).

To illustrate: $33.1481 = (1)(33.7799) - (1.4378)(0.68858) + (2.7863)$ (0.12857), and so on. Thus:

$$Y_0' = 33.1481, \ Y_0'' = 32.782, \text{ and } Y_0''' = 32.6818$$

Now, begin the smoothing in the normal manner to calculate values for time period $t = 1$.

$$Y_1' = (0.4102)(34.60) + (0.5898)(33.1481) = 33.743$$

$$Y_1'' = (0.4102)(33.743) + (0.5898)(32.7820) = 33.176$$

$$Y_1''' = (0.4102)(33.176) + (0.5898)(32.6818) = 32.884$$

These values are the same except for rounding differences, as those presented in Table 3.16.

APPENDIX 3.E COMPUTER PROGRAM TO COMPUTE OPTIMAL WEIGHTS FOR WINTERS' EXPONENTIAL SMOOTHING

```
C WINTERS' METHOD OF SMOOTHING
C  ESTIMATES OF INITIAL INTERCEPT, SLOPE, AND SEASONAL FACTORS
C BASED ON THE FIRST 2 * THE SEASONAL LENGTH OF DATA
C INSERT THE LENGTH OF THE SEASONAL CYCLE IN DATA FILE
      DIMENSION VALUE(100,5),SEAS(20),HOLD(730,4),SHOLD(20)
      WRITE(1,800)
      WRITE(1,801)
      WRITE(1,802)
      WRITE(1,803)
      READ(5,1)N,LEN
    1 FORMAT(I3,2X,I2)
      ANUM=N
      K=N+1
      READ(5,2)(VALUE(J,1),J=2,K)
    2 FORMAT(F5.1)
      KTEST=LEN*2
      IF(KTEST-N)10,10,5
    5 WRITE(1,6)
    6 FORMAT(1H ,2X,'RUN ABORTED TOO FEW OBSERVATIONS')
      GO TO 820
   10 SX1=0
      SX2=0
      X=LEN+0.5
      DO 11 L=1,LEN
      J=L+1
      K=J+LEN
      SX1=SX1+VALUE(J,1)/LEN
   11 SX2=SX2+VALUE(K,1)/LEN
      SLOPE=(SX2-SX1)/LEN
      SINT=(SX1+SX2)/2.-SLOPE*X
      WRITE(1,900)
      WRITE(1,900)
      WRITE(1,905)SLOPE,SINT
  900 FORMAT(1H )
  905 FORMAT(1H ,'INITIAL SLOPE =',F8.5,'    AND INTERCEPT =',F8.5)
      AX=0
      DO 20 J=1,LEN
      KK=J+1
      AX=AX+1
   20 SHOLD(J)=VALUE(KK,1)/(SINT+AX*SLOPE)/2.
      K=LEN+1
      DO 25 J=1,LEN
      KK=KK+1
      AX=AX+1
   25 SHOLD(J)=SHOLD(J)+(VALUE(KK,1)/(SINT+AX*SLOPE)/2.)
```

Appendix 3.E, copyright © 1983 by Charles W. Gross.

```
C WEIGHTS CONSTRAINED TO TENTHS BETWEEN 0.1 AND 0.9
      IHOLD=0
      JTEST=0
      ILOOP=9
      VALUE(1,2)=SINT
      VALUE(1,3)=SLOPE
      DO 90 IA=1,ILOOP
      A=IA/10.
      DO 90 IB=1,ILOOP
      B=IB/10.
      DO 90 IC=1,ILOOP
      C=IC/10.
      IHOLD=IHOLD+1
 30 DO 35 J=1,LEN
 35 SEAS(J)=SHOLD(J)
      IS=0
      DO 60 INUM=1,N
      IVAL=INUM+1
      IS=IS+1
      IF(IS-LEN)45,45,40
 40 IS=1
 45 VALUE(IVAL,2)=A*(VALUE(IVAL,1)/SEAS(IS))+
    1(1.-A)*(VALUE(INUM,2)+VALUE(INUM,3))
      VALUE(IVAL,3)=B*(VALUE(IVAL,2)-VALUE(INUM,2))+
    1(1.-B)*VALUE(INUM,3)
      VALUE(IVAL,4)=C*(VALUE(IVAL,1)/VALUE(IVAL,2))+(1.0-C)*SEAS(IS)
      VALUE(IVAL,5)=(VALUE(INUM,2)+VALUE(INUM,3))*SEAS(IS)
 60 SEAS(IS)=VALUE(IVAL,4)
      IF(JTEST-1)75,150,150
 75 VAR=0
      DO 80 J=1,N
      K=J+1
 80 VAR=VAR+(VALUE(K,1)-VALUE(K,5))**2
      HOLD(IHOLD,1)=VAR
      HOLD(IHOLD,2)=A
      HOLD(IHOLD,3)=B
      HOLD(IHOLD,4)=C
 90 CONTINUE
      JTEST=1
      VARMIN=999999**2
      ISCAN=ILOOP**3
      DO 110 J=1,ISCAN
      IF(VARMIN-HOLD(J,1))110,110,100
100 K=J
      VARMIN=HOLD(J,1)
110 CONTINUE
      A=HOLD(K,2)
      B=HOLD(K,3)
      C=HOLD(K,4)
      JTEST=1
```

```
      GO TO 30
150 VAR=0
    VARMIN=VARMIN/ANUM
    WRITE(1,8060)VARMIN
    K=N+1
    WRITE(1,804)A
    WRITE(1,805)B
    WRITE(1,806)C
    WRITE(1,807)
    WRITE(1,808)VALUE(K,2)
    WRITE(1,809)VALUE(K,3)
    WRITE(1,810)
    DO 190 J=1,LEN
190 WRITE(1,811)J,SEAS(J)
    WRITE(1,812)LEN
    INC=0
    DO 195 J=1,LEN
    INC=INC+1
    FOR=(VALUE(K,2)+VALUE(K,3)*INC)*SEAS(J)
195 WRITE(1,813)J,FOR
    WRITE(1,900)
    WRITE(1,900)
    WRITE(1,910)
    DO 200 J=1,N
    K=J+1
    DIF=VALUE(K,1)-VALUE(K,5)
    DIFSQ=DIF**2
200 WRITE(1,920)J,(VALUE(K,M),M=1,5),DIF,DIFSQ
800 FORMAT(1H ,5X,'OPTIMAL WEIGHT ROUTINE FOR')
801 FORMAT(1H ,5X,'WINTERS',1H','EXPONENTIAL SMOOTHING')
802 FORMAT(1H ,5X,'USES TWO TIMES THE SEASON LENGTH')
803 FORMAT(1H ,5X,'TO INITIALIZE TREND AND SEASONALS')
804 FORMAT(1H ,5X,'OPTIMAL INTERCEPT WEIGHT    =',F3.1)
805 FORMAT(1H ,5X,'OPTIMAL SLOPE WEIGHT        ='F3.1)
806 FORMAT(1H ,5X,'OPTIMAL SEASONAL WEIGHT     =',F3.1)
8060 FORMAT(1H ,5X,'VARIANCE AT OPTIMAL WEIGHTS =',F8.2)
807 FORMAT(1H ,5X,'THE FOLLOWING ARE FINAL ESTIMATES')
808 FORMAT(1H ,5X,'INTERCEPT =',F8.2)
809 FORMAT(1H ,5X,'SLOPE',5X,'=',F8.2)
810 FORMAT(1H ,5X,'SEASONS AHEAD',4X,'INDEX')
811 FORMAT(1H ,9X,I2,10X,F7.5)
812 FORMAT(1H ,'  FORECASTS FOR THE NEXT',I2,' SEASONS:')
813 FORMAT(1H ,9X,I2,7X,F8.3)
910 FORMAT(1H ,'TIME',4X,'ACTUAL',7X,'A',9X,'B',9X,'C',6X,'FOREC.',
   15X,'ERROR',5X,'SQ.ER.')
920 FORMAT(1H ,I3,1X,7(2X,F8.3))
820 CONTINUE
    STOP
    END
```

CASE 3: COMPUTER ENTERPRISES, INC.

Computer Enterprises, Inc. (CEI) is a chain-store organization that sells personal computers to businesses, schools, and consumers. The eight-year-old firm is headquartered in Houston and has franchise stores in 31 states. Last year, sales of these stores came to $784,539,000.

Franchisees (independent business owners) purchase the computers they sell from the franchisor (CEI). In turn, they pay to the franchisor 9% of their total sales. In return for this payment, they receive training programs, the good will of the company name, local and national advertising programs, low prices for computers (because the chain buys them in volume), and specialized assistance in such matters as store location, financing, and interior display. Franchisees agree to adhere to certain standards, such as maintaining specified levels of inventory, providing customer services identified by the company, and constructing the store interior and exterior according to company specifications (all stores thus have a common appearance).

The market for personal computers is large and growing, and has attracted some formidable competition. Some large firms, like IBM and Xerox, sell their models through independent outlets. Others, like Radio Shack, both manufacture computers and sell them through their own stores. Mass retailers, like Sears and J. C. Penney, try to sell low-priced compact machines. This competition can be expected to intensify in the face of a predicted total sales of 10 million personal computers by 1985.

CEI stores orient their efforts toward satisfying small businesses and consumers. Each store has a modern and aesthetically pleasing interior. Various computer models are on display and well-trained sales personnel are available to help customers, who are encouraged to try out computers after a demonstration by a sales representative. The stores also sell software (standardized computer programs). The prices range from $399 for a very basic model computer to $7,999 for a computer with numerous uses and many basic programs. The stores are supported by advertisements in local newspapers and (in large market areas) by television.

Total sales for the company by quarter are as follows (in thousands of dollars):

Year	Sales, $	Year	Sales $
1975 1	52,800	1979 1	77,903
2	63,920	2	79,901
3	59,550	3	78,092
4	78,912	4	83,909
1976 1	67,779	1980 1	91,550
2	81,970	2	99,901
3	70,402	3	93,000
4	81,009	4	107,589
1977 1	71,346	1981 1	113,330
2	78,063	2	143,902
3	64,396	3	139,219
4	83,090	4	159,991
1978 1	75,901	1982 1	127,975
2	77,270	2	209,896
3	70,934	3	207,900
4	82,987	4	238,768

CEI is an aggressive company. Its goals are to expand sales and profits to the fullest extent that is compatible with maintaining high-quality service to customers and not straining its financial position. It is not believed that the latter will act as a serious constraint to growth, at least in the near future, since profits and cash position are secure and the company is well regarded by lending institutions. Its relationships with computer manufacturers are good, so that the firm is able to negotiate favorable prices, terms of sale, and service agreements with these manufacturers.

1. Is time-series forecasting appropriate for this firm? Why or why not?
2. What time-series models would appear to be most appropriate for CEI? Defend your answer. What is your sales forecast for each quarter of 1983?
3. What are the advantages and disadvantages of time-series models, as compared to judgmental models, for this company?

Chapter 4
Regression and Correlation

INTRODUCTION

Two closely related techniques, regression and correlation, are probably the most widely known statistically based procedures used in practical forecasting situations. Their popularity is due to at least two factors. First, the techniques are relatively easy to understand, even for those who are not mathematically inclined. Second, the techniques' results can be very accurate in many situations.

In essence, regression and correlation procedures attempt to examine the mathematical relationship between the forecast variable and at least one other variable. They try to relate changes in the value of one variable to changes in the magnitude of other variables. For example, changes in annual family clothing expenditures may be related to changes in personal income. If a significant relationship is detected, perhaps expected future income levels can be used to predict clothing expenditures. The forecaster first attempts to learn the extent of the relationship and then constructs the forecast accordingly.

SOME DEFINITIONS

Before proceeding into an extended examination of techniques, it is helpful to understand several different types of relationships that may exist between variables. In general, variables can be related in one of two basic forms, complete and incomplete relationships.

Complete Relationships

The first form is the case when one variable exerts a causal influence on a second. This relationship can be termed *complete* because one variable is dependent and the other independent. The latter variable is the causal agent in influencing the value of the dependent variable; one might say that the independent variable causes the magnitude of the dependent variable. For example, the level of an individual's income is one cause of the amount the person spends on a home.

In the case of complete relationships, the forecaster may use both correlation and regression analyses. *Correlation*, which measures the magnitude of the relationship between two or more variables, is often employed to detect the existence of an association between the dependent and independent variable. Then, after an association is detected, *regression* analysis can be employed to predict the value of the dependent variable.

Incomplete Relationships

A second form of relationship may exist, in which it is not known if the level of one variable is caused by the level of the second. Thus, the relationship may be termed *incomplete*. In this case, either variable may be dependent or independent of the other. Both may be dependent on at least one variable not included in the analysis and be independent of each other. For example, an examination of historical data might indicate that birth rates are related to foreign trade balances. Logic suggests that it is doubtful that these variables are complete. A well-conceived analysis generally takes the form of trying to determine if and to what extent an association exists. Correlation analysis can be used for this purpose.

DEPENDENCE DETERMINATION

Logic is often the best indicator of whether a particular variable relationship is complete or incomplete as well as dependent or independent. To illustrate, assume that a forecaster is attempting to analyze national industry sales of snowmobiles. Assume that after several variables are studied in terms of their association to snowmobile sales, it is found that three variables are closely related: average snow depth in the geographic area under consideration, personal income, and whether or not members of households own color television sets. The first association, that of average snow depth, logically appears to be a causal influence on the use of snowmobiles, and hence, on their sales. It is not unreasonable to assume that snowmobiles will be demanded infrequently in areas where little snow exists, and as snow becomes deeper, the need for snowmobiles should increase. Conversely, snowmobile usage exerts little or no influence on the average snow depth in an area. This relationship is complete since it appears that average snow depth is an independent variable that has an impact upon the dependent variable (snowmobile sales).

Income also appears to have a complete association with snowmobile sales. Logically, as a family's income rises, its ability to purchase a snowmobile also rises. Hence, income appears to be an independent variable. On the other hand, the likelihood of snowmobile sales affecting income is quite small. Therefore, the forecaster can assume with reasonable certainty that income is the independent and snowmobile sales the dependent variable and that their relationship is complete.

As you may already have decided, the third variable, color television, occupies a different status. It is unlikely that the purchase of a color television set increases the desire of the buyer for a snowmobile, nor would the purchase of a snowmobile seem to expand the desire to acquire a color television. Their association is incomplete, and some other variable is responsible for the relationship; both may be dependent upon another variable such as income. As a result, a forecaster would be well advised to exercise caution when using data on color television expenditures to predict sales of snowmobiles. Statistical theory suggests that forecasts should not be made on the basis of such variables because of the incomplete association. To illustrate, if preferences for color television sets suddenly shift, there is no logical assurance that preferences for snowmobiles would likewise shift.

In practice, however, analysts do not often have the luxury of unlimited time and resources. Forecasts must be made when they can be used—before the fact. It may be impossible, given time and cost constraints, for example, to find another variable with an equal degree of association with snowmobile sales where completeness can be assumed. Thus, it may be necessary to use a variable such as color television sales as a predictor of snowmobile sales. The analyst must be aware, however, that such an association is incomplete and that resulting forecasts may well contain an element of error, because of possible undetected underlying changes between the variables.

Another type of association, *reverse association*, can be in existence. Consider the relationship between the sales of snowmobiles and of motor oil. Although a very significant and very high degree of association may exist between these variables, it is probably due to the sales of snowmobiles influencing the sales of snowmobile motor oil rather than the reverse.

In this case, the independent variable is sales of snowmobiles and the dependent is sales of snowmobile motor oil. Forecasters will inject error into their estimates if they use reverse associations to predict the value of the forecast variable. Certainly snowmobile motor oil is not a valid predictor of the level of snowmobile sales. There is no logical association for prediction between these variables. With these concepts in mind, let us direct our attention to the analytic techniques that are the working tools of the forecaster.

REGRESSION ANALYSIS

Regression analysis attempts to assess the relationship between at least two variables—one or more independent and one dependent. Its purpose is to predict the value of the dependent variable from the specific magnitude of the independent variable. The basis of this prediction is generally historical data. This technique is best illustrated with an example.

Example: Forecasting Sales of Vacuum Cleaners

Suppose analysts are faced with the task of estimating next quarter's sales of central vacuum cleaners for a firm. An investigation indicates that these units are usually installed as an integral part of the building in which they are housed; the conduit pipe for these vacuum cleaners is usually in a wall or in the floor. Therefore, after buildings have been constructed, installation of central vacuum cleaners is impractical. The analysts' first observation may be that installation would be most readily accomplished during the initial construction of a home or building. Their immediate impression may be that sales of central vacuum cleaners are probably related to new building constructions.

Additional investigation suggests that new building construction, in most cases, requires a building permit. Thus, the analysts may reason that the number of new construction permits is a good potential lead indicator of central vacuum cleaner sales. If a strong relationship is found, it is logical to assume that central vacuum cleaner sales represent the dependent and building permits the independent variable. It would not be logical to assume the reverse. Therefore, any detected association could be termed *complete*.

The first step taken by the regression analysts is to obtain a set of historical data for both variables. Theoretically, the greater the amount of historical data the more accurate the regression output.

In practice, however, most forecasters must make a trade-off. First, the cost of additional historical information may increase rapidly with the growing number of observations. This additional cost may substantially outweigh the advantage in mathematical precision yielded by greater accuracy. (The cost of perfect information, discussed in Chapter 2, is relevant in this evaluation.) Second, and more obviously, regression makes several perhaps naive assumptions. One is that the underlying relationships between the variables either remain constant or change at a constant rate throughout the range of the values of variables being studied. If historical data are chosen from a period with a long time span, this assumption may be less realistic than if a shorter time frame is selected. What constitutes a long or short time span is, of course, relative. In this regard, a thousand years may be a short time when studying various natural phenomena, but an hour may be a long time for a riot. However, within the socioeconomic realm, less than a year is generally considered a short span and more than one year a long span.

The selection of the specific time span to be employed, if time is a relevant variable, must be based on the judgment of the analysts. Suppose that the analysts, because of their experience and familiarity with the market, assume that the past twelve quarters are representative if a relationship is, in fact, determined. The analysts are reasonably confident that underlying factors (awareness of central vacuum cleaners among home builders, economic considerations, and so forth) are relatively constant in terms of their relationship to sales over three years. The investigation has produced the historical sales and construction permits data listed in Table 4.1.

After collecting the data, the analysts should subjectively assess whether or not there appears to exist a relationship between the sales of central vacuum cleaners and new home construction permits. A scatter diagram allows them to inspect visually the data to determine if the variables appear related. Incidentally, a side benefit of the scatter diagram is that it may suggest the type of relationship (linear, exponential, and so on) in existence. The scatter diagram for data presented in Table 4.1 appears in Figure 4.1. Of course, the scatter diagram could have been constructed with the use of a computer.

In using regression, it must be assumed that any relationship detected from *discrete* observations is *continuous*. Essentially, a continuous

Table 4.1 Central Vacuum Cleaner Sales and Construction Permits

Quarter[a] (t)	Central Vacuum Cleaner Sales (in Millions of Dollars)	New Home Construction Permits in the Sales Area for the $t-1$ Quarter (in Thousands of Units)
1	7.0	6.5
2	6.5	7.0
3	5.1	5.0
4	4.0	4.0
5	5.5	4.5
6	6.0	5.5
7	5.3	6.0
8	5.0	4.5
9	7.0	8.2
10	8.1	7.5
11	6.0	6.8
12	7.1	9.0

[a] In this table, 12 represents the current quarter.

Figure 4.1 Scatter Diagram of Central Vacuum Cleaner Sales and Construction Permits

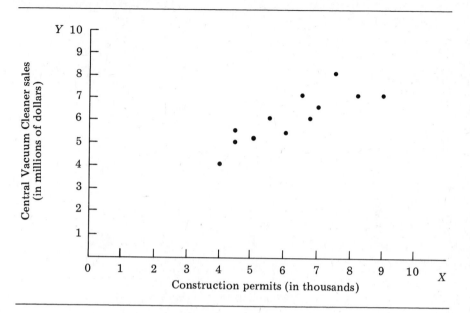

distribution implies that the detected functional relationship between the dependent and independent variables at the points of measurement, the data points, also exists along other points. Discrete, on the other hand, refers to the fact that observations were specific values with spaces (measurement gaps) existing between each value. Continuity assumes that the association detected remains inherent in the data if actual observations had been observed between those present measured observations.

An examination of the discrete observations (the dots) in Figure 4.1 indicates that sales of central vacuum cleaners during one period are linearly related to construction permits issued during the preceding period. This means that a straight line best represents the functional relationship existing between the variables.

After making the observation that a linear relationship exists, a naive forecaster might approach the estimation process by employing the free-hand-smoothing method discussed in Chapter 3. Figure 4.2 presents a freehand-smoothing-function line illustrating the outcome of this process.

The analysts might then obtain the equation of the function determined by the freehand-smoothing method with Equation 3.2 (see Chapter 3). For the example, the equation is

Figure 4.2 Freehand Smoothed Functional Relationship of Central
Vacuum Cleaner Sales and Construction Permits

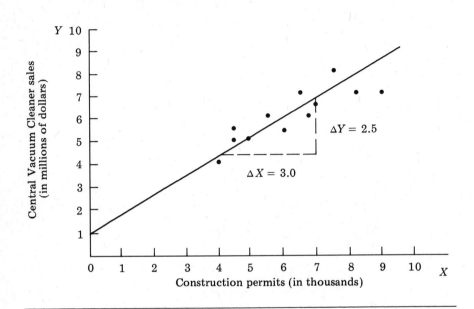

$$y_c = 1.0 + 0.833x$$

where y_c = mean (arithmetic average) vacuum cleaner sales after
relating these sales to construction permits
   x = construction permits issued in the previous quarter

   The above equation could then be used to determine how well the
model fits the historical data. This is done by calculating the y_c value
corresponding to each of the historical measurements of x construction
permits. For $t = 1$, $y_c = 1.0 + (0.833)(6.5) = 6.42$ (see Table 4.2). For
$t = 2$, $y_c = 1.0 + (0.833)(7.0) = 6.83$, and so on. Each of the y_c values
could then be compared to the actual values to calculate the overall
mean squared error (MSE), or variance, as illustrated in Table 4.2.
   There appears to be a relatively small MSE, and thus the model seems
reasonable. Thus, if construction permits were 7.3 thousand this quarter,
sales of central vacuum cleaners for next quarter would be forecast at

$$y_c = 1.0 + (0.833)(7.3) = \$7.08 \text{ million}$$

   Freehand smoothing can lead to reasonably accurate results in cases
where all the observations are near the line. But it really should be

Table 4.2 Assessment of Naive Freehand Smoothing

t	x	y	y_c	Error $(y - y_c)$	Squared Error
1	6.5	7.0	6.42	0.58	0.336
2	7.0	6.5	6.83	(0.33)	0.109
3	5.0	5.1	5.17	(0.07)	0.005
4	4.0	4.0	4.33	(0.33)	0.109
5	4.5	5.5	4.75	0.75	0.563
6	5.5	6.0	5.58	0.42	0.176
7	6.0	5.3	6.00	(0.70)	0.490
8	4.5	5.0	4.75	0.25	0.063
9	8.2	7.0	7.83	(0.83)	0.689
10	7.5	8.1	7.25	0.85	0.723
11	6.8	6.0	6.67	(0.67)	0.449
12	9.0	7.1	8.50	(1.40)	1.960

Summary: MSE $= \$0.473 \times 10^{12}$

$\sqrt{\text{MSE}} = \$0.688$ million

avoided because of the inevitability of error stemming from fitting a line by "eyeball."

There is a widespread availability of machines that perform regression by the least-squares procedure, thus making freehand smoothing essentially obsolete. Fortunately, regression computer software is abundant. Even several inexpensive calculators, which sell below \$30, can perform regression when two variables are being analyzed.

Least-Squares Method

The least-squares method is a relatively simple mathematical technique that ensures that the calculated functional linear equation is the one that best fits the data. A line is said to be the best-fit line when it minimizes, in relation to all other possible lines, the vertical deviations of the observations from that line. This method of regression-function determination is more accurate than freehand smoothing in depicting the relationship of the variable because it employs objective mathematical procedures. The procedure mathematically generates a line that minimizes the sum of the squared deviations of the actual values from this least-squares line. The computations require determining the values of a and b in the regression equation $y_c = a + b_x$. The values of a and b are calculated by solving the following equations.

$$b = \frac{n\Sigma xy - \Sigma x \Sigma y}{n\Sigma x^2 - (\Sigma x)^2} \tag{4.1}$$

$$a = \bar{y} - b\bar{x} \tag{4.2}$$

where n = the number of observations
x = the independent variable
y = the dependent variable
a = the function's intercept of the y axis when x equals 0
b = the slope of the function line
$\bar{x}$ = the mean of x, that is, $\bar{x} = \Sigma x/n$
$\bar{y}$ = the mean of y, that is, $\bar{y} = \Sigma y/n$

Table 4.3 uses data from the example to illustrate the equation-generation process.
Injecting these values into Equations 4.1 and 4.2 produces

$$b = \frac{n\Sigma xy - \Sigma x \Sigma y}{n\Sigma x^2 - (\Sigma x)^2} = \frac{(12)(467.40) - (74.5)(72.6)}{(12)(489.73) - (74.5)^2} = 0.6128$$

$$\bar{x} = \frac{74.5}{12} = 6.2083$$

$$\bar{y} = \frac{72.6}{12} = 6.0500$$

Table 4.3   Relevant Values for Regression

x	y	xy	x^2	y^2
6.5	7.0	45.50	42.25	49.00
7.0	6.5	45.50	49.00	42.25
5.0	5.1	25.50	25.00	26.01
4.0	4.0	16.00	16.00	16.00
4.5	5.5	24.75	20.25	30.25
5.5	6.0	33.00	30.25	36.00
6.0	5.3	31.80	36.00	28.09
4.5	5.0	22.50	20.25	25.00
8.2	7.0	57.40	67.24	49.00
7.5	8.1	60.75	56.25	65.61
6.8	6.0	40.80	46.24	36.00
9.0	7.1	63.90	81.00	50.41
74.5	72.6	467.40	489.73	453.62

and

$$a = \bar{y} - b\bar{x} = 6.05 - (0.6128)(6.2083) = 2.2456$$

The regression equation therefore becomes

$$y_c = 2.2456 + 0.6128x \qquad (4.3)$$

where y_c = the calculated value of the dependent variable for a given value of x.

Table 4.4 presents an assessment of how well the least-squares calculated function fits the historical series. Notice that there is improvement over the MSE associated with the freehand-smoothing method. In fact, no linear function will yield a smaller MSE for this example than that of Table 4.4. The forecast value, y_c, is considered a mean because of the statistical premise upon which the forecast is made. With regression analysis, it is assumed that the calculated function represents the true (theoretical) underlying relationship between variables, and the actual historical data observations represent only a sample drawn from this distribution. Deviations of historical data from

Table 4.4 Assessment of Least Squares

x	y	y_c	Error $(y - y_c)$	Squared Error
6.5	7.0	6.23	0.77	0.593
7.0	6.5	6.54	(0.04)	0.002
5.0	5.1	5.31	(0.21)	0.044
4.0	4.0	4.70	(0.70)	0.490
4.5	5.5	5.00	0.50	0.250
5.5	6.0	5.62	0.38	0.144
6.0	5.3	5.92	(0.62)	0.384
4.5	5.0	5.00	0	0
8.2	7.0	7.27	(0.27)	0.073
7.5	8.1	6.84	1.26	1.588
6.8	6.0	6.41	(0.41)	0.168
9.0	7.1	7.76	(0.66)	0.436

Summary: MSE = 0.348×10^{12}

$\sqrt{\text{MSE}}$ = \$0.590 million

this calculated underlying relationship are assumed to be randomly distributed. A further discussion of this point will be presented later in this chapter.

Again, if the analysts were to predict the level of vacuum cleaner sales based upon 7.3 thousand issued construction permits this quarter, the projection would be (assuming constant prices)

$$y_c = 2.2456 + (0.6128)(7.3) = \$6.72 \text{ million}$$

The forecast of $6.72 million obtained with the least-squares method is almost $400 thousand less than that obtained with the freehand-smoothing technique. This difference of approximately 5% of the forecast value is solely the result of the freehand-smoothing method's inaccuracy. Both procedures attempt to assess the data in an identical manner, but the freehand-smoothing method employs subjective assessment in positioning the function line. Conversely, the least-squares technique derives the function line objectively through mathematical procedures. The difference, therefore, is occasioned by error due solely to the subjective element used in the smoothing technique. Because both these procedures have exactly the same purpose, it is evident that the least-squares technique is superior to the freehand-smoothing method. It is on the basis of this objectivity that the former procedure is preferred.

Variability

The rationale for using least-squares regression analysis is to eliminate some of the variability, or unexplained fluctuation, associated with the forecast variable. That is, it is assumed that by associating the forecast variable with another variable that influences its fluctuation, a better prediction is possible because some of the variability has been explained and can be used to adjust the forecast.

The variability associated with the forecast variable is estimated from the historical data, which is considered a sample.[1] This is accomplished by calculating the unbiased estimate of the standard deviation of Y, identified as $\hat{\sigma}_y$, as follows.[2]

1. Statistical theory suggests that all observations must be randomly selected. A slight modification in assumptions is necessary in the above approach. It is assumed that the periods are selected because of their theoretical similarity in underlying variables and that actual values within this framework are subject to random fluctuations, that is, specific historical values are treated as random variables detected through a sample.
2. Both the unbiased estimate of the standard deviation of Y and the standard deviation of the regression are termed *unbiased estimates* because their value is

$$\hat{\sigma}_y = \sqrt{\frac{\Sigma y^2}{n} - \left(\frac{\Sigma y}{n}\right)^2} \sqrt{\frac{n}{n-1}} \qquad (4.4)$$

For the example,

$$\hat{\sigma}_y = \sqrt{\frac{453.62}{12} - \left(\frac{72.6}{12}\right)^2} \sqrt{\frac{12}{12-1}}$$
$$= \sqrt{37.8016 - 36.6025}\,\sqrt{1.0909}$$
$$= (1.095)(1.0445)$$
$$\hat{\sigma}_y = \$1.144 \text{ million}$$

Assume, for a moment, that sales of central vacuum cleaners are *not* associated with either construction permits or time. Yet, assume that a forecast is needed for the next time period. What would constitute a reasonable forecast?

Without additional information, the best forecast would be mean historical sales, that is, average sales over the time period under consideration. If one assumes that the historical values comprise a sample of the underlying population, then the sample mean is the best estimate of that population's mean. Further, the population's mean has the greatest frequency, or likelihood of occurrence. This is illustrated in Figure 4.3. For the example, therefore, the forecast for the next period is $\bar{y} =$ $6.05 million.

The next logical question is how likely is it that next quarter's sales will exactly equal $6.05 million? The answer is that it is not at all likely for actual sales to exactly equal this mean. We would have very low confidence in the forecast.

Assume that we want to be 95% confident that actual sales will fall within a range of values centered around the mean. Statistical theory tells us that approximately 95% of all the values in a normal distribution fall within approximately $2\hat{\sigma}$ around the mean.[3,4] Therefore, for

calculated from the sample. An adjustment factor that allows for estimations of population parameters is inherent in the formula by the denominator being determined as the number of observations minus the number of variables. Equations 4.3 and 4.4 are those generally used, but are only close estimates of the theoretically correct expressions. The difference is not generally considered significant in practical applications. For further reference, see Ya-lun Chou, *Probability and Statistics for Decision Making* (New York: Holt, Rinehart and Winston, 1972), pp. 459–460.

3. Even if the population is of some other distribution, the sampling means may be assumed to be normally distributed. See any good basic statistics text, such as ibid., Chapter 11.
4. See any table of standard normal distribution function values, such as ibid., p. 608.

Figure 4.3 Estimated Population Distribution

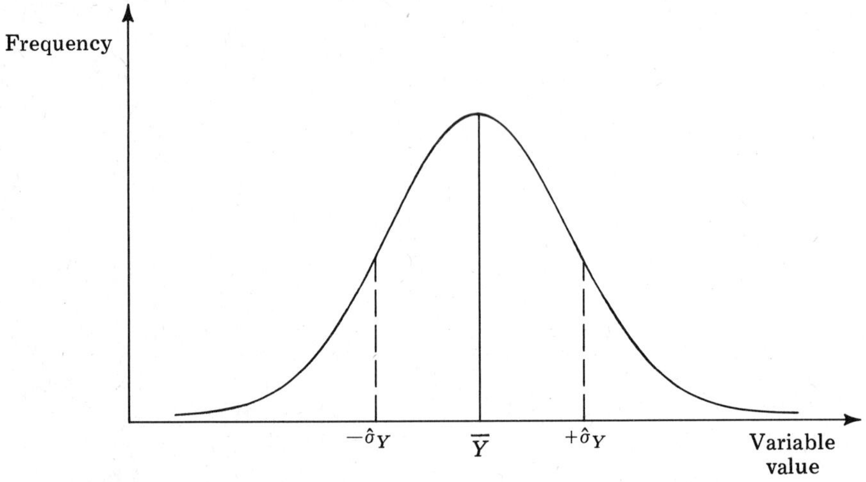

Frequency

$-\hat{\sigma}_Y$ $\overline{Y}$ $+\hat{\sigma}_Y$ Variable value

the example, we would be 95% confident that next quarter's sales of vacuum cleaners will be $6.05 million ± (2)(1.144) million, that is, within the $3.76 million to $8.34 million range.

This range, termed a *confidence band*, is illustrated in Figure 4.4. The deviations of all historic values from the mean are also pictured in the figure. (Note: Do not pay any attention to the fact that a linear relationship exists between sales and construction permits. We are ignoring permits for now. The trend evidenced is only present because the graph was constructed with permits being one axis for convenience.)

Let us now consider the relationship between central vacuum cleaner sales and construction permits. The mean that we use to forecast sales is no longer $\overline{y}$. Instead, it is $y_c = 2.2456 + 0.6128x$, the function we calculated using least squares.

But the question, "How confident are we that the actual value will equal the forecast?" remains. We no longer use $\hat{\sigma}_y$ to answer the question. Instead we use the regression equivalent, termed *standard error of regression* and denoted $\hat{\sigma}_{yx}$. The value of $\hat{\sigma}_{yx}$ is dependent on the strength of the association between dependent and independent variables. If no association exists at all, $\hat{\sigma}_{yx}$ has essentially the same value as $\hat{\sigma}_y$. Perfect association, which is virtually impossible with business economic data, would result in $\hat{\sigma}_{yx} = 0$. That is, every dependent variable value would fall exactly on the regression line. Thus, $\hat{\sigma}_{yx}$ has $\hat{\sigma}_y$ as its upper bound and 0 as its lower bound.

Figure 4.4 Confidence Band, Vacuum Cleaner Sales

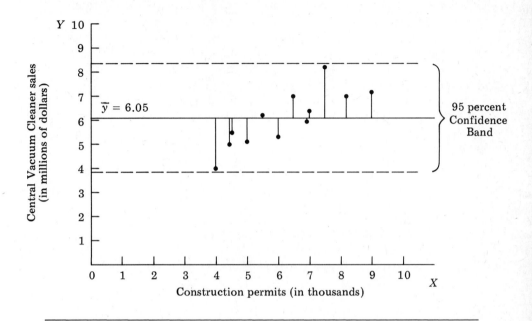

The $\hat{\sigma}_{yx}$ is a measure of the vertical deviations of the dependent, forecast, variable from the regression line. One can calculate the value by summing the squared deviations and dividing by the number of observations less one degree of freedom for each variable analyzed. In the example, there are two variables and twelve observations. The denominator, therefore, is $12 - 2 = 10$. A simpler way to calculate the value directly from the raw data, hence avoiding the need to calculate each y_c corresponding to each value of x, is to use the following equation:

$$\hat{\sigma}_{yx} = \sqrt{\frac{\Sigma y^2 - a\Sigma y - b\Sigma xy}{n - 2}} \tag{4.5}$$

For the example, the standard error of the regression is

$$\hat{\sigma}_{yx} = \sqrt{\frac{453.62 - (2.2456)(72.6) - (0.6128)(467.40)}{12 - 2}}$$

$$\hat{\sigma}_{yx} = 0.646$$

We can now compare $\hat{\sigma}_{yx}$ with $\hat{\sigma}_y$ to get an idea of the value of performing regression. For the example, $\hat{\sigma}_{yx} = 0.646$, which is nearly a

45% reduction from $\hat{\sigma}_y$. This is indeed a sizable improvement. As a
first estimate, the 95% confidence band is $y_c \pm (2)(0.646)$, which is
illustrated in Figure 4.5. Notice that the band is much narrower than
the one pictured in Figure 4.4.

As it turns out, adjustments need to be made to the band pictured
in the figure to reveal the shape of the real confidence band. These are
discussed later in the chapter. Figure 4.5, nonetheless, is useful to
illustrate what is involved in regression.

The MSE, which was presented in Table 4.4, and $\hat{\sigma}_{yx}$ are directly
related. But they are not identical. This is because in calculating $\hat{\sigma}_{yx}$
we take into consideration the loss in degrees of freedom. Theoretically,
they are related as follows:

$$\sqrt{\text{MSE}} \; X \sqrt{\frac{N}{N - V}} = \hat{\sigma}_{yx} \qquad (4.6)$$

where V = the number of variables in the regression

Figure 4.5 Initially Estimated Confidence Band Based Upon Regression

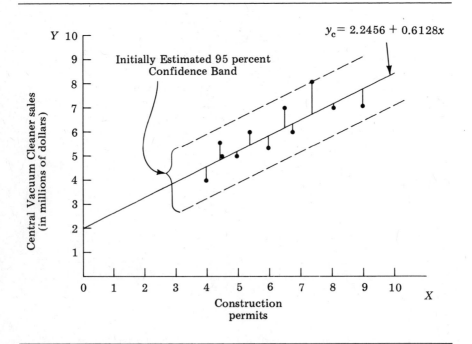

For the example,

$$(0.590) \sqrt{\frac{12}{10}} = 0.646$$

which equals $\hat{\sigma}_{yx}$. This puts the calculation of $\hat{\sigma}_{yx}$ into perspective. Typically $\hat{\sigma}_{yx}$ is used with regression analysis instead of MSE to enable further statistical analysis.

Significance of b

The slope of the regression function b is critical in making predictions. However, it is subject to sampling error because the statistic was computed through the values established by the sample. Hence, it is wise for the forecaster to determine the statistical significance of this statistic. In essence, when conducting a significance test, the analyst is testing whether the population coefficient of b is different from 0, based on the information yielded in this sample at some stated level of probability.

A basic assumption of regression analysis is that the dependent variable is normally distributed about the true population regression line. This leads to the assumption that the sampling distribution of b is normal.

As is generally the case with statistical analysis, when n (the number of observations in the sample) is less than 60, the student's t distribution is used instead of the standard normal distribution. The t distribution is a conservative representation of the normal distribution and is used for small samples. For larger samples, the testing statistic is that of the standard normal distribution and calculated z value. This statistic is computed in a similar manner to the t statistic presented below.

The procedure for large samples will not be presented in this text, primarily for two reasons. First, the computation is very similar to that for smaller samples. Second, the z distribution is approximated by the t distribution when the sample size is large. For all practical purposes, the t value from Appendix 4.A for ∞ degrees of freedom may be used for all samples of greater size than 120 observations (some argue greater than 60), rather than using a z-distribution table. Finally, this text is concerned with forecasting business and economic data. In practical applications, more than 60 historical time periods are not often desirable. One of the assumptions of regression analysis, as previously discussed, is that the variables being analyzed are consistently related throughout all periods of observation. This assumption becomes unreasonable as the number of periods expands beyond 60. Most basic statistics texts may be consulted by the concerned student if the computation and analysis of the z statistic are desired.[5]

5. Chou, *Probability*, pp. 461–462.

The standard deviation of the theoretical distribution, sometimes called the standard error of b, is estimated from the sample data with the unbiased estimator

$$\hat{\sigma}_b = \frac{\hat{\sigma}_{yx}}{\sqrt{\Sigma(x - \bar{x})^2}}$$

Alternately, for ease of computation,

$$\hat{\sigma}_b = \frac{\hat{\sigma}_{yx}}{\sqrt{\Sigma x^2 - (\Sigma x)^2 /n}} \tag{4.7}$$

In the example, the unbiased estimator of the standard error of b is calculated with Equation 4.7 as follows:

$$\hat{\sigma}_b = \frac{0.646}{\sqrt{489.73 - (74.5)^2 /12}}$$

$$= \frac{0.646}{\sqrt{27.209}} = 0.124$$

The unbiased estimate of the standard error of b is used to test the significance of b. The test is designed to determine, at a stated level of probability, if a b of the magnitude detected in the sample could have occurred by chance, if the population parameter is one of no association (that is, a zero relationship). The stated level of probability, called the *alpha level* (α), represents the probability of rejecting the hypothesis of no population association $(\beta = 0)$ if β is, in fact, equal to zero. The t statistic is determined by

$$t = \frac{b - \beta}{\hat{\sigma}_b} \tag{4.8}$$

with $n - 2$ degrees of freedom and

$$\text{Null hypothesis } (H_0)\beta = 0$$
$$\text{Alternate hypothesis } (H_a)\beta \neq 0$$

For the example,

$$t = \frac{0.6128 - 0}{0.124} = 4.942$$

From Appendix 4.A, for ten degrees of freedom and at the 95% confidence level, the critical value of t is 2.228. The degrees of freedom result from subtracting the number of variables from the number of observations ($12 - 2 = 10$). Since $t > t_{0.05}$, the null hypothesis is rejected; that is, the alternate hypothesis that an association does exist in the population is accepted. The best estimate of β is b; hence, this statistic is used in the prediction equation.[6]

Prediction

Regression analysis is used for predicting the dependent variable on the basis of its relation to the independent variable. Suppose that new home construction permits for the period just completed ($t = 12$) were 7.9 thousand units. The predictive equation is

$$Y_c = 2.2456 + (0.6128)(7.9) = \$7.09 \text{ million}$$

Based on the regression analysis, the single best estimate of central vacuum cleaner sales is $7.09 million. This value is obtained from the predictive equation. However, even though this value is the best estimate of sales, a range of possible values at a stated probability is more meaningful, as there is little chance for sales to exactly equal this number.

Careful examination of the previous equations will reveal that all the statistics are based on central-tendency calculations. In calculating $\hat{\sigma}_{yx}$, for example, we measure the deviation about y_c, which is a mean. Thus, it is logical to expect that greater confidence can be given to forecasts when they are near the average.

That is, the closer x is to $\bar{x}$ when making a forecast, the more confident we would be that the forecast will be accurate. Conversely, the more extreme the value of x used to forecast, the lower is our confidence in the forecast's accuracy.

The previously discussed confidence band, based solely upon $\hat{\sigma}_{yx}$, was a good initial approximation of the confidence interval associated with forecasts. But further adjustment is needed to reflect how far away from the mean the forecast is being made.

The concept of the standard deviation of individual values about the estimated values should be used to develop this interval. An unbiased estimator of this parameter is

$$\hat{\sigma}_{y-y_c} = \hat{\sigma}_{yx} \sqrt{1 + \frac{1}{n} + \frac{(x_p - \bar{x})^2}{\Sigma x^2 - \frac{(\Sigma x)^2}{n}}} \tag{4.9}$$

---

6. The a statistic is also subject to sampling error but is generally less critical than b in prediction. Therefore, a significance test for a is not presented.

where x_p = the value of the independent variable used as the basis for prediction

$\bar{x}$ = the mean of the sample x's

For the example,

$$\hat{\sigma}_{y \cdot y_c} = 0.646 \sqrt{1 + \frac{1}{12} + \frac{(7.9 - 6.21)^2}{27.21}}$$

$$= 0.646\sqrt{1.188}$$

$$= 0.704$$

The confidence interval, the linear distance bounded by limits on either side of the prediction, is calculated by multiplying $\hat{\sigma}_{y \cdot y_c}$ by the critical t value for the level of significance employed. For an $\alpha = 0.05$ level, the critical value of t for ten degrees of freedom is 2.228 (see Appendix 4.A).

The confidence interval is established by using the equation:

$$Y_c \pm (t_{0.05})(\hat{\sigma}_{y \cdot y_c}) \tag{4.10}$$

or

$$7.09 \pm (2.228)(0.704)$$

Therefore, the analyst can be 95% confident that the predicted population Y will fall in the range

$$5.52 \leqslant y \leqslant 8.66$$

For illustration, confidence intervals for individual values of $\bar{y}_c$ have been constructed in Table 4.5 based on various values of x_p.

Table 4.5 Computation of 95% Confidence Intervals for Various Values of x_p

x_p	$(x_p - \bar{x})^2$	$\hat{\sigma}_{y \cdot y_c}$	$\bar{y}_c$	$\bar{y}_c \pm 2.228(\hat{\sigma}_{y \cdot y_c})$
4.0	4.88	0.725	4.70	3.08–6.32
5.0	1.46	0.688	5.31	3.78–6.84
6.0	0.04	0.672	5.92	4.42–7.42
7.0	0.62	0.678	6.54	5.03–8.05
8.0	3.20	0.708	7.15	5.57–8.73
9.0	7.78	0.755	7.76	6.08–9.44

Data from Table 4.5 are presented in Figure 4.6 in the form of a confidence band for possible forecast intervals, based on various levels of construction permits. The confidence interval required at a constant level of probability becomes greater as the value of x_p moves away from $\bar{x}$. This is caused by the value of $\hat{\sigma}_{y \cdot y_c}$ being dependent upon $(x_p - \bar{x})^2$. The widening interval as x_p approaches extremes illustrates that we become less sure of the relationship between variables as we move away from their means. Equation 4.10 allows adjustment for this movement.

CORRELATION ⟨10/9⟩

Regression measures the explicit association between a dependent variable and an independent causal variable. However, in many instances, a measure of the association between variables is desired when the causality of one on another cannot be safely assumed. For example, it may be desirable to determine whether there exists an association between the sale of television sets and automobiles. Causality of one of these variables on the other appears doubtful. Any detected association may be the result of a variable or variables that are exogeneous to the analysis—that is, where a third variable excluded from analysis causes each included variable to fluctuate in a related manner.

the smaller the correlation # the closer the correlation is...!!

Figure 4.6   95% Confidence Band for $\bar{y}_c$

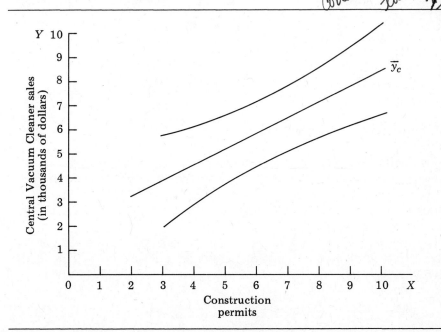

Correlation allows the measurement of such an association. In addition, correlation measures the degree of association between variables when causality is inherent. In essence, strong associations detected through correlation analysis yield narrow confidence intervals around regression-forecast estimates. Conversely, weak associations yield wide intervals. Forecast accuracy, naturally, is improved by selecting variables with strong associations.

The slope of a regression function was designated as b. This b refers to the regression of the variable Y on the basis of the independent variable X. Another regression function can be created by the variable X on the basis of Y. These coefficients of slope are b_{yx} and b_{xy} respectively. The b_{xy} coefficient is computed as follows:

$$b_{xy} = \frac{n\Sigma xy - \Sigma x \Sigma y}{n\Sigma y^2 - (\Sigma y)^2} \tag{4.11}$$

Continuing with the data for the vacuum cleaner–construction permit example:

$$b_{xy} = \frac{(12)(467.4) - (74.5)(72.6)}{(12)(453.62) - (72.6)^2} = \frac{200.1}{172.7} = 1.1587$$

The b_{xy} coefficient by itself may have no apparent meaning or usefulness when causality is inherent in the analysis. However, both coefficients lead to the calculation of the coefficient of correlation (r) as follows, where the sign is the same as b_{yx} :

$$r = \sqrt{(b_{xy})(b_{yx})} \tag{4.12}$$

In the example,

$$r = \sqrt{(1.1587)(0.6128)} = 0.843$$

The Coefficient of Correlation

The coefficient of correlation is a measure of the degree of association between the variables X and Y. It has a maximum theoretical value of 1.0, which means a perfect direct relationship, and –1.0, which may be interpreted as a perfect inverse relationship. A value of 0 means that no relationship exists at all.

More precisely, this coefficient measures the ratio of the b_{yx} coefficient to the unbiased estimate of the standard deviations of Y divided by X, as follows:

$$r = b_{yx} \div \frac{\hat{\sigma}_y}{\hat{\sigma}_x} \qquad\qquad (4.13)$$

For the example,

$$r = 0.6128 \div \frac{1.144}{\sqrt{\dfrac{\Sigma x^2}{n} - \left(\dfrac{\Sigma x}{n}\right)^2}\sqrt{\dfrac{n}{n-1}}}$$

$$= 0.6128 \div \frac{1.144}{\sqrt{\dfrac{489.73}{12} - \left(\dfrac{74.5}{12}\right)^2}\sqrt{\dfrac{12}{11}}}$$

$$= 0.6128 \div \frac{1.144}{\sqrt{2.27}\sqrt{1.09}}$$

$$= 0.6128 \div \frac{1.144}{1.573}$$

$$= 0.843$$

This calculation of r shows that correlation is a measure of the commonality in the variances of each variable. This is exactly what correlation is designed to measure. However, a more precise definition is that r^2, called the *coefficient of determination*, measures the variation in one variable that is explained by the association with the other variable. This coefficient measures the improvement in reducing the total error of X and Y by fitting the regression line.[7] Even when causality between the variables cannot be assumed, the coefficient of determination measures the degree of association between the variables. The value of r^2 can range between 0 and 1.0, the former indicating a complete lack of association and the latter a perfect degree of association.

To illustrate, the total variance of Y prior to the association with X was estimated as $\hat{\sigma}_y^2$, from the sample of observations. This value was calculated on the basis of the deviations of Y from the mean $\bar{y}$, as illustrated in Figure 4.4. However, by associating Y with X, the deviations from Y_c were reduced as in Figure 4.5. This reduction was accomplished by redefining the mean of Y on the basis of particular X values through the regression equation. Part of the total deviation of any one observation of Y was adjusted by the distance between Y_c and the associated value of X. Figure 4.7 presents this graphically for one point.

7. Chou, *Probability*, p. 475.

Figure 4.7 Scatter Diagram Depicting Explained and Unexplained Portions of the Total Deviation of y from $\bar{y}$

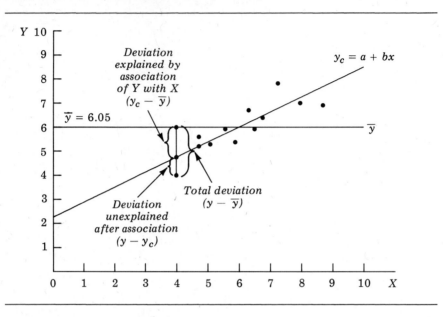

The Coefficient of Determination

The coefficient of determination reflects the proportion of the total variance in y, explained by the regression as follows:

$$r^2 = \frac{\hat{\sigma}^2_{yc}}{\hat{\sigma}^2_y} \qquad (4.14)$$

where

$$\hat{\sigma}^2_{yc} = \frac{\Sigma(y_c - y)^2}{n - 1} \qquad (4.15)$$

A computationally simpler equation for Equation 4.15 is:

$$\hat{\sigma}^2_{yc} = \frac{\Sigma y_c^2 - \dfrac{(\Sigma y)^2}{n}}{n - 1} \qquad (4.16)$$

Table 4.6 presents additional computations required to solve for $\hat{\sigma}^2_{yc}$. Calculations in Table 4.6 are used to solve Equation 4.16.

Table 4.6 Additional Computations Required to Solve for $\hat{\sigma}_{y_c}^{\ 2}$

x	y	y_c	$y_c^{\ 2}$
6.5	7.0	6.23	38.81
7.0	6.5	6.54	42.77
5.0	5.1	5.31	28.20
4.0	4.0	4.70	22.09
4.5	5.5	5.00	25.00
5.5	6.0	5.62	31.58
6.0	5.3	5.92	35.05
4.5	5.0	5.00	25.00
8.2	7.0	7.27	52.85
7.5	8.1	6.84	46.79
6.8	6.0	6.41	41.09
9.0	7.1	7.76	60.22
74.5	72.6		449.45

$$\hat{\sigma}_{yc}^2 = \frac{449.45 - \dfrac{72.6^2}{12}}{11}$$

$$= \frac{10.22}{11} = 0.929$$

and

$$\hat{\sigma}_y^2 = 1.144^2 = 1.309$$

Finally,

$$r^2 = \frac{0.929}{1.309} = 0.71$$

This value of r^2 is the same as that calculated with Equations 4.12 and 4.13 ($0.843^2 = 0.71$). It may be interpreted to mean that 71% of y's variance was explained by associating the variable with X.

Straightforward Correlation Equation[8]

The foregoing equations have been presented to illustrate the link between correlation and regression. In practice, correlation is generally computed by

$$r = \frac{n\Sigma xy - (\Sigma x)(\Sigma y)}{\sqrt{[n\Sigma x^2 - (\Sigma x)^2][n\Sigma y^2 - (\Sigma y)^2]}} \qquad (4.17)$$

Using data from Table 4.3,

$$r = \frac{(12)(467.4) - (74.5)(72.6)}{\sqrt{[(12)(489.73) - (74.5)^2][(12)(453.62) - (72.6)^2]}}$$

$$= \frac{200.1}{\sqrt{(326.51)(172.68)}} = 0.843$$

This equation has two major advantages over those presented earlier. First, the calculation of r is computationally simpler. Second, the direction of association is more easily assessed. If the association is inverse, the r coefficient will automatically be computed as negative. Therefore, r has a possible range of values from -1 to $+1$. The value of r^2 will remain within the range of 0 and 1.

SIGNIFICANCE OF r

Additional calculations are necessary after the correlation coefficient between the variables has been computed. The r detected from a sample may have occurred by chance even if the populations of variables studied have no association, simply as the result of sampling error.

Therefore, a test of r's significance is needed to assess the probability of the populations not exhibiting an association even with the sample detecting one. As with regression analysis, the null hypothesis is one of no association between the populations. When $n \leqslant 60$, the t statistic is used to test the null hypothesis through:

$$t = r\sqrt{\frac{n-2}{1-r^2}} \qquad (4.18)$$

This t statistic is then compared to the critical value of t for $n - 2$ degrees of freedom. This is because there is a one-unit loss in degrees of freedom for each variable in the analysis.

8. The technique used in this text is termed *Pearson product-moment* correlation.

For the example,

$$t = 0.8427 \sqrt{\frac{12 - 2}{1.0 - 0.7101}} = 4.95$$

At the 0.05 level, the critical value of t is 2.228 (see Appendix 4.A). As a result, the null hypothesis is rejected.

An additional statistic important to the forecaster is also relevant to the example. The r^2 statistic of 0.710 indicates that the 71% of the variation in y is explained by the variation in x. This means that X can be used as a fairly strong predictor of Y, assuming causality.

It would also be possible for both b_{yx} and r to be significant when r^2 is small, perhaps as low as 0.04 or less. In this instance, the forecaster is advised to exercise caution because X is not a good predictor of Y at all. In this case, the $\hat{\sigma}_{y \cdot y_c}$ statistic would be very large, indicating substantial variance from the predictions. As a result, the confidence interval would be large, which renders an analysis of questionable value.

When confronted with this situation, the forecaster may select one of several alternatives. First, another forecasting technique may be employed. Techniques such as obtaining expert opinions or sampling of buyer intentions may produce desirable results. Second, Another variable may be examined for possible regression treatment. Third, multiple-regression and correlation techniques may be employed. As their names imply, these procedures examine three or more independent variables. Perhaps the current variable from bivariate analysis may even be retained in the composite analysis. Before we proceed with a discussion of multiple analysis, mention of the fourth alternative available to the analyst will be made; that is, nonlinear techniques may be useful.

NONLINEAR ANALYSIS

A low r^2 may not be the result of a lack of association between the variables. Instead, a nonlinear association may actually exist but not be detected when measured through linear functions. Linear relationships are those capable of geometric presentation through a straight line of a graph, as in Figure 4.2. Nonlinear relationships cannot be depicted graphically by a straight line. Some of the nonlinear relationships possible for two-variable situations are presented in Figure 4.8.

Figure 4.8 Some Common Nonlinear Relationships Among Two Variables

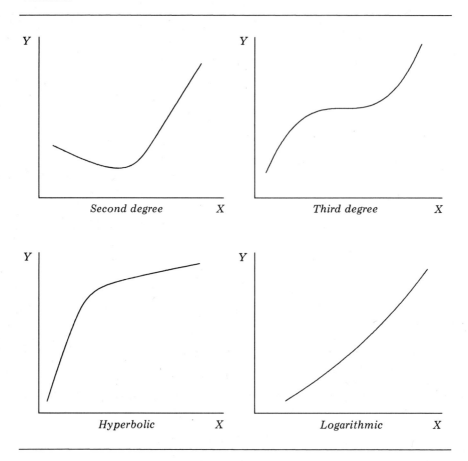

Log-linear Transformation

Table 4.7, to illustrate, presents ten years of equipment sales history of Digital Equipment Corporation. The above regression equations may be used to regress equipment sales on time by substituting t for x. Figure 4.9 depicts a graph of sales and the resulting least-squares linear regression line. The following are other related statistics of the linear analysis.

$$r^2 = 0.892$$
$$\hat{\sigma}_{yt} = \$154.52 \text{ million}$$

The forecast for $t = 11$ is $\$1{,}299.49 \pm 431.53$, in millions, at the 95% confidence level. (Remember, one first needs to calculate $\hat{\sigma}_{y \cdot y_c}$ before determining the confidence band.)

Table 4.7 Sales of Digital Equipment Corporation

Year	t	Sales (in Millions of Dollars)	Natural Log of Sales (in Millions of Dollars)
1970	1	128.0	4.852
1971	2	133.0	4.890
1972	3	166.3	5.114
1973	4	229.1	5.434
1974	5	360.8	5.888
1975	6	433.2	6.071
1976	7	586.7	6.375
1977	8	847.5	6.742
1978	9	1,128.1	7.028
1979	10	1,381.8	7.231

Source: 1979 annual report

The above r^2, 0.892, is really quite large. But so is the confidence interval. This is because of a large standard error of the regression due to the fact that sales are not linearly related to time, as illustrated in Figure 4.9.

Compare the sales graph in Figure 4.9 with the functions pictured in Figure 4.8. Notice the similarity between Digital's historic sales and the logarithmic function. This indicates that transforming raw sales into their logarithm will enable much better linear analysis.

Figure 4.10 depicts the graph of the natural log of equipment sales, from Table 4.7, and time. The figure also pictures the least-squares linear function for the log of sales regressed against time. Now look at how close the fit is. The following are other related statistics of the logarithmic analysis:

$$r^2 = 0.988$$

$\hat{\sigma}_{yt} = \$e^{0.0990}$ million; natural antilogarithm $= \$1.104$ million

The forecast for $t = 11$ is $\$e^{7.5466}$ million, natural antilogarithm $=$ $\$1,894.29 \pm 3.08$, in millions, at the 95% confidence level. (Again, use $\hat{\sigma}_{y \cdot y_c}$.)

Thus, the logarithmic transformation yields a model with a much better fit for this example. Even though there is a closer fit, however, an analyst should be very cautious in using such high-powered mathematical functions, because very large changes may be forecast for future periods. For the example, to illustrate the forecast for $t = 15$, or 1984,

Figure 4.9 Graph of Digital Equipment Corporation Equipment Sales, 1970 through 1979

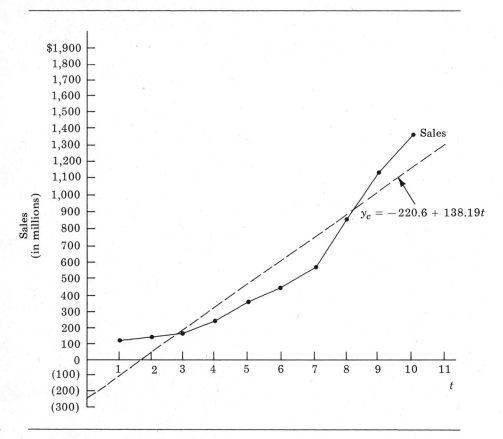

Source: Based on 1979 annual report

is $5,996 million, or more than a quadrupling of equipment sales in five years. Such an increase might be possible but is certainly questionable. However, short-run forecasts resulting from curvilinear models are often more realistic.

Many inexpensive calculators have logarithmic functions. Such calculators, along with widely available computers, greatly simplify the analysis.

Hyperbolic Transformation

Another simple transformation procedure is for a hyperbolic function. The general equation for a hyperbola is

Figure 4.10 Graph of Digital Equipment Corporation Equipment Sales, 1970 through 1979

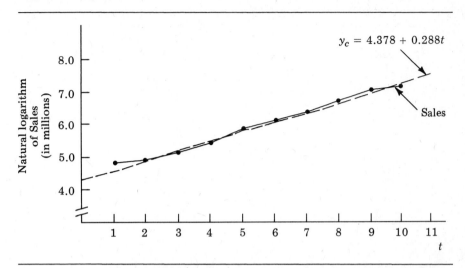

Source: Based on 1979 annual report

$$y = a - \frac{b}{x} \qquad (4.19)$$

Fortunately, the function may be easily transformed into a linear function for analysis. To do this, it is only necessary to define a new variable, x', in terms of the original x as $x' = 1/x$. Everything else remains the same. The linear function used for analysis becomes

$$y = a - bx' \qquad (4.20)$$

To illustrate, Table 4.8 presents historical rental receipts for Kryger Property Management Co.'s Meadowvale Shopping Mall. Figure 4.11 depicts a graph of sales and time, t. A linear least-squares regression line is also pictured. The following are other related statistics of the linear analysis of the raw data (of course, using t instead of x in the equations):

$$r^2 = 0.777$$
$$\hat{\sigma}_{yt} = \$137.24 \text{ hundred thousand}$$

The forecast for $t = 9$ is $\$1,609.8 \pm 425.74$, in hundred thousands, at the 95% confidence level.

Once again the r^2 value is quite large but so is the confidence interval. This is because the data are clearly nonlinear.

Table 4.8 Kryger Property Management Co.'s Rental Receipts from Meadowvale Shopping Mall

Year	t	t'	Rental Receipts (in Hundred Thousands of Dollars)
1975	1	1.0000	603
1976	2	0.5000	963
1977	3	0.3333	1,179
1978	4	0.2500	1,240
1979	5	0.2000	1,299
1980	6	0.1667	1,345
1981	7	0.1429	1,368
1982	8	0.1250	1,396

Figure 4.12 presents the data transformed with Equation 4.20, of course, after substituting t for x. The t' values are listed in Table 4.8. The following are further relevant statistics:

$$r^2 = 0.987$$

$$\hat{\sigma}'_{yt} = \$32.9 \text{ hundred thousand}$$

The forecast for 1983 ($t = 9$), hence $t' = 1/9$, is 1483.3 − (910.0)(1/9) = \$1382.2 ± 88.6, in hundred thousands, at the 95% confidence level.

Thus, there is a considerable improvement in accuracy because the appropriate transformation was made.

Transformation of a Second-Degree Function

A second-degree function takes the form

$$Y = a + bx + cx^2 \tag{4.21}$$

Solving such functional relationships, however, is more difficult than hyperbolic or logarithmic cases. Three equations with three unknowns must be solved simultaneously. This is exactly the procedure that we used in Chapter 3 to estimate the improved initial estimates of a, b, and c in quadratic exponential smoothing. Except in regression analysis, of course, all the historical data would be analyzed. Refer to Appendix 3.D for the procedure.

Figure 4.11 Rental Receipts from Meadowvale Shopping Mall

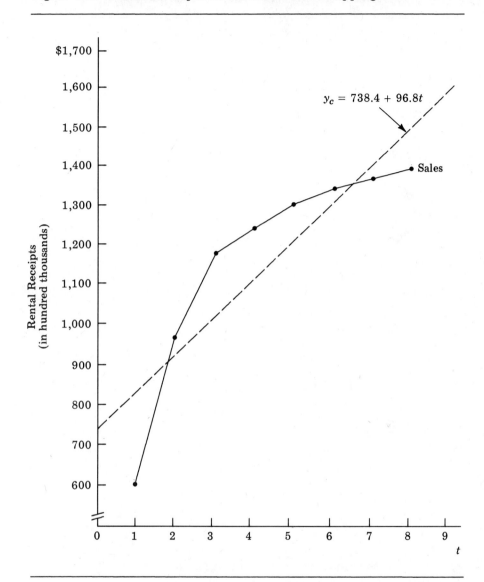

Transformations of More Complex Functions

Regression can be performed with even more complex functions.[9] The more complex models, however, are rarely used in business settings. One

9. For a further discussion, see S. J. Press, *Applied Multivariate Analysis* (New York: Holt, Rinehart and Winston, 1972), Chapter 3.

Figure 4.12 Rental Receipts After Data Transformation

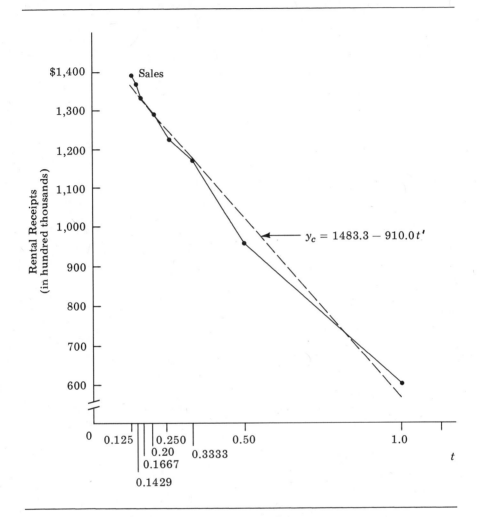

reason is that the model becomes so complex that wild gyrations may be anticipated when one forecasts into the future.

Another reason is that several independent variables are often used simultaneously in regression for forecasting. This is because seldom does any single independent variable explain that much of a forecast variable's fluctuations. The r^2 values in bivariate analysis are typically quite low, often below 0.2. Therefore, it is frequently necessary to use multiple independent variables simultaneously to generate a fairly large overall r^2. And multivariate analysis does not easily lend itself to the careful graphic analysis needed to determine how nonlinear data should be transformed.

MULTIVARIATE ANALYSIS

When the degree of association between two variables is less than acceptable to the analysts, they may decide to select one or more additional
variables for analysis. Rather than finding another variable for bivariate
analysis, multivariate procedures are generally used. If the original
independent variable was found to be statistically significant in its
relationship with the forecast variable, it is retained as one of the inputs.
The calculations become quite complex, but the wide availability of
computers and software have greatly expanded the use of multivariate
procedures over the past several years.

Multivariate regression is used more often than bivariate analysis for
at least two major reasons. First, the degree of association between two
natural or real-world behavioral variables is seldom great, and, consequently, the standard error is often quite large and forecast reliability is
moderate. To combat this problem, other variables are included in the
analysis to improve forecast accuracy.

Second, real-world variables are often related to a multitude of other
variables, particularly in the business and economic setting. Real-world
behavioral relationships, unfortunately, are seldom as precise as textbook examples, which have been selected for illustration of procedures
rather than for application. For example, expenditures for food are
related to factors including but not restricted to income. In addition,
savings, hunger (and physical size), habits, reference-group influence,
expenditures on other items, weather, and religious and ethnic origin
may all have an influence on both the type and amount of food an
individual may consume, along with its related expenditure. It is frequently necessary to include many inputs for analysis to attain accurate
forecasts.

Multivariate Example

Assume that Robinson Appliance, a retail chain in a large West Coast
city, wants to forecast next month's sales of washing machines. Washing
machine sales may be related to many phenomena. Logic is needed to
help identify the variables that appear to be causal factors.

The number of shopping days in a month might be one influence.
The greater the number, the greater is the opportunity to buy. Another
factor is the unemployment rate. One would expect greater sales when
employment is high than when it is low. Still another factor might be
the rate of inflation. With high inflation, people might have to postpone
purchases of durables.

Table 4.9 presents the past 16 months of history of these variables.
As previously indicated, multiple regression is almost always performed

Table 4.9 Robinson Appliance Historical Data

t	Company Unit Sales of Washers	Number of Shopping Days	Unemployment Rate, %	Inflation Rate, %
1	204	28	7.2	1.3
2	268	31	7.0	1.2
3	249	30	7.1	1.2
4	294	31	6.7	1.1
5	305	30	6.3	1.1
6	273	31	6.4	1.1
7	285	31	6.4	1.0
8	295	30	6.3	1.0
9	273	31	6.4	1.1
10	290	30	6.2	1.0
11	282	31	6.3	1.1
12	288	31	6.1	1.0
13	312	28	6.0	1.0
14	308	31	6.1	1.1
15	310	30	6.0	1.0
16	274	31	5.8	0.9

with a computer. This is because hand calculations are complicated and time consuming. Also, multiple-regression computer programs are widely available.

Table 4.10 portrays output from a standard multiple-regression computer package for the Robinson example. The output is in three basic parts.

First, correlation coefficients are presented. Notice that there are two measures of r and r^2, unadjusted and adjusted. The unadjusted values are calculated in a manner similar to Equation 4.17. The adjusted r and r^2 values are calculated as follows:

$$r^2 \text{ (adjusted)} = 1 - (1 - r^2)\frac{n - 1}{n - m - 1} \qquad (4.22)$$

where m = the number of independent variables

Thus, for the example,

$$r^2 \text{ (adjusted)} = 1 - (1 - 0.6118)\frac{16 - 1}{16 - 4 - 1} = 0.4704$$

Table 4.10 Robinson Appliance Sales Regressed Against Time, Days, Unemployment, and Inflation

```
    REGR
* DEP. VAR. : TIME
HOW MANY INDEP. VAR. ? 0
MEAN                   =  8.50000E 00
STD. ERROR OF MEAN     =  1.19024E 00
STD. DEV.              =  4.76095E 00
STD. ERROR PRED. OBS.=  4.90748E 00

> REGR
* DEP. VAR. : SALES
HOW MANY INDEP. VAR. ? 4
INDEP. VAR. 1 : TIME
INDEP. VAR. 2 : DAYS
INDEP. VAR. 3 : UNEMP
INDEP. VAR. 4 : INFL
UPDATING CORR. MATRIX...
COMPUTING REGRESSION...
ANALYZING RESIDUALS...
CHECKING AUTO CORRELATIONS...

> SUMM

             MULTIPLE R   R-SQUARE
UNADJUSTED     0.7822      0.6118
 ADJUSTED      0.6961      0.4707

STD. DEV. OF RESIDUALS = 1.9617E 01
N =   16

> ANOVA

   SOURCE         SS        DF       MS          F
REGRESSION  6.67263E 03     4   1.66816E 03    4.33
RESIDUALS   4.23311E 03    11   3.84828E 02
   TOTAL    1.09057E 04    15   7.27050E 02

> COEF

VARIABLE   B(STD.V)        B      STD.ERROR(B)    T
TIME       -0.5266  -2.9824E 00   2.7617E 00   -1.080
DAYS        0.1064   2.8275E 00   5.1691E 00    0.547
UNEMP      -1.2657  -8.3439E 01   4.4183E 01   -1.888
INFL        0.0616   1.6614E 01   1.1628E 02    0.143
CONSTANT    0        7.3715E 02   2.9329E 02    2.513
```

The adjusted r^2 value is especially important in forecasting situations when using multivariate regression. This is because there are often many variables and not that many observations. As m approaches n, unadjusted r and r^2 become biased by the loss in degrees of freedom. In fact, as m approaches n, r and r^2 approach 1.0. Thus, an adjustment is needed to estimate the underlying population r value. This is precisely what Equation 4.22 accomplishes.

The second section of output, ANOVA, refers to *analysis of variance.* What it means is that the total variation in the dependent variable is broken into two components. The first is that which is explained by the least-squares regression line. The second component is the residual variation, or, more simply, that which is unexplained by the regression. (It might be useful to refer back to Figure 4.7 to visualize this.) The DF column presents the degrees of freedom (usually abbreviated d.f.) related to each of the variation components. The MS column is the mean variation for each component, found by dividing SS (*sum of squares*) by DF. Finally, an F statistic is reported, which is calculated as

$$\frac{1668.16}{384.828} = 4.33$$

Multiple-regression programs use the F statistic instead of the t statistic to measure the significance of r. The number of independent variables equal the degrees of freedom in the numerator, and there are $n - m - 1$ degrees of freedom in the denominator, where m is the number of predictor variables. Thus, for the example, there are 4 d.f. in the numerator and $16 - 4 - 1 = 11$ d.f. in the denominator. From Appendix 4.B, we see that the critical value of F is 2.54, at the 90% confidence level. Since the calculated $F = 4.33$ and exceeds the critical value, we conclude that there is a significant association among the variables.

The next section of output reveals the equation's coefficients. Under the B column we see that[10]

$$y_c = 737.15 - 2.9824t + 2.8275x_1 - 83.439x_2 + 16.614x_3$$

where x_1 = the number of days in the month
x_2 = the unemployment rate
x_3 = the inflation rate
t = the time period

10. Note the coefficients listed below "B(STD.V)" refer to unit normal transformations of the original values. These are calculated by substituting for each value
of a variable that amount minus the mean then divided by the variable's
standard deviation. This transforms all data to a unit normal space with the
intercept at the origin.

If all the variables were statistically significant, we would use this equation to forecast sales. But the question of whether all the variables are each statistically significant remains. The question is answered by looking at the computed t values, also reported in Table 4.19. To evaluate them, there are

$$n - m - 1 \text{ degrees of freedom} \qquad (4.23)$$

From Appendix 4.A, we see that the critical value of $t = 1.790$, at the 90% confidence level, with $16 - 4 - 1 = 11$ degrees of freedom. Since we ignore signs, only the unemployment rate's calculated t exceeds the critical value. This means all the other variables are *not* associated with sales at a statistically significant level, provided that the unemployment rate is considered. Thus, we should only use the unemployment rate to explain sales for the example, unless, of course, some other variables are found significant.

The next step in the analysis, therefore, is to regress sales against the unemployment rate while ignoring the remaining variables. Table 4.11 presents the output.

Notice that all the statistics are now statistically significant. Also notice that while the raw r values are smaller than in Table 4.10, the adjusted r values are higher. This further confirms that more would be lost by including these other variables than would be gained by including them.

Thus, the final regression equation is

$$\text{Sales} = 596.58 - 49.221x$$

where x is the unemployment rate

Table 4.12 presents the results of calculating the estimated sales, "FITTED," for the historical series on the basis of Equation 4.23. "RESIDU" means residual, or error. We can see that the error is relatively small. If management believes that it is still too large, other variables would have to be found to reduce the error. If the error is acceptable (53% of the variation has been explained, $r^2 = 0.5258$ from Table 4.11), the regression equation would be used. If x, the unemployment rate, were 6.1%, the illustrated sales would be forecast at $596.58 - (49.221)(6.1) = 296$ units.

Dummy Variable Multiple Regression

Some variables are not very quantifiable in a strict sense, at least as precisely as is needed for regression. To illustrate, a strike may have occurred, or a recession, or a major publicity story, or a special sale, and so on.

Table 4.11 Robinson Appliance Sales Regressed Against Unemployment Rate

```
REGR
 * DEP. VAR. : SALES
 HOW MANY INDEP. VAR. ? 1
 INDEP. VAR. 1 : UNEMP
 COMPUTING REGRESSION...
 ANALYZING RESIDUALS...
 CHECKING AUTO CORRELATIONS...


 > SUMM

               MULTIPLE R   R-SQUARE
 UNADJUSTED      0.7466      0.5574
  ADJUSTED       0.7251      0.5258

 STD. DEV. OF RESIDUALS = 1.8567E 01
 N =   16

 > ANOVA

   SOURCE         SS         DF       MS          F
 REGRESSION   6.07936E 03     1   6.07936E 03   17.63
 RESIDUALS    4.82638E 03    14   3.44742E 02
   TOTAL      1.09057E 04    15   7.27050E 02

 > COEF

 VARIABLE   B(STD.V)       B        STD.ERROR(B)    T
 UNEMP       -0.7466    -4.9221E 01   1.1721E 01   -4.199
 CONSTANT      0         5.9658E 02   7.5085E 01    7.945
```

Such variables can influence sales. Further, they reduce the relationship of sales to other variables. Yet, at first glance, they are difficult to quantify.

Dummy variable regression might help in such cases. Dummy variable regression involves the creation of a variable having dichotomous values, say 0 and 1 or −1 and +1. One of the values is assigned to the dummy variable every time one type of condition occurs. The other value is assigned when the other condition is present.

Table 4.12 Robinson Appliance, Estimated Historical Sales,
Based on Regression, Compared with Actual Sales

```
    PRTF
WANT FITTED VALUES ONLY ? N
TO PRINT ONE COL OF DATA PLUS
FITTED AND RESIDUAL VALUES, GIVE
+ COLUMN OF DATA MATRIX TO BE PRINTED : SALES
```

ROW	SALES	FITTED	RESIDU
* 1 *	204.00000	242.19089	-38.19089
* 2 *	268.00000	252.03500	15.96500
* 3 *	249.00000	247.11298	1.88702
* 4 *	294.00000	266.80115	27.19885
* 5 *	305.00000	286.48938	18.51062
* 6 *	273.00000	281.56732	-8.56732
* 7 *	285.00000	281.56732	3.43268
* 8 *	295.00000	286.48938	8.51062
* 9 *	273.00000	281.56732	-8.56732
* 10 *	290.00000	291.41144	-1.41144
* 11 *	282.00000	286.48938	-4.48938
* 12 *	288.00000	296.33350	-8.33350
* 13 *	312.00000	301.25549	10.74451
* 14 *	308.00000	296.33350	11.66650
* 15 *	310.00000	301.25549	8.74451
* 16 *	274.00000	311.09967	-37.09967

MEAN	281.87500	281.87482	0.00000
S.DEV	26.96386	20.13183	18.56727

To illustrate, Table 4.13 presents General Motors' sales of Cadillacs, in units, from 1965 through 1974. Table 4.14 presents computer output providing the regression unit sales on time. Although there is a significant relationship at the 90% confidence level, the association is not very strong.

There happened to be recessions in years $t = 3$, $t = 6$, and $t = 10$. This information can be used to form a dummy variable. This dummy variable has the value of 1 in the above three years and value of 0 in the remaining years. Table 4.15 presents the multiple regression of sales against time and the dummy variable.

Table 4.13 Unit Sales of Cadillacs

t	Unit Sales	t	Unit Sales
1	189,661	6	165,042
2	196,498	7	253,002
3	209,546	8	257,795
4	205,593	9	285,709
5	243,905	10	219,993

Source: Ward's Automotive Yearbook

Table 4.14 Cadillac Sales Regressed Against Time

```
   REGR
+ DEP. VAR. : SALES
HOW MANY INDEP. VAR. ? 1
INDEP. VAR. 1 : TIME
COMPUTING REGRESSION...
ANALYZING RESIDUALS...
CHECKING AUTO CORRELATIONS...


> SUMM

             MULTIPLE R   R-SQUARE
UNADJUSTED     0.6004      0.3605
 ADJUSTED      0.5297      0.2806

STD. DEV. OF RESIDUALS = 3.1158E 04
N =   10

> ANOVA

   SOURCE        SS        DF       MS           F
REGRESSION  4.37873E 09    1   4.37873E 09     4.51
RESIDUALS   7.76648E 09    8   9.70810E 08
   TOTAL    1.21452E 10    9   1.34947E 09

> COEF

VARIABLE   B(STD.V)     B       STD.ERROR(B)    T
TIME       0.6004    7.2853E 03  3.4304E 03    2.124
CONSTANT   0         1.8261E 05  2.1285E 04    8.579
```

Table 4.15 Cadillac Sales Regressed Against Time and a Dummy
Variable for Recessions

```
> REGR
* DEP. VAR. : SALES
HOW MANY INDEP. VAR. ? 2
INDEP. VAR. 1 : TIME
INDEP. VAR. 2 : RECESS
COMPUTING REGRESSION...
ANALYZING RESIDUALS...
CHECKING AUTO CORRELATIONS...


> SUMM

              MULTIPLE R   R-SQUARE
UNADJUSTED      0.8380      0.7022
 ADJUSTED       0.7856      0.6172

STD. DEV. OF RESIDUALS = 2.2730E 04
N =   10

> ANOVA

   SOURCE         SS        DF        MS          F
REGRESSION   8.52879E 09    2    4.26439E 09    8.25
RESIDUALS    3.61642E 09    7    5.16631E 08
   TOTAL     1.21452E 10    9    1.34947E 09

> COEF

VARIABLE   B(STD.V)      B        STD.ERROR(B)    T
TIME         0.7135   8.6574E 03   2.5488E 03    3.397
RECESS      -0.5954  -4.5279E 04   1.5976E 04   -2.834
CONSTANT      0       1.8864E 05   1.5673E 04   12.036
```

Notice that now the regression is much more significant. The amount
of variation that is explained is increased dramatically. The forecast with
the model for $t = 1$ is as follows:

a. No recession assumed

Sales = 188640 + (8657.4)(11) – (45279)(0) = 283871 units

b. Recession assumed

Sales = 188640 + (8657.4)(11) – (45279)(1) = 238592 units

The use of such dummy variables greatly expands the use of multiple regression as a forecasting tool.

SOME LIMITATIONS AND ASSUMPTIONS TO REGRESSION AND CORRELATION

Regression and correlation techniques are extremely powerful tools that aid the accuracy of forecasts. The uses and strength of regression analysis have increased tremendously in past years.

However, limitations to the use of regression and correlation analysis do exist. Managers are often in the best position to determine the extent of the limitations to their specific situations. This determination is often based not on technical expertise but on judgment, which should be the manager's area of strength.

Constant Relationships

One rather obvious limitation is that the underlying relationships being analyzed are assumed to remain constant throughout the period in question, including the forecast span. As an example, if the sale of watermelons is related to temperature, it is assumed in using these techniques that the relationship holds true and remains constant over the period of time analyzed.

In general, this assumption becomes more unlikely as the time span increases. The solution is complicated by the problem of reduced reliability resulting from small sample sizes, as is the case with all statistical inferences.

Autocorrelation

Second, autocorrelation may exist within the data. Autocorrelation refers to the condition where the value of the forecast variable is related to its preceding value. Regression analysis assumes random variable values, not those that are ordered by past values of the same variable. Consistent over- or underprediction may result from such ordering.

This does not generally present a problem in most business and economic forecasting situations, however. It is true that sales at one point in time are typically influenced by past levels. But explicit notice of this is taken by including the time period, t, as one of the regression's independent variables. In so doing, one tends to factor out the overall impact of the time-related autocorrelation. Thus, it is a good idea in general to use time as one variable when using regression to forecast sales. This often accounts for any trend present.

Further, other time-related systematic influences should also be eliminated from the data. Seasonal and cyclical indexes, for example, can be used to eliminate these factors. Seasonality was briefly treated in Chapter 3, and both are considered in Chapter 5. The point here is that combinations of techniques are often desirable for increasing forecast accuracy.

Multicolinearity

Multicolinearity is the third major limitation to regression and correlation analysis. This condition exists when some or all of the independent variables in the analysis are causally related to each other as well as to the dependent variable. This condition is often the case in business and economic data. For instance, the multivariate example in this chapter is likely to contain multicolinearity. The unemployment and inflation rates both influence each other.[11] The existence of multicolinearity does not materially affect, for all practical purposes, the total analysis and relationship of all the independent variables to the forecast variable. The effects of multicolinearity on the forecast itself may be ignored for most practical purposes, but multicolinearity does alter each of the separate independent variables' computed relationship to the dependent variable. In other words, if multicolinearity exists, each of the b coefficients of the predictive regression equation as well as the coefficient of correlation between bivariate cases may be seriously distorted.

In practice, the effect of this distortion may be considered balanced out or eliminated in the multiple relation. Essentially all extensive multivariate problems involving economic data contain multicolinearity.

The existence of this condition theoretically invalidates the use of *stepwise* regression and correlation. This technique, which is widely available on most computers that have regression programs, consists of first assessing all bivariate comparisons and then building the multivariate analysis one variable at a time in descending order of relationship magnitude. That is, the strongest bivariate relationship is first regressed, then the second strongest, and so forth. Stepwise regression

11. For a discussion of and tests to detect multicolinearity, see Press, *Applied Multivariate Analysis*, pp. 193, 272. Also see J. Johnston, *Econometric Methods*, 2nd ed. (New York: McGraw-Hill, 1972).

procedures usually contain provisions that, if one variable is not significantly related, it is eliminated from analysis. Despite its theoretical limitations, stepwise regression is often used in practice as a method designed to allow attention to be focused only on the most influential variables. Much more will be said about multicolinearity in Chapter 9.

Causality

Regression problems require the analysis of independent and dependent variables; the magnitude of one variable must have a causal effect on the magnitude of another. If causality does not exist, regression analysis should theoretically not be used for forecasting. There is no way of being assured that the detected relationships will continue in the future unless causality is inherent.

But in most cases, it is impossible to be certain that causality exists. Controlled experimental studies, or possibly longitudinal studies, are required to test for causality. Unfortunately, these techniques are not often available to the forecaster. Time constraints and the inability to control accurately many of the variables of most problems are deterrents. Instead, causal relationships are most often inferred on the basis of logic, as in the examples in this chapter.

As a practical matter, it might be necessary to forecast with regression even when causality is highly suspect. A historically high r^2 between the forecast variable and some questionable causal factor might be the only clue available to the analyst. The assumption might be made, therefore, that the relationship was caused by some exogenous variable, the real causal agent, and that it will hold true in the future.

Forecasting on the basis of such a historic relationship, even if it is not a causal one, may be better than to forecast by pure guess. But one must anticipate the possibility that the relationship may not hold true in the future.

Other Limitations

Other assumptions and limitations to regression analysis exist. Most of these relate to the statistical assumptions required, such as independent observations, normal distribution of deviations, unbiased measurement, and random observations. These assumptions are generally required for all statistical analyses and will not be presented in this text. They are not unique to forecasting problems.

SUMMARY

Regression and correlation techniques are among the most widely used and most powerful methods of forecasting. Accuracy of forecasts and technique have been greatly enhanced since the advent of the computer, which has greatly expanded the possible number of variables for analysis and corresponding forecast accuracy.

The first step in using these techniques is to determine logically those variables possibly associated with the forecast variable. Experience and familiarity with the forecast variable greatly enhances this phase of forecasting.

After selecting the key variables to be used in analysis, it is important to determine whether or not these variables are independent and causal influencers of the forecast variable. If causality may be assumed, regression analysis may be used to predict the value of the forecast variable from the independent variables. However, it may be necessary in practice to make predictions using regression even if causality cannot be assumed. It may be better to make such a prediction than merely to guess.

Correlation serves only the function of determining if variables are associated. Correlation is useful to assess the magnitude of the association of the variables being analyzed. If the coefficient of determination (r^2) between the variables being analyzed is small, extreme caution should be taken in accepting the forecast. In this case, analysis should continue with other (or more) variables, if possible. On the other hand, if the coefficient is large, forecast accuracy becomes more reliable.

A low correlation does not necessarily mean that an association does not really exist between the variables. It might result from using linear analysis on nonlinearly related data. Data transformation procedures may be used to convert nonlinearly related data into their linear counterparts. Or more complex nonlinear least-squares procedures may be used.

Nonlinear analysis may be useful in bivariate cases. More frequently, linear multivariate analysis is used in business settings. Sales and other forecast variables are generally influenced by a multitude of factors, hence the need for multivariate treatment. And multivariate problems do not easily lend themselves to nonlinear analysis. Computers are virtually always used to solve multivariate regression and correlation problems, as hand calculations are tedious and very time consuming.

After analysis, care must be taken in interpreting results. Several major limitations to regression and correlation may exist. Experience and familiarity with the forecast and environmental variables are also essential in assessing whether or not the necessary assumptions are realistic. If they are, these techniques can be used as important management aids that provide guides for decision making.

DISCUSSION QUESTIONS

1. Name some of the variables that might be used to forecast the sales of:
   a. Automobiles
   b. New homes
   c. Clothing at the regional level
   d. Refrigerators
   e. Sheet steel
   f. Pencils
   g. Round-trip European vacations
2. Why is it necessary to determine whether a relationship between two variables is complete or incomplete? In practice, is it ever advisable to forecast on the basis of incomplete relationships?
3. New Center Theater for ten days has kept track of attendance and sales of buttered popcorn, with the following results:

Day	Sales of Buttered Popcorn	Movie Attendance
1	$26.50	83
2	17.00	56
3	19.30	63
4	24.50	75
5	33.90	92
6	35.00	108
7	41.50	148
8	37.80	125
9	30.10	110
10	37.00	119

   a. Are sales of buttered popcorn and movie attendance related? How related? Explain the concepts behind the calculations.
   b. Forecast buttered popcorn sales for an attendance of 114 people. Construct a confidence interval at the 95% level and explain its meaning.
4. Verify that the $r^2 = 0.892$, $\hat{\sigma}_{yt} = \$154.52$ million, and the forecast $= \$1,299.49 \pm 431.53$ million numbers for the Digital example, as presented in the chapter.
5. Verify the comparable results of the Digital example presented in the chapter after logarithmic transformations are made.

6. Verify the results, both linear and after data transformation, presented in the chapter for the Kryger example.

In questions 7 through 12, first use a scatter diagram to identify the appropriate relationship.

7. Forecast sales for $t = 11$ for the following:

t	Unit Sales	t	Unit Sales
1	10.0	6	16.3
2	11.0	7	17.9
3	12.2	8	19.9
4	13.5	9	22.1
5	14.4	10	24.0

8. Forecast sales for $t = 9$ for the following:

t	Unit Sales	t	Unit Sales
1	29.0	5	45.7
2	40.0	6	46.1
3	43.1	7	47.0
4	44.8	8	48.1

9. Forecast sales for $t = 9$ for the following:

t	Unit Sales	t	Unit Sales
1	12.1	5	19.8
2	13.8	6	22.3
3	15.9	7	24.2
4	18.3	8	25.7

10. Forecast sales for $t = 11$ for the following:

t	Unit Sales	t	Unit Sales
1	7.0	6	34.8
2	11.0	7	44.2
3	15.9	8	53.3
4	20.8	9	64.6
5	26.9	10	77.4

11. Forecast sales for $t = 11$ for the following:

t	Unit Sales	t	Unit Sales
1	5.3	6	12.8
2	6.1	7	14.5
3	7.5	8	17.7
4	8.6	9	21.8
5	10.3	10	26.3

12. Forecast sales for $t = 11$ for the following:

t	Unit Sales	t	Unit Sales
1	58	6	72
2	67	7	69
3	73	8	64
4	74	9	56
5	75	10	49

Questions 13 through 19 relate to the following problem:

The Horner Company has asked you to assist them in preparing a sales forecast for their candy bar named Zanzibar. The following monthly data have been collected:

t	Cartons Sold (in Thousands of Units)	Advertising in Previous Month (in Thousands of Dollars)	Leading Competitor's Advertising in Previous Month (in Thousands of Dollars)
1	7.2	4.3	5.8
2	8.3	4.8	5.3
3	8.0	4.5	5.7
4	7.6	4.2	6.0
5	8.2	4.3	5.6
6	8.6	4.5	5.4
7	8.1	4.4	5.9
8	8.4	4.5	5.8
9	8.9	4.8	5.5
10	8.7	4.7	6.0
11	9.3	4.9	5.7
12	9.2	4.9	6.3
13	9.5	4.9	6.1
14	9.4	5.0	6.4
15	9.8	5.1	6.0

13. Are sales related to company advertising? How strongly?
14. Are sales related to competitor advertising? How strongly?
15. How strongly are sales related to time?
16. Is there any benefit in considering all the variables when analyzing sales?
17. Forecast sales for $t = 16$. Assume that company advertising was $4.7 thousand during $t = 15$ and that the leading competitor spent $6.2 thousand in the same period.
18. Interpret any interrelationships among the variables. Is this information useful to management in shaping strategy?
19. Horner used a famous actor in its advertising during the months $t = 9$, $t = 13$, and $t = 15$. Assume that there is a $50 profit to Horner per carton of Zanzibars sold. The famous actor charges a $3,000 premium, per month, in his fee over the "regular" actors used during the other months. Is the premium worth the added cost to the company?

RECOMMENDED READINGS

Batsell, Richard, and Leonard M. Lodish. "A Model and Measurement Methodology for Predicting Individual Consumer Choice." *Journal of Marketing Research*, 17 (February 1981), 1-12.

Chou, Ya-lun. *Probability and Statistics for Decision Making*. New York: Holt, Rinehart and Winston, 1972, Chapters 17, 20.

Chou, Ya-lun. *Statistical Analysis: With Business and Economic Application*. New York: Holt, Rinehart and Winston, 1969, Chapters 19, 20.

Hamburg, Morris. *Statistical Analysis for Decision Making*, 2nd ed. New York: Harcourt Brace Jovanovich, 1977, Chapter 9.

Hoel, Paul G., and Raymond J. Jessen. *Basic Statistics for Business and Economics*, 2nd ed. Santa Barbara, Calif.: John Wiley and Sons, 1977, Chapters 9-11.

Johnston, J. *Econometric Methods*, 2nd ed. New York: McGraw-Hill Book Company, 1972.

Mason, Robert D. *Statistical Techniques in Business and Economics*. Homewood, Ill.: Richard D. Irwin, 1970, Chapters 16-17.

Press, S. James. *Applied Multivariate Analysis*. New York: Holt, Rinehart and Winston, 1972, Chapters 8, 11, and Appendix A.

Reibstein, David J. "The Prediction of Individual Probabilities of Brand Choice." *Journal of Consumer Research*, 5 (December 1978), 163-168.

Snedecor, George W., and William G. Cochran. *Statistical Methods*. 6th ed. Ames, Iowa: Iowa State University Press, 1967, Chapters 6, 7, 10, 13, 14, 15.

APPENDIX 4.A Table of Critical Values of *t*

df	Level of Significance for One-Tailed Test					
	0.10	0.05	0.025	0.01	0.005	0.0005
	Level of Significance for Two-Tailed Test					
	0.20	0.10	0.05	0.02	0.01	0.001
1	3.078	6.314	12.706	31.821	63.657	636.619
2	1.886	2.920	4.303	6.965	9.925	31.598
3	1.638	2.353	3.182	4.541	5.841	12.941
4	1.533	2.132	2.776	3.747	4.604	8.610
5	1.476	2.015	2.571	3.365	4.032	6.859
6	1.440	1.943	2.447	3.143	3.707	5.959
7	1.415	1.895	2.365	2.998	3.499	5.405
8	1.397	1.860	2.306	2.896	3.355	5.041
9	1.383	1.833	2.262	2.821	3.250	4.781
10	1.372	1.812	2.228	2.764	3.169	4.587
11	1.363	1.790	2.201	2.718	3.106	4.437
12	1.356	1.782	2.179	2.681	3.055	4.318
13	1.350	1.771	2.160	2.650	3.012	4.221
14	1.345	1.761	2.145	2.624	2.977	4.140
15	1.341	1.753	2.131	2.602	2.947	4.073
16	1.337	1.746	2.120	2.583	2.921	4.015
17	1.333	1.740	2.110	2.567	2.898	3.965
18	1.330	1.734	2.101	2.552	2.878	3.922
19	1.328	1.729	2.093	2.539	2.861	3.883
20	1.325	1.725	2.086	2.528	2.845	3.850
21	1.323	1.721	2.080	2.518	2.831	3.819
22	1.321	1.717	2.074	2.508	2.819	3.792
23	1.319	1.714	2.069	2.500	2.807	3.767
24	1.318	1.711	2.064	2.492	2.797	3.745
25	1.316	1.708	2.060	2.485	2.787	3.725
26	1.315	1.706	2.056	2.479	2.779	3.707
27	1.314	1.703	2.052	2.473	2.771	3.690
28	1.313	1.701	2.048	2.467	2.763	3.674
29	1.311	1.699	2.045	2.462	2.756	3.659
30	1.310	1.697	2.042	2.457	2.750	3.646
40	1.303	1.684	2.021	2.423	2.704	3.551
60	1.296	1.671	2.000	2.390	2.660	3.460
120	1.289	1.658	1.980	2.358	2.617	3.373
∞	1.282	1.645	1.960	2.326	2.576	3.291

The table of critical values of *t* is taken from Table III of Fisher and Yates: *Statistical Tables for Biological, Agricultural and Medical Research*, published by Longman Group Ltd., London (previously published by Oliver and Boyd, Edinburgh), and by permission of the authors and publishers.

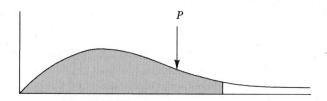

Percentiles of the F Distribution[a] $[F_{0.90}(n_1, n_2); \alpha = 0.1]$

[a] n_1 = degrees of freedom for numerator; n_2 = degrees of freedom for the denominator.

n_1 / n_2	1	2	3	4	5	6	7	8	9
1	39.86	49.50	53.59	55.83	57.24	58.20	58.91	59.44	59.86
2	8.53	9.00	9.16	9.24	9.29	9.33	9.35	9.37	9.38
3	5.54	5.46	5.39	5.34	5.31	5.28	5.27	5.25	5.24
4	4.54	4.32	4.19	4.11	4.05	4.01	3.98	3.95	3.94
5	4.06	3.78	3.62	3.52	3.45	3.40	3.37	3.34	3.32
6	3.78	3.46	3.29	3.18	3.11	3.05	3.01	2.98	2.96
7	3.59	3.26	3.07	2.96	2.88	2.83	2.78	2.75	2.72
8	3.46	3.11	2.92	2.81	2.73	2.67	2.62	2.59	2.56
9	3.36	3.01	2.81	2.69	2.61	2.55	2.51	2.47	2.44
10	3.29	2.92	2.73	2.61	2.52	2.46	2.41	2.38	2.35
11	3.23	2.86	2.66	2.54	2.45	2.39	2.34	2.30	2.27
12	3.18	2.81	2.61	2.48	2.39	2.33	2.28	2.24	2.21
13	3.14	2.76	2.56	2.43	2.35	2.28	2.23	2.20	2.16
14	3.10	2.73	2.52	2.39	2.31	2.24	2.19	2.15	2.12
15	3.07	2.70	2.49	2.36	2.27	2.21	2.16	2.12	2.09
16	3.05	2.67	2.46	2.33	2.24	2.18	2.13	2.09	2.06
17	3.03	2.64	2.44	2.31	2.22	2.15	2.10	2.06	2.03
18	3.01	2.62	2.42	2.29	2.20	2.13	2.08	2.04	2.00
19	2.99	2.61	2.40	2.27	2.18	2.11	2.06	2.02	1.98
20	2.97	2.59	2.38	2.25	2.16	2.09	2.04	2.00	1.96
21	2.96	2.57	2.36	2.23	2.14	2.08	2.02	1.98	1.95
22	2.95	2.56	2.35	2.22	2.13	2.06	2.01	1.97	1.93
23	2.94	2.55	2.34	2.21	2.11	2.05	1.99	1.95	1.92
24	2.93	2.54	2.33	2.19	2.10	2.04	1.98	1.94	1.91
25	2.92	2.53	2.32	2.18	2.09	2.02	1.97	1.93	1.89
26	2.91	2.52	2.31	2.17	1.08	2.01	1.96	1.92	1.88
27	2.90	2.51	2.30	2.17	2.07	2.00	1.95	1.91	1.87
28	2.89	2.50	2.29	2.16	2.06	2.00	1.94	1.90	1.87
29	2.89	2.50	2.28	2.15	2.06	1.99	1.93	1.89	1.86
30	2.88	2.49	2.28	2.14	2.05	1.98	1.93	1.88	1.85
40	2.84	2.44	2.23	2.09	2.00	1.93	1.87	1.83	1.79
60	2.79	2.39	2.18	2.04	1.95	1.87	1.82	1.77	1.74
120	2.75	2.35	2.13	1.99	1.90	1.82	1.77	1.72	1.68
∞	2.71	2.30	2.08	1.94	1.85	1.77	1.72	1.67	1.63

n_1 / n_2	10	12	15	20	24	30	40	60	120	∞
1	60.19	60.71	61.22	61.74	62.00	62.26	62.53	62.79	63.06	63.33
2	9.39	9.41	9.42	9.44	9.45	9.46	9.47	9.47	9.48	9.49
3	5.23	5.22	5.20	5.18	5.18	5.17	5.16	5.15	5.14	5.13
4	3.92	3.90	3.87	3.84	3.83	3.82	3.80	3.79	3.78	3.76
5	3.30	3.27	3.24	3.21	3.19	3.17	3.16	3.14	3.12	3.10

continued

n_1 / n_2	10	12	15	20	24	30	40	60	120	∞
6	2.94	2.90	2.87	2.84	2.82	2.80	2.78	2.76	2.74	2.72
7	2.70	2.67	2.63	2.59	2.58	2.56	2.54	2.51	2.49	2.47
8	2.50	2.50	2.46	2.42	2.40	2.38	2.36	2.34	2.32	2.29
9	2.42	2.38	2.34	2.30	2.28	2.25	2.23	2.21	2.18	2.16
10	2.32	2.28	2.24	2.20	2.18	2.16	2.13	2.11	2.08	2.06
11	2.25	2.21	2.17	2.12	2.10	2.08	2.05	2.03	2.00	1.97
12	2.19	2.15	2.10	2.06	2.04	2.01	1.99	1.96	1.93	1.90
13	2.14	2.10	2.05	2.01	1.98	1.96	1.93	1.90	1.88	1.85
14	2.10	2.05	2.01	1.96	1.94	1.91	1.89	1.86	1.83	1.80
15	2.06	2.02	1.97	1.92	1.90	1.87	1.85	1.82	1.79	1.76
16	2.03	1.99	1.94	1.89	1.87	1.84	1.81	1.78	1.75	1.72
17	2.00	1.96	1.91	1.86	1.84	1.81	1.78	1.75	1.72	1.69
18	1.98	1.93	1.89	1.84	1.81	1.78	1.75	1.72	1.69	1.66
19	1.96	1.91	1.86	1.81	1.79	1.76	1.73	1.70	1.67	1.63
20	1.94	1.89	1.84	1.79	1.77	1.74	1.71	1.68	1.64	1.61
21	1.92	1.87	1.83	1.78	1.75	1.72	1.69	1.66	1.62	1.59
22	1.90	1.86	1.81	1.76	1.73	1.70	1.67	1.64	1.60	1.57
23	1.89	1.84	1.80	1.74	1.72	1.69	1.66	1.62	1.59	1.55
24	1.88	1.83	1.78	1.73	1.70	1.67	1.64	1.61	1.57	1.53
25	1.87	1.82	1.77	1.72	1.69	1.66	1.63	1.59	1.56	1.52
26	1.86	1.81	1.76	1.71	1.68	1.65	1.61	1.58	1.54	1.50
27	1.85	1.80	1.75	1.70	1.67	1.64	1.60	1.57	1.53	1.49
28	1.84	1.79	1.74	1.69	1.66	1.63	1.59	1.56	1.52	1.48
29	1.83	1.78	1.73	1.68	1.65	1.62	1.58	1.55	1.51	1.47
30	1.82	1.77	1.72	1.67	1.64	1.61	1.57	1.54	1.50	1.46
31	1.76	1.71	1.66	1.61	1.57	1.54	1.51	1.47	1.42	1.38
32	1.71	1.66	1.60	1.54	1.51	1.48	1.44	1.40	1.35	1.29
33	1.65	1.60	1.55	1.48	1.45	1.41	1.37	1.32	1.26	1.19
34	1.60	1.55	1.49	1.42	1.38	1.34	1.30	1.24	1.17	1.00

Percentiles of the F Distribution[a] (Continued) [$F_{0.95}(n_1, n_2)$; $\alpha = 0.05$]

n_1 / n_2	1	2	3	4	5	6	7	8	9
1	161.4	199.5	215.7	224.6	230.2	234.0	236.8	238.9	240.5
2	18.51	19.00	19.16	19.25	19.30	19.33	19.35	19.37	19.38
3	10.13	9.55	9.28	9.12	9.01	8.94	8.89	8.85	8.81
4	7.71	6.94	6.59	6.39	6.26	6.16	6.09	6.04	6.00
5	6.61	5.79	5.41	5.19	5.05	4.95	4.88	4.82	4.77
6	5.99	5.14	4.76	4.53	4.39	4.28	4.21	4.15	4.10
7	5.59	4.74	4.35	4.12	3.97	3.87	3.79	3.73	3.68
8	5.32	4.46	4.07	3.84	3.69	3.58	3.50	3.44	3.39
9	5.12	4.26	3.86	3.63	3.48	3.37	3.29	3.23	3.18
10	4.96	4.10	3.71	3.48	3.33	3.22	3.14	3.07	3.02
11	4.84	3.98	3.59	3.36	3.20	3.09	3.01	2.95	2.90
12	4.75	3.89	3.49	3.26	3.11	3.00	2.91	2.85	2.80
13	4.67	3.81	3.41	3.18	3.03	2.92	2.83	2.77	2.71
14	4.60	3.74	3.34	3.11	2.96	2.85	2.76	2.70	2.65
15	4.54	3.68	3.29	3.06	2.90	2.79	2.71	2.64	2.59
16	4.49	3.63	3.24	3.01	2.85	2.74	2.66	2.59	2.54
17	4.45	3.59	3.20	2.96	2.81	2.70	2.61	2.55	2.49
18	4.41	3.55	3.16	2.93	2.77	2.66	2.58	2.51	2.46
19	4.38	3.52	3.13	2.90	2.74	2.63	2.54	2.48	2.42

continued

n_2 \ n_1	1	2	3	4	5	6	7	8	9
20	4.35	3.49	3.10	2.87	2.71	2.60	2.51	2.45	2.39
21	4.32	3.47	3.07	2.84	2.68	2.57	2.49	2.42	2.37
22	4.30	3.44	3.05	2.82	2.66	2.55	2.46	2.40	2.34
23	4.28	3.42	3.03	2.80	2.64	2.53	2.44	2.37	2.32
24	4.26	3.40	3.01	2.78	2.62	2.51	2.42	2.36	2.30
25	4.24	3.39	2.99	2.76	2.60	2.49	2.40	2.34	2.28
26	4.23	3.37	2.98	2.74	2.59	2.47	2.39	2.32	2.27
27	4.21	3.35	2.96	2.73	2.57	2.46	2.37	2.31	2.25
28	4.20	3.34	2.95	2.71	2.56	2.45	2.36	2.29	2.24
29	4.18	3.33	2.93	2.70	2.55	2.43	2.35	2.28	2.22
30	4.17	3.32	2.92	2.69	2.53	2.42	2.33	2.27	2.21
40	4.08	3.23	2.84	2.61	2.45	2.34	2.25	2.18	2.12
60	4.00	3.15	2.76	2.53	2.37	2.25	2.17	2.10	2.04
120	3.92	3.07	2.68	2.45	2.29	2.17	2.09	2.02	1.96
∞	3.84	3.00	2.60	2.37	2.21	2.10	2.01	1.94	1.88

n_2 \ n_1	10	12	15	20	24	30	40	60	120	∞
1	241.9	243.9	245.9	248.0	249.1	250.1	251.1	252.2	253.3	254.3
2	19.40	19.41	19.43	19.45	19.45	19.46	19.47	19.48	19.49	19.50
3	8.79	8.74	8.70	8.66	8.64	8.62	8.59	8.57	8.55	8.53
4	5.96	5.91	5.86	5.80	5.77	5.75	5.72	5.69	5.66	5.63
5	4.74	4.68	4.62	4.56	4.53	4.50	4.46	4.43	4.40	4.36
6	4.06	4.00	3.94	3.87	3.84	3.81	3.77	3.74	3.70	3.67
7	3.64	3.57	3.51	3.44	3.41	3.38	3.34	3.30	3.27	3.23
8	3.35	3.28	3.22	3.15	3.12	3.08	3.04	3.01	2.97	2.93
9	3.14	3.07	3.01	2.94	2.90	2.86	2.83	2.79	2.75	2.71
10	2.98	2.91	2.85	2.77	2.74	2.70	2.66	2.62	2.58	2.54
11	2.85	2.79	2.72	2.65	2.61	2.57	2.53	2.49	2.45	2.40
12	2.75	2.69	2.62	2.54	2.51	2.47	2.43	2.38	2.34	2.30
13	2.67	2.60	2.53	2.46	2.42	2.38	2.34	2.30	2.25	2.21
14	2.60	2.53	2.46	2.39	2.35	2.31	2.27	2.22	2.18	2.13
15	2.54	2.48	2.40	2.33	2.29	2.25	2.20	2.16	2.11	2.07
16	2.49	2.42	2.35	2.28	2.24	2.19	2.15	2.11	2.06	2.01
17	2.45	2.38	2.31	2.23	2.19	2.15	2.10	2.06	2.01	1.96
18	2.41	2.34	2.27	2.19	2.15	2.11	2.06	2.02	1.97	1.92
19	2.38	2.31	2.23	2.16	2.11	2.07	2.03	1.98	1.93	1.88
20	2.35	2.28	2.20	2.12	2.08	2.04	1.99	1.95	1.90	1.84
21	2.32	2.25	2.18	2.10	2.05	2.01	1.96	1.92	1.87	1.81
22	2.30	2.23	2.15	2.07	2.03	1.98	1.94	1.89	1.84	1.78
23	2.27	2.20	2.13	2.05	2.01	1.96	1.91	1.86	1.81	1.76
24	2.25	2.18	2.11	2.03	1.98	1.94	1.89	1.84	1.79	1.73
25	2.24	2.16	2.09	2.01	1.96	1.92	1.87	1.82	1.77	1.71
26	2.22	2.15	2.07	1.99	1.95	1.90	1.85	1.80	1.75	1.69
27	2.20	2.13	2.06	1.97	1.93	1.88	1.84	1.79	1.73	1.67
28	2.19	2.12	2.04	1.96	1.91	1.87	1.82	1.77	1.71	1.65
29	2.18	2.10	2.03	1.94	1.90	1.85	1.81	1.75	1.70	1.64
30	2.16	2.09	2.01	1.93	1.89	1.84	1.79	1.74	1.68	1.62
31	2.08	2.00	1.92	1.84	1.79	1.74	1.69	1.64	1.58	1.51
32	1.99	1.92	1.84	1.75	1.70	1.65	1.59	1.53	1.47	1.39
33	1.91	1.83	1.75	1.66	1.61	1.55	1.50	1.43	1.35	1.25
34	1.83	1.75	1.67	1.57	1.52	1.46	1.39	1.32	1.22	1.00

Percentiles of the F Distribution[a] (Continued) [$F_{0.99}(n_1, n_2)$; $\alpha = 0.01$]

n_2 \ n_1	1	2	3	4	5	6	7	8	9
1	4052.	4999.5	5403.	5625.	5764.	5859.	5928.	5982.	6022.
2	98.50	99.00	99.17	99.25	99.30	99.33	99.36	99.37	99.39
3	34.12	30.82	29.46	28.71	28.24	27.91	27.67	27.49	27.35
4	21.20	18.00	16.69	15.98	15.52	15.21	14.98	14.80	14.66
5	16.26	13.27	12.06	11.39	10.97	10.67	10.46	10.29	10.16
6	13.75	10.92	9.78	9.15	8.75	8.47	8.26	8.10	7.98
7	12.25	9.55	8.45	7.85	7.46	7.19	6.99	6.84	6.72
8	11.26	8.65	7.59	7.01	6.63	6.37	6.18	6.03	5.91
9	10.56	8.02	6.99	6.42	6.06	5.80	5.61	5.47	5.35
10	10.04	7.56	6.55	5.99	5.64	5.39	5.20	5.06	4.94
11	9.65	7.21	6.22	5.67	5.32	5.07	4.89	4.74	4.63
12	9.33	6.93	5.95	5.41	5.06	4.82	4.64	4.50	4.39
13	9.07	6.70	5.74	5.21	4.86	4.62	4.44	4.30	4.19
14	8.86	6.51	5.56	5.04	4.69	4.46	4.28	4.14	4.03
15	8.68	6.36	5.42	4.89	4.56	4.32	4.14	4.00	3.89
16	8.53	6.23	5.29	4.77	4.44	4.20	4.03	3.89	3.78
17	8.40	6.11	5.18	4.67	4.34	4.10	3.93	3.79	3.68
18	8.29	6.01	5.09	4.58	4.25	4.01	3.84	3.71	3.60
19	8.18	5.93	5.01	4.50	4.17	3.94	3.77	3.63	3.52
20	8.10	5.85	4.94	4.43	4.10	3.87	3.70	3.56	3.46
21	8.02	5.78	4.87	4.37	4.04	3.81	3.64	3.51	3.40
22	7.95	5.72	4.82	4.31	3.99	3.76	3.59	3.45	3.35
23	7.88	5.66	4.76	4.26	3.94	3.71	3.54	3.41	3.30
24	7.82	5.61	4.72	4.22	3.90	3.67	3.50	3.36	3.26
25	7.77	5.57	4.68	4.18	3.85	3.63	3.46	3.32	3.22
26	7.72	5.53	4.64	4.14	3.82	3.59	3.42	3.29	3.18
27	7.68	5.49	4.60	4.11	3.78	3.56	3.39	3.26	3.15
28	7.64	5.45	4.57	4.07	3.75	3.53	3.36	3.23	3.12
29	7.60	5.42	4.54	4.04	3.73	3.50	3.33	3.20	3.09
30	7.56	5.39	4.51	4.02	3.70	3.47	3.30	3.17	3.07
40	7.31	5.18	4.31	3.83	3.51	3.29	3.12	2.99	2.89
60	7.08	4.98	4.13	3.65	3.34	3.12	2.95	2.82	2.72
120	6.85	4.79	3.95	3.48	3.17	2.96	2.79	2.66	2.56
∞	6.63	4.61	3.78	3.32	3.02	2.80	2.64	2.51	2.41

n_2 \ n_1	10	12	15	20	24	30	40	60	120	∞
1	6056.	6106.	6157.	6209.	6235.	6261.	6287.	6313.	6339.	6366.
2	99.40	99.42	99.43	99.45	99.46	99.47	99.47	99.48	99.49	99.50
3	27.23	27.05	26.87	26.69	26.60	26.50	26.41	26.32	26.22	26.13
4	14.55	14.37	14.20	14.02	13.93	13.84	13.75	13.65	13.56	13.46
5	10.05	9.89	9.72	9.55	9.47	9.38	9.29	9.20	9.11	9.02
6	7.87	7.72	7.56	7.40	7.31	7.23	7.14	7.06	6.97	6.88
7	6.62	6.47	6.31	6.16	6.07	5.99	5.91	5.82	5.74	5.65
8	5.81	5.67	5.52	5.36	5.28	5.20	5.12	5.03	4.95	4.86
9	5.26	5.11	4.96	4.81	4.73	4.65	4.57	4.48	4.40	4.31
10	4.85	4.71	4.56	4.41	4.33	4.25	4.17	4.08	4.00	3.91
11	4.54	4.40	4.25	4.10	4.02	3.94	3.86	3.78	3.69	3.60
12	4.30	4.16	4.01	3.86	3.78	3.70	3.62	3.54	3.45	3.36
13	4.10	3.96	3.82	3.66	3.59	3.51	3.43	3.34	3.25	3.17
14	3.94	3.80	3.66	3.51	3.43	3.35	3.27	3.18	3.09	3.00

continued

	10	12	15	20	24	30	40	60	120	∞
15	3.80	3.67	3.52	3.37	3.29	3.21	3.13	3.05	2.96	2.87
16	3.69	3.55	3.41	3.26	3.18	3.10	3.02	2.93	2.84	2.75
17	3.59	3.46	3.31	3.16	3.08	3.00	2.92	2.83	2.75	2.65
18	3.51	3.37	3.23	3.08	3.00	2.92	2.84	2.75	2.66	2.57
19	3.43	3.30	3.15	3.00	2.92	2.84	2.76	2.67	2.58	2.49
20	3.37	3.23	3.09	2.94	2.86	2.78	2.69	2.61	2.52	2.42
21	3.31	3.17	3.03	2.88	2.80	2.72	2.64	2.55	2.46	2.36
22	3.26	3.12	2.98	2.83	2.75	2.67	2.58	2.50	2.40	2.31
23	3.21	3.07	2.93	2.78	2.70	2.62	2.54	2.45	2.35	2.26
24	3.17	3.03	2.89	2.74	2.66	2.58	2.49	2.40	2.31	2.21
25	3.13	2.99	2.85	2.70	2.62	2.54	2.45	2.36	2.27	2.17
26	3.09	2.96	2.81	2.66	2.58	2.50	2.42	2.33	2.23	2.13
27	3.06	2.93	2.78	2.63	2.55	2.47	2.38	2.29	2.20	2.10
28	3.03	2.90	2.75	2.60	2.52	2.44	2.35	2.26	2.17	2.06
29	3.00	2.87	2.73	2.57	2.49	2.41	2.33	2.23	2.14	2.03
30	2.98	2.84	2.70	2.55	2.47	2.39	2.30	2.21	2.11	2.01
31	2.80	2.66	2.52	2.37	2.29	2.20	2.11	2.02	1.92	1.80
32	2.63	2.50	2.35	2.20	2.12	2.03	1.94	1.84	1.73	1.60
33	2.47	2.34	2.19	2.03	1.95	1.86	1.76	1.66	1.53	1.38
34	2.32	2.18	2.04	1.88	1.79	1.70	1.59	1.47	1.32	1.00

Percentiles of the F Distribution[a] (Continued) [$F_{0.975}(n_1, n_2)$; $\alpha = 0.025$]

n_2 \ n_1	1	2	3	4	5	6	7	8	9
1	647.8	799.5	864.2	899.6	921.8	937.1	948.2	956.7	963.3
2	38.51	39.00	39.17	39.25	39.30	39.33	39.36	39.37	39.39
3	17.44	16.04	15.44	15.10	14.88	14.73	14.62	14.54	14.47
4	12.22	10.65	9.98	9.60	9.36	9.20	9.07	8.98	8.90
5	10.01	8.43	7.76	7.39	7.15	6.98	6.85	6.76	6.68
6	8.81	7.26	6.60	6.23	5.99	5.82	5.70	5.60	5.52
7	8.07	6.54	5.89	5.52	5.29	5.12	4.99	4.90	4.82
8	7.57	6.06	5.42	5.05	4.82	4.65	4.53	4.43	4.36
9	7.21	5.71	5.08	4.72	4.48	4.32	4.20	4.10	4.03
10	6.94	5.46	4.83	4.47	4.24	4.07	3.95	3.85	3.78
11	6.72	5.26	4.63	4.28	4.04	3.88	3.76	3.66	3.59
12	6.55	5.10	4.47	4.12	3.89	3.73	3.61	3.51	3.44
13	6.41	4.97	4.35	4.00	3.77	3.60	3.48	3.39	3.31
14	6.30	4.86	4.24	3.89	3.66	3.50	3.38	3.29	3.21
15	6.20	4.77	4.15	3.80	3.58	3.41	3.29	3.20	3.12
16	6.12	4.69	4.08	3.73	3.50	3.34	3.22	3.12	3.05
17	6.04	4.62	4.01	3.66	3.44	3.28	3.16	3.06	2.98
18	5.98	4.56	3.95	3.61	3.38	3.22	3.10	3.01	2.93
19	5.92	4.51	3.90	3.56	3.33	3.17	3.05	2.96	2.88
20	5.87	4.46	3.86	3.51	3.29	3.13	3.01	2.91	2.84
21	5.83	4.42	3.82	3.48	3.25	3.09	2.97	2.87	2.80
22	5.79	4.38	3.78	3.44	3.22	3.05	2.93	2.84	2.76
23	5.75	4.35	3.75	3.41	3.18	3.02	2.90	2.81	2.73
24	5.72	4.32	3.72	3.38	3.15	2.99	2.87	2.78	2.70
25	5.69	4.29	3.69	3.35	3.13	2.97	2.85	2.75	2.68
26	5.66	4.27	3.67	3.33	3.10	2.94	2.82	2.73	2.65
27	5.63	4.24	3.65	3.31	3.08	2.92	2.80	2.71	2.63
28	5.61	4.22	3.63	3.29	3.06	2.90	2.78	2.69	2.61
29	5.59	4.20	3.61	3.27	3.04	2.88	2.76	2.67	2.59

continued

n_2 \ n_1	1	2	3	4	5	6	7	8	9
30	5.57	4.18	3.59	3.25	3.03	2.87	2.75	2.65	2.57
40	5.42	4.05	3.46	3.13	2.90	2.74	2.62	2.53	2.45
60	5.29	3.93	3.34	3.01	2.79	2.63	2.51	2.41	2.33
120	5.15	3.80	3.23	2.89	2.67	2.52	2.39	2.30	2.22
∞	5.02	3.69	3.12	2.79	2.57	2.41	2.29	2.19	2.11

	10	12	15	20	24	30	40	60	120	∞
1	968.6	976.7	984.9	993.1	997.2	1001.	1006.	1010.	1014.	1018.
2	39.40	39.41	39.43	39.45	39.46	39.46	39.47	39.48	39.49	39.50
3	14.42	14.34	14.25	14.17	14.12	14.08	14.04	13.99	13.95	13.90
4	8.84	8.75	8.66	8.56	8.51	8.46	8.41	8.36	8.31	8.26
5	6.62	6.52	6.43	6.33	6.28	6.23	6.18	6.12	6.07	6.02
6	5.46	5.37	5.27	5.17	5.12	5.07	5.01	4.96	4.90	4.85
7	4.76	4.67	4.57	4.47	4.42	4.36	4.31	4.25	4.20	4.14
8	4.30	4.20	4.10	4.00	3.95	3.89	3.84	3.78	3.73	3.67
9	3.96	3.87	3.77	3.67	3.61	3.56	3.51	3.45	3.39	3.33
10	3.72	3.62	3.52	3.42	3.37	3.31	3.26	3.20	3.14	3.08
11	3.53	3.43	3.33	3.23	3.17	3.12	3.06	3.00	2.94	2.88
12	3.37	3.28	3.18	3.07	3.02	2.96	2.91	2.85	2.79	2.72
13	3.25	3.15	3.05	2.95	2.89	2.84	2.78	2.72	2.66	2.60
14	3.15	3.05	2.95	2.84	2.79	2.73	2.67	2.61	2.55	2.49
15	3.06	2.96	2.86	2.76	2.70	2.64	2.59	2.52	2.46	2.40
16	2.99	2.89	2.79	2.68	2.63	2.57	2.51	2.45	2.38	2.32
17	2.92	2.82	2.72	2.62	2.56	2.50	2.44	2.38	2.32	2.25
18	2.87	2.77	2.67	2.56	2.50	2.44	2.38	2.32	2.26	2.19
19	2.82	2.72	2.62	2.51	2.45	2.39	2.33	2.27	2.20	2.13
20	2.77	2.68	2.57	2.46	2.41	2.35	2.29	2.22	2.16	2.09
21	2.73	2.64	2.53	2.42	2.37	2.31	2.25	2.18	2.11	2.04
22	2.70	2.60	2.50	2.39	2.33	2.27	2.21	2.14	2.08	2.00
23	2.67	2.57	2.47	2.36	2.30	2.24	2.18	2.11	2.04	1.97
24	2.64	2.54	2.44	2.33	2.27	2.21	2.15	2.08	2.01	1.94
25	2.61	2.51	2.41	2.30	2.24	2.18	2.12	2.05	1.98	1.91
26	2.59	2.49	2.39	2.28	2.22	2.16	2.09	2.03	1.95	1.88
27	2.57	2.47	2.36	2.25	2.19	2.13	2.07	2.00	1.93	1.85
28	2.55	2.45	2.34	2.23	2.17	2.11	2.05	1.98	1.91	1.83
29	2.53	2.43	2.32	2.21	2.15	2.09	2.03	1.96	1.89	1.81
30	2.51	2.41	2.31	2.20	2.14	2.07	2.01	1.94	1.87	1.79
31	2.39	2.29	2.18	2.07	2.01	1.94	1.88	1.80	1.72	1.64
32	2.27	2.17	2.06	1.94	1.88	1.82	1.74	1.67	1.58	1.48
33	2.16	2.05	1.94	1.82	1.76	1.69	1.61	1.53	1.43	1.31
34	2.05	1.94	1.83	1.71	1.64	1.57	1.48	1.39	1.27	1.00

Source: E. S. Pearson and H. O. Hartley, eds., *Biometrika Tables for Statisticians*, 2nd ed. (New York: Cambridge University Press, 1972), I, 177–180.

CASE 4: THE NIAGRA BOOK COMPANY

The Niagra Book Company has been in existence since 1962. This firm operates a book club, whose members receive books through the mail at prices lower than those charged at most retail bookstores. New members obtain their first six books for a total price of $2.99. Thereafter, they agree to buy at least four books every year that they are a member, at the price set forth in the firm's advertising. The volumes are mostly best sellers, and sports, cooking, exercise, and mystery books.

This company is unusual in that all its promotion efforts take place through the mail. New members are reached through magazine advertising; old members are contacted through a club magazine, which lists books on hand from which the member selects four for the coming year. Top executives in the company and key members of its advertising agency are convinced that the firm does an excellent job, both in attracting new members and in retaining old ones.

Niagra executives have found that the market for the kind of books they sell is expanding. Increased leisure time and the "me generation" ethos contribute to the purchase and reading of books of this nature. On the other hand, competition from bookstores, other retailers, and other book clubs is intense.

Company executives have found that it is not difficult to forecast sales to old club members. They average a purchase rate of six books per year at an average price of $12.50. Thus, the estimate of sales to old club members is 6 × $12.50 = $75, times the number of members who can be expected to retain their membership for the forecast period (one year). An analysis of company records shows that, of individuals who are members during a given year, 60% will be members the following year. Thus, if there were 2 million members in a year, sales to old customers for the following year would be forecasted at 2,000,000 × .60 = 1,200,000 × $75.00 = $90,000,000. As the price of books increases due to inflation, the $75 figure, of course, will have to be adjusted upward.

The firm forecasts sales to new members through a regression model. The dependent variable is total sales to new members, while the independent variable is total company advertising for the year. Following are the data and the computations that led to the derivation of the regression equations:

Year	Advertising (in 10s of thousands of dollars) x	Sales to new customers (in millions of books) y	xy	x^2
1962	$ 41	32	$ 1,312	$ 1,681
1963	35	20	700	1,225
1964	34	35	1,190	1,156
1965	40	24	960	1,600
1966	33	27	891	1,089
1967	42	28	1,176	1,764
1968	37	31	1,147	1,369
1969	42	33	1,386	1,764
1970	30	26	780	900
1971	43	41	1,763	1,849
1972	38	29	1,102	1,444
1973	38	33	1,254	1,444
1974	46	36	1,656	2,116
1975	36	23	828	1,296
1976	32	22	704	1,024
1977	43	38	1,634	1,849
1978	42	26	1,092	1,764
1979	30	20	600	900
1980	41	30	1,230	1,681
1981	45	30	1,350	2,025
Totals	$768	584	$22,755	$29,940

$$b = \frac{20(22{,}755) - (768)(584)}{20(29{,}940) - (768)(768)} = .734$$

$$a = \frac{584}{20} - .734\ \frac{768}{20} = 1.01$$

95 = LOW 28.124 = HIGH 38.8

Thus, if the firm plans to spend $440,000 in advertising, expected sales to new customers is:

$$y_c = 1.01 \times .734(44) = 33.306 = 33{,}306{,}000 \text{ books.}$$

The calculated standard error of regression is 4.78.

These methods for estimating sales to both new and old members have been employed by the firm for some time. Essentially, their validity has never been challenged. Some members of the management team wonder if other methods might be better, however.

1. Evaluate the forecasting efforts of the Niagra book company.
2. Is regression a useful tool in this case? Why or why not?
3. What is the confidence interval for the forecast of 33,306,000 books with planned advertising of $440,000?
4. How might the forecasting program of this firm be improved?

Chapter 5
Time-Series Analysis: Decomposition

INTRODUCTION

Chapter 3 introduced time-series analysis, the process of identifying systematic fluctuation in the forecast variable over time. In Chapter 4, we focused on identifying any relationship between two or more variables, one of which might be time. In this chapter, we shall bring together all these concepts and return to the examination of time-series analysis.

It is important in beginning to consider some of the operational implications of using the forecasting models discussed so far. This should help in understanding the different approaches.

Regression models have high intuitive appeal because they "explain"; they focus on causality. Further, many variables can be brought into a solution simultaneously. Adding additional significant variables enables us to "chip away" at the unexplained variance, or mean squared error, until it reaches some "acceptable" level.

But there are problems with using regression. In addition to the typical statistical caveats of any technique, there are the operational difficulties of identifying which independent variables to use. There are virtually as many possibilities as there are things to measure. Further, data for such variables may be difficult or expensive to come by. Sales of GE light bulbs, for instance, are probably a function of many factors including consumer brand awareness. Collecting such information, despite any inherent imprecision, is expensive and time consuming.

Untold hours, weeks, or even months can be spent in finely developing a regression model. Once it is refined, considerable time and effort is still often required for periodic updating. This time and effort may be worth the price when the dollar values and the related costs of being wrong are large, such as at the overall firm level or perhaps the product group level. At the individual product level, however, it is often far too costly to spend such time and effort. This is especially true for multiproduct, multimarket companies like Texas Instruments. Nonetheless, forecasts are still needed and the more accurate the better, given time and cost constraints.

Time-series techniques, in contrast, may have less intuitive appeal since they focus only on time as the influencing factor. But the techniques have the decided advantage of being relatively simple to use. Further, the data are comparatively simple to collect. And they can generate relatively accurate forecasts. These techniques, consequently, are especially useful at the individual product level, where numerous forecasts are needed every period. The time-series techniques presented in Chapter 3 can be the simplest of all to use. Once the appropriate model is formulated, forecasts in subsequent periods can be made with only the previously determined weight(s), the most recent actual value, and its corresponding forecast. A new model is needed only when forecasts exceed the tracking signal.

The decomposition techniques presented in this chapter focus directly on examining the specific components of a time series one at a time. After each component is separately analyzed, they are then amalgamated into one combined forecast. Because decomposition looks at each specific component directly, the procedure often leads to better results than the methods of Chapter 3. Usually, however, decomposition techniques also involve a complete reanalysis of the series at the end of each period when new information is made available.

COMPONENTS

The traditional decomposition approach is to break a historical time series into four basic components: trend, seasonal, cyclical, and erratic. To illustrate, Figure 5.1 pictures Phone-Matic Co.'s quarterly sales of model 241-L telephone answering devices over the past four years.

The first component is that of *trend*. It consists of the long-run pattern of decline or growth of a set of historical data. An example of this element may be the diffusion of an innovation's acceptance or rejection through its potential market over the long run. For instance, the demand for hand-held electronic calculators in the United States has rapidly increased throughout the past decade. Figure 5.2 shows that sales of Phone-Matic's model 241-L have, in general, increased over the four-year historical series.

A second component is *seasonal variation*. This adjusts the forecast to reflect the effects of seasonal buying patterns. For example, the sale of swim wear is greater in the spring than in fall or early winter. When seasonal influence is taken into consideration, forecast accuracy may be improved for many products, even those in the industrial sector.

The length of the time period used in seasonal analysis varies and is dependent on such factors as buying patterns, production schedules, delivery schedules, and storage operations. Demand patterns may repeat themselves on a weekly or bimonthly basis, and the seasonal component should reflect a 7- or 14-day length. An example of weekly seasons may be demand for hunting licenses. A few weeks before the season starts,

Figure 5.1 Historical Sales of Phone-Matic Co.'s Model 241-L

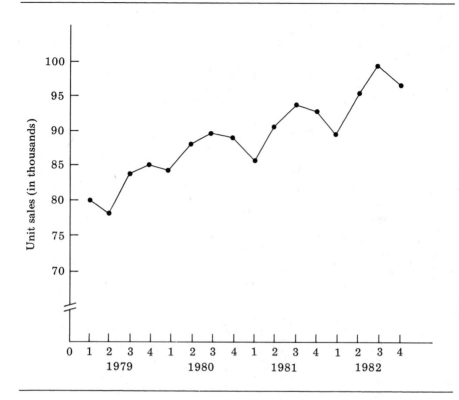

demand generally begins to accelerate and to change dramatically each week. In other situations, six months may be the appropriate season duration. An example of a lengthy duration may be demand for seasonal food products, such as vegetables.

Expert experience and judgment applied to the pattern of data fluctuations most often serve as the best guides for establishing appropriate lengths of time. Most often, however, seasonal lengths are either months or quarters, because these time periods correspond with calendar periods. Most people regulate their buying habits for many items on the basis of calendar periods. For example, the spring and early summer are traditionally periods in which many people search for new housing. Vacations, holidays, and other periods are all related to the calendar.

Figure 5.3 presents a graph reflecting quarterly seasonal fluctuations. Notice that sales vary throughout the entire series, but each corresponding season's changes are somewhat constant. Seasonal analysis examines the relationship of each corresponding season's effects on the forecast variable.

Figure 5.2 Historical Sales of Phone-Matic Co.'s Model 241-L

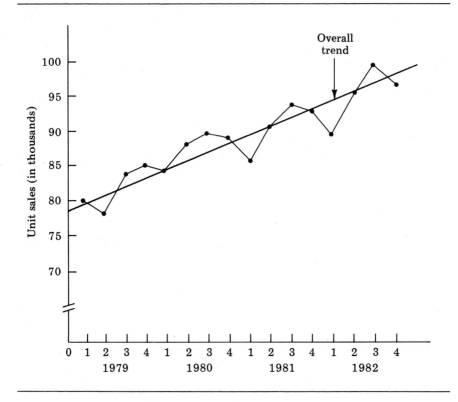

Figure 5.3 Seasonal Fluctuations

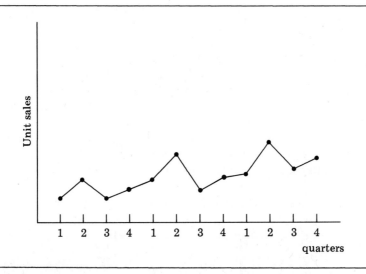

Third, *cyclical effects* are a basic component of time series. This is perhaps the most difficult to define. Figure 5.4 presents a graph containing a cyclical component.

Cyclical fluctuations ". . . comprise a series of repeated sequences, just as a wheel goes round and round."[1] However, the length of time of the fluctuation is different than that of the seasons. In Figure 5.4, the wavelike fluctuations are quite apparent but they are not related to the seasons. An example of a cyclical change in demand is the increase and then decline in demand for durable goods every few years. Some specific products that are especially vulnerable to cycles are homes, automobiles, and recreational vehicles.

The final component is the *erratic*. This element represents nonsystematic, or random, fluctuations of the data. Figure 5.5 illustrates the erratic in relation to all components. The erratic component is that which cannot be explained by the other components. In the long run, erratic components balance each other. For this reason and because they are random, they are not used to make the forecast; the erratic components are considered instead in analyzing historical data in order to calculate the remaining elements more accurately.

Figure 5.4 Cyclical Fluctuations

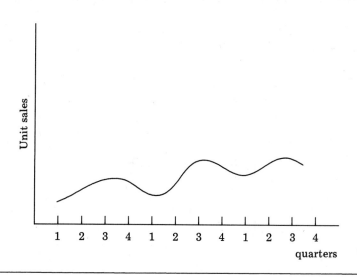

1. Ya-lun Chou, *Probability and Statistics for Decision Making* (New York: Holt, Rinehart and Winston, 1972), p. 491.

Figure 5.5 Erratic and Other Components

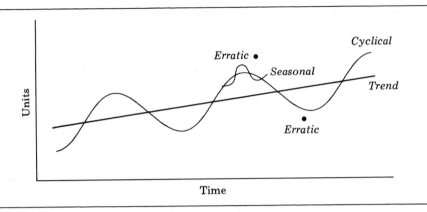

MODELS

Many possible models may be used to represent the time series being analyzed. The relationships may be linear or nonlinear. Several possible nonlinear functions were presented in Figure 4.8 in the preceding chapter. These and other functions are all possible candidates for the time-series model. However, linear analysis is most often employed in practice.

Linear time-series analysis may take two basic forms. The model may be additive or multiplicative. The additive model is as follows:

$$Y_t = T_t + S_t + C_t + E_t$$

where Y_t = the value of the time series at period t
T_t = the value of the trend component at period t
S_t = the value of the seasonal component at period t
E_t = the value of the erratic component at period t
C_t = the value of the cyclical component at period t

Using the same definitions in the multiplicative model, Y_t is the product of each of the components as follows:

$$Y_t = T_t \times S_t \times C_t \times E_t \qquad (5.1)$$

The latter model is most often used in actual situations because of computational ease and validity. The S, C, and E elements represent indices in this model. Accuracy is generally increased by using indices because relationships automatically remain in perspective as the value of the forecast variable fluctuates. The multiplicative model will be used in this chapter because it is the most commonly used in business.

CLASSICAL DECOMPOSITION

Decomposition involves the breaking down of a time series into its components. Each component is then analyzed separately in order to isolate its unique pattern of behavior and resulting influence on the forecast variable. Because each component is often found to have different behavior patterns over time, separate analysis often increases forecast accuracy.

Traditionally, four major steps are taken to decompose a time series. First, the seasonal component is determined and its effects are eliminated from the raw data. Second, the long-term trend is computed and its effects are eliminated from the deseasonalized data. Third, the erratic component is calculated and eliminated from the remaining data. Finally, the cyclical component is analyzed.

To illustrate, the Donnovax Corporation is trying to forecast sales of its brand of lawn chairs next month. Table 5.1 presents historical sales, as collected from company records.

As in regression analyses, the time span covered by the historical data varies according to the situation. The analyst must weigh the statistical desirability of more information and the increased probability that the underpinnings of the relationship change as time increases. Usually a time period exceeding four years is used, although four years are sufficient to demonstrate the analytical framework of time-series analysis.

Table 5.1 Unit Sales of the Donnovax Corporation

	Year			
Month	1979	1980	1981	1982
January	4,674	3,811	5,419	5,157
February	5,364	4,081	6,106	6,408
March	5,589	4,772	6,401	6,936
April	6,315	5,361	7,343	7,581
May	6,698	6,650	7,515	7,536
June	7,098	7,096	7,697	8,499
July	5,971	5,793	6,846	7,004
August	6,212	6,430	7,308	7,958
September	6,436	6,860	7,620	8,217
October	5,550	7,082	6,479	7,682
November	5,502	6,812	4,413	7,124
December	3,592	4,589	3,467	4,771
Total for year	69,001	69,337	76,614	85,873

Seasonal Component

The first step in the decomposition of the time series is to eliminate the seasonal effects from the historical data. This is done before attempting to isolate any of the other components because the removal of seasonal fluctuations allows the trend computation to be made from deseasonalized data, which increases forecast accuracy.

In selecting seasonal time periods, the analyst should first construct a scatter diagram and inspect it for seasonal patterns, as shown in Figure 5.6. In the case of the Donnovax Corporation, it is assumed that the relevant time period constituting a season is one month. This is based upon the following analysis.

Careful examination of Figure 5.6 reveals that sales tend to increase over the four-year period, but fluctuate widely within each year. The general direction of sales from one month to the next relates to changes experienced over the same period during other years. Therefore, each month within the year appears to contain a seasonal influence.

The objective of seasonal analysis is to develop an index of seasonal variation that meets the following criteria:

1. Only the seasonal components should be analyzed.
2. Changes in seasonal patterns should be reflected in the index. That is, the strength of a certain season's effect may be increasing or

Figure 5.6 Scatter Diagram of Donnovax Sales

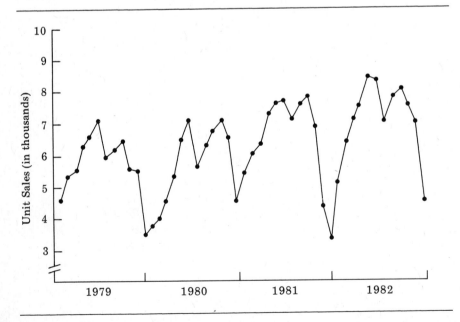

diminishing over the time period. The index should reflect this possible change. Since the model (Equation 5.1) is multiplicative, a value of 1.0 means no influence.

3. Erratic elements of the seasonal fluctuations should be dampened. One effective way to accomplish this is to average a seasonal impact.

One method that satisfies these criteria is termed the *ratio of a two-item average on a 12-month moving average.*[2] This method is accomplished by calculating a 12-month moving total (the sum of the monthly sales for 6 months before and after the midpoint between 2 months), summing two consecutive 12-month moving totals and then dividing by 24 months to obtain a 12-month moving average.

This latter figure is termed *centered* because it represents a moving average for the whole month, resulting from the 13-month time span that leads to the two-year moving total. This type of calculation is required because an even number of months exists in the year, and a simple 12-month moving average would represent the second half of 1 calendar month and the first half of the next. When the year is divided into an odd number of seasons, such as every 4 months, the simple moving-average procedure is sufficient. Table 5.2 presents data from Table 5.1 along with computations required for the calculation of seasonal indices for the example.

To illustrate, the sum of the first 12 seasons, a moving total, is $4,674 + 5,374 + \cdots + 3,592 + 69,001$. The sum of the next 12 seasons is $5,364 + 5,589 + \cdots + 3,811 = 68,138$. The figures in this column are considered uncentered. This is because they conform to the middle of one month to the middle of the next due to an even number of seasons. An average of 69,001, for instance, would correspond to the middle of June through mid-July.

The third column contains sums of two 12-month moving totals—to illustrate, $69,001 + 68,138 + 137,139$. These figures are considered centered as they now align with the beginning to the end of a month period. Notice that 24 monthly sales figures were summed to yield these values, although only 13 months of chronology were included. The first and thirteenth months were each counted once and the middle 11 months were counted twice.

The two-year moving totals are divided by 24 to determine the 12-month moving averages, which are also centered. Actual sales for a month is divided by the month's moving average, presented in column 5 of Table 5.2. This figure represents each individual month's seasonal index.

---

2. C. T. Clarke and L. L. Schkade, *Statistical Methods for Business Decisions* (Cincinnati: South-Western, 1969), pp. 657–690.

Table 5.2 Donnovax Corporation—Seasonal Index Computations

Month		Unit Sales (a)	Twelve-Month Moving Total (b)	Two-Year Moving Total (c)	Twelve-Month Moving Average, Centered (c ÷ 24) (d)	Ratio to Twelve-Month Moving Average (a ÷ d)
1979	Jan.	4,674				
	Feb.	5,364				
	March	5,589				
	April	6,315				
	May	6,698				
	June	7,098				
	July	5,971	69,001	137,139	5,714	1.045
	Aug.	6,212	68,138	134,993	5,625	1.104
	Sept.	6,436	66,855	132,893	5,537	1.162
	Oct.	5,550	66,038	131,122	5,463	1.016
	Nov.	5,502	65,084	130,120	5,422	1.015
	Dec.	3,592	65,036	130,070	5,420	0.663
1980	Jan.	3,811	65,034	129,890	5,412	0.704
	Feb.	4,081	64,856	129,930	5,414	0.754
	March	4,772	65,074	130,572	5,441	0.877
	April	5,361	65,498	132,528	5,522	0.971
	May	6,650	67,030	135,370	5,640	1.179
	June	7,096	68,340	137,677	5,737	1.237
	July	5,793	69,337	140,282	5,845	0.991
	Aug.	6,430	70,945	143,915	5,996	1.072
	Sept.	6,860	72,970	147,569	6,149	1.116
	Oct.	7,082	74,599	151,180	6,299	1.124
	Nov.	6,812	76,581	154,027	6,418	1.061
	Dec.	4,589	77,446	155,493	6,479	0.708
1981	Jan.	5,419	78,047	157,147	6,548	0.828
	Feb.	6,106	79,100	159,078	6,628	0.921
	March	6,401	79,978	160,716	6,697	0.956
	April	7,343	80,738	160,873	6,703	1.095
	May	7,515	80,135	157,871	6,578	1.142
	June	7,697	77,736	154,350	6,431	1.197
	July	6,846	76,614	152,966	6,374	1.074
	Aug.	7,308	76,352	153,006	6,375	1.146
			76,654			

continued

Table 5.2 Donnovax Corporation—Seasonal Index Computations *continued*

Month		Unit Sales (a)	Twelve-Month Moving Total (b)	Two-Year Moving Total (c)	Twelve-Month Moving Average Centered (c ÷ 24) (d)	Ratio to Twelve-Month Moving Average (a ÷ d)
	Sept.	7,620		153,843	6,410	1.189
	Oct.	6,479	77,189	154,616	6,442	1.006
	Nov.	4,413	77,427	155,875	6,495	0.679
	Dec.	3,467	78,448	157,698	6,571	0.528
			79,250			
1982	Jan.	5,157		158,658	6,611	0.780
	Feb.	6,408	79,408	159,466	6,644	0.964
	March	6,936	80,058	160,713	6,696	1.036
	April	7,581	80,655	162,513	6,771	1.120
	May	8,536	81,858	166,427	6,934	1.231
	June	8,499	84,569	170,442	7,102	1.197
	July	7,004	85,873			
	Aug.	7,958				
	Sept.	8,217				
	Oct.	7,682				
	Nov.	7,124				
	Dec.	4,771				

As in Table 5.2, it is most common to use monthly data in time-series analysis, for two reasons. For one, lengthier periods are less useful to management for the scheduling of production, anticipating cash flows, and so on. For another, shorter periods usually offer little opportunity for more accuracy. Weekly sales, to illustrate, are seldom measured as accurately as are monthly sales. But it is possible for other than monthly data to be most appropriate for a given application. Identifying the appropriate season lengths to use is part of the forecasting task. The procedures of decomposition are parallel regardless of the season lengths. We will primarily use monthly data for convenience.

Seasonal-Index Evaluation

A multitude of an individual month's seasonal ratios, or indices, is not useful to the analyst. Instead, these ratios must be analyzed in a manner that eliminates their variation from each other. One possible procedure used to develop a single seasonal index is to employ regression analysis to predict a specific month's value. For instance, if sales for January 1983 are to be forecast, a regression analysis would be performed on all the individual historical January ratios calculated. One of the principal advantages of using this procedure, in addition to its averaging effect, is that trends in seasonal effects may be detected. A disadvantage is that there may not be enough observations to make the regression of each season meaningful.

Probably a better method, especially when the number of observations is small, is to use some type of moving average. A moving average of each January index, for example, could be used to project an index for January 1983.

A third method is to employ an exponential-smoothing model. This might involve the use of a different weighting factor for each of the seasons.

Finally, a fourth method is to calculate the simple arithmetic average of individual ratios for each of the seasons. This method allows for the dampening effect of random fluctuations as do the previous methods. However, it does not allow for trends in seasonal effects to be included. This is not a serious weakness if the analyst is reasonably sure that seasonal effects are not changing substantially over time. Another rationale is that when historical information is rather limited and the other methods are therefore inappropriate, this method can be used. Without sufficient data, regression and moving-average methods are not possible. Table 5.3 applies this method to the Donnovax Corporation data.

Numbers in the first column of Table 5.3 represent the raw mean ratios for each respective month. For instance, the figure of 0.771 for January represents the arithmetic average of the three ratios for January in Table 5.2.

These averages, however, are not always final. The sum of all the average ratios must equal 12.0. This is because the seasonal indices serve as weighting factors which balance out throughout the year. Therefore, if the sum of the averages is either greater or less than 12.0, each of the average ratios must be adjusted by 12.0 divided by the total. The adjustment factor is 1.003, which is determined by multiplying each of the average ratios by 1.003. The adjusted values are those used for the seasonal indices.

Table 5.3 Computation of Donnovax Seasonal Indices

Month	Average of Month's Ratios (a)	Adjusted Index (a × 1.003)
Jan.	0.771	0.773
Feb.	0.880	0.883
March	0.956	0.959
April	1.062	1.065
May	1.184	1.188
June	1.210	1.214
July	1.037	1.040
Aug.	1.107	1.110
Sept.	1.156	1.160
Oct.	1.049	1.052
Nov.	0.918	0.921
Dec.	0.633	0.635
Total	11.963	12.000

$$\text{Adjustment} = \frac{12.000}{11.963} = 1.003$$

Deseasonalized Sales

The objective of developing seasonal indices is to be in a position to eliminate seasonal influences from the data, thus allowing more accurate trend analysis. To accomplish this, individual historical values are divided by the appropriate month's seasonal index. The resulting value may be expressed as $Y_t = T_t \times C_t \times E_t$. Column 3 of Table 5.4 presents the deseasonalized sales for the Donnovax Corporation.

Deseasonalized sales from Table 5.4 have been used to construct the scatter diagram presented in Figure 5.7. It is evident that fluctuation in sales remains after adjustment for the seasonal component. A component of Figures 5.7 and 5.6 reveals, however, that the magnitude of the fluctuations has been dampened by the seasonal adjustment.

Trend

The next major step in decomposition analysis is to determine the extent of a trend existing within the deseasonalized data. Several types

Table 5.4 Donnovax Corporation Deseasonalized Sales

Month		Unit Sales	Seasonal Index	Deseasonalized Unit Sales $Y_t = T_t \times C_t \times E_t$
1979	Jan.	4,674	0.773	6,047
	Feb.	5,364	0.883	6,075
	March	5,589	0.959	5,828
	April	6,315	1.065	5,930
	May	6,698	1.188	5,638
	June	7,098	1.214	5,847
	July	5,971	1.040	5,741
	Aug.	6,212	1.110	5,596
	Sept.	6,436	1.160	5,548
	Oct.	5,550	1.052	5,276
	Nov.	5,502	0.921	5,974
	Dec.	3,592	0.635	5,657
1980	Jan.	3,811	0.773	4,930
	Feb.	4,081	0.883	4,622
	March	4,772	0.959	4,976
	April	5,361	1.065	5,034
	May	6,650	1.188	5,598
	June	7,096	1.214	5,845
	July	5,793	1.040	5,570
	Aug.	6,430	1.110	5,793
	Sept.	6,860	1.160	5,914
	Oct.	7,082	1.052	6,732
	Nov.	6,812	0.921	7,396
	Dec.	4,589	0.635	7,227
1981	Jan.	5,419	0.773	7,010
	Feb.	6,106	0.883	6,915
	March	6,401	0.959	6,675
	April	7,343	1.065	6,895
	May	7,515	1.188	6,326
	June	7,697	1.214	6,340
	July	6,846	1.040	6,583
	Aug.	7,308	1.110	6,584
	Sept.	7,620	1.160	6,569
	Oct.	6,479	1.052	6,159
	Nov.	4,413	0.921	4,792
	Dec.	3,467	0.635	5,460

continued

Table 5.4 Donnovax Corporation Deseasonalized Sales *continued*

	Month	Unit Sales	Seasonal Index	Deseasonalized Unit Sales $Y_t = T_t \times C_t \times E_t$
1982	Jan.	5,157	0.773	6,671
	Feb.	6,408	0.883	7,257
	March	6,936	0.959	7,233
	April	7,581	1.065	7,118
	May	8,536	1.188	7,185
	June	8,499	1.214	7,001
	July	7,004	1.040	6,735
	Aug.	7,958	1.110	7,169
	Sept.	8,217	1.160	7,084
	Oct.	7,682	1.052	7,302
	Nov.	7,124	0.921	7,735
	Dec.	4,771	0.635	7,513

Figure 5.7 Donnovax Deseasonalized Sales

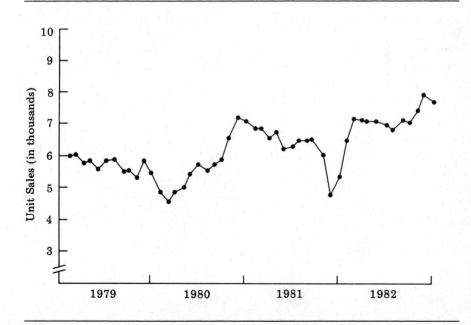

of procedures are available to determine trend. As with regression analysis, the relationship may be nonlinear or linear. Linear analysis is presented here.

Recall that the least-squares method is the procedure used to develop a trend equation. However, minor adjustments in the data are possible to make the analysis easier. The time periods may be coded so that the sum of the codes equals zero ($\Sigma t = 0$). This is done by assigning positive and negative codes to data before and after the midpoint of the time series. When there is an odd number of time periods, coding is accomplished as follows:

Date	Code t
1	-2
2	-1
3	0
4	1
5	2
	0

In the foregoing case, each code unit represents one time period. Another procedure is used when there is an even number of dates in the time series. In this instance, the midpoint is designated as possessing half of one of the periods nearest the middle and half of the other period. The unit of measurement when approached in this fashion represents one half of a time period. This coding procedure is accomplished as follows:

Date	Code t
1	-5
2	-3
3	-1
4	1
5	3
6	5
	0

Once the coding procedure has been applied to the data and the sum of the assigned X values equals zero, the equations used to determine the trend line become:

$$a = \frac{\Sigma Y}{n} \qquad (5.2)$$

and

$$b = \frac{\Sigma t Y}{\Sigma t^2} \qquad (5.3)$$

where
$\quad t$ = coded time data
$\quad Y$ = deseasonalized sales
$\quad n$ = the number of time periods
$\quad a$ = the y axis intercept
$\quad b$ = the slope of the trend line

Table 5.5 presents calculations for Donnovax.

Table 5.5 Donnovax Corporation, Trend and CXE Components

(1) Coded Dates t	(2) Deseasonalized Unit Sales Y_t	(3) tY_t	(4) t^2	(5) T_t	(6) (2 ÷ 5) $C_t \times E_t$
-47	6,047	$-284,209$	2,209	5,360	1.128
-45	6,075	$-273,375$	2,025	5,399	1.125
-43	5,828	$-250,604$	1,849	5,438	1.072
-41	5,930	$-243,130$	1,681	5,477	1.083
-39	5,638	$-219,882$	1,521	5,516	1.022
-37	5,847	$-216,339$	1,369	5,554	1.053
-35	5,741	$-200,935$	1,225	5,593	1.026
-33	5,596	$-184,668$	1,089	5,632	0.994
-31	5,548	$-171,988$	961	5,671	0.978
-29	5,276	$-153,004$	841	5,710	0.924
-27	5,974	$-161,298$	729	5,749	1.039
-25	5,657	$-141,425$	625	5,788	0.977
-23	4,930	$-113,390$	529	5,826	0.846
-21	4,622	$-97,062$	441	5,865	0.788
-19	4,976	$-94,544$	361	5,904	0.843
-17	5,034	$-85,578$	289	5,943	0.847
-15	5,598	$-83,970$	225	5,982	0.936

Table 5.5 Donnovax Corporation, Trend and CXE Components
continued

(1) Coded Dates t	(2) Deseasonalized Unit Sales Y_t	(3) tY_t	(4) t^2	(5) T_t	(6) $(2 \div 5)$ $C_t \times E_t$
-13	5,845	-75,985	169	6,021	0.971
-11	5,570	-61,270	121	6,059	0.919
-9	5,793	-52,137	81	6,098	0.950
-7	5,914	-41,398	49	6,137	0.964
-5	6,732	-33,660	25	6,176	1.090
-3	7,396	-22,188	9	6,215	1.190
-1	7,227	-7,227	1	6,254	1.156
1	7,010	7,010	1	6,292	1.114
3	6,915	20,745	9	6,331	1.092
5	6,675	33,375	25	6,370	1.048
7	6,895	48,265	49	6,409	1.076
9	6,326	56,934	81	6,448	0.981
11	6,340	69,740	121	6,487	0.977
13	6,583	85,579	169	6,525	1.009
15	6,584	98,760	225	6,564	1.003
17	6,569	111,673	289	6,603	0.995
19	6,159	117,021	361	6,642	0.927
21	4,792	100,632	441	6,681	0.717
23	5,460	125,580	529	6,720	0.813
25	6,671	166,775	625	6,759	0.987
27	7,257	195,939	729	6,797	1.068
29	7,233	209,757	841	6,836	1.058
31	7,118	220,658	961	6,875	1.035
33	7,185	237,105	1,089	6,914	1.039
35	7,001	245,035	1,225	6,953	1.007
37	6,735	249,195	1,369	6,992	0.963
39	7,169	279,591	1,521	7,030	1.020
41	7,084	290,444	1,681	7,069	1.002
43	7,302	313,986	1,849	7,108	1.027
45	7,735	348,075	2,025	7,147	1.082
47	7,513	353,111	2,209	7,186	1.046
0	301,105	715,719	36,848		

Data from Table 5.5 along with Equations 5.2 and 5.3 are used to solve for the least-squares function as follows:

$$a = \frac{301{,}105}{48} = 6{,}273 \text{ units}$$

and

$$b = \frac{715{,}719}{36{,}848} = 19.42 \text{ units}$$

Using the foregoing, expected trend values for sales T_t were calculated and presented in Table 5.5 with the following equation:

$$T_t = 6{,}273 + 19.42t \text{ units} \tag{5.4}$$

For example, calculations for January and February of 1979 ($t = -47$ and $t = -45$, respectively) are as follows:

Jan. 1979: $T_{-47} = 6{,}273 + 19.42(-47) = 5{,}360$ units

Feb. 1979: $T_{-45} = 6{,}273 + 19.42(-45) = 5{,}399$ units

The coded time periods in Table 5.5 must be used to calculate each of the T_t values.

The deseasonalized figures of Table 5.5 could now be used in a number of ways, all to see how sales relate to something ignoring seasonal influences. One would be in regression analysis to see how sales relate to one or more variables. Another would be to use one of the time-series models of Chapter 3. Still another is to continue with decomposition, as discussed below.

Erratic-Component Elimination

The sixth column of Table 5.5 ($C_t \times E_t$) presents a combination of the cyclical and erratic components for each period. These were obtained by dividing the deseasonalized sales (column 2) by the trend value T_t. The next major step in the analysis is to eliminate the erratic component, thereby yielding the cyclical indices.

Again, several techniques are available to accomplish this task. One involves calculation of a moving average of the combined cyclical and erratic indices. The analyst must select the number of time periods to average in this calculation. The longer the time span being averaged, the greater is the capability of the procedure to eliminate erratic

fluctuations. The longer the time span being averaged, the more dampening the effect on true cyclical fluctuations. This procedure, including
the foregoing steps, is termed the classical decomposition method.

Table 5.6 presents the results of the classical decomposition method
for the Donnovax example. The third column contains a three-month
moving average of the combined $C_t \times E_t$ component of Table 5.5; the
fourth column is the trend, calculated with Equations 5.2 and 5.3; and
the fifth column contains the seasonal factors. The next column presents
the corresponding forecasts. These are the products of the corresponding
$C_t \times T_t \times S_t$ values. Finally, the last two columns contain the actual
values and the forecast errors. Figure 5.8 graphically illustrates how well
the calculated forecasts match the actual values.

Figure 5.8 Graph on Donnovax Sales and Classical Decomposition
Forecasts

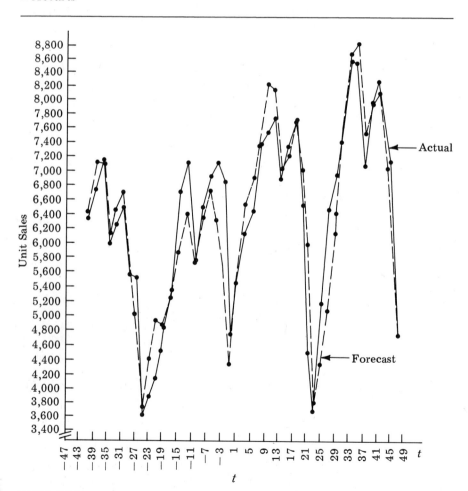

Table 5.6 Classical Decomposition of Donnovax Sales

t	$C_t \times E_t$	Three-Month Moving-Average Estimate of C_t	T_t	S_t	Forecast $C_t \times T_t \times S_t$	Actual	Error, Actual Minus Forecast
-47.000	1.128	—	—	—	—	—	—
-45.000	1.125	—	—	—	—	—	—
-43.000	1.072	—	—	—	—	—	—
-41.000	1.083	1.108	5476.779	1.065	6462.705	6315.000	-147.705
-39.000	1.022	1.093	5515.619	1.188	7161.942	6698.000	-463.942
-37.000	1.053	1.059	5554.460	1.214	7140.955	7098.000	-42.955
-35.000	1.026	1.053	5593.300	1.040	6125.333	5971.000	-154.333
-33.000	0.994	1.034	5632.140	1.110	6464.230	6212.000	-252.230
-31.000	0.978	1.024	5670.979	1.160	6736.214	6436.000	-300.214
-29.000	0.924	0.999	5709.819	1.052	6000.721	5550.000	-450.721
-27.000	1.039	0.965	5748.659	0.921	5109.205	5502.000	392.795
-25.000	0.977	0.980	5787.500	0.635	3601.561	3592.000	-9.561
-23.000	0.846	0.980	5826.340	0.773	4413.684	3811.000	-602.684
-21.000	0.788	0.954	5865.180	0.883	4940.721	4081.000	-859.721
-19.000	0.843	0.870	5904.020	0.959	4925.899	4772.000	-153.899
-17.000	0.847	0.826	5942.859	1.065	5227.871	5361.000	133.129
-15.000	0.936	0.826	5981.699	1.188	5869.769	6650.000	780.231
-13.000	0.971	0.875	6020.539	1.214	6395.315	7096.000	700.685
-11.000	0.919	0.918	6059.380	1.040	5785.010	5793.000	7.990
-9.000	0.950	0.942	6098.220	1.110	6376.418	6430.000	53.582
-7.000	0.964	0.947	6137.060	1.160	6741.680	6860.000	118.320
-5.000	1.090	0.944	6175.899	1.052	6133.209	7082.000	948.791
-3.000	1.190	1.001	6214.739	0.921	5729.497	6812.000	1082.503
-1.000	1.156	1.081	6253.579	0.635	4292.674	4589.000	296.326
1.000	1.114	1.145	6292.420	0.773	5569.325	5419.000	-150.325

Table 5.6 Classical Decomposition of Donnovax Sales *continued*

t	$C_t \times E_t$	Three-Month Moving-Average Estimate of C_t	T_t	S_t	Forecast $C_t \times T_t \times S_t$	Actual	Error, Actual Minus Forecast
3.000	1.092	1.153	6331.260	0.883	6445.847	6106.000	-339.847
5.000	1.048	1.121	6370.100	0.959	6848.104	6401.000	-447.104
7.000	1.076	1.085	6408.939	1.065	7405.686	7343.000	-62.686
9.000	0.981	1.072	6447.779	1.188	8211.477	7515.000	-696.477
11.000	0.977	1.035	6486.619	1.214	8150.370	7697.000	-453.370
13.000	1.009	1.011	6525.460	1.040	6861.128	6846.000	-15.128
15.000	1.003	0.989	6564.300	1.110	7206.221	7308.000	101.779
17.000	0.995	0.996	6603.140	1.160	7629.001	7620.000	-9.001
19.000	0.927	1.002	6641.979	1.052	7001.334	6479.000	-522.334
21.000	0.717	0.975	6680.819	0.921	5999.207	4413.000	-1586.207
23.000	0.813	0.880	6719.659	0.635	3754.945	3467.000	-287.945
25.000	0.987	0.819	6758.499	0.773	4278.716	5157.000	878.284
27.000	1.068	0.839	6797.340	0.883	5035.720	6408.000	1372.280
29.000	1.058	0.956	6836.180	0.959	6267.436	6936.000	668.564
31.000	1.035	1.038	6875.020	1.065	7600.124	7581.000	-19.124
33.000	1.039	1.054	6913.859	1.188	8657.201	8536.000	-121.201
35.000	1.007	1.044	6952.699	1.214	8811.961	8499.000	-312.961
37.000	0.963	1.027	6991.539	1.040	7467.521	7004.000	-463.521
39.000	1.020	1.003	7030.380	1.110	7827.129	7958.000	130.871
41.000	1.002	0.997	7069.220	1.160	8175.692	8217.000	41.308
43.000	1.027	0.995	7108.060	1.052	7440.287	7682.000	241.713
45.000	1.082	1.016	7146.899	0.921	6687.608	7124.000	436.392
47.000	1.046	1.037	7185.739	0.635	4731.772	4771.000	39.228

Summary: MSE = 284,619 units   Square root of MSE = 533,497 units

Forecast

Forecasts for future periods under the classical approach are made in a manner identical to the way the series was decomposed in the first place, one component at a time. To illustrate, the forecast for January 1983 ($t = 49$) is as follows:

$$T_{49} = 6{,}273 + (19.42)(49) = 7{,}224.58 \text{ units}$$

$$S_{49} = S_{\text{Jan.}} = 0.773$$

$$C_{49} = \frac{1.027 + 1.082 + 1.046}{3} = 1.052$$

$$\text{Forecast} = 7{,}224.58 \times 0.773 \times 1.052 = 5{,}875 \text{ units}$$

The square root of the MSE is useful in estimating a confidence interval. At a 95% confidence level, such an interval is approximately $2\sqrt{\text{MSE}}$. Thus, such a forecast for January would be 5875 ± 1067 units, or a range of $4{,}808 \leqslant$ actual value $\leqslant 6942$ units.

If the confidence interval is too great for management to accept, then some other techniques must be explored. One possibility is to regress the $C_t \times E_t$ factors against some predictor variables, such as the unemployment rate, GNP, and so on. A very accurate forecasting model can result from linking decomposition and regression in such a way, providing, of course, that a strong association is found among the variables. Another possibility is to use a more advanced form of decomposition. The following is a discussion of such a method.

CENSUS II DECOMPOSITION

Census II is a widely employed decomposition procedure that was developed by the federal government. The method has been used quite successfully by both the Federal Reserve System and the Bureau of the Census for forecasting national trends in income, consumption, sales of durables, and so on. The complete computer program for the method can be acquired from the government, and modified versions are available elsewhere.

Census II does not differ much from classical decomposition. Where it does differ is in methodological execution. The procedure uses a multitude of moving averages of varied numbers of base periods in the decomposition. This provides many benefits. For one, it enables more detailed analyses of seasonal factors. Adjustments can be made for extreme values that appear to be anomalies. These are termed *outliers*. Considerably improved results can be derived by removing such outliers from influencing the model.

Another benefit is that the process helps an analyst forecast the cycle. Many assumptions are required in the classical method, and one involves the appropriate number of periods to include in the base periods for the moving averages. But a different number may be far more effective. Census II evaluates many scenarios and helps the analyst identify the best of these.

Essentially, Census II is a large computer program that is rather cumbersome to use by the inexperienced user. The program and its use can be quite complex. Further, there is not a wide program availability. Thus, we shall not focus on the program directly.[3]

However, it is possible to closely approximate the Census II process and results by using a combination of techniques already discussed, plus the explicit removal of outliers. In fact, we have found that this process provides even better results than Census II in some cases. For lack of a better name, we take the liberty of calling the procedure a modified version of Census II. We will continue with the Donnovax example for illustration.

Outlier Removal

Reconsider the seasonal indices that were calculated for Donnovax and presented in Table 5.2. These are repeated in a systematic way in Table 5.7. The top two sections of the table contain the raw indices of Table 5.2. Look at them closely. For example, consider those for November. Two of the values are greater than 1.0, whereas one is below 0.7. It is apparent that other irregularities are also evident.

Such irregularities could occur for numerous reasons. Unusual weather conditions, strikes, economic conditions, or even pure chance could be the cause of a particular extreme value at one time period. Including them, as we did in the classical approach, only serves to bias the factors.

One way to exclude outliers is to eliminate the extreme values within a season. For the example, this results in the medial value being selected because there are only three ratios for each season. When more periods are available, it is wise to use the average of all the ratios within a season after the outliers are removed.

Notice how this eliminates the obvious outliers, such as for November. But also notice that it does not materially affect the results where there may not be obvious outliers, as in June. The selected ratios are then adjusted so that their total sums to 12.0, at the bottom of the table.

3. Interested readers are referred to: R. L. McLaughlin, *Time Series Forecasting: A New Computer Technique for Company Sales Forecasting* (Chicago: American Marketing Association, 1962).

The adjusted ratios are then used to deseasonalize sales in a manner identical to classical decomposition. Table 5.8 presents the results. To illustrate with $t = -47$, actual sales equal 4674 (the next to last column) $\div 0.771 = 6062.257$.

Table 5.7 Donnovax, Seasonal Factors Adjusted to Eliminate Outliers

July	Aug.	Sept.	Oct.	Nov.	Dec.
1.045	1.104	1.162	1.016	1.015	0.663
0.991	1.072	1.116	1.124	1.061	0.708
1.074	1.146	1.189	1.006	0.679	0.528

Jan.	Feb.	Mar.	April	May	June
0.704	0.754	0.877	0.971	1.179	1.237
0.828	0.921	0.956	1.095	1.142	1.197
0.780	0.964	1.036	1.120	1.231	1.197

Month	Medial Ratios	Adjusted
Jan.	0.780	0.771
Feb.	0.921	0.911
March	0.956	0.946
April	1.095	1.083
May	1.179	1.166
June	1.197	1.184
July	1.045	1.033
Aug.	1.104	1.092
Sept.	1.162	1.149
Oct.	1.016	1.005
Nov.	1.015	1.004
Dec.	1.663	0.656
Total	12.133	12.000

$$\text{Adjustment} = \frac{12.000}{12.133} = 0.989$$

Table 5.8 Modified Census II Decomposition of Donnovax

t	S	Deseasonalized Sales	T_t	$C_t \times E_t$	C_t	Forecast $T_t \times S_t \times C_t$	Actual	Error Actual-Forecast
-47.000	0.771	6062.257	5362.522	1.130	1.098	4539.684	4674.000	134.316
-45.000	0.911	5888.035	5400.704	1.090	1.112	5471.084	5364.000	-107.084
-43.000	0.946	5908.033	5438.887	1.086	1.096	5639.124	5589.000	-50.124
-41.000	1.083	5831.024	5477.068	1.065	1.051	6234.178	6315.000	80.822
-39.000	1.166	5744.426	5515.250	1.042	1.051	6758.749	6698.000	-60.749
-37.000	1.184	5994.933	5553.433	1.080	1.062	6982.927	7098.000	115.073
-35.000	1.033	5780.251	5591.614	1.034	1.022	5903.210	5971.000	67.790
-33.000	1.092	5688.646	5629.796	1.010	1.020	6270.689	6212.000	-58.689
-31.000	1.149	5601.393	5667.979	0.988	1.011	6584.144	6436.000	-148.144
-29.000	1.005	5522.389	5706.160	0.968	0.989	5671.607	5550.000	-121.607
-27.000	1.004	5480.079	5744.343	0.954	0.961	5542.394	5502.000	-40.394
-25.000	0.656	5475.610	5782.524	0.947	0.935	3546.768	3592.000	45.232
-23.000	0.771	4942.932	5820.706	0.849	0.741	3325.432	3811.000	485.568
-21.000	0.911	4479.692	5858.889	0.765	0.834	4451.430	4081.000	-370.430
-19.000	0.946	5044.397	5897.070	0.855	0.944	5266.224	4772.000	-494.224
-17.000	1.083	4950.139	5935.252	0.834	0.898	5772.232	5361.000	-411.232
-15.000	1.166	5703.259	5973.435	0.955	0.926	6449.611	6650.000	200.389
-13.000	1.184	5993.244	6011.616	0.997	0.932	6633.744	7096.000	462.256
-11.000	1.033	5607.938	6049.798	0.927	0.954	5961.966	5793.000	-168.966
-9.000	1.092	5888.279	6087.980	0.967	0.941	6255.836	6430.000	174.164
-7.000	1.149	5970.409	6126.162	0.975	0.929	6539.191	6860.000	320.809
-5.000	1.005	7046.767	6164.345	1.143	1.073	6647.411	7082.000	434.589
-3.000	1.004	6784.860	6202.526	1.094	1.172	7298.437	6812.000	-486.437
-1.000	0.656	6995.428	6240.708	1.121	1.117	4572.890	4589.000	16.110
1.000	0.771	7028.535	6278.891	1.119	1.117	5407.422	5419.000	11.578

continued

Table 5.8 Modified Census II Decomposition of Donnovax *continued*

t	S	Deseasonalized Sales	T_t	$C_t \times E_t$	C_t	Forecast $T_t \times S_t \times C_t$	Actual	Error Actual-Forecast
3.00	0.911	6702.525	6317.072	1.061	1.080	6215.238	6106.000	-109.238
5.00	0.946	6766.385	6355.254	1.065	1.058	6360.768	6401.000	40.232
7.00	1.083	6780.240	6393.437	1.060	1.080	7478.017	7343.000	-135.017
9.00	1.166	6445.111	6431.618	1.002	1.015	7611.753	7515.000	-96.753
11.00	1.184	6500.846	6469.801	1.005	0.994	7614.280	7697.000	82.720
13.00	1.033	6627.299	6507.982	1.018	0.994	6682.408	6846.000	163.592
15.00	1.092	6692.309	6546.164	1.022	1.001	7155.557	7308.000	152.443
17.00	1.149	6631.854	6584.347	1.007	1.001	7572.978	7620.000	47.022
19.00	1.005	6446.767	6622.528	0.973	0.986	6562.460	6479.000	-83.460
21.00	1.004	4395.418	6660.710	0.660	0.775	5182.697	4413.000	-769.697
23.00	0.656	5285.062	6698.893	0.789	0.713	3133.258	3467.000	333.742
25.00	0.771	6688.716	6737.074	0.993	0.899	4669.660	5157.000	487.340
27.00	0.911	7034.029	6775.256	1.038	0.972	5999.433	6408.000	408.567
29.00	0.946	7331.924	6813.438	1.076	1.111	7160.962	6936.000	-224.962
31.00	1.083	7000.000	6851.620	1.022	1.092	8102.970	7581.000	-521.970
33.00	1.166	7320.755	6889.803	1.063	1.032	8290.578	8536.000	245.422
35.00	1.184	7178.210	6927.984	1.036	1.064	8727.703	8499.000	-228.703
37.00	1.033	6780.251	6966.166	0.973	1.022	7354.360	7004.000	-350.360
39.00	1.092	7287.547	7004.349	1.040	1.113	8513.055	7958.000	-555.055
41.00	1.149	7151.436	7042.530	1.015	1.108	8965.785	8217.000	-748.785
43.00	1.005	7643.781	7080.712	1.080	1.036	7372.292	7682.000	309.708
45.00	1.004	7095.617	7118.895	0.997	1.051	7511.884	7124.000	-387.884
47.00	0.656	7272.866	7157.076	1.016	0.972	4563.579	4771.000	207.421

Summary: MSE = 97,161 units

Square root of MSE = 311.7 units

The trend column, T_t, results from applying Equations 5.2 and 5.3. The following are relevant calculations:

$$a = \frac{\Sigma Y}{n} = \frac{300470.4}{48} = 6259.8 \text{ units} \qquad (5.5)$$

$$b = \frac{\Sigma tY}{\Sigma t^2} = \frac{703456.5}{36848} = 19.091 \text{ units} \qquad (5.6)$$

Thus, the estimated trend value $T_{-47} = 6259.8 + (19.091)(-47) = 5362.52$.

The combined $C_t \times E_t$ column was obtained in the usual manner, that is, by dividing the deseasonalized sales estimates by the trend estimate. To illustrate, $C_{-47} \times E_{-47} = 6062.257 \div 5326.522 = 1.130$.

The next task in this modified version of Census II is to evaluate the combined $C_t \times E_t$ component to estimate the cycle. Figure 5.9 graphs the $C_t \times E_t$ components of Table 5.8 against time. The solid line connects the individual components. Notice that there seems to be somewhat of a pattern evident, though not an exact one. There are 16 periods between peaks 2 and 4, 21 between peaks 1 and 4 and 3 and 5, and 22 periods between peaks 4 and 6. Similarly, there are 16 periods between troughs 2 and 3 and 21 periods between troughs 1 and 3.

What Census II does is use several moving averages to evaluate such patterns. In this modified version, Winters's exponential smoothing is used instead. In other words, we can use Winters's model in place of the moving averages. We could also use some other exponential-smoothing model, but that of Winters has the advantage of enabling us to focus specifically on estimating cyclical indices. Instead of treating the indices of the model as seasonals, we treat them as cyclical. (Refer to Chapter 3 for a discussion of Winters's model.)

With monthly data, it is customary to use 12 as the number of periods for seasonality with Winters's. This is because sales tend to follow some monthly pattern. When using the method to evaluate cycles, however, another base should be used, since seasonality has already been considered.

The exact number of periods to use to demarcate a full repetition of cycles is somewhat fuzzy. Certainly, the process of identifying cycles is imprecise. But the observations made of Figure 5.9 provide a good start. The computer program for the model (Appendix 3.E) was used to evaluate the combined $C_t \times E_t$ components of Figure 5.9. Several different cycle lengths—all those between 16 and 24 periods long—were attempted. As it turned out, a cycle length of 22 yielded the smallest MSE. The optimal weights were $\alpha = 0.6$, $\beta = 0.1$, and $\gamma = 0.1$. And the forecasts over the historical series are presented in column 6 of Table 5.8 as the estimated C_t values. These values are also plotted in Figure 5.9. The dashed line connects the points. It is clear in the figure that the method is a good indicator of the combined $C_t \times E_t$ component. Therefore, we shall use Winters's model to forecast the cycle.

Returning to Table 5.8, the forecasts over the time series appear in column 7. They are simly the product of $T_t \times S_t \times C_t$. The last two columns contain the actual and error values over the series. Figure 5.10 graphs the forecast and actual values. Notice that the forecasts are much closer to the actuals than in classical decomposition (see Figure 5.8).

Finally, the bottom of Table 5.8 presents the summary statistics. Notice the dramatic improvement in the MSE over that of classical decomposition. This is further evidence that this model fits the data better than the less complex model.

Figure 5.9 Donnovax Corporation $C_t \times E_t$ Combined Components

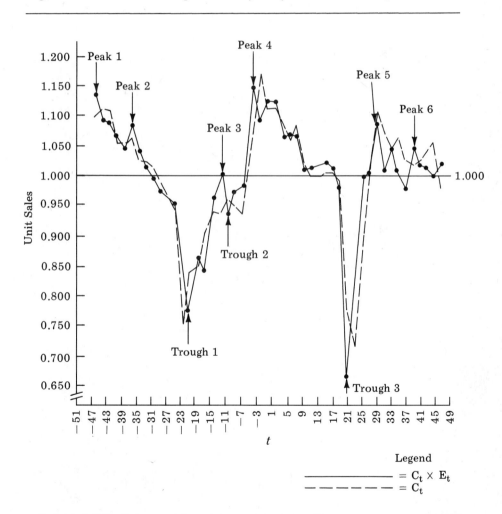

Figure 5.10 Graph of Donnovax Sales and Modified Census II Results

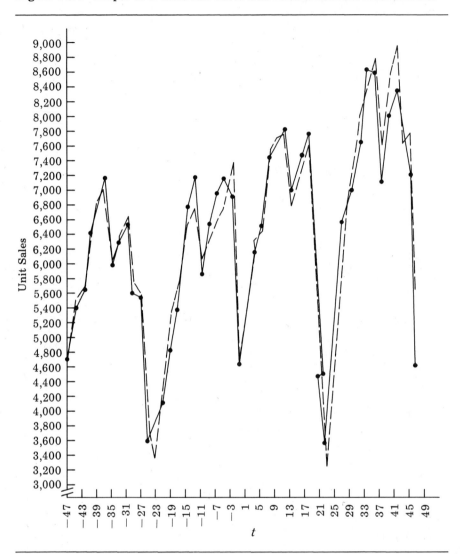

Forecast

Forecasts for future periods with the modified Census II method are made in a manner similar to classical decomposition. One difference is that the output of the Winters's model is used in estimating the cyclical factor. Table 5.9 presents selected computer output of the model (from Appendix 3.E) for the Donnovax example.

Table 5.9 Forecasts of Cyclical Factors for Donnovax, Based on Winters's Model

Forecasts for the Next 22 Seasons:			
1	1.036	12	0.816
2	1.027	13	0.636
3	1.012	14	0.649
4	0.971	15	0.764
5	0.953	16	0.766
6	0.959	17	0.824
7	0.905	18	0.812
8	0.888	19	0.792
9	0.876	20	0.790
10	0.861	21	0.761
11	0.841	22	0.845

The forecast for January 1983 ($t = 49$), to illustrate, is made as follows:

- Trend, from Equations 5.5 and 5.6

$$T_{49} = 6259.8 + (19.09)(49) = 7195.26$$

- Seasonal, from Table 5.7 for January

$$S_{49} = 0.771$$

- Cycle, from Table 5.9 for the next period

$$C_{49} = 1.036$$

$$\text{Forecast} = T_{49} \times S_{49} \times C_{49}$$
$$= 7195.26 \times 0.771 \times 1.036 = 5{,}747 \text{ units}$$

Successive forecasts are made in a similar manner.

Caution

We have discussed many forecasting techniques, several of which are potentially useful for cases like Donnovax. Winters's model itself could be used on the raw data. In fact, Winters's model used on the actual historical sales values results in a MSE = 272,622 units at the optimal weights of $a = 0.9$, $\beta = 0.1$, and $\gamma = 0.3$ (from the program in Appendix 3.E). The forecast for January 1983 is 5,034 units.

The classical decomposition approach results in a MSE of 284,619 units and a forecast of 5,875 units for January 1983. And the modified Census II method results in a MSE = 97161 units and a forecast of 5,747 units. Thus, there are considerable differences in the results of the various methods.

The differences stem largely from the treatment of the cyclical factor. Winters's model ignores cycle, whereas the decomposition models do not. Consequently, it is tempting to accept automatically the decomposition results as they treat cyclical influences explicitly. Further, the MSE is generally smaller from a decomposition model than a pure smoothing model. This can further lead to blind acceptance of the results.

Such a conclusion can be unwarranted, however. The process of evaluating and forecasting a cycle is not exact. Unlike seasonal influences, which tend to remain relatively stable over time for most products, cyclical influences tend to vary somewhat erratically over time. To illustrate, there was a short recession in 1970, a stronger, but still relatively short, recession in 1973, a boom period of six plus years, then a major recession in 1979 through 1982. The point is that such business cycles tend to be somewhat erratic over time. And trying to estimate their influence in a decomposition model can lead to faulty conclusions. The cycles are likely not to repeat themselves in exactly the same way. Thus, one must be very cautious in interpreting the results.

One can take several steps to try to avoid the problem in practice. One is to *validate* a model. This involves the building of a model on the first half to two-thirds of the historical series. The model is then used to see how well it forecasts the remaining of the series. The model that best forecasts the remaining series is chosen to forecast the future.

Another step that can be taken is to use regression analysis to analyze the cycle components. This is the preferred step, because if the economic causes of the cycle can be isolated, using them to forecast future cyclical factors can lead to the best results. The problem is that such detailed analysis is generally cost-prohibitive on an individual product basis. Such models should be explored for aggregate forecasts, such as at the corporate division or major product group level. But the cost of obtaining greater accuracy is generally not worth the benefit at the individual product level.

Third, one can recognize that the past is a better predictor of the near future than of the distant future. Time-series techniques are best used on monthly or weekly data. Forecasts for the next period or two generally have the greatest reliability. By reapplying the method and updating all the calculations at the end of each period, one is able to provide revised forecasts on a continuing basis. Further, such revision generates factors adjusted to reflect any emerging changes in historical patterns. With experience, one is then able to assess how well a particular approach is working in fact.

Finally, one can recognize that no model can substitute for good, solid business judgment. Managers cannot hide under a rock and blindly follow any model. They should use judgment and be familiar with good information sources like the *Wall Street Journal, Business Week,* and so on. If it appears that new cycles are emerging, their adjustments should be made judgmentally to model outputs. Certainly models do not replace judgment, they only help to assure systematic analysis. In this regard, all the time-series techniques can be invaluable tools.

OTHER TIME-SERIES TECHNIQUES

The methods presented in this book are the workhorses of time-series techniques. They have received the most widespread attention, and their use is growing. But there are also other methodologies, which are covered below.

Spectral Analysis

One approach to evaluating time-series data is through the use of *spectral analysis.* The technique was originally developed in engineering, where wavelengths and frequencies are analyzed into their components. With economic data, a time series is broken down into its components in terms of individual exact sine and cosine waves after the series is smoothed. The transformations required to develop the smoothed series are made by means of integral transformations. Spectral analysis has not experienced widespread business application, because most business (and other social) data are aperiodic. Business cycles rise and fall; but not in as regular a manner as required by this form of analysis.[4]

Box-Jenkins

A very complex time-series analysis approach is termed *Box-Jenkins.*[5] The general model is a complicated mix of autoregressive (a variable

---

4. For further reference, see R. B. Blackman and J. W. Tukey, *The Measurement of Power Spectra* (New York: Dover Press, 1958).
5. G. E. P. Box and G. M. Jenkins, *Time Series Analysis: Forecasting and Control,* rev. ed. (San Francisco: Holden Day, 1976).

regressed against itself at a previous time) and moving-average methods. Essentially, therefore, smoothing models are special cases of the general model.

The approach begins by correlating values at period t with those at $t - 1$, then values at t with $t - 2$, then with $t - 3$, and so on. The results help in identifying systematic patterns. For example, assume that monthly data containing strong seasonality are analyzed. It is logical to expect that the correlation would be high between the values at t and those at $t - 12$.

Similarly, if there is a strong trend in existence, we would expect that there would be a stronger correlation the closer the previous period is to t. For example, values at t should correlate more strongly with those at $t - 1$ than those at $t - 2$. In turn, those at $t - 2$ should correlate more strongly with those at t than those at $t - 3$, and so on.

On the other hand, the autocorrelations may be *stable*. This means that values at t correlate about equally with those at previous periods. This suggests that there is neither trend nor seasonality. Or there may be no strong correlations except between values at t and $t - 12$. This, of course, suggests no trend but a seasonal pattern of 12. Such correlations, therefore, help the analyst in selecting the right kind of model for the series.

The approach continues until the autocorrelations become relatively stable. Suppose a strong linear trend exists, for example. One would expect that the above autocorrelations would go from strongly positive to strongly negative between values at t and values at $t - v$, as v becomes large.

But, one could define a new variable termed *1st difference*, or d'. The definition is

$$d'_t = x_t - x_{t-1} \qquad (5.7)$$

where x_t is the actual value at period t.

One could then correlate d'_t with d'_{t-1} and with d'_{t-2}, and so on. If the trend is linear, and ignoring any seasonality, one would expect that the autocorrelations would now become stable. This is because the differences are values that are affected by the slope.

To illustrate, consider the following linear time series:

$$5, 10, 15, 20, 25, 30, 35 \qquad d'_1 = 5, d'_2 = 5, \cdots, d'_6 = 5$$

Thus, the autocorrelations would be stable.

Now, if the first difference is unstable, one could take the second difference or d''_2, defined as

$$d''_t = d'_t - d''_t \qquad (5.8)$$

A quadratic trend is signaled by stable autocorrelations of the second differences, assuming that the previous autocorrelations were unstable.

This process could continue for many such differences. But usually no more than the third differences is analyzed. Any further differencing might only result in too complex a model to be considered very reliable for forecasting future periods.

Autocorrelation analysis represents only the identification phase of Box-Jenkins. The next phase is to estimate the parameters of the moving-average autoregressive model. This essentially involves finding the weighting factors that produce the smallest MSE. Further, autocorrelations of the residuals, or errors, are analyzed to ensure that there is no systematic pattern.

Needless to say, Box-Jenkins involves calculations of tremendously cumbersome proportions. Thus, a relatively large, high-speed computer is essential. Evidence seems to suggest that the approach works well for large aggregate forecasts.[6] But other studies suggest that the method does not outperform simpler and less costly techniques at the individual product level.[7]

As a practical matter, we have found there to be several operational problems with the approach in many companies. In the first place, we have found that many of the computer packages that have been acquired do not work properly. This is a real problem because the programs are so complex that they are difficult to fix. Second, the model tends to be very complex, causing one to be suspicious of future forecasts. Third, relatively highly skilled users are generally needed, as well as large amounts of both user and computer time. Finally, the results tend to be not much, if any, better than those of other techniques, especially decomposition.

We have, however, found the autocorrelation analysis to be very useful in identifying the existence and shape of a trend, along with seasonal and cyclical lengths. Once these are known for a particular product, the choice of which smoothing or decomposition model to use, along with certain parameters like season length, becomes simplified.

A very similar approach is termed *adaptive filtering*.[8] The major difference from Box-Jenkins is that the weights in the adaptive filtering model change with every observation, whereas those of Box-Jenkins do not.

6. H. O. Steckler, "Forecasting with Economic Models: An Evaluation," *Econometrica*, 36 (July–October 1968), 437–63.
7. M. D. Guerts and I. B. Ibrahim, "Comparing the Box-Jenkins Approach with the Exponential Smoothed Forecasting Model Application to Hawaii Tourist," *Journal of Marketing Research*, 12 (May 1975), 182–188.
8. For further reference, see B. Widrow, "Adaptive Filtering I: Fundamentals," Center for Systems Research, Technical Report No. 6764-6 (Stanford, Calif.: Stanford University, 1966). Also see S. Makridakis and S. C. Wheelwright, *Interactive Forecasting: Univariate and Multivariate Methods*, 2nd ed. (San Francisco: Holden-Day, 1978), Chapter 17.

Other Smoothing Techniques

There are also several other smoothing techniques used in time-series analysis. Adaptive response rate exponential smoothing is one of them.[9] The method is similar to single exponential smoothing except that the weight changes from period to period. The basis of this change is dependent upon the ratio of the actual error values to the absolute error values. In essence, both are smoothed to reduce bias in consistent under- or overestimation.

Another is termed Holt's two-parameter linear exponential smoothing.[10] The technique is something like Winters's model in that a separate smoothing constant is used for the slope and another for the intercept. Both of these smoothing methods can be useful, but the improved initialization schemes and optimal weight routines contained in Chapter 3's appendices virtually eliminate the need for the different approaches.

Several other time-series techniques have been proposed. Most tend to be some variant of those discussed in this book, including regression against time. All the important basic essentials concerning time-series analysis have been covered in this chapter.

SOME LIMITATIONS

Time-series analysis is not without its limitations. Perhaps most important, the underpinnings of the analysis may change. In time-series analysis, it is assumed that time is causally related to the forecast variable, but this may not be the case. The argument is the same as that presented in Chapter 4 for correlation. The underlying relationship between the variables may change either throughout the time series or in the future. However, if time-series analysis produces forecasts more accurately than other methods, it should, of course, be used.

The second limitation is that of the quantitative procedures. Time series is perhaps more loaded with subjective judgment than other methods. For example, the derived seasonal indices are naturally dependent on the time period, defined as a season. It would be virtually impossible to analyze all candidates for seasons, and all seasons would not necessarily contain the same duration of time. Once judgment enters the analysis, results become subject to bias. Perhaps seasons other than

9. D. W. Trigg and D. H. Leach, "Exponential Smoothing with an Adaptive Response Rate," *Operational Research Quarterly*, 18 (1967), 53–59.
10. C. C. Holt, *Forecasting Seasonal and Trends by Exponentially Weighted Moving Averages* (Pittsburgh: Carnegie Institute of Technology, 1957).

those selected would best describe the behavior of the variable being analyzed. This limitation is compounded by the analyst's tendency to regard output as quantitative and beyond criticism. The forecaster must realize that, at best, time-series analysis represents a synergy between judgment and quantitative methods.

Finally, there is a tendency to regard time-series analysis as an either/or procedure. That is, many analysts use either time series or another tool, perhaps regression analysis. There is no reason to assume that these methods cannot be combined, either jointly or separately. A joint combination is one in which one technique is used as input factor to a second procedure. The trend portion of time series, or another portion, for that matter, could be based on multiple-regression analysis where time is considered as only one of the inputs. In the Donnovax case, other variables might be income levels, temperature, or amount of sunshine, in addition to time periods. Much greater accuracy may be gained in this manner. In a separate combination, two or more techniques are used separately. Each individual forecast is then used as a check on the reasonableness of others. An almost infinite number of quantitative and judgmental mixtures exist, which, in turn, make forecasting an art and extremely adaptive.

SUMMARY

This chapter concludes the investigation into time-series analysis. Attention was focused on decomposition techniques, which involve the breaking down of a time series into specific components which are then separately analyzed. The customary components studied are the seasonal, trend, cyclical, and erratic factors. Swimsuit sales, for example, are heaviest in months leading into summer. Trend involves the long-run change in the overall series. The cycle component refers to something between seasonal and trend, sort of a mid-run pulsation.

First discussed was the classical decomposition approach, which involves the use of centered moving averages to extract seasonal indices. These indices are then evaluated and used to deseasonalize the historical values. Next, least squares is used to extract the trend. The ratios of the deseasonalized values to the trend values are then defined as the combined cycle and error factors. Finally, a moving average is used to estimate the cyclical factor.

Next, the Census II method was discussed. This technique involves the extensive use of multiple moving averages. It also has the capability of removing outliers, or sporadic occurrences, from consideration.

In a modified version of Census II, outliers were omitted by ignoring the extremes when calculating seasonal indices. Further, instead of using many different moving averages, Winters's exponential smoothing was used to evaluate the cyclical component.

Perhaps the most important limitation of time-series analysis is that historical time relationships may not hold true in the future. This is especially true regarding the evaluation of cyclical fluctuations, where time relationships are not exact. It is possible to develop a more sophisticated model to overcome this limitation by linking regression analysis to decomposition to forecast the cycle. Management must decide whether or not the benefit is worth the cost.

DISCUSSION QUESTIONS

1. How do decomposition techniques differ from other time-series methods?
2. Contrast the classical and the modified Census II decomposition models.

The following table refers to questions 3, 4, and 5:

Historical Sales of the Crabner Company

Year	Quarter	Sales (in Millions of Dollars)
1979	1	80.0
	2	77.7
	3	64.7
	4	61.2
1980	1	90.6
	2	82.9
	3	75.4
	4	52.5
1981	1	85.6
	2	78.6
	3	71.0
	4	68.2
1982	1	90.7
	2	81.3
	3	75.9
	4	70.4

3. Use the classical method of decomposition to forecast sales in the first two quarters of 1983.

4. Use the modified Census II method to forecast sales in the first two quarters of 1983.

5. Use Winters's exponential smoothing on the raw data itself to forecast sales in the first two quarters of 1983. Assess the differences between the forecasts and the methods of this and the previous two questions. Which forecast would you use?

The following data may relate to the chapter's Donnovax example.

t	Interest Rate	t	Interest Rate	t	Interest Rate	t	Interest Rate
-47	11.8	-23	13.0	1	12.3	25	12.3
-45	12.0	-21	13.2	3	12.3	27	12.5
-43	11.9	-19	13.2	5	12.4	29	12.9
-41	11.8	-17	13.5	7	12.5	31	12.8
-39	12.0	-15	13.6	9	12.5	33	12.8
-37	11.9	-13	13.1	11	12.4	35	12.6
-35	12.1	-11	13.0	13	12.4	37	12.7
-33	12.2	- 9	13.2	15	12.3	39	13.0
-31	12.5	- 7	13.2	17	12.2	41	12.9
-29	12.3	- 5	13.1	19	12.0	43	12.2
-27	12.4	- 3	12.7	21	11.9	45	13.1
-25	12.5	- 1	12.6	23	11.3	47	12.7

6. Do the interest rates above relate very strongly with the combined $C_t \times E_t$ factors found in decomposition? If so, use regression analysis to estimate the cyclical factors. (Use the results of the modified Census II method.) How do the results compare with decomposition? Which method would you use to forecast sales?

The following table refers to questions 7 and 8.

Season	Sales	Season	Sales
1	38.2	1	43.6
2	24.3	2	29.8
3	54.8	3	57.4
4	58.3	4	61.3
1	40.6	1	42.8
2	28.8	2	32.4
3	56.4	3	59.8
4	60.7	4	68.7

7. Forecast sales for the next period using the classical decomposition approach.
8. Forecast sales for the next period using the modified Census II approach.

RECOMMENDED READINGS

Blackman, R. B., and J. W. Tukey. *The Measurement of Power Spectra.* New York: Dover Press, 1958.

Box, G. E. P., and G. M. Jenkins. *Time Series Analysis, Forecasting and Control.* Rev. ed. San Francisco: Holden-Day, 1976.

Brown, R. G. *Smoothing, Forecasting and Prediction of Discrete Time Series.* Englewood Cliffs, N.J.: Prentice-Hall, 1963.

Chambers, J. C. et al. "How to Choose the Right Forecasting Technique." *Harvard Business Review,* 49 (July–August 1971), 45–74.

Chou, Ya-lun. *Probability and Statistics for Decision Making.* New York: Holt, Rinehart and Winston, 1972.

Guerts, M. D., and I. B. Ibrahim. "Comparing the Box-Jenkins Approach with the Exponential Smoothed Forecasting Model Application to Hawaii Tourists." *Journal of Marketing Research,* 2 (May 1975), 182–188.

Holt, C. C. *Forecasting Seasonal and Trends by Exponentially Weighted Moving Averages.* Pittsburgh: Carnegie Institute of Technology, 1957.

McLaughlin, R. L. *Time Series Forecasting: A New Computer Technique for Company Sales Forecasting.* Chicago: American Marketing Association, 1962.

Makridakis, S., and S. C. Wheelwright. *Interactive Forecasting: Univariate and Multivariate Methods.* 2nd ed. San Francisco: Holden-Day, 1978.

Steckler, H. O. "Forecasting with Economic Models: An Evaluation." *Econometrica,* 36 (July–October 1968), 437–463.

Thomopolis, N. *Applied Forecasting Methods.* Englewood Cliffs, N.J.: Prentice-Hall, 1980.

Trigg, D. W., and D. H. Leach. "Exponential Smoothing with an Adaptive Response Rate." *Operational Research Quarterly,* 18 (1967), 53–59.

CASE 5: COPPALA BELT COMPANY

The Coppala Belt Company produces rubber belts for manufacturing facilities throughout the United States. The company's headquarters is located in Detroit; distribution warehouses are located in Los Angeles, Dallas, and Cleveland. Most of the firm's customers are manufacturers and represent a variety of industries.

Coppala has approximately fifty competitors, most of whom are located in the northeastern and midwestern United States. Four of the competitors manufacture a similar product line and service the same consumers. Competition, therefore, often focuses on pricing and delivery since the offerings of one firm are essentially the same as those of others. Coppala has been effective in the area of customer service— deliveries are rapid and reliable, and sales representatives go to considerable effort to insure customer satisfaction.

The rubber belt industry has been relatively stable over the past few decades. It has not suffered the same degree of economic expansion and contraction as have other industrial-goods industries, such as machine parts, steel, and heavy equipment. It is expected that this trend will continue into the future.

The firm has determined that an effective pricing strategy is for them to absorb some freight charges. Prices are quoted at the buyer's warehouse, but Coppala does not charge customers the full cost of the freight from its warehouse to the customer. This has enabled the company to compete even in markets where they have no warehouses.

Another factor in the firm's success is prompt delivery. Coppala owns its own fleet of trucks, making it possible for them to provide the on-time delivery desired by customers. Competitors rely upon for-hire carriers.

Sales of Coppala Belt Co. (in Thousands)					
1977	1	$147	1980	1	$172
	2	$189		2	$197
	3	$120		3	$119
	4	$122		4	$126
1978	1	$166	1981	1	$163
	2	$199		2	$180
	3	$114		3	$106
	4	$115		4	$105
1979	1	$168	1982	1	$179
	2	$197		2	$191
	3	$115		3	$120
	4	$118		4	$133

The company has used regression analysis for forecasting purposes, but this technique has not been sufficiently accurate. At present, management is considering the use of decomposition time series.

1. Is decomposition time series a potentially good forecasting tool for this firm? Why or why not?
2. What decomposition model would appear to be the best? Support your answer. What are your sales forecasts for each quarter of 1983?
3. What are the possible disadvantages of Coppala's use of decomposition time series?

Chapter 6
Forecasting by Surveys and Test Markets

INTRODUCTION

Two means of providing forecasts, in addition to those discussed previously, are surveys and test markets. Both techniques are in wide use, especially when firms are considering either introducing new products or expanding the sales areas of existing products. The problem is to decide whether the product can be expected to generate sufficient sales volume to justify distribution.

This chapter outlines the process of using surveys and test markets as forecasting tools, explaining the rationale and weaknesses of their use and the methodologies involved.

The chapter, however, does not cover all or even most of the important materials offered in a marketing research course. It provides only an overview of this key topic.

SURVEYS

Surveys consist of systematic efforts to elicit information from specified groups, such as consumers, distributors, or economists. Some well-known examples are the public opinion surveys conducted by firms like Gallup and Robinson. These enterprises solicit the opinions of individuals about such issues as inflation, tax increases, unemployment, and hazards to the physical environment, like air pollution. Similarly, surveys can be used for sales forecasting purposes. The analyst can, for instance, survey the buying plans of purchasing agents or the probable reaction of ultimate consumers to a new product, both toward the end of estimating future sales.

Rationale for Surveys

In general, analysts use surveys for forecasting purposes in cases where historical data either are judged not to be indicative of the future or do not exist at all. The auto industry illustrates the first case. The demand for cars with large engines increased steadily from the early 1950s through the mid-1970s. Rapid and hefty increases in gasoline prices, however, quickly reversed the trend. Thus, forecasts based on historical trends were wrong, and Detroit was left with untold numbers of "gas guzzlers" in inventory.

A prime example of the second case is the introduction of a new product or brand, as in 1980, when executives of the Beatrice Foods Company, Clark Division, tried to determine if they should introduce a "sunpower" candy bar. In this situation, historical data, such as past sales or market share, are not available, thus making the use of regression and trend-analysis techniques impossible. Analysts might elect to employ judgmental methods under such circumstances, of course. Or they might assume that sales of the product in question will parallel past sales of similar products. These methods can lead to serious error, however. The makers of television sets, for instance, discovered that color set sales were much lower and did not grow as fast as did those of black-and-white sets following the introduction of each. Those firms that assumed sales of color sets would grow in a fashion similar to sales of black-and-white sets were seriously in error.

One use of the survey technique by an advertising agency located in a medium-sized city in the Rocky Mountains illustrates its application to new-product planning. In 1983, the agency had one person on its payroll who had some experience and training in marketing research. Management was considering offering marketing research services to local firms but was uncertain about the revenue that could be expected from research offerings. A survey of over a hundred local firms was conducted. Respondents were asked if they would use research consulting, what kinds of research they were interested in, and the approximate amounts of money they would be willing to pay. The survey indicated that there was virtually no interest in the research product in the community. The level of sales estimated by the technique was below that required to justify acquiring research facilities and personnel. The new-product idea was dropped from further consideration.

In another case, a savings and loan association was, in 1980, trying to decide what services to make available to its shareholders. It conducted a survey that showed substantial demand for NOW accounts, interest-bearing checking accounts.

Surveys like these are an alternative when historical data do not exist. In some cases, historical data may be available but may not provide useful indicators of the future. For example, they may have been inaccurately tabulated, recorded, or transcribed. More commonly, conditions may have changed to the degree that the past is no longer a valid predictor of the future: rivals may have introduced new products or inflation may have changed consumer spending patterns.

There are many examples of external changes that counterindicate the use of past data. Consider the case of TKD, Inc., a large manufacturer of kitchen and bathroom cabinets. In the past, conditions in the industry have remained fairly stable, and the analyst has been able to use time series with a high degree of accuracy in estimating both short- and long-run sales. The analyst has decided that time series is not likely to produce accurate estimates for 1985, however, because

1. Lumber prices have risen significantly, producing higher kitchen cabinet prices.
2. One large competitor has increased the size of its sales force substantially.
3. Residential construction activity appears to be decreasing at an abnormally rapid rate.
4. Cabinet imports are advancing considerably.

Under these conditions, the manufacturer probably would not rely on past data for forecasting purposes. Instead, a survey might satisfy the firm's need.

In many cases, surveys are employed as adjuncts to estimates based on historical data. In this instance, the analyst generates a forecast by using data but feels insecure as to its validity. Under these circumstances, a survey forecast may help in testing the validity. If, for instance, the survey produces approximately the same estimate as does a regression analysis, the legitimacy of the latter is reinforced.

Finally, surveys frequently produce valuable input for other methods of forecasting. Chief among these is model building and simulation, the subject matter of Chapter 8.

Weaknesses of Surveys

Surveys, like all forecasting techniques, are not without shortcomings. Certainly, one is a possible lack of predictive power. This is not an inherent weakness, but one that can result from inadequate data-collection procedures. Thus, many surveys ask the respondents for predictions of their own behavior or that of others. Experience indicates that respondents frequently find this to be a difficult if not impossible task.[1] Individuals cannot easily provide valid answers to questions like these:

1. Would you purchase a new menthol-flavored toothpaste?
2. How many boxes of presweetened cereal will you buy next year?
3. Will you purchase a golf club set next year?
4. How likely is it that you will switch brands of canned soup?

Commonly, industrial buyers are capable of responding to forecast surveys more readily than are ultimate consumers, since buyers attempt

---

1. Charles J. Stokes, *Economics for Managers* (New York: McGraw-Hill Book Company, Inc., 1979), p. 279.

to objectively anticipate their future needs through forecasts and subjective estimates. Still, they often find it difficult to estimate their future procurement behavior, for it may diverge radically from the forecast should company policy or tactics or environmental forces change. Buyers, for instance, may alter purchase volumes in response to changes in sales and production levels in their own company or in prices and terms of sales of suppliers. In 1980, for instance, buyers for the Brunswick Corporation sharply cut back on purchases of supplies for its marine motor business.[2]

Another problem with some surveys is high cost. Expenses are incurred in determining the survey plan, training and compensating interviewers or mailing questionnaires, and tabulating, analyzing, and interpreting data. These expenses may be substantial, especially when the sample size is large and/or tabulation and analysis are extensive, for example, when long and intricate questionnaires are used.

Surveys can be very time consuming. More than a year may pass from the time the survey plan begins until the responses have been received and processed into forecast data. For this reason, surveys may be inappropriate when estimates must be prepared within very short time periods.

To summarize, surveys have shortcomings as well as advantages. An analyst contemplating their use should consider the impact of their advantages and disadvantages as they apply to a particular forecasting task.

Survey Procedure

Following are the steps involved in generating survey forecasts:

1. Defining informational needs
2. Determining appropriate information sources
3. Ascertaining modes of gathering data
   a. Personal interviews
   b. Telephone interviews
   c. Direct mail
   d. Observation
   e. Panels and group interviews
4. Developing and pretesting the measuring instrument
5. Formulating the sample
6. Acquiring information
7. Tabulating and analyzing the data

2. "Brunswick: Caught in a Shrinking Consumer Market for Boat Motors," *Business Week*, October 27, 1980, pp. 139–140.

Defining Informational Needs

The first step to be undertaken by the analyst is to determine precisely the nature of the information needed. This is probably the most important phase of the survey, because if it is poorly implemented, all subsequent steps will be to no avail.

Obviously, informational needs vary in dimension from one survey to another. Among the types of information sought are: (1) future buying plans, (2) attitudes toward the forecaster's firm, (3) preferences of one brand or product over others, and (4) sales or production expected to be generated by the respondents' concern.

The choice of a particular type of sought information depends on the assumptions about reality that have been adopted by the analyst. The forecaster for the Rollins-American Corporation, a large producer of black-and-white and color television sets, for instance, believes that consumer buying plans accurately predict actual television purchases for following years. As a corollary of this belief, the forecaster each year forwards the following questionnaire to a representative sample of consumers:

1. Do you plan to purchase a new television set next year?
    Yes _____ No _____
2. If yes, what type? black and white _____ color _____
3. What brand do you favor at this time? _____

Other forecasters attempt to estimate sales by indirect methods, for example, by assessing consumers' attitudes toward the brand. They assume that attitudes and purchasing are closely related—highly favorable attitudes signifying probable purchases and negative or neutral attitudes signaling improbable purchases. Under these circumstances, the analyst's sought information might consist of consumers' favorableness of attitude toward the Rollins-American brand, as measured by scales such as the following:

> *Instructions:* Please evaluate Rollins-American television sets on the following scale. Indicate, on each line, your feelings about Rollins-American by placing an X on the appropriate blank. If you have a strong feeling, place an X in the blank next to the description (Have a clear picture X _ _ or _ _ X Have an unclear picture). If your feeling is not strong or is neutral, place an X on the middle space.

Rollins-American Television Sets

Have a clear picture	_ _ _	Have an unclear picture
Have a clear tone	_ _ _	Have an unclear tone
Have a durable picture tube	_ _ _	Have a short-lived picture tube

Have a good warranty	_ _ _	Have a poor warranty
Are low priced	_ _ _	Are high priced
Are easy to service	_ _ _	Are difficult to service

Consumer evaluations of Rollins-American television sets, when compared to evaluations of rivals' sets, can be used as indicators of future shares of market expected to be achieved by each. These, in turn, can be applied to industry forecasts for individual brands. If, for instance, numerous current owners of very old Rollins-American sets have very negative attitudes toward the brand, the future company market share is likely to decline.

We have illustrated only two of the many possible types of sought data. We are not implying that these are necessarily superior to others; each analyst must determine the kinds of information that appear to be most predictive for the brand and company in question.

Determining Appropriate Information Sources

Once analysts have ascertained the nature of the sought information, they are faced with determining information sources; they must decide which individuals are to be surveyed. More than one source may be expected to have and be willing to divulge the sought information.

In the Rollins-American example, the analysts could survey company dealers, other dealers, jobbers, or ultimate consumers to forecast sales. Once the analysts have chosen a general source—such as ultimate consumers—they are faced with a choice of specific individuals. Should both husbands and wives be surveyed? If the general source is company dealers, should the survey include retail managers, merchandise managers, or buyers?

The choice of general and individual source is best accomplished by answering the questions: (1) Who is most likely to be in possession of the sought information in the form specified? (2) Who is most likely to divulge this information? Rollins-American might decide that heads of household are the best source of information regarding attitudes toward brands of television sets since, in most families, they exercise paramount authority in committing the family to major purchase decisions. Conversely, if past Rollins-American survey experience has indicated that men are reluctant to provide meaningful attitudinal information, wives might be surveyed.

Ascertaining Modes of Gathering Data

Following the determination of source, the analyst chooses a mode or modes of acquiring survey information. The basic methods are the following:

1. Personal interview
2. Telephone interviews
3. Direct mail
4. Observation
5. Panels and group interviews

Personal Interviews   In personal interviewing, interviewers contact potential respondents, solicit their cooperation, and ask them to respond to questions. This technique can be effective in eliciting information, as many individuals respond more readily to personal interviews than to mail questionnaires or telephone interviews. Furthermore, the interviewer is in a position to answer questions, to probe for additional information, and, if desired, to explain the goals of the interview.

The chief weakness of personal interviewing is its cost. Expenditures are required to recruit, select, train, motivate, compensate, supervise, and pay expenses for interviewers.

Another drawback of personal interviewing is that it is time consuming, especially when respondents are dispersed geographically. Although interviews in and of themselves can be time consuming, cost in time is magnified when interviewers must engage in extensive travel. It is not unusual for them to be unable to complete more than ten interviews in an eight-hour day. Both the time and the expenses required in interviewing may be minimized by contracting field work to a professional interviewing organization.

Telephone Interviews   An alternative to conducting interviews in person is to use the telephone for reaching a large number of individuals in a short period of time, especially when they are geographically dispersed.

On the other hand, refusal rates are higher for telephone than for personal interviews, since it is relatively easy for an individual to hang up the telephone when asked to respond to an interviewer. Telephone surveys are often mistaken for selling schemes disguised as surveys. Also, some households either do not own telephones or have unlisted numbers. Finally, the length of the telephone interview must be short or the cooperation of the respondent is likely to be lost.

Direct Mail   Like the telephone method, mail surveys are effective in reaching subjects who are widely separated geographically. When many questions are to be asked, mail is preferable to telephone because respondents can take their time in filling out the questionnaire. The cost of a mail survey may be moderate, provided that repeated waves of questionnaires do not have to be forwarded to nonrespondents.

Unfortunately, response to mail surveys often is small. It is common to experience response rates as low as 10 to 20% in surveys of households. The characteristics of nonrespondents can also differ significantly from respondents. Respondents tend to possess higher levels of education and income and, in many cases, interest in the survey's subject matter. Analysts may often increase response through such devices as monetary rewards, sending second and third waves of questionnaires to nonrespondents, sending cover letters signed by the researchers, enclosing stamped and self-addressed return envelopes, explaining the worth of the survey's objectives, and promising a copy of the survey results to those who respond.[3]

Observation   The analyst may obtain information by observing rather than by questioning. In a literal sense, observation is not really a survey method, although its implementation closely resembles that of surveys. Observation may be conducted mechanically by electronic traffic counters at retail store entrances or counters of automobile traffic, or human observers may be used. They may engage in such activities as observing customers in retail store parking lots, for example.

Observation is advantageous in that it is relatively objective; it is free from weaknesses in questionnaire design, interviewer bias, and invalid responses. However, its use is limited in forecasting; it primarily provides a data base from which projections can be formulated. The A. C. Nielsen Company, for instance, provides estimates of retail sales of specific brands through the employment of retail audits (inventory counts). These allow Nielsen to estimate sales based on the following equation:

$$\text{Sales} = \text{beginning inventory} + \text{purchases} - \text{ending inventory}$$

The sales estimates can be accumulated for a period of years and then be injected into a mathematical model, such as trend analysis. Of course, the observations as such do not constitute forecasts.

Panels and Group Interviews   Panels are made up of a group of individuals, such as consumers or retailers, who agree to provide information to the sponsoring organization over a period of time. Normally, members record in a diary which brands were purchased and where, prices paid,

3. See Chris T. Allen, Charles D. Schowe, and Gostg Wijk, "More on Self-Perception Theory's Foot Technique in the Pre-Cell/Mail Survey Setting," *Journal of Marketing Research*, 17 (November 1980), 498–502; and William J. Whitmore, "Mail Survey Premiums and Response Bias," *Journal of Marketing Research*, 13 (February 1976), 46–50.

and other variables, and submit this information on a periodic basis, such as every two weeks.

Some commercial research concerns offer panel information services to others for a fee. Examples are Market Research Corporation of America and National Family Opinion, Inc. These enterprises maintain very large panels and provide questionnaire formulation and data processing facilities to clients. On the other hand, company panels are maintained by some firms engaged in forecasting. One Yugoslavian cigarette manufacturer, for instance, supports a panel of consumers who agree to smoke and evaluate on an ongoing basis the quality of existing and new brands offered by the sponsor.

The unique attribute of a panel is that it is a source of longitudinal information—information provided over a period of time—as contrasted with conventional one-time survey information. The panel sponsor is able to develop trends in brand usage, attitudes toward its brands, changes in shopping patterns, and other variables indicative of future sales. Panel members are readily available for submission of periodic surveys, and their response rate is much more favorable than that of the population at large.

Obviously panels are not the answer to all survey needs. They are not necessary in cases where longitudinal information is not needed, that is, where one-shot surveys are adequate. The cost of panels can be high, especially since members usually are remunerated for their services. Finally, the analyst must take steps to ensure that panel members behave like typical consumers and do not come to view themselves as experts in consumer matters.

Panels are not to be confused with *focus group*-interview surveys. In the latter, the interviewer simultaneously interviews a number of individuals, usually 5 to 15, in a group-discussion setting. The interviewers introduce the subject matter and then act as discussion leaders and moderators. They ask few direct questions, however. Rather, their function is to galvanize group discussion and to see that it does not diverge too far off the subject matter or languish because of lack of interest. Group discussion can be advantageous in that the interaction process often brings forth sincere opinions rather than the stereotyped and rationalized responses sometimes elicited in conventional interviews and questionnaires. In the group interview, comments by one interviewee often stimulate others to reveal information that otherwise might be held in confidence—the group setting can be a synergistic one.

Group interviews may be time consuming and expensive. In many cases, the group members must be compensated in money or in merchandise. Considerable time is involved in organizing the group as well as in conducting the sessions. Some respondents are reluctant to join in group discussion or to reveal facts that might be considered personal or potentially embarrassing.

When considering which survey method to use, analysts should consider the applicability of each to the specific forecasting need. Each method has its applications for certain products, territories, and time periods and is not necessarily suited to others.

Developing and Pretesting the Measuring Instrument

The acquisition of survey information requires some sort of measuring instrument, such as a questionnaire, interview guide, or observation guide. The first is a written document on which information is recorded by the respondent, whereas interview and observation guides are forms that set forth instructions to interviewers and observers and provide space for their notations.

Table 6.1 is a mail questionnaire designed to gather information on consumers' expected automobile purchases for the upcoming year.

Table 6.1 Automobile Purchase Survey

The Decker and Stone research firm is conducting a survey to estimate consumers' expected automobile purchases for the 1983 calendar year. We would appreciate your completing this questionnaire and forwarding it in the enclosed stamped envelope. As compensation for your efforts, please accept the fifty-cent piece which is affixed to this letter. Do not place your name on the questionnaire; we will completely disguise the sources of information. There is no way in which information given confidentially by you can be revealed.

Automobile-Purchase Questionnaire

1. What make and model of automobile do you presently own?

   Make _____
   Model _____

2. How old is the automobile?

   _____

3. How long have you owned it?

   _____

4. This may be difficult, but think ahead about the upcoming year—1983. What is the probability that you will purchase an automobile during this year?

   100 percent   _____
   90–99 percent   _____
   80–89 percent   _____
   70–79 percent   _____
   60–69 percent

continued

Table 6.1 Automobile-Purchase Survey   *continued*

50–59 percent _____	Manager, official, or proprietor _____
40–49 percent _____	Supervisor _____
30–39 percent _____	Skilled blue-collar worker _____
20–29 percent _____	Unskilled blue-collar worker _____
10–19 percent _____	White-collar worker _____
0–9 percent _____	Farm owner or worker _____
No chance at all _____	Professional _____
Don't know _____	Armed services _____
	Retired _____
	Other (specify) _____

5. If you do purchase next year, what make and model will you buy?

Make _____
Model _____
Don't know _____

6. Age of head of household

15–20 _____
21–26 _____
27–32 _____
33–38 _____
39–44 _____
45–50 _____
51–56 _____
57–62 _____
63–68 _____
69 and over _____

7. Total number of persons in household

1 _____
2 _____
3 _____
4 _____
5 _____
6 _____
7 _____
8 _____
9 _____
10 _____
11 or more _____

8. Occupation of head of household

9. Marital status

Married _____
Single _____

10. If married, do both wife and husband work?

Yes _____
No _____

11. Education

Less than four years of elementary school _____
Less than eight years of elementary school _____
Less than two years of high school _____
Less than four years of high school _____
High school graduate _____
Less than two years of college _____
Less than four years of college _____
College graduate—bachelor's degree _____
College graduate—advanced degree

Written Instructions   Analysts frequently issue written instructions to interviewers. These may be placed on the questionnaire or on a separate document. The automobile-purchase survey, if conducted by interviews rather than by mail, might include instructions for selecting respondents, obtaining cooperation, conducting the interview, and handling finished questionnaires. In conducting the interview, for instance, the interviewer might be directed to do the following:

1. Avoid placing inflection on particular words in asking questions.
2. Ask the questions in the order given.
3. Allow the interviewee to view the questionnaire as the interviewer asks the questions.
4. Avoid suggesting answers to respondents.
5. Record entries in an unambiguous manner; for example, place marks clearly on intended spaces (X) not in a position where the marking is not clear (_ X _).
6. Avoid taking more than 30 minutes for an interview.
7. Attempt to conduct the interview in a friendly and informal manner that keeps the respondent at ease.
8. Encourage respondents to provide accurate information and to avoid guesses.
9. If respondents are reluctant to respond to some questions, remind them that the results of the interview are to be held in strict confidence and that their responses will not be identified with them.
10. Be alert for obvious cases of dishonest replies; for example, a respondent lives in a home obviously in bad repair and in a low-income neighborhood, and has a 1975 Ford automobile parked in front of the home, yet claims to own a 1983 Cadillac.

In determining which items to place on a questionnaire, the analysts must ask themselves, "Exactly what do we need to know in order to prepare a forecast?" The tendency to include interesting but nonessential questions should be avoided.

Types of Questions   Three kinds of questions appear on the questionnaire—identification, demographic, and direct. Identification information is used to identify individual respondents. A questionnaire number serves to identify each response.

Demographic information is used to categorize the responses in order to divide them into meaningful subclasses to permit comparison. Questions 1-3 and 6-11 in the questionnaire in Table 6.1 are classification questions. Responses to question 6 will allow the analyst to determine automobile purchase plans of persons in various age groups, whereas responses to question 7 will allow categorization for various family sizes.

Direct information is that which is actually used to provide forecasts. Questions 4 and 5 request such information. Tabulation of these will elicit expected purchases of automobiles.

The analyst has several question forms from which to choose. One form is the dichotomous, or two-category, question, as exemplified by marital status:

Married   _____
Single   _____

Where more detail is desired, multiple-choice questions can be employed:

What kind of automobile do you now own? (Check one.)

Two-door sedan   _____
Four-door sedan   _____
Compact   _____
Subcompact   _____
Station wagon   _____
Sports car   _____

When the analyst desires direct comparison, ranking can be used. For example:

Rank the following station wagon brands, in order of their relative desirability to you:

Brand   *Rank (in descending order of desirability)*

Fairmont   _____
Cutlass   _____
Aries   _____
Reliant   _____
Skylark   _____
Zephyr   _____

In cases where respondents find it difficult to rank large numbers of objects, paired comparisons may be used. Here each item is compared to every other item, and the total number of points accumulated by each is tabulated. In the foregoing example, Aries, for instance, would be compared with each of the other brands. Overall, 15 comparisons would take place. Each brand's score is the number of times it is preferred over another brand.

When analysts require measurements of distance on a continuum between two extremes, they may choose to employ scales. For example:

Evaluate the Cutlass station wagon (relative to other brands) on each of the following scales. (Place an X on the appropriate blank.)

	Very Good	Good	Fair	Poor	Very Poor
Power	_____	_____	_____	_____	_____
Passenger space	_____	_____	_____	_____	_____
Durability	_____	_____	_____	_____	_____
Price	_____	_____	_____	_____	_____
Economy of operation	_____	_____	_____	_____	_____
Attractiveness	_____	_____	_____	_____	_____

Finally, the analyst may use open-ended questions to which possible answers are not provided. This ensures that respondents are spontaneous in providing information, but they make tabulation more difficult and expensive since the data are not prearranged into categories. An example of an open-ended question is:

How impressed are you with the new Reliant two-door sedan? _____
_____
_____

The questionnaire designer must take care to ensure that the format of the document provides for clear understanding on the part of respondents, has a professional appearance, and includes sufficient space for recording information. Usually, uncomplicated and nonembarrassing questions appear first, allowing the respondent to warm up to the more difficult ones.

Generally, question wording should be oriented to characteristics of respondents. If the respondents possess less than average formal schooling, for instance, the questionnaire formulator should use simple words and phrases. Other question-formulation principles consist of avoiding statements that are ambiguous or that suggest an answer to the respondent. Both of these can introduce serious error in survey results.

The question sequence should follow a logical pattern, where specific questions follow general questions, and where a chronological sequence is maintained. Most respondents find it meaningful, for instance, to answer questions in an order like this:

1. What brand automobile did you first own? _____
2. What brands have you purchased since owning your first car?_____
   _____
3. What brand do you now own?_____

The overall objective is to elicit cooperation in attaining valid responses, and all aspects of questionnaire formulation should be oriented to this end.

Questionnaires should be pretested. This involves testing them on a group of individuals before employing them in an actual data-gathering effort. Pretesting often indicates that some questions are ambiguous or misleading and should be changed. The validity of the pretest is enhanced by conducting it with respondents who are members of the universe to be sampled.

Formulating the Sample

Most surveys involve sampling-gathering information from a representative portion of the total universe. This conserves time and money and is, of course, vital where the population is widely dispersed.[4]

Sampling requires first a definition of the universe, namely, the group from which information is sought. Thus in forecasting sales of cake mix, the analysts might define the universe as "all females who are eighteen years of age or older and who prepare meals at home." A definition of the universe, then, requires precise designation.

After defining the universe, the analyst constructs a frame that identifies members of that particular universe. Thus, the frame for households in a city might consist of a city directory or phone book, or a map that identifies city blocks. A frame is needed as a vehicle for sampling because elements of the sample are drawn from it, for example, selecting names from the city directory.

In sampling, the analyst tries to keep statistical error (or lack of reliability) to a minimum and still keep the cost of the survey within budgeted limits. Statistical error takes place when the sample is not representative of the population from which it was taken. Thus, if by chance, the analyst happens to choose for inclusion in the sample wealthy respondents who plan to purchase expensive automobiles next year, whereas most of the rest of the population does not plan any purchase, random error exists.

Random error can be minimized by (1) choosing an appropriate sampling method, and (2) selecting a sufficiently large sample. Unfortunately, however, efforts taken to keep error at a minimum, such as selecting a large sample, may result in high survey costs. In practice, the analyst usually strikes a balance resulting in acceptable (usually not

---

4. An extensive discussion of sampling is beyond the scope of this text. For a more detailed explanation of this field, see Paul G. Hoel and Raymond J. Jessen, *Basic Statistics for Business and Economics* (New York: John Wiley and Sons, 1977), pp. 150–169.

optimal) levels of error and cost. The choice of an appropriate sampling method is one way of achieving such a balance. Following are some of the more widely employed methods.

Probability Samples   Some samples are termed *probability samples.* In these, the probability of selecting any one member of the population is known. For instance, when a jar contains 99 green marbles and 1 white marble and the marbles are thoroughly mixed, the probability of drawing a white marble from the jar is 0.01. The measure of random error or reliability for a probability sample is the standard error.[5] When analysts compute mean sales values, for instance, the measure of reliability is standard error of the mean. When they compute percentages, the measure is standard error of the percentage. In the case of *nonprobability sampling*, random error cannot be computed. All the sampling methods, with the exception of convenience and quota, discussed in the following are probabilistic in nature. The analyst who is highly concerned with developing precise measures of reliability is likely to choose one of these. Conversely, analysts who are highly concerned with minimizing the cost, effort, and time consumed by the research often use nonprobability methods.

Random Samples   One method of sampling is the simple random method, where each member of the universe has an equal chance of being selected. This is exemplified by identifying each member of the population by a number, recording these on equal-size slips of paper, thoroughly mixing these in a bowl, and selecting numbers from the bowl. Other simple random-sampling methods are facilitated with tables of random numbers and computer random-number generators.

In many cases, a random sample will fulfill the needs of the analyst. Sometimes, however, other methods are more reliable, less expensive, or less time consuming. This being the case, we will examine some of these methods, beginning with stratified samples.

Stratified Samples   When the population is made up of closely defined groups whose memberships do not overlap and differ according to the information sought, stratified sampling may be appropriate. This requires subdividing the population into mutually exclusive groups and taking a random sample from each. The effect of this may be to increase the reliability of the estimates (to reduce random error). In the

---

5. Defined as the square root of the averages of the squares of the deviations from the measure of central tendency, the mean.

automobile-purchase study, the analyst might decide that three strata are appropriate: (1) low-income households, (2) intermediate-income households, and (3) upper-income households. Provided that members of each group have somewhat similar purchase plans and that the groups differ in average purchase plans, stratified sampling could be expected to improve sampling precision. In addition, it will provide separate sample statistics for each of the groups under study.

Area Samples   A special kind of stratified sampling is area sampling, in which the strata are geographical areas, as identified by a map. Thus, the analysts can place a grid on a map of a city and subdivide it into sectors. Following this, they can select a sample of areas and interview all households within each. Or they can sample within strata, as is the case when only a sample of the households are interviewed within the areas chosen. Area sampling can greatly reduce survey expense, since interviewers have to travel in only a portion of the universe. Conversely, area sampling can be less precise than simple random sampling when different portions of the area are heterogeneous with regard to the variables under study. It might be expected, for instance, that auto-mobile purchase plans of inner-city residents differ from those in the suburbs. The results of the survey may be misleading if the former are selected by the sample and the latter are not.

Systematic Samples   Systematic sampling is a probability method that can be used to select a sample from a list in which the elements are randomly distributed with respect to the variable in question. The analyst might, for instance, choose every tenth name listed in a city directory for inclusion in a survey. Systematic sampling is advantageous in that the sample-selection process can be conducted quickly and at low cost. The disadvantages are that a list may not be available and the elements of the universe may not be randomly distributed. In computing the interval for systematic sampling, the analyst divides population size by desired sample size. If, for instance, the population size is 42,170 and the sample size is 1,000, the interval is 42.17. A number between 1 and 42 (42.17 rounded to the next smallest integer) is randomly selected. Assume that this number is 2. Since the interval is 42 (42.17 rounded), the sample would consist of the 2nd, 44th, 86th, and so on, listings.

Convenience Samples   Sometimes convenience sampling is employed. This is a nonprobability method in which the analyst acquires information from individuals who can be conveniently contacted. Examples are members of a PTA group or students in a class. Unfortunately, members of convenient-to-contact groups are often not representative of the population at large. Thus, the results are often meaningless. On the other hand, convenience sampling reduces the cost and effort involved in gathering data. This makes them quite useful in pre-testing.

Quota Samples   Another nonprobability method is quota sampling. Here the analysts select a sample in accord with quotas of respondents having various characteristics. They might, for instance, specify a sample of consumers made up of 40% female, 60% male, 70% under age 65, and 30% age 65 and over. In this case, if the sample size is 300, its composition would be as follows:

	Under 65	65 and Over	Total
Male	126	54	180
Female	84	36	120
Total	210	90	300

Interviewers are asked to try to select respondents in accordance with quotas. Thus, once 210 individuals believed to be under 65 have been interviewed, only those 65 and over are queried. This process continues until all quotas are filled. This method enables the analyst to include the mix of respondents desired in the study. In the foregoing case, for instance, the analyst may have discovered through previous research that 60% of the consumers of the product in question are male and 70% are under age 65. The sampling plan fits the sample into these proportions. It is a nonprobability method, however, because objectivity is lost in granting to interviewers the authority to choose who will be included in the sample. It cannot be ensured that they are capable of distinguishing between individuals in accordance with the quotas. In the foregoing case, for instance, interviewers may find it to be difficult to judge the ages of potential respondents. When subjective interviewer judgment is substituted for a systematic and impartial sampling method, the sample is nonprobability.

Determination of Sample Size   The determination of sample size is an important determinant of the time consumed in a survey, its cost, and its validity. One means of doing this, when large sample statistics are used, is to rely on the rule of thumb that the number of respondents falling into a given classification of data should not fall below 20.[6] Thus, the following subdivision would be valid:

Age of Head of Household	Number of Respondents
15–20	31
21–26	47
27–32	106
33–38	212
39–44	301
45–50	280
51–56	264
57–62	97
63–68	28
69 and older	22
Total	1388

Following this rule of thumb, sampling continues until each category has at least 20 subjects.

One can estimate how large the total sample should be by solving for n (sample size) in the measure of dispersion formula that the analyst has adopted. Thus, assume that the analyst plans to survey housewives, asking each for the number of pounds of brand X coffee the household is expected to consume in 1984. The analyst wants measures of the mean. For a simple random sample, the proper measure of dispersion in the case of the mean is the standard error of the mean, defined as:

$$\sigma_{\bar{x}} = \frac{\sigma}{\sqrt{n}} \tag{6.1}$$

where
$\sigma_{\bar{x}}$ = standard error of the mean
σ = standard deviation of the population
n = sample size

Solving for n in the formula produces an equation for required sample size, which is:

$$n = \frac{\sigma^2}{\sigma_{\bar{x}}^2} \tag{6.2}$$

---

6. Some statisticians are of the opinion that this figure should be 30.

With this in mind, the following steps are taken:

1. Specify the amount of error (e) that can be allowed. This is the magnitude of difference between the sample mean ($\bar{x}$) and the true population mean (μ) that can be tolerated. $\bar{x} \pm e$, therefore, defines an interval within which μ will lie with some specified level of confidence. For the example, assume that the maximum error tolerable is 1.0 pound per year ($e = 1.0$).
2. Specify the desired level of confidence. For the example, assume that a 95% confidence level is desired.
3. Determine the number of standard errors (Z values) that are associated with the confidence level. Z values are found in tables of probabilities for a normal distribution. They may also be estimated with a t table at infinite degrees of freedom (see Appendix 4.A). For the example, $Z = 1.96$.
4. Estimate the standard deviation of the population. Past studies and pilot studies may be useful in this regard. Means tend to change over time, but standard deviations tend to remain stable. Another means of estimating is with the rule of thumb for a normally distributed variable that the standard deviation is approximately one-sixth of the range.[7] It is reasonable to assume for the example that average coffee consumption is normally distributed with a range of from 0 to 100 pounds per year, or 100 pounds. One-sixth of the range, therefore, is 16.67 pounds.
5. Calculate the sample size using Equation 6.2. One standard error of the mean is set equal to the allowable error ($e = 1$ pound) divided by the approximate Z value ($Z = 1.96$) as follows:

$$\sigma_{\bar{x}} = \frac{e}{Z} = \frac{1.0}{1.96} = 0.5102 \qquad (6.3)$$

This ensures that the interval to be computed around the eventual sample will have a 95% chance of being within ± 1 pound of the true population mean.
6. Solve for n using Equation 6.2:

$$n = \frac{\sigma^2}{\sigma_{\bar{x}}^2} = \frac{16.67^2}{0.5102^2} = 1,068$$

Thus, a randomly selected sample of 1,068 households would be needed for the example, assuming that none of the eventual cells will contain fewer than 20 subjects.

Notice that the appropriate sample size is affected by three major factors. The inherent standard deviation of the population, over which

7. Gilbert A. Churchill, *Marketing Research: Methodological Foundations*, 2nd ed. (Hinsdale, Ill.: Dryden Press, 1979), p. 341.

we have no control, is one of them. The other two result from our decisions, however.

The first of these is our tolerable error. If we had been willing to accept a 2.0-pound interval, the appropriate sample size would have been only 267 households. Similarly, if we had desired a 1.0-pound interval but had been willing to accept a 90% confidence level, the appropriate size would have been 752 households. (Readers are urged to verify these numbers.) Thus, management must make a trade-off between precision and survey cost.

The foregoing sample-size-determination procedure is appropriate in situations where means are estimated, which is the most common case in forecasting. In situations where other sampling methods and statistics are involved, the procedure is identical; it consists of locating the appropriate formula for a measure of dispersion, solving for n, and estimating the values in the equation.[8]

Acquiring Information

The acquisition of information can be a time-consuming and expensive process. In the case of mail questionnaires, letters are forwarded and their return anticipated. When interviewing is involved, the analyst has a more active role, namely that of supervising the interviewing process.

Direction of this function requires recruiting, selecting, training, compensating, motivating, and controlling the field force. Sometimes portions of or all these functions are best transferred to a professional research organization like Market Facts or Burke Marketing Research, as they are staffed with professionals.

Sources of interviewers include housewives, students, elementary and high-school teachers, and retirees. Middle-aged housewives have proved to be especially proficient and adapted to this function. If executives or professionals are to be interviewed, the analysts themselves may decide to collect the data.

The extent and composition of interviewer training vary from one survey to another. Normally, however, trainees are informed of the purpose of the study and instructed in techniques of selecting respondents, eliciting cooperation, asking questions, and recording information. Training techniques include lectures, practice interviews, and role playing. Organizations that engage in periodic surveys often use the same set of interviewers for each survey to moderate training cost.

Methods of compensation vary. Some concerns pay a piece rate, which bases compensation on the number of completed interviews. Others prefer hourly wages, based on the assumption that piece rates

8. For a discussion of sampling, see Paul E. Green and Donald S. Tull, *Research for Marketing Decisions* (Englewood Cliffs, N.J.: Prentice-Hall, 1978), Chapter 7.

produce low-quality work, such as hastily completed and incomplete interviews.

Since interviewers usually work alone and often travel, their working conditions are similar to those of many salespeople. Like salespeople, they cannot be directly supervised; usually supervision consists of periodic visits by supervisors and examination of completed question-naires that have been submitted. The latter process (editing) requires diligent search for evidence of interviewer dishonesty or lack of adher-ence to instructions.

Tabulating and Analyzing the Data

Once the data have been received, they must be tabulated. In some cases, this is done manually, by counting the number of responses in each category and recording the count. More frequently, calculators and computers are used.[9]

Analyzing involves breaking data down into categories and subjecting them to tests of significance. In the coffee example presented earlier, for instance, the analyst wants to determine the significance of the estimates of the means. This requires applying measures of significance to each and developing confidence intervals that stipulate the range within which the population value is expected to lie. The output of this is the ability to make statements such as "the probability is 0.95 that the population mean is between 12 and 28." Such statements provide an indication of the reliability of the sample estimates.

Analysis requires proper choice of a statistical test, one that will indicate whether the sampling statistic is significant or, on the other hand, could have resulted from chance alone. A technical presentation of the various statistical tests and their respective formulas are beyond the scope of this text. Judgment and background enables analysts and managers to determine which test is appropriate in a given case.[10]

Very frequently, analysts deal with means, for example, when they ask a sample of consumers for their expected number of purchases of a brand in a forthcoming period (such as a year) and compute the mean number of expected purchases. Here, they are concerned with testing the null hypothesis that the sample mean differs significantly from a hypothesized population mean or from another sample mean. The appropriate statistical test is usually the t test, which requires

9. An extensive discussion of statistical analysis is beyond the scope of this volume. For such a discussion, see Wayne W. Daniel, *Introductory Statistics with Applications* (Boston: Houghton Mifflin Company, 1980).
10. For a detailed description, see Leonard J. Kozmier, *Basic Statistics for Business and Economics* (New York: McGraw-Hill Book Company, 1978), Chapters 14 and 15.

computation of a derived value of t emanating from the sample and comparing this to a tabled critical value of t.

Sometimes analysis requires assessment of the significance of a percentage or proportion, for example, when the analyst determines the proportion of a sample of consumers who plan to purchase a brand X automobile next year. If the sample is large (the number in each category exceeds 20) the t test is relevant. Where sample size is small, the chi-square test is appropriate. The latter, however, has a higher risk of accepting a false null hypothesis. Thus, where merited, the t test is preferable.

In some cases, analysts want to assess the significance of differences between a large number of means. They could employ t tests to assess the difference between each pair of means, but this becomes tedious when the number of means is large (exceeding four). The appropriate test, under these circumstances, is the analysis of variance, which indicates the overall difference between the group of means considered as a whole. The analysis of variance involves application of the F test, which compares the variance between means with the variance between individual observations.

The tests set forth to this point, with the exception of chi-square, are called *parametric*. They require certain assumptions, such as normal distribution of the underlying data and similarity of variances between groups to be compared. In contrast, nonparametric tests place few or no restrictions on the nature of the underlying distribution.[11] They may be used where sample size is small, where the distribution of the data departs substantially from the normal, and where the data are in ordinal, as contrasted to interval or ratio, form.

The prime disadvantage of nonparametric tests, in comparison to their metric counterparts, is that they are more likely to produce an acceptance of a false null hypothesis. In the opinion of many analysts, however, the advantages set forth in the foregoing overcome this defect.

It is beyond the scope of this text to outline the nature of the numerous nonparametric tests in existence. Suffice it to say that most of these assess hypotheses concerning the median, rank order, percentages, and proportions.

TEST MARKETS

Another technique closely allied to survey methods is the test market. Here the analyst arranges for the placement of a new product or brand,

---

11. For an excellent discussion of nonparametric tests, see Robert D. Mason, *Statistical Techniques in Business and Economics* (Homewood, Ill.: Richard D. Irwin, 1978), Chapters 14, 15, and 19.

or a modification of an existing one, in cities believed to be representative of the firm's geographical target market. The analyst measures
sales behavior in the test market over a period of time, and often compares it to sales in control markets, those in which a different product
or brand is being offered or a different marketing strategy is being
used. The test market may be one in which particular merchandising,
pricing, promotion, or distribution tactics are being employed, and the
control markets are where they are not. The basic objective is to observe
sales in a small-scale setting, and the basic assumption is that behavior
in this setting will predict that of the market at large. The Shulton, Inc.
International Division, for instance, test marketed its line of men's
fragrance and grooming products in several British cities in 1979. The
test was very positive, so the firm elected to sell the line throughout
Britain.[12] In another test, Andersen, Clayton and Co. successfully
introduced "New Age" imitation cheese slices in five southern cities and,
basing its decision upon the test, decided to distribute the slices throughout the Southeast and the Southwest.[13]

Conducting a Test Market

The Eagle Travel Agency, Inc., is considering offering packaged tours to
senior citizens from Florida. Management feels that members of this age
group might be expected to respond favorably to packages—two- or
three-week excursions in Europe, the Bahamas, Hawaii, and southern
Asia. The package would include services of an experienced guide, air
travel, hotel accommodations, local bus and boat tours, meals, and
entertainment, and would be limited to senior citizens.

Before embarking on such a plan, management feels that revenues
should be estimated. Thus, it decides to engage in sales testing. This
involves offering the senior citizens' package in St. Petersburg, Florida,
believed to embody a senior citizen market that is typical of the state
at large. The test is conducted in 1982. If the results are favorable,
Eagle plans to promote the excursion heavily and regularly throughout
the state, beginning in 1983.

Management arranges with the various service purveyors—an air
carrier, numerous hotels, American Express, several bus carriers, and a
number of restaurants—to provide accommodations in Western Europe
during June 1982. The tour is promoted through newspaper advertising,
displays and pamphlets in Eagle's offices, and direct-mail advertisements
to the local chapter of the National Association of Retired Persons and

---

12. "Shulton's Sales More than Double in Seven Years," *International Business*, 4
    (July/August 1979), 4.
13. "Flankers Flare in October Test," *Advertising Age*, 51 (November 3, 1980), 20.

several senior citizens' clubs. These activities result in over 400 inquiries and 250 bookings for the tour. Management views these results as substantially more favorable than that yielded by other packages in 1982 and decides to adopt the package as its feature service. The sales test has suggested that this new product will generate sufficient revenues to justify its continuance.

Advantages and Disadvantages

Sales tests are advantageous because they depict reality by measuring what consumers do (in buying products and services) rather than what they say (as in a survey). In this sense, they are perhaps one of the better forecasting techniques. In addition, the sales tests allow management to measure the impact of various prices, promotion programs, and product variations upon sales.

On the other hand, some weaknesses of sales tests are evident. One is the length of time consumed; it is not unusual for a sales test to last as long as two years. A certain minimum time must pass during which the product is used initially and reused by consumers, thus establishing some form of stable purchasing pattern. The minimum effective time is probably six months. This may delay important decisions, such as new product introductions or additions to plant capacity.

Sales tests also can be expensive. They require production of the product, distribution to sales test cities, and promotion and merchandising expenses within the test cities. This is in contrast to the fairly moderate costs incurred in conducting most surveys.

In the case of new products, test markets can aid competitors. Introduction of an offering at the retail level tips off rivals as to the probable forthcoming strategy of the firm and can enable them to emulate or retaliate to this strategy. Sometimes competitors attempt to invalidate sales tests by influencing their results so that the testing firm obtains misleading results. Competitors may alter prices, increase promotion expenditures, or increase personal selling activities to upset test results. Or competitors may purchase large volumes of the products being tested, thereby inflating the expected sales levels.

Finally, sales tests may not be indicative of the behavior of the market at large. This is especially likely if consumer composition or retail structure is not representative of the whole. If management has not introduced the product in test markets using exactly the same marketing strategy as it will in the entire market, the results of the former may be misleading. Thus, the firm should take care to ensure that test market expenditures and procedures for advertising, sales promotion, and personal selling are commensurate with those in the market at large.

SUMMARY

Surveys and test markets are useful forecasting devices, especially when historical data are lacking or are unreliable. New-product forecasts are illustrative of such conditions. Survey shortcomings include lack of predictive power, cost, and time consumption.

Surveys require the following series of steps:

1. Ascertain sought information—determine precisely the nature of the information needed.
2. Ascertain information sources—decide what persons are the best providers of the needed information.
3. Ascertain modes of gathering data:
   a. Personal interviews—conducted on a person-to-person basis
   b. Telephone surveys—where the interviewing takes place over the telephone
   c. Mail surveys—where questionnaires are mailed to respondents
   d. Observation—where observers note the behavior of respondents
   e. Panels—where groups of consumers record their purchasing behavior in diaries over a period of time
   f. Group interviews—where groups of respondents are interviewed simultaneously
4. Develop and pretest measuring instrument—generate and test a questionnaire, interview guide, or observation guide.
5. Formulate the sample—determine size and type of sampling plan to be utilized.
6. Acquire information—organize the activities of the field force and monitor its performance. (Sometimes this function is contracted to outside firms)
7. Tabulate information—count the data obtained in the survey or test market.
8. Analyze information—break the data down into categories and subject them to tests of significance, both parametric and nonparametric.

Each step requires a multitude of decisions. If each is carefully carried out, the results can have a high degree of predictive power.

In the case of test markets, analysts arrange for the placement of a company offering in cities believed to be representative of the actual market. Sales are observed over a period of time and are often compared with control markets. Inferences concerning expected future sales may then be made. The test markets do provide realism. On the other hand, they can be expensive and time consuming, may tip off competitors, and may generate misleading forecasts.

DISCUSSION QUESTIONS

1. What is meant by the term *survey*?
2. Why are surveys used by sales forecasters?
3. Would you expect surveys to be useful in forecasting the sales of an established cereal brand, such as Kellogg's Corn Flakes? Why or why not?
4. What are the disadvantages of survey forecasts?
5. Describe what is involved in each of the following survey procedures:
   a. Ascertaining sought information
   b. Ascertaining information sources
   c. Ascertaining mode of gathering data
   d. Developing and pretesting the measuring instrument
   e. Formulating sample
   f. Acquiring information
   g. Tabulating and analyzing data
6. Design a question that could be used to determine consumers' favorableness of attitude toward Hershey candy bars (use more than one question, if necessary). How could the company use such a question as a sales forecasting tool?
7. Assume that a computer manufacturer is attempting to sell an expensive computer to community colleges, four-year colleges, and universities. A survey is to be used as a sales forecasting device. Which individuals, within the educational institutions, should the firm survey?
8. What are the principal strengths and weaknesses of:
   a. Personal interviews
   b. Telephone interviews
   c. Mail surveys
   d. Observation
   e. Panels
   f. Group interviews
9. Describe the procedure involved in acquiring forecasting data through test markets.
10. Assume that you are a manager for Cannon Mills, Inc. (a manufacturer of bed sheets and pillowcases), and that you are considering the introduction of a new offering that is 40% cotton and 60% polyester and that has some unique new color and pattern combinations not yet in existence in the industry. Cite the reasons for and against generating a sales forecast through a test market.
11. What are some of the more important written instructions that should be given to interviewers?
12. Describe and provide an example of each of the following types of questions:
    a. Identification information
    b. Demographic information
    c. Direct information

13. Provide an example of each of the following types of questions:
    a. Dichotomous
    b. Multiple choice
    c. Ranking
    d. Paired comparison
    e. Scales
    f. Open ended
14. What guidelines should be followed in planning the sequence of questions in a questionnaire?
15. Distinguish between probability and nonprobability samples.
16. What might be a useful sampling frame if the universe consists of heads of household in a particular city?
17. Describe each of the following types of samples:
    a. Simple random
    b. Stratified
    c. Area
    d. Systematic
    e. Convenience
    f. Quota
18. Assume that you are conducting a sample survey designed to provide a forecast of sales for a maker of toothpaste. How might you stratify the sample?
19. Provide a hypothetical example of a systematic sample.
20. In a survey, an analyst wants to employ a quota sample that is 60% blue-collar and 40% white-collar worker, and is 70% union member and 30% non-union member. The sample size will be 1,000. What are the numbers (sample breakdown) in each group?
21. A heating and refrigeration supplies wholesaler desires to conduct a survey to generate a sales forecast for the following year, given the following information:
    a. The sample statistic is the mean.
    b. The analysts want to be about 95% sure that the universe mean is not more than five units larger or smaller than the sample mean.
    c. The estimated range is 50.
    What sample size should be taken?
22. A producer of microwave ovens plans to conduct a survey of customers to develop an estimate of mean purchases. It is desired that management be around 99% sure that the population mean is not more than three units larger or smaller than the sample mean. The estimated standard deviation is 11. What should be the sample size?
23. Distinguish between parametric and nonparametric tests.

RECOMMENDED READINGS

Ackoff, Russell L., S. K. Gupta, and J. Sayre Minas. *Scientific Method: Optimizing Applied Research Decisions.* New York: John Wiley and Sons, 1962, Chapters 1 and 2.

Allen, Chris T., Charles D. Schewe, and Gosta Wijk. "More on Self Perception Theory's Foot Technique in the Pre-Call Mail Survey Setting." *Journal of Marketing Research*, 17 (November 1980), 498–502.

Becker, Boru W., and Patrick E. Comper. "Values and Behavior of Research Subjects: Yeasaying Response Style." *1976 Proceedings, American Marketing Association Educators' Conference.* Chicago: American Marketing Association, 1977, 41–44.

Childers, Terry C., William M. Pride, and O. C. Ferrell. "A Reassessment of the Effects of Appeals on Response to Mail Surveys." *Journal of Marketing Research*, 17 (August 1980), 365–370.

Churchill, Gilbert A. *Marketing Research: Methodological Foundations.* 2nd ed. Hinsdale, Ill.: Dryden Press, 1979.

Churchman, C. West, and P. Ratoosh (eds.). *Measurement: Definitions and Theories.* New York: John Wiley and Sons, 1959, Chapter 2.

Dolde, Walter, Richard Staelin, and Tsu Yao. "Estimating Response Rates for Different Market Segments from Questionnaire Data." *Journal of Marketing Research*, 17 (May 1980), 245–252.

Erdos, Paul. *Professional Mail Surveys.* New York: McGraw-Hill Book Company, 1971.

Green, Paul T., and Donald S. Tull, *Research for Marketing Decisions.* 4th ed. Englewood Cliffs, N.J.: Prentice-Hall, 1978.

Groves, Robert M., and Robert L. Kahn. *Surveys by Telephone—A National Comparison with Personal Interviews.* New York: Academic Press, 1979.

Hye, G. P., and J. R. McKenzie. "Effect of Underreporting by Consumer Panels on Level of Repeat Purchasing of New Products." *Journal of Marketing Research*, 13 (February 1976), 80–86.

Jones, Wesley H., and Gerald Lind. "Multiple Criteria Effects in a Mail Survey Experiment." *Journal of Marketing Research*, 16 (May 1978), 280–284.

Mendeshall, W. L. Ott, and R. Sheaffer. *Elementary Survey Sampling.* Belmont, Calif.: Wadsworth Publishing Co., 1971.

Selltiz, Claire, Marie Jehoda, Morton Deutsch, and Stuart W. Cook. *Research Methods in Social Relations.* New York: Henry Holt and Company, 1959, Chapters 1, 6, 7, and 11.

Shouksmith, G. *Assessment Through Interviewing.* New York: Pergamon Press, 1978.

Sudman, Seymour. "Improving the Quality of Shopping Center Sampling." *Journal of Marketing Research*, 16 (November 1980), 423–431.

Wiseman, Frederick, and Philip McDonald. "Noncontact and Refusal Rates in Consumer Telephone Surveys." *Journal of Marketing Research*, 16 (November 1979), 478–484.

Wolfe, Lee M. "Characteristics of Persons with and without Home Telephones." *Journal of Marketing Research*, 16 (August 1979), 421–425.

CASE 6: COLUMBIA BAKING COMPANY

The Columbia Baking Company is a Seattle-based producer of cookies and crackers, with customers in Washington, Oregon, Northern California, Montana, and Idaho. The customers are wholesalers who sell to food retailers and large supermarket chains in the target market area.

In the trade, Columbia has a reputation for producing very high quality products. Management believes that this reputation is, in fact, earned. In the snack-cracker area, for instance, Columbia puts a higher proportion of eggs into its crackers and more chocolate chips in its chocolate chip cookies than does any other firm in the industry. These strategies, while winning customer support for company products, have pushed up direct material costs to a high level. Coupled with the impact of inflation, these costs have impelled management to increase, on the average, the prices of cookies by 15% and crackers by 14% during the past year.

Columbia has considerable competition from very large firms like General Foods and Nabisco, regional producers that are about the same size as Columbia, and a small group of small producers who sell in a very restricted area (such as a city) and who usually specialize in a particular kind of cookie. The competition has prevented Columbia from raising its prices any further. It has also impelled the company to undertake a well-conceived advertising plan and to employ an aggressive sales force.

The firm owns a fleet of trucks which move products from the plant in Seattle to several company-leased warehouses in the major markets and to warehouses owned by supermarket chains the firm serves. The company-leased warehouses serve primarily the smaller grocery outlets. They are equipped with local-delivery trucks, and are modern and efficient, with inventory-control procedures to keep the product line fresh.

Columbia advertises in several places. It uses spot television commercials in major market areas like Seattle and Portland, Oregon. Another medium is Sunday newspaper magazine supplements and newspaper ads. The advertisements feature the product taste, potential uses (such as entertaining guests), and the fact that all products are packaged to ensure freshness.

The firm orients its products to consumers who are willing to pay a little extra in order to obtain a superior product. This group includes middle- and upper-income families, white-collar workers, executives, and professionals. Company-sponsored research has shown that the bulk of the consumers have total family incomes exceeding $25,000, live in the suburbs of a large city or in a smaller city, and seek value over price when purchasing cookies and crackers.

Columbia's sales over the past ten years are as follows:

1973	$ 7,645,800
1974	7,782,250
1975	8,309,000
1976	9,693,750
1977	11,109,400
1978	11,972,950
1979	13,891,150
1980	15,665,750
1981	17,923,000
1982	19,336,750

One company manager has proposed that Columbia consider the introduction of a new snack cracker that would contain mostly natural ingredients. The baking production facilities are such that this product could easily be made by the firm, although the direct labor costs would be higher than for other crackers currently offered for sale. The new offering would be triangular-shaped, packed in cellophane, and targeted to consumers who are health-conscious. Management has developed a plan for producing and marketing the product. The major question confronting management, however, is, would the product generate adequate sales? Accordingly, a survey of ultimate consumers is planned.

The objectives of the survey are to determine if consumers would accept the new product and to gather other information that might be of value in devising promotion, distribution, merchandising, and price strategies. Questionnaires are to be mailed to 2,000 residents of Seattle, Spokane, and Tacoma, Washington; Sacramento, California; Bozeman and Missoula, Montana; and Boise, Idaho. They will be sent to heads of households who, according to the city directory, are professionals, businesspeople, or well-paid white-collar workers, and will include self-addressed, stamped return envelopes.

A copy of the questionnaire follows:

COLUMBIA BAKING COMPANY

Attitude Survey

1. Do you buy snack crackers?   Yes _____   No _____

2. If yes, when do you normally eat them?
   - Lunch _____
   - Afternoon _____
   - Evening _____

3. What brand of snack cracker do you prefer? _____

4. Would you be interested in a new triangular-shaped snack cracker with natural ingredients?

- Yes _____
- No _____
- Maybe _____

5. When would you consume such a cracker?

- Lunch _____
- Afternoon _____
- Evening _____

6. (*If you have children*) Do you think that your children would be interested in such a cracker?

- Yes _____
- No _____
- Maybe _____

7. (*If you are married*) Do you think that your husband or wife would be interested in such a cracker?

- Yes _____
- No _____
- Maybe _____

8. What would be the maximum price that you would pay for a 12-ounce box of such a cracker? _____

9. In what kind of store do you normally buy snack crackers? _____ _____

10. What snack crackers flavors do you prefer? _____

11. In what medium have you experienced snack cracker advertising?

- Radio _____
- Television _____
- Newspaper _____
- Magazine _____
- Billboard _____
- Other _____

12. Age _____

13. Total family income last year _____

14. Number of persons in family _____

15. Occupation _____

16. Numbers of years at present residence _____

17. Number of years of education completed _____

18. Ages of children, if any: _____ _____ _____ _____

Cover Letter to Accompany Questionnaire

Dear _____

The Columbia Baking Company is conducting a survey concerning consumer attitudes about snack crackers. Your name was randomly selected for inclusion in the sample. We would appreciate your filling out and returning the enclosed questionnaire in the self-addressed return envelope. All information that you supply will be held in strict confidence. Thank you.

Sincerely,

Richard Rathmell

Richard Rathmell, Product Manager

1. What is your overall evaluation of this research effort?
2. Comment on the sampling plan.
3. Are mail questionnaires the best medium for gathering the desired information? Why or why not?
4. Is this a good questionnaire? Why or why not?
5. What are the risks associated with relying on forecasts derived from such a survey?

Chapter 7
Models Based on Learned Behavior

INTRODUCTION

To this point, we have not discussed any of the numerous aspects of consumers' behavior when they are making product decisions in the marketplace. Consumption, which is the source of sales, is a form of learned behavior. Individuals do not objectively evaluate each competing product every time they make a purchase decision. They tend instead to repeat their past activities, that is, they become loyal to certain product types as well as specific brands. Some, however, tend to seek other brands and products.

Models based on market share for existing products, brand switching, market share and new products, and product life cycles are based on the fact that buying behavior is learned. These models, the subject of this chapter, are often very useful for forecasting sales.

MARKET SHARE

Most companies exist in an oligopolistic or nearly oligopolistic setting in which there are two or more competing firms within an industry. Sales of a particular firm often depend on its position relative to the other enterprises within its industry. There is a tendency for firms within an industry to share the market with each other at a relatively constant rate. Changes in market shares exist, but shares held during one period often serve as starting points to divide the pie during the next period.

Current market shares are a function of past shares for several reasons. First, any market share can be considered a result of past competitive efforts. Earlier decisions about promotion, distribution, product design, and so forth have an impact upon the current market share. At the same time, these past determinations tend to influence future decisions. As a result, future shares of the market tend to be a function of existing shares.

Second, customers tend to develop loyalty to a particular product or ∨ retail outlet. Satisfactory past service results in favorable attitudes, which increase the probability of a repurchase of the same product, often at the same store.

Third, distribution and production systems tend to restrict wide fluctuations in market share from one period to the next. Some stores selectively or exclusively carry some product brands, whereas others carry those of the competition. Such a distribution system often does not rapidly adjust to market conditions. To illustrate, many department stores carry only a few lines of furniture. To purchase a different brand, a customer must find another store that carries a competitor's line. This retards substantial shifts in market share. Also, the production system is often incapable of rapid shifts to meet substantially increased demand. If, for example, the entire market suddenly preferred General Motors cars, GM's production facilities would be incapable of meeting the demand. Many people would purchase competitors' cars because of the lack of availability of those from GM. It could take several years to substantially increase production facilities and, thereby, allow a major shift in relative position within the market.

The concept of market share implies that, as a total industry's sales change, the various firms' sales tend to change in relation to the overall movement. Market share is a guarded objective within all industries, and this phenomenon can be used in the forecasting process.

Consider Table 7.1, which presents hypothetical sales of the monofilament fishing line industry. Sales for all three leaders in the industry were up in 1982 over 1981. However, this does not necessarily mean that all three of the companies improved performance. Instead, both Acme and Leader companies lost ground to competition. In analyzing results, the managements of these two companies should try to determine the reason for their decline in market share.

Table 7.1 Sales of the Monofilament Fishing Line Industry

Firm	1981 Sales (in Millions of Dollars)	Market Share	1982 Sales (in Millions of Dollars)	Market Share
Acme	189	0.35	194.7	0.33
Leader	135	0.25	135.7	0.23
Alright	108	0.20	135.7	0.23
All others	108	0.20	123.9	0.21
Total	540	1.00	590.0	1.00

MARKET SHARE AND EXISTING PRODUCTS

We discuss the market share concept because it can be used in forecasting future sales. The greatest use of market share analysis is for existing products for which product (or firm), historical, and industry information is available for calculations. We shall consider both static and dynamic methods. Static methods assume a constant pattern of brand loyalty and switching behavior, whereas dynamic models consider a changing pattern of preferences.

Static Market Share Forecasts

Static market share forecasts consist of projecting market share into a future period and then applying this projection to forecast industry sales, yielding an estimate of anticipated firm sales. The Strictor Manufacturing Company, for example, produces rain gutters for residential buildings and uses such a method to forecast sales. Table 7.2 presents historical market shares for Strictor over the past ten years.

All the time-series techniques are candidate methods for forecasting future market shares. Because there is a linear trend present in Strictor's shares, double exponential smoothing and regression against time appear to be the most suited. Strictor's management has found that regressing the shares against time has worked well in the past and feels that it should be used again.

Table 7.2 Strictor Market Shares

Year	Market Share
1973	0.275
1974	0.281
1975	0.284
1976	0.283
1977	0.288
1978	0.291
1979	0.295
1980	0.293
1981	0.296
1982	0.299

The following statistics relate to the example:

$$r^2 = 0.948$$
$$b = 0.00245$$
$$a = 0.275$$

The forecast for 1983 ($t = 11$), therefore, is

$$0.275 + (11)(0.00245) = 0.302$$

This market share estimate is then multiplied by a forecast of industry sales in order to forecast company sales. To illustrate, assume industry sales are forecast at $7,350,000 in 1983. Strictor's sales forecast would then be $7,350,000 × 0.302 + $2,219,700.

A major advantage of forecasting the market shares instead of sales dollars directly is that quite reliable industry forecasts might be available. Trade associations, government agencies, foundations, several large banks, and several universities are among the many institutions that have developed large-scale, complex models to forecast sales volumes of certain industries. Such models are often much more complex and accurate than those that individual companies can build efficiently. Using these forecasts indirectly, therefore, can increase a company's forecast accuracy. Further, such forecasts serve as comparisons against which one can assess the reasonableness of any internally generated forecasts.

Dynamic Market Share Forecasts (Markov Chains)

Dynamic market share forecasts attempt to reflect buyer brand loyalty and switching behavior. This method is considered dynamic because it recognizes the impact of these forces in determining market share. The method is often termed *Markov analysis*, or *Markov chains*.

The forecasting analyst for General Products Company's Chewing Gum Division is analyzing market share data to estimate sales of their gum, the Tasty Chew brand. The analyst has used various methods to estimate market shares in the past, but none has been totally satisfactory; customer interaction among brands may be the reason for past inaccuracies. Market share data for the three major firms and all others in the industry as of May 31, 1982, are as follows:

Brand	Market Share Percentage
Tasty Chew	40.0
Eatwell	30.0
Maple	20.0
All others	10.0
Total	100.0

The Tasty Chew analyst conducted a sample of gum purchasers in June and found, as suspected, that some sales were lost to and some gained from the competition. The sample consisted of a stratified random sample of 1,000 gum purchasers. The sample was stratified in accordance with the May 31 market share percentages. That is, subjects were randomly selected within categories of purchase such that their stated aggregate May purchases were in accordance with the end of May market shares. Results of the sample are presented in Table 7.3.

Table 7.3 Sample Gains and Losses of Customers During June

Brand	May 31 Customers	Customers Purchasing Same Brand During June	Customers Gained from Other Brands in June
Tasty Chew	400	350	20
Eatwell	300	270	40
Maple	200	160	55
All others	100	80	25
Total	1,000	860	140

Customers Lost to Other Brands in June	Net Gain or Loss	Customers of Brand at June 30	June 30 Market Shares, %
50	-30	370	37.0
30	10	310	31.0
40	15	215	21.5
20	5	105	10.5
140	0	1,000	100.0

This information is not sufficient in and of itself to forecast sales of Tasty Chew gum during July. It is also necessary to learn from which company new sales were attained and to which company sales were lost. The relative sizes of each company as well as the probability of capturing (or losing) customers determine the expected number of customer gains or losses, which in turn influence market share.

Table 7.4 presents these data, as obtained from the sample. The table indicates that Tasty Chew gained a total of 20 customers. The total was made up of 10 customers obtained from Eatwell, 8 customers from Maple, and 2 from all others. At the same time, 20 customers were lost to Eatwell, 25 to Maple, and 5 to all others. The bottom of Table 7.4 presents essentially the same data as the top. From the bottom, we see that Eatwell lost 10 customers to Tasty Chew during the month, and we see that Tasty Chew has gained 10 customers from Eatwell during the month, depicted on the top of the table. The same is true for all entries on either side of the table. Results of the sample, detailed in Tables 7.3 and 7.4, are summarized in Table 7.5. Such brand-switching patterns have obvious strategic implications. Knowing which brands are most competitive can help in making good product positioning decisions. The brand-switching patterns are also very useful in the forecasting process, as we shall see.

Transition Probabilities

The retained, gained, and lost data obtained from the sample may be converted into probabilities to make forecasts. Each entry in Table 7.5 may be divided by the number of customers each brand attracted at May 31. This figure represents the fractional allocation of those customers retained, lost, or gained throughout the period. To illustrate, Tasty Chew had 400 customers at May 31. Of these 400, 350 were retained at June 30 (350/400 = 0.8750), 20 went to Eatwell (20/400 = 0.0500), 25 went to Maple (25/400 = 0.0625) and 5 went to other competitors (5/400 = 0.0125). These figures represent the transition, in relative terms, of May 31 customers.

Because the transitions may be expressed in fractional terms, the sum of which equals 1.00, each may be considered the probability of customers entering each state. 0.8750 may be considered to be the probability of a Tasty Chew customer buying the same brand at the end of the period, 0.0500 may be considered the probability of a customer becoming one of Eatwell's at the end of the period, and so forth. Table 7.6 presents the transitional probabilities for all brands in a transitional matirix.

The interpretation of the columns in the transitional probability matrix have already been explained. The following illustrate the

Table 7.4 Sources of Gains and Locations of Losses

Brand	Total Customers Gained	Gained from			
		Tasty Chew	Eatwell	Maple	All Others
Tasty Chew	20	0	10	8	2
Eatwell	40	20	0	15	5
Maple	55	25	17	0	13
All others	25	5	3	17	0
Total	140	50	30	40	20

Brand	Total Customers Lost	Lost to			
		Tasty Chew	Eatwell	Maple	All Others
Tasty Chew	50	0	20	25	5
Eatwell	30	10	0	17	3
Maple	40	8	15	0	17
All others	20	2	5	13	0
Total	140	20	40	55	25

Table 7.5 Summary of Sample Findings

Customers Retained or Gained (Rows)	Customers Retained or Lost to Brand (Columns)				
	Tasty Chew	Eatwell	Maple	All Others	Customers of Brand at June 30
Tasty Chew	350	10	8	2	370
Eatwell	20	270	15	5	310
Maple	25	17	160	13	215
All others	5	3	17	80	105
Customers at May 31	400	300	200	100	1,000

Table 7.6 Transitional Probability Matrix

Probability of Customers Being Retained or Gained (Rows)	Probability of Customers Being Retained or Lost (Columns)			
	Tasty Chew	Eatwell	Maple	All Others
Tasty Chew	0.8750	0.0333	0.0400	0.0200
Eatwell	0.0500	0.9000	0.0750	0.0500
Maple	0.0625	0.0567	0.8000	0.1300
All others	0.0125	0.0100	0.0850	0.8000

interpretation of the rows. Of the May 31 customers, Eatwell gains 5% of Tasty Chew's, 7.5% of Maple's, and 5% of all others' customers. Eatwell retains 90% of its own. These gains, retentions, and losses, in addition to the May 31 shares, reflect market shares at June 30.

Use of the Transitional Probability Matrix

The transitional probability matrix is used to calculate market share. To illustrate, Tasty Chew held 40% of the market at May 31. Of this 40%, 8.75% were retained. Tasty Chew gained 3.33% of Eatwell's 30%, 4% of Maple's 20% of the market, and 2% of the all-other category's 10% of the market. The June 20 market share of Tasty Chew is, therefore, calculated to be as follows:

Retention	$0.8750 \times 0.40 = 0.3500$
Gain from Eatwell	$0.0333 \times 0.30 = 0.0100$
Gain from Maple	$0.0400 \times 0.20 = 0.0080$
Gain from all others	$0.0200 \times 0.10 = 0.0020$
Total	0.3700

This figure is identical to the June 30 market share, as detected in the sample.

Eatwell's market share is as follows:

Gain from Tasty Chew	$0.0500 \times 0.40 = 0.0200$
Retention	$0.9000 \times 0.30 = 0.2700$
Gain from Maple	$0.0750 \times 0.20 = 0.0150$
Gain from all others	$0.0500 \times 0.10 = 0.0050$
Total	0.3100

A multiplication operation in matrix algebra is accomplished in the foregoing calculations. The transformation matrix is multiplied by the matrix representing original market shares as follows:

$$\begin{pmatrix} 0.8750 & 0.0333 & 0.0400 & 0.0200 \\ 0.0500 & 0.9000 & 0.0750 & 0.0500 \\ 0.0625 & 0.0567 & 0.8000 & 0.1300 \\ 0.0125 & 0.0100 & 0.0850 & 0.8000 \end{pmatrix} \begin{pmatrix} 0.40 \\ 0.30 \\ 0.20 \\ 0.10 \end{pmatrix}$$

A detailed discussion of matrix algebra will not be presented in this text. The reference to matrix multiplication is made merely to aid in reducing the number of tables required for explanation. To continue with the calculation of the June 30 market share, the related matrices will be used. Maple's market share at June 30 may be calculated as follows:

$$(0.0625 \quad 0.0567 \quad 0.8000 \quad 0.1300) \begin{pmatrix} 0.40 \\ 0.30 \\ 0.20 \\ 0.10 \end{pmatrix}$$

To perform this multiplication operation one has to sum the product of the first element in the row matrix times the first (top) element in the column matrix, the second element of the row matrix times the second element of the column matrix, and so on. There must be the same number of elements in the row matrix as there are in the column matrix. This should always be the case if the transformational probability matrix is constructed from Table 7.5 or its equivalent. These operations may be summarized as follows:

$$0.0625 \times 0.40 = 0.0250$$
$$0.0567 \times 0.30 = 0.0170$$
$$0.8000 \times 0.20 = 0.1600$$
$$0.1300 \times 0.10 = \underline{0.0130}$$
$$0.2150$$

The final calculation required is that for all others. The appropriate matrices and solution are

$$(0.0125 \quad 0.0100 \quad 0.0850 \quad 0.8000) \begin{pmatrix} 0.40 \\ 0.30 \\ 0.20 \\ 0.10 \end{pmatrix} = 0.1050$$

All the matrix operations may be summarized as

$$\begin{pmatrix} 0.8750 & 0.0333 & 0.0400 & 0.0200 \\ 0.0500 & 0.9000 & 0.0750 & 0.0500 \\ 0.0625 & 0.0567 & 0.8000 & 0.1300 \\ 0.0125 & 0.0100 & 0.0850 & 0.8000 \end{pmatrix} \begin{pmatrix} 0.40 \\ 0.30 \\ 0.20 \\ 0.10 \end{pmatrix} = \begin{pmatrix} 0.3700 \\ 0.3100 \\ 0.2150 \\ 0.1050 \end{pmatrix}$$

The matrix resulting from the multiplication represents the final market shares for June 30 for the companies in the same order as the respective rows in the transitional probability matrix.

Future Periods

The discussion thus far has concentrated on the calculation of the transitional matrix obtained from the sample data and an explanation of its use for calculating resulting market shares. A logical extension of the use of the transitional probability matrix is for forecasting future period market shares. The transitional matrix has been defined as being composed of probabilities relating to various possibilities of behavior on the part of individuals (remain loyal or switch, and if a switch, to which brand). These probabilities may again be used to forecast market shares for July 31. The mathematical procedure is simply to multiply the transitional probability matrix by the June 30 market share matrix to yield the forecast market share matrix. For the example, we have

$$\begin{pmatrix} 0.8750 & 0.0333 & 0.0400 & 0.0200 \\ 0.0500 & 0.9000 & 0.0750 & 0.0500 \\ 0.0625 & 0.0567 & 0.8000 & 0.1300 \\ 0.0125 & 0.0100 & 0.0850 & 0.8000 \end{pmatrix} \begin{pmatrix} 0.370 \\ 0.310 \\ 0.215 \\ 0.105 \end{pmatrix}$$

The solution of the foregoing matrix multiplication is as follows:

Row 1 $0.8750 \times 0.370 = 0.3238$
$0.0333 \times 0.310 = 0.0103$
$0.0400 \times 0.215 = 0.0086$
$0.0200 \times 0.105 = \underline{0.0021}$

  Sum   0.3448

Row 2 $0.0500 \times 0.370 = 0.0185$
$0.9000 \times 0.310 = 0.2790$
$0.0750 \times 0.215 = 0.0161$
$0.0500 \times 0.105 = \underline{0.0053}$

  Sum   0.3189

Row 3   0.0625 × 0.370 = 0.0231
0.0567 × 0.310 = 0.0176
0.8000 × 0.215 = 0.1720
0.1300 × 0.105 = 0.0136
_____

Sum   0.2263

Row 4   0.0125 × 0.370 = 0.0046
0.0100 × 0.310 = 0.0031
0.0850 × 0.215 = 0.0183
0.8000 × 0.105 = 0.0840
_____

Sum   0.1100

The forecast market share for July 31, therefore, is as follows:

Brand	Market Share Percentage
Tasty Chew	34.48
Eatwell	31.89
Maple	22.63
All others	11.00
Total	100.00

The market share forecasts may then be used to generate a specific forecast of sales. If industry sales are forecast to be $81,760,000, obtained through regression analysis or some other technique, the forecast of sales for Tasty Chew is $28,191,000 ($81,760,000 × 0.3448).

Sample Discrepancy

The June 30 market shares used to calculate both the transitional matrix and the forecast of July 31 shares were based on those obtained from the sample. However, actual market shares for June 30 are probably known at that time as well. Suppose actual market shares for the industry were the following:

Brand	Actual Market Share Percentage at June 30th
Tasty Chew	37.25
Eatwell	30.50
Maple	21.40
All others	10.85
Total	100.00

These data differ slightly from those obtained from the sample. The question should be raised, "Was the sample representative of the population?" If not, the transitional probability matrix should not be used to forecast market share. Instead, another, perhaps larger, sample should be drawn and the process should begin again. Various methods may be used to test whether or not the difference in the data could have been caused by chance. If the difference can in fact be explained by chance, the transition matrix may be used to make the forecast. Two methods are recommended—the chi-square and Kolmogorov-Smirnov procedures—to test whether or not the difference in sample and population market shares may be explained by chance (see Appendix 8.A).

When the actual market shares are slightly different but not at a statistically significant level, a mixed approach in making the forecast is generally used in practice. That is, forecast market shares should be made by multiplying the transitional probability matrix by a matrix of actual market shares rather than those obtained for the final period from the sample. This step simply means that the forecast is made on the basis of as much current information as possible. For the chewing gum industry example, the market share forecast becomes (the reader is urged to verify these figures):

$$\begin{pmatrix} 0.8750 & 0.0333 & 0.0400 & 0.0200 \\ 0.0500 & 0.9000 & 0.0750 & 0.0500 \\ 0.0625 & 0.0567 & 0.8000 & 0.1300 \\ 0.0125 & 0.0100 & 0.0850 & 0.8000 \end{pmatrix} \begin{pmatrix} 0.3725 \\ 0.3050 \\ 0.2140 \\ 0.1085 \end{pmatrix} = \begin{pmatrix} 0.3468 \\ 0.3146 \\ 0.2259 \\ 0.1127 \end{pmatrix}$$

The specific forecast of Tasty Chew sales is $28,354,000 ($81,760,000 × 0.3468).

This represents a slight departure from most discussions of Markov chains. Markov analysis is used to explain what happened in an entire population as well as to forecast future conditions. Theoretically, the entire population should be accounted for when using this technique. Unfortunately, forecasters of business data do not often have the luxury of total information and, instead, must rely on samples. From a practical perspective, the deviation from the theoretical analysis is often necessary and is justified, provided forecasts prove more accurate than they would have been without the technique at all.

Equilibrium

Most Markov models will result in a final equilibrium level where changes in market share will no longer result with the passing of time. To obtain this equilibrium, the transitional probability matrix can be multiplied by successive product matrices (forecast market share matrices) until no further changes in market shares result. Another way to find the equilibrium condition is through the *substitution method*, which simply and algebraically substitutes one equation for another until all values are found.

However, the final equilibrium and its derivation will not be presented in this text. These concepts have very little practical application because the equilibrium condition assumes no changes in competitive efforts on the part of participants within the industry. This assumption is unreasonable for most, if not all, industries. As market share declines, some reaction must assuredly be expected. The application of the transition matrix toward equilibrium assumes functionally linear loyalty and switching behavior on the part of customers. It assumes that if market share falls from 30% to 10%, the probability of switching to another brand remains constant. This is also unreasonable, since loyalty is a matter of degree. The first to switch as market share declines are those who are the least brand loyal. After they switch, those remaining tend to be more loyal and, accordingly, less likely to change brands. Finally, Markov analysis is generally only successful for forecasting market shares in the near future. Distant forecasts, after many time periods, are generally not very reliably forecast by this method.

Problems with Markov Analysis

Markov analysis has, to an extent, fallen into disfavor with some analysts because of its limiting assumptions. In theory, the following assumptions must be made:[2]

1. A firm's retention, switching-out, and switching-in rates at a given time depend on the current state only, not the prior history of the process.

1. For a presentation of equilibrium derivation, see Marvin A. Jolson and Richard T. Hise, *Quantitative Techniques for Marketing Decisions* (New York : Macmillan Company, 1973), pp. 100–102.
2. Ibid., p. 93.

2. The last purchase pattern observed will continue.
3. Consumers purchase at regular intervals.
4. Consumers all purchase equal quantities of the product in a given time period.
5. The same loyalty and switching rates apply to all purchasers.
6. The market size remains constant.
7. No new competitors enter the market.
8. All consumers purchase the product.

These assumptions appear to be rather formidable at first glance. However, most are not that difficult to deal with in practical situations. Assumptions 3 and 8 may technically be handled by creating an artificial category into which or from which individuals may be considered to switch or remain loyal (a slack variable based on potential market). Assumption 6 may be dealt with by handling an increased market in the same technical manner or by simply assuming that new customers enter the market by purchasing in the same proportion as the current market share existing at the time of their entrance. Assumption 4 may be dealt with by assuming instead that, within each quantity level of purchasers, loyalty and switching behavior are identical to those indicated in the transformational probability matrix. In a very large market, this assumption is less restrictive than in a small one. Assumption 5 is less restrictive for forecasts in the short run, where it is likely to be realistic. The hard-core unswitchables would not be as proportionately, or significantly, greater as a short period progresses as would be the case in the long run.

Many of the assumptions may be made less restrictive in practical application. Sampling regularly to construct a new transformational probability matrix generally increases the accuracy of forecasts made via this method. Many of the restrictive theoretical assumptions may be practically overcome with frequent updating of the matrices as obtained from new data.

Higher-Order Markov Chains

The Markov analysis presented was that of a first-order process. We assumed that a customer's probability of purchasing a brand was dependent solely on his or her most recent purchase. This situation is not always characteristic of brand selection behavior. Instead, an individual's behavior may be a function of past as well as most recent behavior. Higher-order Markov analytic techniques are available to handle these types of situations. However, these techniques are more complex, and a complete discussion of Markov process is beyond the scope of this text. More important, these refinements do not generally offer substantially improved forecasts in practice.

MARKET SHARE AND NEW PRODUCTS

You may be surprised to learn that market share techniques are not exclusively limited to forecasting for existing products. A slightly different application is available for new products. For instance, the Hanlon Detergent Company is planning to introduce a new lanolin hand soap called Kleanands. This soap may be used to remove grease and grime from extremely dirty hands. Kleanands may also be used for bathing because of its low abrasive qualities. The latter use, however, is estimated to be small because of its low perfume content, although, because of the soap's lathering ease, some use for bathing may be expected in areas that have extremely hard water. Table 7.7 presents industry data for soap.

Table 7.7 1982 Personal Detergent Industry Data

Market-Firm	Sales (in Millions of Dollars)	Market Shares, % Segment	Industry
Hand soap			
Wipe Clean	53.7	47.4	7.3
Dirt-Off	26.2	23.1	3.6
Eliminate	16.8	14.8	2.3
Dad's Good Ol' Soap	12.5	11.1	1.7
All others	4.1	3.6	0.6
Total hand soap	113.3	100.0	15.5
General-usage soaps			
Tally	207.1	41.9	28.3
Creamy	169.3	34.3	23.1
Floaty	101.0	20.5	13.8
Sinks-in-the-Tub	12.9	2.6	1.8
All others	3.6	0.7	0.5
Total general usage	493.9	100.0	67.5
Bathing			
Soft and Cuddly	62.8	50.3	8.6
Hug Me	53.1	42.5	7.2
Tender Skin	7.5	6.1	1.0
All other	1.4	1.1	0.2
Total bathing	124.8	100.0	17.0
Total industry sales	732.0		100.0

The marketing manager of Hanlon has decided that, should the product be introduced nationally, the best introductory program is to distribute free samples of the detergent along with a brief description of the product. Limited market testing and knowledge obtained from introducing new products in the past suggest additional information, presented in Table 7.8, for the proposed new product. The optimistic, pessimistic, and most likely estimates may be based on judgment, as discussed in Chapter 2, or on confidence limits established from a sample. They serve to establish a range within which the actual new product market share is very likely to fall at the end of the first year. Table 7.9 presents the calculations necessary to obtain the range of forecast market shares at the end of the introduction.

These forecasts of market share may be used to forecast sales of the proposed new product for the first full year of sales (after the first to buy and then adopt have done so). Industry sales are forecast to be $750,000,000 during the forthcoming year, as obtained through time-series analysis. It is expected that each market segment will account for the same percentage of industry sales as it did in 1982. The forecast of sales is presented in Table 7.10 (in dollars, not in millions). The market manager must decide, on the basis of this analysis, whether or not these forecasts of sales are worth the cost and effort necessary to introduce the product.

The Kleanands example was simplified for illustration. The number of trials to stabilize, switching after initial stabilization, and gradual acceptance of the product are all factors that increase the complexity

Table 7.8 Additional Hanlon New Product Information

Percentage of the market reached with free samples:

Hand soap	25.0
General usage	40.0
Bathing	20.0

Percentage of those reached buying the product the first time:

	Optimistic	Pessimistic	Most Likely
Hand soap	2.50	0.50	1.50
General usage	1.00	0.20	0.60
Bathing	0.20	0.05	0.13

Percentage of those buying the first time who continue to purchase throughout the first year:

Hand soap	50.0
General usage	35.0
Bathing	15.0

Table 7.9 Calculation of Forecast Market Share

Market Segment	Percentage Reached	Percentage of Market Buying First Time[a]			Percentage Buying the Second Time[b]		
		Optimistic	Pessimistic	Most Likely	Optimistic	Pessimistic	Most Likely
Hand soap	25.0	0.625	0.125	0.375	0.3125	0.0625	0.1875
General usage	40.0	0.400	0.080	0.240	0.1400	0.0280	0.0840
Bathing	20.0	0.040	0.010	0.026	0.0060	0.0015	0.0039

[a] Percentage reached times percentage buying after being reached, as listed in Table 7.8.
[b] Percentage of market buying first time times percentage repeating, as listed in Table 7.8.

Table 7.10 First-Year Sales Forecast for Kleanands

Market Segment	Industry Sales (in Millions of Dollars)	Forecast Sales[a]		
		Optimistic, $	Pessimistic, $	Most Likely, $
Hand soap	116.25	363,280	72,660	217,970
General usage	506.25	708,750	141,750	425,250
Bathing	127.50	7,650	1,910	4,970
Total	750.00	1,079,680	216,320	648,190

[a] Forecast market share, as presented in Table 7.9, times forecast segment sales.

of the analysis. Nevertheless, Kleanands serves to illustrate the use of reasonably attainable market shares in forecasting for new products.

PRODUCT LIFE CYCLES

Products do not simply enter the market with instant success or suddenly depart without warning. Rather, they have life cycles which typify their sales. After introduction, successful products experience a rapid increase during initial time periods, then a leveling, and finally a decline in sales. The typical life cycle of a product is characterized in Figure 7.1, which indicates that the rate of change in sales differs throughout the entire life of the product. For many products, the analyst must take into consideration this changing rate when preparing a forecast.

The importance of the product life cycle in influencing sales in the immediate future is dependent upon the time period covered. For some products, such as certain clothing fashions, the entire product life cycle is rather short-lived. For other products, such as coal, the life cycle is lengthy, and may be ignored for all practical purposes. Many analysts are primarily concerned with forecasts of only a few years. The underlying life cycle may have an insignificant impact on forecasts for such products. With relatively short-lived products, however, the stage of the life cycle may be a very important consideration when preparing the forecast.

From a forecasting perspective, the recognition of product life cycles does not necessitate additional forecasting techniques. Technically, a product's life cycle is a trend that must be analyzed in making a forecast. Trend analysis was considered in Chapters 3, 4, and 5.

Figure 7.1 Life Cycle of a Typical Product

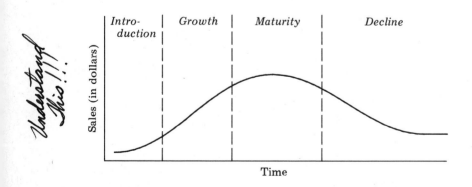

Source: Philip Kotler, *Marketing Management: Analysis, Planning, and Control*, 4th ed. (Englewood Cliffs, N.J.: Prentice-Hall, 1980), Chapter 12.

SUMMARY

This chapter dealt with techniques that relate to the market's decisions among competing products within an industry. A firm's relative sales position with respect to competition within an industry is dependent upon its past position. Customers become loyal to certain brands and certain stores, and this loyalty influences future decisions. Historical market shares within an industry are often good indicators of future sales and may be used in the forecasting process. Simple market shares may be used to forecast sales in the future, or an analysis of shares may be made in greater depth. That is, customers may be analyzed to learn of switching and loyalty behavior. These data may, in turn, be used to forecast market shares and related sales with greater accuracy. In-depth analysis of brand loyalty and switching also enhances the development of marketing strategies and plans in that further insight into the strengths and weaknesses of brands in attracting and holding customers is often obtained. The interplay between brands may be highlighted by examining switching behavior. This enables marketing strategists to focus efforts on areas of relative strength and weakness.

DISCUSSION QUESTIONS

1. Summarize what may be learned by analyzing customer brand switching and loyalty behavior.
2. What impact does a proposed new competing product have on market share forecasts?

The following January market shares relate to questions 3 through 5.

Firm	Percent Share
A	27.0
B	23.0
C	20.0
D	16.0
All others	14.0
Total	100.0

A stratified random sample of 1,000 subjects during February yields the following results:

| | Customers Gained from | | | | | |
Firm	A	B	C	D	All Others	Total
A	0	20	30	25	10	85
B	35	0	20	50	20	125
C	60	15	0	20	20	115
D	80	10	10	0	20	120
All others	5	10	5	20	0	40
Total	180	55	65	115	70	485

| | Customers Lost to | | | | | |
Firm	A	B	C	D	All Others	Total
A	0	35	60	80	5	180
B	20	0	15	10	10	55
C	30	20	0	10	5	65
D	25	50	20	0	20	115
All others	10	20	20	20	0	70
Total	85	125	115	120	40	485

Actual market share at February 28:

Firm	Percent Share
A	18.5
B	29.0
C	24.0
D	16.5
All others	12.0
Total	100.0

continued

3. What is the transitional probability matrix? How is it beneficial, by itself, in helping management to gain an understanding of competitive interactions in the marketplace?
4. Forecast market share at March 31st for each competitor.
5. Was the sample representative of the population? If not, what should be done?

Firm	Customers Gained from					
	A	B	C	D	All Others	Total
A	0	15	25	20	5	65
B	30	0	20	30	10	90
C	60	10	0	15	20	105
D	70	15	15	0	10	110
All others	5	15	15	15	0	45
Total	165	55	70	80	45	415

Assume the above and that the January 31 and February 28 market shares remain the same as before, for questions 6 through 10.

6. Now interpret the loyalty patterns.
7. Was the sample representative of the population?
8. Assume that the sample was representative. Forecast market shares for March 31.
9. What is the best estimate possible at the end of February of market shares on April 30?
10. What is the problem with using brand loyalty and switching patterns for forecasts into distant periods?

RECOMMENDED READINGS

Day, Ralph L., and Leonard J. Parsons (eds.). *Marketing Models: Quantitative Applications.* Scranton, Pa.: Intext Educational Publishers, 1971.

Jolson, Marvin A., and Richard T. Hise. *Quantitative Techniques for Marketing Decisions.* New York: Macmillan Company, 1973.

Kesavan, Ram. "Empirical Tests of Two Stochastic Models of Consumer Brand Choice." *Journal of the Academy of Marketing Science*, 8 (Summer 1980), 264–276.

King, William R. *Quantitative Analysis for Marketing Management.* New York: McGraw-Hill Book Company, 1967.

Kotler, Philip. *Marketing Decision Making: A Model Building Approach.* New York: Holt, Rinehart and Winston, 1971.

Kotler, Philip. *Marketing Management: Analysis, Planning and Control.* Englewood Cliffs, N.J.: Prentice-Hall, 1980.

Kuehn, Alfred A., and Ralph L. Day. "Probabilistic Models of Consumer Buying Behavior." *Journal of Marketing*, 28 (October 1964), 27–31.

Levin, Richard I., and Charles A. Kirkpatrick. *Quantitative Approaches to Management*. 3rd ed. New York: McGraw-Hill Book Company, 1974, Chapter 13.

Morrison, Donald G. "Testing Brand-Switching Models." *Journal of Marketing Research*, 3 (November 1966), 401–409.

Siegel, Sidney. *Nonparametric Statistics for the Behavioral Sciences*. New York: McGraw-Hill Book Company, 1956.

CASE 7: DEL BURKE LUMBER COMPANY

The Del Burke Lumber Company is a lumberyard located in a midwestern city of over 120,000 population. The firm was founded in 1947 by Del Burke and his two sons. In 1982, Burke retired, and the sons took over as managers. Burke, however, still spends a few hours each day in the lumberyard, doing odd jobs and acting as an adviser.

The firm's managers are ambitious and hope to expand sales and profits. There are six other lumberyards in the city and adjacent area, two of which are large enough to pose considerable competition. One of the competitors operates on a "low-price, no-frills" basis, whereby customers who are willing to do without certain services, such as loading and delivery, can purchase lumber and related products at a price well below the market average. This competitor is located in a remote section of the city, operates out of an older building that needs renovating, and has fewer employees relative to its sales position than the other firms. The second large lumberyard follows the opposite strategy, offering many services and a skilled work force but at relatively higher prices. These two large competitors and two of the smaller ones advertise extensively in the local newspaper and on the radio station.

Over the years, Del Burke has tried to maintain a profile about halfway between the two major competitors described above. The firm's services, offered through an average sales force, are adequate but not extensive; its location is less remote than that of the low-priced competitor; and its prices, for most of its inventory, falls midway between those of the other two firms.

Burke's firm tries to attract the business of both individual consumers and industrial customers. In the first category, it aims primarily at married couples aged 20 to 50 with average incomes. In the second category, it serves construction companies and some miscellaneous service, manufacturing, and retail businesses. In 1982, 20% of the company's business came from individual consumers, 75% from construction companies, and 5% from other sources.

Sales data for the Del Burke lumberyard are as follows:

Year	Sales (in Thousands of Dollars)	Year	Sales (in Thousands of Dollars)
1947	35	1965	119
1948	39	1966	127
1949	42	1967	130
1950	48	1968	136
1951	57	1969	149
1952	64	1970	157
1953	64	1971	172
1954	69	1972	189
1955	72	1973	198
1956	79	1974	225
1957	70	1975	259
1958	81	1976	290
1959	83	1977	329
1960	85	1978	358
1961	89	1979	377
1962	91	1980	394
1963	102	1981	436
1964	114	1982	457

Share of market data (estimated, because management can only estimate total city sales—there are no established data on this variable) are as follows:

Year	Share of Market, %
1947	5
1957	8
1967	10
1977	12
1978	11
1979	10
1980	12
1981	11
1982	13

The Del Burke management believes that, despite its many years of operations, the firm is still in the growth phase of its life cycle. Sales (and profits) are growing at a steady pace. If the growth continues, it may be necessary to purchase additional land, enlarge the lumberyard buildings, and hire additional employees.

1. Would you recommend sales forecasting by estimating future shares of market? Why or why not?
2. Could Markov analysis provide effective sales forecasts? Why or why not?
3. Do you believe that the firm is in the growth stage of its life cycle? Defend your answer.

Chapter 8
Model Building and Simulation

INTRODUCTION

The term *simulation* appeared in the literature of business administration within the past two decades. Simulation is a computer-age technique for analyzing systems. It involves the building of a mathematical model representing a real-world system, which is analyzed by manipulating the model. For example, a model airplane is usually built and analyzed in a wind tunnel before the first real plane is built. Inferences about the real plane are made on the basis of the wind tunnel tests. Business systems may also be simulated in a similar manner except that mathematical relationships are used instead of physical models.

Model-building and simulation techniques have many applications for analyzing business systems, including inventory control, production and quality control, and human behavior settings. A brief look into the simulation process, some especially useful applications to forecasting, and the reason for its use are discussed in this chapter.

STATIC FORECASTING

Thus far, this text has dealt primarily with the static forecast, which is a forecast made of a particular variable for a specific point in time. For example, forecasters for the Hi-Tech Semiconductor Company use a simple bivariate regression model to forecast sales for the next quarter. Historical data for the last twelve quarters are presented in Table 8.1.

From the data in Table 8.1, the following regression equation was calculated by using the techniques presented in Chapter 4:

$$y_c = a + bx = -53.72 + (0.5872)x,$$

$$\text{with adjusted } r^2 = 0.826$$

The First Quarter

If the forecast GNP for next quarter is \$269.8 (obtained from government sources), the forecast of Hi-Tech's sales becomes

Table 8.1 Hi-Tech Semiconductor Company Historical Data

Time Period	GNP (in Billions of Dollars)	Sales (in Millions of Dollars)
t	x	y
1	225.1	82.8
2	249.8	87.3
3	237.3	85.4
4	256.0	93.2
5	253.2	92.1
6	259.8	97.6
7	260.4	98.3
8	258.7	98.1
9	264.1	102.2
10	262.7	101.6
11	265.3	105.4
12	266.5	107.6

$$y_c = -53.72 + (0.5872)(269.8) = \$104{,}707{,}000$$

This value, subject to a possible evaluation of its variability, is the forecast for the following quarter, which is used by management as a basis for planning. The forecast of $104,707,000 is used to plan production, purchases, inventory levels, shipping and distribution, and so on. These other variables may be adjusted for other conditions or may even be forecast by themselves, but the forecast of sales is used as one, if not the most, influential factor in scheduling activity for the coming quarter.

The Second Quarter

At the end of the next quarter, the process is again repeated, with an attempt to forecast the next static value. Table 8.2 presents updated data to reflect one additional quarter's information.

Careful comparison of Tables 8.1 and 8.2 reveals that they are essentially the same. Their difference stems from the fact that one quarter's worth of new information is now available and is entered into the historical data set. All other data are pushed one quarter back. In addition, the oldest quarter's data in Table 8.1 (that for $t = 1$) was deleted for convenience.

Table 8.2 Hi-Tech Semiconductor Historical Data Updated

Time Period	GNP (in Billions of Dollars)	Sales (in Millions of Dollars)
t	x	y
1	249.8	87.3
2	237.3	85.4
3	256.0	93.2
4	253.2	92.1
5	259.8	97.6
6	260.4	98.3
7	258.7	98.1
8	264.1	102.2
9	262.7	101.6
10	265.3	105.4
11	266.5	107.6
12	296.2	104.9

If the forecast GNP for next quarter (again obtained from govern-ment sources) is $271.1, the following forecast of sales is made after the regression equation is recalculated for the current information:

$$y_c = a + bx$$
$$= -6.877 + (0.4013)x$$
$$y_c = -6.877 + (0.4013)(271.1) = \$101,915,000$$

The planning process is again activated.

Problems with Static Forecasts

The process of forecasting values for specific periods, after updating historical information, continues until either a better technique is found or until conditions change and result in altered forecast needs. Success-ful applications of this type of forecasting are dependent on at least two factors.

The first of these concerns forecast accuracy. Measurements of mean squared error, MSE, address this issue. The second, and perhaps even more important, is that operations must be flexible enough to be adjusted to changes in expected conditions if the forecast is to be useful at all. If sales are projected to be at a lower level for the next period, operations must also be flexible enough to be adjusted downward to reflect anticipated sales for the forecast to be of great value.

PROCESS FORECASTS

Another type of requirement is placed on forecasts when flexibility cannot be assumed. Chevrolet, for example, must use forecasts in designing new assembly plants. Once a plant is built, however, it is very inflexible. A part of the plant cannot mysteriously disappear simply because demand is expected to decline in a following quarter. Further, if demand suddenly increases, lost sales may materialize as a result of an inability to satisfy all customers.

The forecast of optimum plant size is complicated by the consideration of the cost of building and maintaining a plant. If a plant is built to meet the largest expected demand for the foreseeable future, costs will be unnecessarily high during those periods when demand is lower than the full-capacity level. The objective of making a decision about plant size in this environment is to balance the cost of carrying additional plant size during periods of low demand with the opportunity costs (lost profits) of being out of inventory during peaks in demand.

Forecasting that considers variables like these is slightly different from the static types discussed in earlier chapters. The objective of this analysis is to determine desirable operation alternatives, given that a variation may be expected to exist in key variables such as demand and days required to receive an order. These forecasts are needed for capital-budgeting decisions. Variables and constraints are forecast for the purpose of determining desirable operating levels of certain processes and resources, such as equipment, plant, inventories, and inventory reorder points, which are ongoing over many periods.

THE BUSINESS THROUGHPUT SYSTEM

Analysts trying to forecast operational levels by using simulation techniques must take an approach that differs from static forecasting in structuring their problems. They must recognize that they are attempting to analyze a system of variables that are all interrelated as a set of interacting components.

The analyst's first task is to identify the components that are essential in the system. To illustrate, if a study is being made of a boat marina to forecast the optimal number of gasoline fuel pumps, diesel fuel pumps, and dock footage to maintain, several relevant variables must be considered, such as boat traffic, size of passing boats, length of time to fill tanks, and number of gasoline versus diesel fuel pumps. To complicate

matters further, each of these components has an impact on demand
for the marine facilities. The system of components interrelates because
the size of the facilities also influences demand. If too few facilities are
provided, boats will be backed up in a waiting line. If the line is too
long, some people may never return for repeat business. Conversely, if
the facility is very large, it may attract many customers, but substantial
spaces may be idle too often. As a consequence, maintenance costs may
be prohibitive. Also, if some of the facilities become run down, customers may avoid the marina in the future.

After identifying relevant components, the analyst's next step is to
attempt to specify the relationships existing between each of them. For
the boat marina, it is necessary to determine the weighting factors that
should be assigned to each of the variables, such as traffic, boat size,
and fueling time, in relation to total demand on the facility. These
represent an analysis of the inputs into the system.

Outputs must also be considered. In a simplified case, this may be
merely the number of gallons delivered and the resulting profit. However,
in the true-system sense, most variables are *circularly* related. To continue with the marina, the number and size of fuel tanks, number and
location of pumps, number of attendants, linear feet of docking space
and prices all affect inputs. If prices are excessive, traffic and demand
will decline. If too few spaces are available for docking, the size of the
waiting line and use of the facilities will tend to rise but total demand
may decline.

Input as well as output variables may influence each other. Boat size
may affect traffic patterns. If many large boats pass, there may be a
tendency for small boats to stay away. Also, large boats may tend to
stay out of the harbor longer than small boats and thereby reduce
traffic.

These variables and interrelationships are not complete. Nevertheless,
they are sufficiently comprehensive to suggest that the prediction
problem is much more complex than those presented in earlier chapters.
The circular influence existing in the relationships among variables
means that inputs, outputs, and the entire conversion process must be
analyzed in total. The process for which we are forecasting optimal
facilities consisting of entities and relationships may be termed the
business *throughput system*. This term emphasizes the conversion of
inputs into outputs (number of pumps into gallons delivered) that exists
in most managed continuous-process business systems.

After an examination of the actual system, the analyst prepares a
model to represent this system. There are many types of models:
physical (model airplanes), schematic (graphs), mathematical (equations),
and so forth. The types used most often by analysts of business throughput systems are mathematical models, which attempt to convey the
essence of the process represented. To illustrate, if an average of 12
boats pass in front of the marina every hour, we may define the number

is there another marina in the area?

of expected boats passing in front of the marina by Y in X hours as $Y = 12X$. This equation represents the nucleus of a set of equations which model the throughput system.

MOVEMENT THROUGH TIME

Simply developing a model of the throughput system is not enough. The reason for making the analysis in the first place is to attempt to determine the impact of various decision alternatives *over time.* A restaurant might be constructed in such a manner that it could hold the number of seats estimated to be needed on the first Monday after the grand opening. If the forecast of demand is accurate, this seating configuration might be perfect on that Monday. However, the questions must be asked, "Will this seating arrangement be proper for other Mondays?" "Will it be adequate during the other six days of the week?" It is obvious that the restaurant's seating capacity should be based on demand over the long run and not just for one Monday.

Simulation represents a process of moving a model through time. The model is solved for a particular time period, and these solved values are, in turn, used to solve for values in a series of succeeding time periods. Inferences are made about the implications of real-world decision alternatives on the basis of their simulated outcomes found by moving the model artificially through time. To illustrate, in preparing for moon launchings, astronauts practiced approach procedures in a lunar lander simulator. This machine allowed the astronauts to become familiar with the anticipated impact of exercising various controls during actual descent. To be sure, many simulated crashes occurred as a result of reactions improper to surface alterations during practice sequences. Various procedures were established that optimized the chances of success on the basis of numerous repeated trials in the simulator.

Like practicing in the simulator, inferences about throughput systems are made on the basis of measurement of numerous repeated trials obtained by analyzing the model through time. For the restaurant's number of seats, the analyst might simulate the impact of 50 seats by analyzing anticipated demand for the next several years on a daily basis. The reader should not be alarmed by the number of days involved. Demand is not statically forecast for each and every day for the entire simulated period. Instead, probability distributions of demand are used, perhaps a separate one for each day in the week, to estimate demand over time. For instance, after the profitability of 50 seats is assessed, the simulation may be repeated for 51 seats. This process continues until the number of seats is found that appears to maximize profits. At that point, provided the model was constructed accurately, the proper number of seats for profit maximization may be provided for in the construction of the building. The model could also be employed to maximize other variables, such as sales or contribution margin.

PROBABILITY

The preceding section indicated that probability distributions may be used to estimate variable *states*. A state refers to the value of a variable at a particular point in time. For the restaurant example, the state of the daily demand was estimated.

The use of probability frequency distributions to estimate variable states is a major part of simulation. If exact variable states were known (daily demand), optimal solutions could be calculated by straightforward mathematical techniques. By introducing various probability factors for one or more variables, the solution becomes much more complex. Relationships between variables become difficult to specify. Instead of making calculations on the basis of expected values and variability for each variable, the model that is moved through time is made to assume an actual state and its effects on the throughput system are calculated. Afterward, another state in the next time period is assumed and its related effects are determined.

This process of assuming one state, calculated through a probability distribution, and determining its impact on the overall system is continued for many periods of time. After each decision alternative is analyzed in a similar manner, expected values or other measures for the entire period may be compared and the most valued alternative selected.

There is considerable complexity in relationships caused by both the great number of variables and by the introduction of probabilistic considerations necessary to analyze most real-world throughput systems. The state of each variable, as influenced by all the relationships with other variables, must be updated for each successive time period in the analysis. Simple examples containing few variables and only limited degrees of interrelationships are presented in this chapter for illustration. These examples are of limited scope in relation to most actual simulations, but they do serve to illustrate what is needed. The seriously interested student, however, is urged to delve into books that concentrate on simulation in depth.[1]

1. For an excellent introductory approach, see Claude McMillan and Richard Gonzalez, with a contributed chapter by Thomas Schriber, *Systems Analysis: A Computer Approach to Decision Models*, 3rd ed. (Homewood, Ill.: Richard D. Irwin, 1973).

MONTE CARLO SIMULATION

The Monte Carlo technique of simulation is based on generating random numbers, each with an equal probability of uniformly distributed occurrence, to be used to represent a variable's state at a particular point in time. This technique presumably got its name because many examples, and even some applications, use gaming devices for the generation of random numbers. For instance, the rolling of dice or the spinning of a roulette wheel can serve to generate a simulation's random numbers.

Conversion to Other Distributions

The generation of random numbers results in a uniformly distributed frequency of digits, or fractions, where each digit has an equal probability of occurrence on a given trial. For example, if the field of digits was limited to all nonnegative integers with one characteristic, the digit field consists of 0, 1, 2, . . ., 9. Each of these digits has an equal probability (0.10) of occurring at any particular trial in the long run.

However, uniform frequency distributions are not usually representative of real-world business throughput systems. For instance, customers do not generally arrive at a retail store at equal rates throughout the day. In many stores, a small group of customers arrives during the first few minutes, and arrivals then stabilize and taper off until noon. During the lunch hour break, many people do some shopping. A slow period for retail stores is around 5:30 P.M., when many families are home for dinner. In summary, demands for a store's services fluctuate in a pattern that is somewhat repetitive each day. Differences in flows may exist between certain days; weekend and weekday patterns are usually different.

Fortunately, uniformly distributed random numbers may be adjusted to fit the nonuniform conditions described above, provided, of course, that they tend to be regular and predictable. For example, each Tuesday morning is slower in terms of customer traffic than the evening. An adjustment is accomplished by selecting a range of possible random digits to represent the occurrence of the simulated variable event on the basis of that variable's assumed frequency, determined from theoretical or historical sources. The frequency of historical occurrence or theoretical occurrence of the various possible states of a variable is used to adjust random digits to represent the underlying process being analyzed.

Assigning Random Digits

Suppose that an analyst wants to simulate through the use of random digits the sum of two dice being repeatedly rolled. A random-digit table is a list of randomly generated digits, as presented in Appendix 8.B. Such a listing is used by randomly selecting the first digit anywhere from the table. Succeeding digits are then obtained by following a fixed order (such as every number of a diagonal from lower right to upper left) which has been established before the initial selection.

Assuming that the dice are fair, the analyst knows the theoretical distribution of summed-dice scores. These have been calculated and appear in Table 8.3. The basis for random-digit selection is obtained from the cumulative frequency function. The range of random digits used to represent each event (summed-dice total) is presented in Table 8.4.

To obtain the conversion from Table 8.3 to 8.4, the cumulative frequency functions were multiplied by 1,000 to convert the figures into integers. As such, three character digits must be selected from Appendix 8.B to represent the random equivalent.

It should be noted that 1.0 has been subtracted from each of the converted frequencies to establish the range because 000 is considered a digit. Hence, 1,000 digits terminate with 999. By converting the cumulative frequencies into a range of random digits, the analyst has established a distribution of random digits that has relative frequencies identical to that for the theoretical distribution of summed-dice scores.

Table 8.3 Theoretical Die-Roll Frequencies

Summed Value of Dice	No. of Ways/ Possible Ways	Relative Frequency[a]	Cumulative Frequency
2	1/36	0.028	0.028
3	2/36	0.055	0.083
4	3/36	0.083	0.166
5	4/36	0.111	0.277
6	5/36	0.139	0.416
7	6/36	0.168	0.584
8	5/36	0.139	0.723
9	4/36	0.111	0.834
10	3/36	0.083	0.917
11	2/36	0.055	0.972
12	1/36	0.028	1.000
		1.000	

[a] Rounded

Table 8.4 Assignment of Random Digits to Events

Event	Random-Digit Range
2	000–027
3	028–082
4	083–165
5	166–276
6	277–415
7	416–583
8	584–722
9	723–833
10	834–916
11	917–971
12	972–999

Simulation of Dice Rolls

It is now possible to use the random-digit table and Table 8.4 to simulate the rolling of dice. For the random-digit-selection strategy, the analyst in this instance begins with the first number in the lower left-hand corner in the table of Appendix 8.B and selects every number from the bottom to the top of each column in a left-to-right columnar order. There are five digits in each number. It does not matter which three digits are used as the generated random digit, as long as a consistent and predetermined strategy is employed. In this case, the middle three digits are used.

The first random digit from Appendix 8.B is 838. Table 8.4 indicates that this digit may be interpreted to mean that the number 10 has been simulated for the first event. In this simulation model, there is no need for concern with the order of the dice, only their total. However, order could have been considered. The next simulated dice score is seven, the third is seven, and so forth. The simulation would continue for successive events in this manner until the process has simulated all the events desired. Table 8.5 presents the number of times that each summed total occurs for this model when 180 events are simulated in the manner outlined.

Compare the relative frequencies simulated with the model to their theoretical counterparts in Table 8.3. The slight differences are due largely to the sample size, which involved simulating only 180 events. The theoretical frequency distribution represents those values that may be expected to occur as a result of repeated rolls over the long run. If we were to simulate 1,000 events, the actual and theoretical frequencies

Table 8.5 Summary of 180 Events

Event	Number of Occurrences	Relative Frequency
2	6	0.033
3	7	0.039
4	13	0.072
5	23	0.128
6	22	0.122
7	29	0.161
8	26	0.145
9	24	0.134
10	13	0.072
11	13	0.072
12	4	0.022
Total	180	1.000

would probably be more closely matched; 10,000 events should be still closer.

Over the long run, a real frequency distribution is practically identical to the theoretical. Gambling casinos operate on this principle. In the long run, they are able to make a profit because the odds, as established by the theoretical distribution, are slightly in their favor. It is also possible to determine statistically whether or not differences in the simulated and theoretical distributions may be explained by chance. Appendix 8.A contains two tests that may be used.

Number of Events

In order for the Monte Carlo simulation to be meaningful, the number of events to be simulated must be large enough to allow the actual to approach the theoretical distribution. Unfortunately, for many simulations, the theoretical distribution is not known. For instance, if a simulation of a proposed new assembly line is being made in order to obtain insight into its down time, the actual frequency of breaks in the process would not be known. As a result, the analyst cannot compare results obtained from the simulation to a theoretical distribution to determine if enough events have been simulated. Instead, the analyst must determine the number of events ahead of time.

There are no hard and fast rules to follow when deciding upon the number of events to be simulated. A sufficiently large number is required

to allow the simulation to represent the long-run distribution of the
actual process. Essentially, a balance must be struck between excessive
computer time (and related cost) and an inadequate representation of
the long-run implications of the throughput system being analyzed.
Generally, the greater the number of possible outcomes for an event
and the smaller their probability of occurrence, the greater should be
the number of events simulated. For many simulations, however,
between 5,000 and 10,000 time periods are considered a sufficiently
large number.

HARD DATA

Simulations are frequently made when actual input data are available. A
base of experience can often be determined from company stock
records, sales slips, deliveries, orders, time records, and cash register
figures. These data can be combined with externally developed data,
such as machine performance specifications as presented by the manufacturer, for the development of the model to be simulated.

Production Planning

The Orelle Company manufactures aluminum combination screen and
storm doors. At present, management is in the analysis stage of a
proposal to replace manufacturing equipment. Their current machines
have recently broken down and, primarily because of their age, are
beyond repair. Consequently, management must evaluate the alternative
courses of action that might be undertaken.

Recently Builtwell Machines Company salespeople proposed to sell
Orelle the two required machines: the first is a shaper and trimmer
which stamps the design on a sheet of aluminum and trims it, and the
second is a sprayer for painting the door. Orelle has requested bids from
all known sources, and only Builtwell has responded. Therefore, Orelle
is faced with the decision of either to buy the Builtwell machines or to
close the plant for an indefinite period to search for another supplier.
The purchasing agent for Orelle is aware that comparable machines will
not be found at a lower cost anywhere, and the chief engineer knows
that the proposed Builtwell machines will last as long and are as inexpensive to operate as those produced by other companies. Therefore,
cost of the machines and their operating costs may be ignored in the
decision.

Downtime is another relevant matter. Orelle is under contract to
supply all of the doors that the Levine & Rowpenny Company sells.
Levine & Rowpenny is a large national department store with a

catalogue-selling operation. They are Orelle's only customer, so they must fill the annual demand for aluminum doors, which is 50,000 units. Seasonal fluctuation may be ignored because Levine & Rowpenny has agreed to carry the inventory of the aluminum doors and accept shipment on a relatively even basis throughout the year.

Orelle's main concern is whether or not the machines proposed by Builtwell will be able to meet the annual demand of Levine & Rowpenny. If the machines are not satisfactory, Orelle might subcontract the manufacture of the doors to several smaller shops until they can find another source for the machines and be able to retain the Levine account. However, because of cost and the risk of not finding suitable subcontractors, management wishes to avoid this alternative.

Specifications for the Builtwell machines are as follows:

Machine	Daily Capacity	Probability of Breakdown
Shaper and trimmer	250 units	0.10
Sprayer	250 units	0.10

These specifications represent the composite of over 1,000 installations of Builtwell equipment and are expected to fulfill the characteristics of Orelle's machines, should they be ordered.

The probability-of-breakdown figure indicates the estimated chances the respective machine will malfunction during any one day. For simplicity, it is assumed that all breakdowns occur immediately at the start of the day, last all day, and are repaired by the start of the next day. The number of breakdowns of each machine is independent of that of the other machines. Orelle operates 234 days per year and, because of a recent union settlement, overtime cannot be scheduled.

Simulation can be used to help Orelle management decide whether or not to buy the Builtwell machines. Figure 8.1 represents a visual daily model of the throughput system about which Orelle must make a decision.

A random-number generator is needed to estimate whether or not each machine is operating on a given simulated day. A single random digit is sufficient for the Orelle example because of the one-in-ten probability of a breakdown. The use of any random digit to simulate a breakdown would be fine, but for simplicity, let us assume that 0 represents a breakdown, and the digits 1, 2, . . ., 9 represent a day when a machine is running. Table 8.6 presents the results of 20 days of operation simulated with random digits from Appendix 8.B (reading left to right, top to bottom, and using the last digit in each field of 5).

Figure 8.1   Builtwell Machines

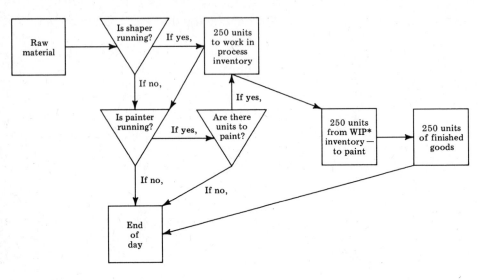

*Work-in-Process (WIP)

    Of course, a sample of only 20 days is not enough to render a decision possible. Neither is one year of simulated events enough, since results obtained at the end of one year represent only one probabilistic chance. Rather, it is the composite of many years' worth of simulated experience with the throughput system that provides insight into the system's characteristics of decision making. The computer program in Figure 8.2 was used to simulate Orelle's throughput system for 1,000 years, where each year is assumed to be the first year with no beginning inventories.[2]

2. RANDU(IX,IY,YFL) represents a system function on many computers for generating a uniformly distributed pseudorandom fraction within the range $0 \leqslant \text{YFL} < 1.0$. To use this function, it is necessary to initialize the generator by setting IX equal to a beginning random integer (preferably an odd integer divisible by 5). After each CALL, it is necessary to set IX equal to IY (which is a uniformly distributed pseudorandom integer). Some argue that RANDU should not be used because it contains bias. For a discussion of random number generation and tests of pseudorandom numbers, see J. W. Schmidt and R. E. Taylor, *Simulation and Analysis of Industrial Systems* (Homewood, Ill.: Richard D. Irwin, 1970), Chapter 6.

Table 8.6 First 20 Days of Operation

Day	Random Digits	Is the Machine Working? Shaper & Trimmer	Is the Machine Working? Painter	End of Day WIP Inventory*	Final Production Cumulative Total
1	1,1	Yes	Yes	0	250
2	6,0	Yes	No	250	250
3	3,8	Yes	Yes	250	500
4	9,6	Yes	Yes	250	750
5	7,6	Yes	Yes	250	1,000
6	0,9	No	Yes	0	1,250
7	5,4	Yes	Yes	0	1,500
8	2,7	Yes	Yes	0	1,750
9	9,2	Yes	Yes	0	2,000
10	0,0	No	No	0	2,000
11	8,0	Yes	No	250	2,000
12	1,3	Yes	Yes	250	2,250
13	9,4	Yes	Yes	250	2,500
14	2,1	Yes	Yes	250	2,750
15	9,0	Yes	No	500	2,750
16	4,2	Yes	Yes	500	3,000
17	1,8	Yes	Yes	500	3,250
18	5,5	Yes	Yes	500	3,500
19	3,3	Yes	Yes	500	3,750
20	5,6	Yes	Yes	500	4,000

*WIP = Work in progress

Figure 8.2 Fortran Program for the Orelle Company

```
            DIMENSION PROD(1001),DIST(1000,2)
            IX=5
            DO 1 J=1,1001
   1 PROD(J)=0.
            DO 2 J=1,1000
            DO 2 K=1,2
   2 DIST(J,K)=0
            DO 22 J=1,1000
            IWP=0
            IFG=0
            DO 20 K=1,234
            CALL RANDU(IX,IY,YFL)
            IX=IY
            MACH1=10.0*YFL
            CALL RANDU(IX,IY,YFL)
            IX=IY
            MACH2=10.0*YFL
            IF(MACH1-1)7,5,5
   5 IWP=IWP+250
   7 IF(MACH2-1)20,9,9
   9 IF(IWP-250)20,11,11
  11 IWP=IWP-250
            IFG=IFG+250
  20 CONTINUE
  22 PROD(J)=IFG
            DO 28 J=1,999
            K=J+1
            SMALL=PROD(J)
            INDEX=J
            DO 26 L=K,1000
            TEST=PROD(L)
            IF(TEST-SMALL)24,26,26
  24 SMALL=TEST
            INDEX=L
  26 CONTINUE
            PROD(INDEX)=PROD(J)
  28 PROD(J)=SMALL
            KOUNT=0
            DO 38 J=1,1000
            NUM=0
            K=J+1
            IF(PROD(J))38,38,30
  30 KOUNT=KOUNT+1
            NUM=NUM+1
            DO 36 L=K,1001
            IF(PROD(L))36,36,32
  32 IF(PROD(J)-PROD(L))36,34,36
  34 NUM=NUM+1
            PROD(L)=0
  36 CONTINUE
            DIST(KOUNT,1)=PROD(J)
            DIST(KOUNT,2)=NUM
  38 CONTINUE
            WRITE(3,54)
  54 FORMAT(1H0,2X,'THE FOLLOW. IS THE PROD. FREQ. DIST.')
            WRITE(3,56)
  56 FORMAT(1H0,4X,'UNITS',6X,'FREQUENCY',8X,'CUM. FREQ.')
            TOT=0
            DO 58 J=1,KOUNT
            A=DIST(J,2)/1000.
            TOT=TOT+A
            I=DIST(J,1)
  58 WRITE(3,60)I,A,TOT
  60 FORMAT(1H ,3X,I6,7X,F6.4,11X,F6.4)
            RETURN
            END
```

Analysis of Results

Figure 8.3 presents the computer output of the simulation of Orelle's throughput system. The figure indicates the range of probable output units from 48,250 to 54,400 units in one year. Any output below the 50,000-unit level does not meet Orelle's requirements. However, Figure 8.3 indicates that the cumulative frequency of output being lower than 50,000 units is 0.068. If one constructed the model to correctly reflect the Builtwell machines, this figure may be interpreted as meaning that there is only a 0.068 chance of not meeting the required demand. Or, from another vantage point, there is a 0.932 probability of being able to produce at least the required 50,000 units that Levine & Rowpenny may be expected to demand.

Whether or not the Builtwell machines should be purchased depends on management's interpretation of the risk of not meeting demand. The 0.068 probability of not producing enough units, and the consequent possibility of losing the Levine & Rowpenny account, must be evaluated by management. Certainly the decision is complicated by the lack

Figure 8.3 Results of 1,000 First Years

```
          THE FOLLOW. IS THE PROD. FREQ. DIST.

        UNITS          FREQUENCY           CUM. FREQ.
        48250          0.0010              0.0010
        48500          0.0020              0.0030
        48750          0.0050              0.0080
        49000          0.0040              0.0120
        49250          0.0060              0.0180
        49500          0.0210              0.0390
        49750          0.0290              0.0680
        50000          0.0280              0.0960
        50250          0.0400              0.1360
        50500          0.0670              0.2030
        50750          0.0630              0.2660
        51000          0.0820              0.3480
        51250          0.1010              0.4490
        51500          0.0890              0.5380
        51750          0.1000              0.6380
        52000          0.0950              0.7330
        52250          0.0900              0.8230
        52500          0.0510              0.8740
        52750          0.0420              0.9160
        53000          0.0290              0.9450
        53250          0.0250              0.9700
        53500          0.0090              0.9790
        53750          0.0120              0.9910
        54000          0.0030              0.9940
        54250          0.0050              0.9990
        54500          0.0010              1.0000
```

of other bids. Management must also weigh the risks of not finding a supplier with better machines, the possible loss of the Levine & Rowpenny account because of inaction (continued search for the best machines), and the probability of finding other customers if the Levine & Rowpenny account is lost. An element of risk prevails in most business decisions, and forecasting does not always specify precisely what alternative course of action management should undertake, as in the Orelle case. Instead, it provides information to management in order to enhance the quality of decision making. At least, when management makes a decision about the Builtwell machines, it should be aware of the attendant risks.

Verifying Results

The Orelle example is obviously a very limited and simple case of a computer simulation. In most real-world simulations, many additional variables enter the picture. Nevertheless, the analytical principles are essentially the same. A system was described and mathematically modeled, and the model was simulated, or moved, through time. The final step should be the follow-up after implementation.

In Orelle's case, production should be monitored on a daily basis to assess the accuracy of the original assumptions of the model. It was assumed that each machine had a failure rate of 0.10 and a daily output of 250 units was assumed for both machines if they were operating. All these initial assumptions must be verified on a continuing basis after installation.

If it is found that the initial assumptions are unwarranted for the specific case of Orelle, the model should be retrieved from storage and altered in accordance with information. Quick and early detection of a problem in the system may allow steps to be taken before incorrect output is acted upon by management. Verifying results is perhaps the most important step to effective operations analysis, but it is often the first to be overlooked.

OTHER SIMULATION APPLICATIONS

Simulation is the art of management science (operations research), and its applications are as broad and plentiful as analysts' ability to perceive real-world problems and their relationships. In turn, model building of these relationships often depends on analysts' creativity rather than on their knowledge of hard and fast truisms. Several areas, however, that have received widespread attention by business analysts are related to forecasting.

Production scheduling and facilities planning, for instance, are broad areas of particular interest to the business forecaster. The Orelle Company was an example of this general-problem category.

Most simulation problems are generally a subset of those typically analyzed in management science courses. A duplication of these materials is not needed here. Therefore, only a brief discussion of some types of these problems that are particularly related to the interests of forecasters are presented. Most simulation problems are much more complex than that of the Orelle Company. Models of these problems must usually be specifically designed for each special case. Canned programs are seldom helpful in building useful computer models because each analysis must be tailor-made to fit each unique situation. Developing the computer and mathematical skills required for simulation would require an entire course in itself.[3]

Inventory Problems

Inventory problems are particularly adaptable to simulation because the system's components and their interactions may be identified more readily than in many other business systems. Certainly the demand for improved inventory management procedures is much greater today than it was a decade ago. High interest rates, warehouse costs, taxes, obsolescence, breakage, and pilferage have made inventory costs an especially important factor in today's profit-and-loss statements.

Some central inventory problems consist of attempting to determine the appropriate levels of inventory to carry, optimal reorder levels and optimal reorder timing, and appropriate reserve stock sizes (for contingencies) if they are to exist at all. The number (centralization versus decentralization) and location of inventories as well as logistics considerations are part of the general inventory problem.

There are obvious costs of carrying an inventory on hand. Interest must either be paid or lost from an alternative investment opportunity. Warehousing expenses, obsolescence and loss, and transportation expenses are all part of the cost of an inventory. If an inventory is not sufficient, lost sales will result. Orders may be placed to take advantage of quantity discounts and terms of payment discounts where possible. If orders are made too frequently, ordering costs may outweigh the savings from not carrying a large inventory.

These factors are complicated by fluctuations in demand and the number of days it takes to receive shipments from a supplier as well as by differences between suppliers. Hence, accurate sales forecasts are

3. For further reference, see H. L. Verma and C. W. Gross, *Introduction to Quantitative Methods: A Managerial Emphasis* (New York: John Wiley and Sons, 1978).

necessary for effective inventory decisions. Some balance of minimizing these costs while satisfying demand must be made. For most inventories, then, a solution is complicated by a multitude of variables. It is no exaggeration to state that inventory problems are among the most complex of those simulated in business. A tremendous number of components and interactions is required to simulate an inventory system for firms with diverse product lines, such as a department store or a multiline wholesaler, because of the numerous products, brands, sizes, colors, and so forth. Forecasting the effects of various inventory policies is an area toward which businesspeople are increasingly turning their attention.

Queuing Problems

Queuing-problem studies attempt to analyze the effects on demand and cost of waiting lines. Frequently bottlenecks exist in a system because of random events. The back-up at these bottlenecks is termed a *waiting line.*

A classic example of a queuing problem is a car wash installation. Customers arrive at the facility at varying frequencies throughout the day, but the car wash requires a relatively fixed amount of time to clean each car. As a result, there are times when a waiting line develops because capacity for the facility has been reached. If the line is too long, some customers become impatient and leave, and immediate sales or even customers are lost. In contrast, if the facility is built so large that a line never becomes long enough to drive customers away, equipment may sit idle for long periods, resulting in reduced profitability.

The work-in-process inventory in the Orelle Company could have become a waiting line if changes in the relationship between machines occurred. If breakdown rates, daily production rates, time of breakdown during the day, or length of time for repairs were different, either in mean or in distribution among machines, a queuing problem could have ensued.

Queuing analysis is used for facilities planning, production scheduling, manpower planning, and even transportation problems. The emphasis is directed toward analyzing the number of satisfactory units of final output as well as the size and characteristics of the queue. Such factors as overall size of the queue, average length of time in the queue, and number of unsatisfied or rejected demands on the system are all important factors in forecasting a proper facilities level.

Decision Models

Simulation techniques can be useful to the manager as a tool in aiding planning. Two well-known applications are CPM (Critical Path Method) and PERT (Program Evaluation and Review Technique). Both of these techniques attempt to analyze an entire new project (such as marketing research or a new building construction project) and forecast its expected time of completion. A total project is analyzed in terms of possible sequences of subprojects required for its completion. PERT goes one step farther by attempting to generate estimates of variances in time related to each of the subprojects as well as to the entire project. These techniques were discussed in Chapter 2.

SOFT DATA

It is often necessary and even desirable to include estimates and judgment in the data base used for simulation. These data are termed *soft* because they do not represent hard objectively determined facts. Forecasts derived from such simulations must be interpreted with greater caution than if all the facts are known. For instance, PERT analysis requires estimates of probabilities for the completion of subprojects. Because PERT is used to forecast for new projects, actual information is seldom available during the simulation and planning stage, and as a result estimates are required for analysis. Similarly, other types of simulation may include subjective judgmental data as inputs. The Orelle Company simulation, for instance, required estimates of downtimes along with machine output specifications. In fact, most simulations include the use of estimations. Chapter 2 dealt with subjective judgmental methods of forecasting and is equally relevant to situations involving simulation.

SUMMARY

The forecast methods presented in this chapter represented a departure from the static forecast procedures described in preceding chapters. Static forecasts are used to plan levels of activities around what is expected to occur during one, or perhaps a succeeding, period in the future. With a forecast of sales, for example, production, purchases, and inventories are planned around the level expected during the forecast period. Decisions resulting from the use of static forecasts relate to levels of operation during the forecast period. This chapter was concerned primarily with forecasting desirable levels of scale that best facilitate various stages of probable activity. These forecasts are more dynamic in that many time periods are usually considered.

Of course, most forecasting techniques may be used interchangeably for many types of situations. Nevertheless, simulation can be instrumental in forecasting desirable process levels. Simulation begins with developing a mathematical model to represent the system being analyzed. Components of the system and their interrelationships must be explicitly stated during this stage. The next step is to drive or move the model through time to observe the model's reaction to various conditions. On the basis of the model's behavior, inferences about the real-world system's behavior are made.

Because of the nature of simulation problems, a model must be built specifically for each application. Each real-world system has a unique set of variables and interactions which must be described in order to understand its behavior. There are no hard and fast rules or formulas to follow when using simulation. Each simulation model must reflect the uniqueness of the situation.

Simulations may also be made where data are obtained through the use of subjective judgmental methods. As such, simulation represents more of an approach to a problem than a specific technique. The systems approach to problem solving is an integral element of simulation.

DISCUSSION QUESTIONS

1. Explain in your own words how simulation differs from forecasting techniques discussed in other chapters.
2. Some critics of simulation disagree about its usefulness because of its low degree of scientific rigor (formulas, rules, etc.). Comment.
3. Why do simulations depend on the particular situation? What types of situations lend themselves to simulation?
4. What are some of the variables that appear interrelated and central to simulating the following?
   a. An automobile service garage
   b. A manufacturer's assembly line
   c. The use of a university's computer
   d. University classrooms
   e. An airline terminal
5. Suppose the Orelle Company has received a bid from a second supplier of machinery. Everything pertaining to bids and specifications from both suppliers are identical except for the following changes relating to equipment of the second bid:
   a. The probability of a machine breakdown is 0.07 for each of the machines. A breakdown of one machine remains independent of the activity of the other machine.
   b. If a machine breaks down, the following repair times may be experienced:

Event	Probability
Repairs completed at end of day—production resumes the beginning of next day	0.3
Repairs completed at end of second day—production resumes the beginning of the third day	0.5
Repairs completed at end of third day—production resumes the beginning of the fourth day	0.2

    c. Daily output of each machine is 275 units. Which bid should Orelle accept?

6. Is there a statistically significant difference in the simulated outputs?
7. Suppose daily output of the above machines is only 260 units. Is there a statistically significant difference in the simulated outputs?
8. Assume that daily output of the machines related to the second bid are not fixed. Instead, suppose there is an expected distribution of output, as follows:

Daily Output	Probability
250	0.01
255	0.05
260	0.12
265	0.18
270	0.25
275	0.27
280	0.09
285	0.02
290	0.01

    Now which bid is best?

9. Why is it important to follow up a forecast situation when new information is made available? How can this lead to better decision making?

RECOMMENDED READINGS

Bierman, Harold, Charles P. Bonini, and Warren H. Hausman. *Quantitative Analysis for Business Decisions.* 5th ed. Homewood, Ill.: Richard D. Irwin, 1977.
Clark, William A., and Donald Sexton. *Marketing and Management Science: A Synergism.* Homewood, Ill.: Richard D. Irwin, 1970.

Day, Ralph L., and Leonard J. Parsons (eds.). *Marketing Models: Quantitative Applications.* Scranton, Pa.: Intext Educational Publishers, 1971.

Gross, C. W., and H. L. Verma. *Introduction to Quantitative Methods: A Managerial Emphasis.* New York: John Wiley and Sons, 1978.

McMillan, Claude, and Richard F. Gonzalez, with a chapter by Thomas Schriber. *Systems Analysis: A Computer Approach to Decision Models.* 3rd ed. Homewood, Ill.: Richard D. Irwin, 1973.

Plane, Donald R., and Gary A. Kochenberger. *Operations Research for Managerial Decisions.* Homewood, Ill.: Richard D. Irwin, 1972.

Schmidt, J. W., and R. E. Taylor. *Simulation and Analysis of Industrial Systems.* Homewood, Ill.: Richard D. Irwin, 1970.

Trueman, Richard E. *An Introduction to Quantitative Methods for Decision Making.* New York: Holt, Rinehart and Winston, 1974, Chapter 14.

Wagner, Harvey M. *Principles of Operations Research: With Applications to Managerial Decisions.* 2nd ed. Englewood Cliffs, N.J.: Prentice-Hall, 1975.

Webster, Frederick. "Management Science in Industrial Marketing." *Journal of Marketing,* 42 (January 1978), 21–27.

Taff, Charles A. *Management of Physical Distribution and Transportation.* Homewood, Ill.: Richard D. Irwin, 1978. p. 284.

APPENDIX 8.A TESTING WHETHER OR NOT THE DIFFERENCE BETWEEN THE SIMULATED AND THEORETICAL FREQUENCIES MAY BE EXPLAINED BY CHANCE

Chi-Square Test (χ^2) The first test that may be employed is the chi-square test. This is a nonparametric test, one that deals with numbers representing classification data, and it is relatively simple to administer. To use this test, one must be able to specify the frequencies expected, and the analyst must specify the null hypothesis as the proportion of objects falling in each of the categories in the theoretical population. The χ^2 technique assesses whether or not the simulated occurrences are sufficiently close to the expected ones to be explained by chance.

The H_O may be tested by[4]

$$\chi^2 = \sum_{i=1}^{k} \frac{(O_i - E_i)^2}{E_i}$$

where $\quad O_i$ = observed number of cases in ith category
$\qquad E_i$ = expected number of cases in ith category

$\displaystyle\sum_{i=1}^{k}$ directs one to sum over all k categories

Table 8.7 presents the expected (relative frequency from Table 8.3 times 180 events) and simulated (from Table 8.5) objects or events of the dice-roll example.

The calculated χ^2 value is obtained from Table 8.7 as follows:

$$\chi^2 = \frac{(6 - 5.04)^2}{5.04} + \frac{(7 - 9.90)^2}{9.90} + \cdots + \frac{(4 - 5.04)^2}{5.04}$$

$$\chi^2 = 4.44$$

The computed χ^2 value is compared to the chi-square distribution to determine if the difference may be explained by chance. Table 8.8 presents critical values of the chi-square distribution.

To interpret Table 8.8, it is necessary to determine first the degrees of freedom (d.f.) (the number of categories -1). In this example, there are 11 categories (one for each possible score on a given roll), so there are $11 - 1 = 10$ d.f.

From Table 8.8 for 10 d.f. it can be seen that a $\chi^2 = 4.44$ has a probability of occurrence by chance of between 0.90 and 0.95.

---

4. Sidney Siegel, *Nonparametric Statistics for the Behavioral Sciences* (New York: McGraw-Hill Book Company, 1956).

Table 8.7 Expected and Simulated Objects

Expected	Simulated	Category (Sum of Dice)
5.04	6	2
9.90	7	3
14.94	13	4
19.98	23	5
25.02	22	6
30.24	29	7
25.02	26	8
19.98	24	9
14.94	13	10
9.90	13	11
5.04	4	12
180.00	180	

Therefore, if the α level established is 0.05, we would reject the H_O because the probability is less than 0.95 (determined by $1.0 - a$). This means that the model does not accurately represent the rolling of dice. This, however, is probably caused by the small number of events simulated.[5]

Kolmogorov-Smirnov Test (D) A major weakness of the chi-square test is that much information is lost by the combination of categories. A major discrepancy may exist for one of the categories, but be diluted by only minor differences for the others. The Kolmogorov-Smirnov test is far superior in testing such information. It is based on testing the category with the greatest distance between the observed and the expected.

The null hypothesis for this test is that there is no difference between observed and expected distributions. The H_O may be tested by[6]

$$D = \max|F_O(X) - S_N(X)|$$

5. It is also likely to mean that the random-number generator is not truly random. For tests of random-number generators, see J. W. Schmidt and R. E. Taylor, *Simulation and Analysis of Industrial Systems* (Homewood, Ill.: Richard D. Irwin, 1970), Chapter 6.
6. Siegel, *Nonparametric Statistics*, p. 48.

Table 8.8 Critical Values of the Chi-Square Distribution

df	Probability Under H_O that $\chi^2 \geqslant$ Chi Square												
	0.99	0.98	0.95	0.90	0.80	0.70	0.50	0.30	0.20	0.10	0.05	0.02	0.01
1	0.00016	0.00063	0.0039	0.016	0.064	0.15	0.46	1.07	1.64	2.71	3.84	5.41	6.64
2	0.02	0.04	0.10	0.21	0.45	0.71	1.39	2.41	3.22	4.60	5.99	7.82	9.21
3	0.12	0.18	0.35	0.58	1.00	1.42	2.37	3.66	4.64	6.25	7.82	9.84	11.34
4	0.30	0.43	0.71	1.06	1.65	2.20	3.36	4.88	5.99	7.78	9.49	11.67	13.28
5	0.55	0.75	1.14	1.61	2.34	3.00	4.35	6.06	7.29	9.24	11.07	13.39	15.09
6	0.87	1.13	1.64	2.20	3.07	3.83	5.35	7.23	8.56	10.64	12.59	15.03	16.81
7	1.24	1.56	2.17	2.83	3.82	4.67	6.35	8.38	9.80	12.02	14.07	16.62	18.48
8	1.65	2.03	2.73	3.49	4.59	5.53	7.34	9.52	11.03	13.36	15.51	18.17	20.09
9	2.09	2.53	3.32	4.17	5.38	6.39	8.34	10.66	12.24	14.68	16.92	19.68	21.67
10	2.56	3.06	3.94	4.86	6.18	7.27	9.34	11.78	13.44	15.99	18.31	21.16	23.21
11	3.05	3.61	4.58	5.58	6.99	8.15	10.34	12.90	14.63	17.28	19.68	22.62	24.72
12	3.57	4.18	5.23	6.30	7.81	9.03	11.34	14.01	15.81	18.55	21.03	24.05	26.22
13	4.11	4.76	5.89	7.04	8.63	9.93	12.34	15.12	16.98	19.81	22.36	25.47	27.69
14	4.66	5.37	6.57	7.79	9.47	10.82	13.34	16.22	18.15	21.06	23.68	26.87	29.14
15	5.23	5.98	7.26	8.55	10.31	11.72	14.34	17.32	19.31	22.31	25.00	28.26	30.58
16	5.81	6.61	7.96	9.31	11.15	12.62	15.34	18.42	20.46	23.54	26.30	29.63	32.00
17	6.41	7.26	8.67	10.08	12.00	13.53	16.34	19.51	21.62	24.77	27.59	31.00	33.41
18	7.02	7.91	9.39	10.86	12.86	14.44	17.34	20.60	22.76	25.99	28.87	32.35	34.80
19	7.63	8.57	10.12	11.65	13.72	15.35	18.34	21.69	23.90	27.20	30.14	33.69	36.19
20	8.26	9.24	10.85	12.44	14.58	16.27	19.34	22.78	25.04	28.41	31.41	35.02	37.57

continued

Table 8.8 Critical Values of the Chi-Square Distribution *continued*

df	\multicolumn{13}{c}{Probability Under H_O that $\chi^2 \geqslant$ Chi Square}

df	0.99	0.98	0.95	0.90	0.80	0.70	0.50	0.30	0.20	0.10	0.05	0.02	0.01
21	8.90	9.92	11.59	13.24	15.44	17.18	20.34	23.86	26.17	29.62	32.67	36.34	38.93
22	9.54	10.60	12.34	14.04	16.31	18.10	21.24	24.94	27.30	30.81	33.92	37.66	40.29
23	10.20	11.29	13.09	14.85	17.19	19.02	22.34	26.02	28.43	32.01	35.17	38.97	41.64
24	10.86	11.99	13.85	15.66	18.06	19.94	23.34	27.10	29.55	33.20	36.42	40.27	42.98
25	11.52	12.70	14.61	16.47	18.94	20.87	24.34	28.17	30.68	34.38	37.65	41.57	44.31
26	12.20	13.41	15.38	17.29	19.82	21.79	25.34	29.25	31.80	35.56	38.88	42.86	45.64
27	12.88	14.12	16.15	18.11	20.70	22.72	26.34	30.32	32.91	36.74	40.11	44.14	46.96
28	13.56	14.85	16.93	18.94	21.59	23.65	27.34	31.39	34.03	37.92	41.34	45.42	48.28
29	14.26	15.57	17.71	19.77	22.48	24.58	28.34	32.46	35.14	39.09	42.56	46.69	49.59
30	14.95	16.31	18.49	20.60	23.36	25.51	29.34	33.53	36.25	40.26	43.77	47.96	50.89

Source: Sir Ronald A. Fisher, *Statistical Methods for Research Workers*, 14th ed., copyright © 1970 University of Adelaide, Hafner Publishing Company, Darien, Conn., 1970.

where $F_O(X)$ = the theoretical cumulative distribution
       $S_N(X)$ = the actual cumulative distribution
       D = the maximum absolute deviation for any of the categories between $F_O(X)$ and $S_N(X)$

Table 8.9 presents the cumulative frequencies (see Tables 8.3 and 8.5) and the absolute value of the difference. From Table 8.9, it can be seen that $D = 0.029$ for these data. This D is compared against the levels of significance in Table 8.10.

If we establish an $\alpha = 0.05$ for this test, we may compute the critical value for this example as follows:

$$CV = \frac{1.36}{\sqrt{180}} = \frac{1.36}{13.42} = 0.101$$

Because $D = 0.029$ is less than 0.101, we cannot reject the null hypothesis and therefore conclude that the model accurately simulates the rolling of dice. For this example, the chi-square test was more sensitive to differences than was the Kolmogorov-Smirnov test. If either or both tests reject the null hypothesis, the analyst should examine the model.

Limited Use of Tests   The major limitation to using statistical procedures to test the model in simulation is that it is first necessary to know

Table 8.9 Cumulative Frequencies

Category	Theoretical	Simulated	Absolute Difference
2	0.028	0.033	0.005
3	0.083	0.072	0.011
4	0.166	0.144	0.022
5	0.277	0.272	0.005
6	0.416	0.394	0.022
7	0.584	0.555	0.029
8	0.723	0.700	0.023
9	0.834	0.834	0
10	0.917	0.906	0.011
11	0.972	0.978	0.006
12	1.000	1.000	0

(or suspect) the theoretical distribution. In many instances, however, the theoretical distribution is not known. When this is the case, the analyst's hands are tied. The analyst must often rely on value judgments to assess whether or not the output of the model appears to be reasonable.

After a model is built, statistical tests may be employed to test for changes. A standard type of analysis is to allow variation in some of the variables to determine effects on the system. Statistical tests may be used to see whether or not the effects are significant.

Table 8.10 Significance Levels of D in the Kolmogorov-Smirnov Test

Sample Size (N)	Level of Significance for D = Maximum $[F_O(X) - S_N(X)]$				
	0.20	0.15	0.10	0.05	0.01
1	0.900	0.925	0.950	0.975	0.995
2	0.684	0.726	0.776	0.842	0.929
3	0.565	0.597	0.642	0.708	0.828
4	0.494	0.525	0.564	0.624	0.733
5	0.446	0.474	0.510	0.565	0.669
6	0.410	0.436	0.470	0.521	0.618
7	0.381	0.405	0.438	0.486	0.577
8	0.358	0.381	0.411	0.457	0.543
9	0.339	0.360	0.388	0.432	0.514
10	0.322	0.342	0.368	0.410	0.490
11	0.307	0.326	0.352	0.391	0.468
12	0.295	0.313	0.338	0.375	0.450
13	0.284	0.302	0.325	0.361	0.433
14	0.274	0.292	0.314	0.349	0.418
15	0.266	0.283	0.304	0.338	0.404
16	0.258	0.274	0.295	0.328	0.392
17	0.250	0.266	0.286	0.318	0.381
18	0.244	0.259	0.278	0.309	0.371
19	0.237	0.252	0.272	0.301	0.363
20	0.231	0.246	0.264	0.294	0.356
25	0.21	0.22	0.24	0.27	0.32
30	0.19	0.20	0.22	0.24	0.29
35	0.18	0.19	0.21	0.23	0.27
Over 35	$\dfrac{1.07}{\sqrt{N}}$	$\dfrac{1.14}{\sqrt{N}}$	$\dfrac{1.22}{\sqrt{N}}$	$\dfrac{1.36}{\sqrt{N}}$	$\dfrac{1.63}{\sqrt{N}}$

Source: F. J. Massey, Jr., *The Kolomogorov-Smirnov Test for Goodness of Fit,* © The Journal of the American Statistical Association, 46 (1951), 70.

APPENDIX 8.B

2,250 Random Digits

```
54941  72711  39406  94620  27963  96478  21559  19246  88097  44026
02349  71389  45608  60947  60775  73181  43264  56895  04232  59604
98210  44546  27174  27499  53523  63110  57106  20865  91683  80688
11826  91326  29664  01603  23156  89223  43429  95353  44662  59433
96810  17100  35066  00815  01552  06392  31437  70385  45863  75971

81060  33449  68055  83844  90942  74857  52419  68723  47830  63010
56135  80647  51404  06626  10042  93629  37609  57215  08409  81906
57361  65304  93258  56760  63348  24949  11839  29793  37457  59377
24548  56415  61927  64416  29934  00755  09418  14230  62887  92683
66504  02036  02922  63569  17906  38076  32135  19096  96970  75917

45068  05520  56321  22693  35089  07694  04252  23791  60249  83010
99717  01542  72990  43413  59744  44595  71326  91382  45114  20245
05394  61840  83089  09224  78530  33996  49965  04851  18280  14039
38155  42661  02363  67625  34683  95372  74733  63558  09665  22610
74319  04318  99387  86874  12549  38369  54952  91579  26023  81076

18134  90062  10761  54548  49505  52685  63903  13193  33905  66936
92012  42710  34650  73236  66167  21788  03581  40699  10396  81827
78101  44392  53767  15220  66319  72953  14071  59148  95154  72852
23469  42846  94810  16151  08029  50554  03891  38313  34016  18671
35342  56119  97190  43635  84249  61254  80993  55431  90793  62603

55846  18076  12415  30193  42777  85611  57635  51362  79907  77364
22184  33998  87436  37430  45246  11400  20986  43996  73112  88474
83668  66236  79665  88312  93047  12088  86937  70794  01041  74867
50083  70696  13558  98995  58159  04700  90443  13168  31553  67891
97765  27552  49617  51734  20849  70198  67906  00880  82899  66065
```

APPENDIX 8.B *continued*

49988	13176	94219	88698	41755	56216	66832	17748	04963	54859
78257	86249	46134	51865	09836	73966	65711	41699	11732	17173
30946	22210	79302	40300	08852	27528	84648	79589	95295	72895
19468	76358	69203	02760	28625	70476	76410	32988	10194	94917
30806	80857	84383	78450	26245	91763	73117	33047	03577	62599
42163	69332	98851	50252	56911	62693	73817	98693	18728	94741
39249	51463	95963	07929	66728	47761	81472	44806	15592	71357
88717	29289	77360	09030	39605	87507	85446	51257	89555	75520
16767	57345	42285	56670	88445	85799	76200	21795	38894	58070
77516	98648	51868	48140	13583	94911	13318	64741	64336	95103
87192	66483	55649	36764	86132	12463	28385	94242	32063	45233
74078	64120	04643	14351	71381	28133	68269	65145	28152	39087
94119	20108	78101	81276	00835	63835	87174	42446	08882	27067
62180	27453	18567	55524	86088	00069	59254	24654	77371	26409
56199	05993	71201	78852	65889	32719	13758	23937	90740	16866
04994	09879	70337	11861	69032	51915	23510	32050	52052	24004
21725	43827	78862	67699	01009	07050	73324	06732	27510	33761
24305	37661	18956	50064	39500	17450	18030	63124	48061	59412
14762	69734	89150	93126	17700	94400	76075	08317	27324	72723
28387	99781	52977	01657	92602	41043	05686	15650	29970	95877

Source: "Table of 105,000 Random Decimal Digits," Statement No. 4914, File No. 261-A-1, Interstate Commerce Commission (Washington, D.C., 1949).

CASE 8: NATIONAL MOTOR PRODUCTS   *PRIECE of ERNIE CLAY*

The National Motor Products company is headquartered in Pittsburgh. This concern produces and sells high-quality industrial electric motors (ranging from 25 to 75 horsepower). These are efficient engines—most have an efficiency range of from 86% to 93%. Major customers are in the defense, food processing and packaging, textile, and chemical processing industries.

National maintains a 50–50 balance between original equipment (OEM) and replacements (including parts). OEM sales primarily are made directly to end users, whereas replacements are sold through industrial distributors. Both markets are growing rapidly.

National advertises aggressively in trade magazines and through direct mail. The ads are designed to appeal to specific markets and highlight the benefits that National purchasers enjoy. These include dependable performance, long product life, low initial costs, ability to perform in hostile environments, and savings in power costs.

The company has numerous competitors, many of which are relatively small firms. It has six immediate rivals, two of which are in direct competition with the firm.

Sales of the company's products have been as follows:

Year	Sales (in Millions of Dollars)
1970	21
1971	23
1972	29
1973	42
1974	51
1975	56
1976	71
1977	94
1978	120
1979	140
1980	164
1981	191
1982	248

National's sales are, of course, a function of derived demand. OEM sales are a function of the sales of customers, the product life of existing motors, the state of the economy, and the actions of competitors.

Replacement sales depend heavily upon the useful life of existing machines, the state of the economy, the aggressiveness of company-utilized distributors, and the actions of competitors. The company marketing research department has gathered extensive data on all these variables over a period of 15 years. To date, the major use of this data has been for the purpose of formulating marketing strategy.

National has utilized a variety of forecasting methods over the years, including linear regression, multiple regression, exponential smoothing, and time series. No one method has proved to be especially effective, however; the mean square error is deemed to be excessive by management. More refined forecasting methods are now being sought.

At one time, company managers felt that their sales representatives and distributor sales representatives might be in a position to supply good sales forecasts. An experiment was attempted during the 1972–1974 time period wherein each sales representative was asked to estimate next year's sales, and these were totaled to derive a company forecast. The method turned out to be very imprecise—the sales estimates departed substantially from actual sales—and the experiment was aborted.

The sales manager has long been an advocate of share-of-market analysis as a method of sales forecasting. When this was tried, it also failed, for a company's share of market rises and falls dramatically as do industry sales, and neither movement could be forecast.

As mentioned earlier, the firm has also employed regression, exponential smoothing, and time series for forecasting purposes. The most accurate of these was multiple regression, but even there, the mean square error was very large. One executive has proposed that perhaps the forecast accuracy could be improved through model building and simulation.

1. Would you recommend model building and simulation in this case? Why or why not?
2. Why might static forecasts be inadequate in this case?
3. How might one go about building a model for this firm's forecasting?

Chapter 9
Indirect Methods:
Econometric and Others

11/20/89

INTRODUCTION

In general, an analyst can proceed in either of two directions when
developing a forecast. The first, the *direct* approach, focuses upon
information contained within the company's own records. Time-
series analysis is perhaps the most straightforward example, because
the input data are observations of historical sales, as reported in internal
documents. Regressing sales on advertising or some other company
promotion activity is also considered to be direct because it relies
primarily on internal data.

historical data

The second, the *indirect* approach, entails deriving forecasts from
historical or projected measures of economic activity that originate in
information sources outside the firm. Measures of GNP, the consumer
price index, and interest rates are among the multitude of such measures
which might prove to be useful. Such an approach is labeled as indirect
because it involves the use of external information. Further, it often
requires utilizing the analytical results of others.

for econometric models / used to predict something

The reason for using the indirect approach is so that consideration
may be given to forces outside the firm that influence its sales. International Harvester, for example, nearly became insolvent during 1980
and 1981. The primary problem was the economy's exorbitant interest
rates of nearly 20% which caused industrywide sales of trucks, farm,
and construction equipment to grind to a halt. Using indirect methods
can yield far greater forecast accuracy whenever major forces outside a
company affect its sales.

This chapter explores the indirect approach. It describes the
approach, suggests useful sources of information, and depicts procedures for generating forecasts through this group of techniques.

prices going up-inflation / industrial matl prices

ECONOMIC INDICATORS

Economic indicators are measures of economic activity, usually for
some aggregate, such as the entire country, a smaller geographic
region, or an industry. These sometimes prove to be useful in

forecasting situations. Indicators may reflect history, the current time period, forecasts of the future, or all three.

In most instances, individual business firms do not try to forecast the level of economic indicators. The task is complex, and forecasts—many of which are very extensive and carefully prepared—are available in government, trade association, foundation, commercial and university publications. Gross national product, the money supply, and the prime lending rate are three of the best known indicators. Economic indicators are statistics that tend to increase or decrease in value ahead of, at the same relative time as, or after the series being forecast. These groups of statistics are termed *lead, coincident,* and *lag indicators,* respectively. Figure 9.1 depicts the relationship of these indicators to a historical trend. Leading indicators move in the same direction as the series being forecast, but they do so ahead of time. Changes in the money supply, to illustrate, typically precede interest rate changes, and hence capital expenditure outlays, by several months. Leading indicators can be of substantial value in forecasting. In this regard, known measurements taken in current periods, and even past ones, can be used in forecasting future sales.

Coincident indicators move at the same time as the forecast variable, and lagging variables follow behind. The question might be asked, "Of what value are coincident and lagging variables since they occur during

Figure 9.1 Lead, Coincident, and Lag Indicators

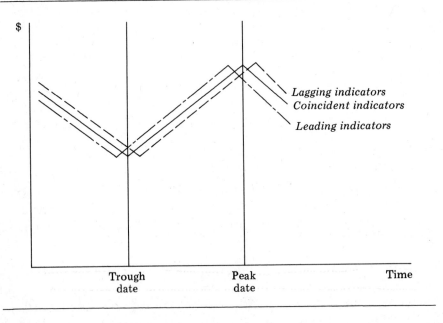

or after the fact of the variable of interest, the forecast variable?" The answer is that it depends upon the situation.

Some forecasts are made of large aggregates, such as total sales of a large conglomerate and national GNP. A problem arises in that measurements of the actual value when the period ends are complicated because components need to be made for items like internal transfers. Consolidated financial statements for large, diverse companies, to illustrate, are often not completed for two or three months after the fact. The same is true for the government.

Both coincident and lagging indices, however, are typically reported on time. They can be used, therefore, to provide adjustments to forecasts that were generated in the past through the use of leading indicators.

A different situation is found when component levels of forecasts are made, such as at the individual product level. Here the measurement problem is not that great and actual sales are typically known promptly. Thus, there is little need to focus on coincident and lagging indices. Here, the analyst is primarily concerned with leading indicators.

Many indicators are reported in the literature. Most are labeled as leading, but still others are reported as lagging. It is important to note, however, that the category within which a particular index actually should fall is situationally dependent. In essence, the indices are labeled as such because of their usefulness in forecasting the overall economy.

A decline in overall activity, for example, may be undesirable to most businesses but may increase the demand for the output of others. A substantial rise in the price of gasoline might serve to trigger a slump in the sale of power boats as well as in the economy in general, but it might trigger a demand for sailboats. In this case, the price of gasoline may be a lead indicator for much of the economy, but the direction of the relationship is opposite to that for sailboats.

Sources of Indicators

An abundant number of indicator sources are available. The following lists some that are commonly used and widely available. In fact, most of these sources can be found in either the government-document or business sections of any reasonably large library.

1. *Resources for the Future* publishes a variety of long-range forecasts of such variables as population, income, and the output of various industries. Some estimates are for as far in the future as the year 2080.
2. *Bureau of the Census, United States Department of Commerce* produces a wide variety of data that can be employed for forecasting purposes. It also furnishes population forecasts by state. The data are set forth in the various periodical census reports and

in interim reports between the periodical census years. Valuable
data on a variety of topics, including population, employment, GNP,
national income, and value added (sales less cost of purchases), are
contained in

   A. *The Census of Population* ✓
   B. *The Census of Manufacturers*
   C. *The Census of Business*
   D. *The Census of Agriculture*

3. *The Federal Reserve Board* makes available an index of industrial
   production, which gauges the output of the manufacturing sector
   of the economy.
4. *The U.S. Department of Agriculture* provides information on the
   output, distribution, and sale of farm products in the United States.
5. *The U.S. Department of Commerce* publishes various series on
   manufacturers' shipments, orders, and inventories. In addition, the
   department publishes the *Survey of Current Business*, which contains data on most of the national income accounts—GNP, national
   income, personal income, and disposable income.
6. *The Bureau of Labor Statistics* produces the *Monthly Labor Review*.
   This contains data on wholesale and retail prices, length of the
   work week, employment and unemployment, and related variables.
7. *The Council of Economic Advisors* publishes *Economic Indicators*
   on a monthly basis. This gives historical data for all the national
   economic indicators. Some annual forecasts are provided.
8. *Business Week* publishes weekly data on production, trade, prices,
   finance, and other economic indicators. The data are for latest
   week, previous week, month ago, year ago, and the average figures
   for the past six years.
9. *Predicasts* publishes forecasts of the future for industries in various
   fields.
10. *F. W. Dodge* reports the level and dollar aggregate of construction
    contracts awarded.
11. *The National Industrial Conference Board* publishes the *Conference
    Board Business Record*. This summarizes the performances of the
    economy in important spheres, such as the balance of trade and
    business expenditures on inventory and investment. The board also
    publishes an annual publication, *The Business Outlook*, which
    contains the views of top economists on the probable future state of
    the economy.
12. *The 12 Federal Reserve Banks* publish data on the performance of
    the economy in the region served by each bank.
13. Many *commercial banks* provide similar data and forecasts per-
    taining to the area served by the bank.
14. *Universities* often provide economic indicator data and projections
    (both state and national). Included in this group are the projections
    of GNP generated by the Wharton School of the University of
    Pennsylvania.

This list of sources is by no means exhaustive, but it does include a cross section of those that are heavily utilized. There are also several commercial sources, like the *Blue Chip Economics Indicators*, a monthly newsletter.[1] One distinctive advantage of the *Blue Chip* and some others is that they compare indicators published by many sources. Table 9.1 presents such a comparison. Another advantage is that they highlight key changes that may be of special interest to the analyst, as illustrated in Figure 9.2, which depicts changes in the automobile and television industries over time.

A disadvantage of such sources, however, is that they often lack great detail. The purpose of many of them is to inform managers of general overall economic conditions. Thus, they focus on relatively few key, large aggregates and do not provide the detail that analysts require. Hence, there is often a need for more precise measures.

Specific Indicators Available

There exist many published indicators relating to specific variables and sectors of the economy. An excellent cross representation of them is published by the U.S. Department of Commerce in its monthly *Business Conditions Digest*. It reports over 200 principal indicators in all. These are subdivided into several divisions, including 9 categories of cyclical indicators and 14 groups of other important economic measures. Table 9.2 presents a sample of these.

The *Business Conditions Digest* also sets forth several other important information facets. It indicates how well the indices compare with their reference overall economic series at various lead- and lag-time lengths, which are the time differences between actual values and index values. Figure 9.3 presents such a comparison for one set of indices. (Remember that leading, lagging, and coincident indicators, as well as the lag periods, are situationally dependent.) Rates of change are also presented. Finally, monthly data are listed for up to 43 years of history for selected series.

Econometric Models

Usually, the forecaster selects for analysis a manageable number of indicators that are expected to be logically related to sales. The objective is to discover which series are closely associated with sales. Once found, the related series can then be employed for the actual forecasting

1. Special thanks is given to Robert J. Eggert Economic Enterprises in Sedona, Arizona, for graciously providing us with several useful materials for this chapter.

Table 9.1 Sample of Comparisons from the *Blue Chip Economic Indicators*, September 10, 1980, p. 2.

Real GNP Consensus for 1981 Now Advancing to a Plus 0.9%

September 1980 Forecast for 1981 Source:	Percent Change 1981 from 1980								4th Quarter Avg. — 1981			Total Units — 1981	
	1	2	3	4	5	6	7	8	9	10	11	12	13
	Real GNP (Con. $) (Output)	GNP Deflator (Prices)	Total GNP (Cur. $)	Personal Income (Cur. $)	Profits Pretax (Cur. $)[a]	Plant Equip. Spend[b]	Indus. Prod. (Total)	Cons. Price Index	Interest Rates Short Term[c]	Interest Rates Long Term[d]	Unempl. % of Labor Force	Housing Starts (Mil.)	Auto Sales (Mil.)[e]
LaSalle National Bank	3.4H	8.3	12.0	12.0H	15.0	4.5	2.0	8.6	8.5	9.5	7.5	1.50	9.9
Moseley, Hallgarten, E. & W.	3.0	8.7	11.9	11.2	13.4	15.8H	3.1	9.4	8.6	11.6	7.2	1.56	9.7
Irving Trust	2.7	7.9L	10.9	10.4	16.7	9.8	2.2	8.9	7.0L	9.8	7.3	1.64	10.5
Cahners Publishing Co.	2.5	8.6	11.3	10.5	15.0	5.0	1.2	9.3	8.0	10.0	7.3	1.55	10.3
Evans Economics Inc.	2.3	9.5	12.1H	11.5	16.6	5.6	4.5	11.9	10.8	13.2	7.1L	1.70	9.4
Wharton Econometric Forecstg.	2.3	9.2	11.7	12.0H	2.7	4.4	3.2	10.3	10.6	12.7	8.1	1.73H	9.3
Citibank	2.3	8.3	10.8	10.2	17.0	3.3	2.4	7.8L	8.0	9.8	7.7	1.70	10.0
Morgan Guaranty	2.0	8.6	10.8	10.7	1.9	7.1	1.3	8.8	N/A	N/A	8.0	1.56	10.3
EGGERT ECONOMIC ENTERPRISES	1.8	9.6	11.6	10.9	9.0	5.5	3.0	9.6	8.8	10.2	7.5	1.70	10.5
Arnhold and S. Bleichroeder	1.8	8.5	10.3	11.0	26.0H	11.0	4.2	8.0	9.5	11.2	7.5	1.33	9.9
National City Bk. Cleveland	1.4	8.6	10.2	9.2	7.4	3.4	1.8	9.0	9.0	10.5	7.8	1.50	10.3
UCLA Forecasting Project	1.2	10.0	11.4	11.8	3.9	10.4	0.8	10.1	9.9	12.2	7.6	1.55	10.2
E. I. Du Pont	1.2	9.3	10.8	10.0	1.0	0.7	2.8	9.9	7.0L	10.0	7.1L	1.45	9.9
U.S. Trust	1.2	9.0	10.2	10.0	14.2	1.6	-0.5	10.0	10.3*	11.0*	7.8	1.60	9.5
The Conference Board	1.1	8.1	9.3	8.9	11.7	4.0	1.5	9.1	N/A	N/A	7.6	1.30	N/A
Peter L. Bernstein Inc.	1.1	8.0	9.2	9.2	14.8	0.0	7.8H	8.5	10.0	11.5	8.0	1.30	9.0L
U. of Michigan MQEM	1.0	9.4	10.6	9.7	-1.9	2.9	-0.8*	12.2	9.8	11.5	8.8	1.30	9.9
Equitable Life	1.0	8.8	10.0	10.0	2.0	5.0	2.0	9.3	9.3	10.8	8.4	1.50	9.8
Chase Manhattan Bank	1.0	8.5	9.6	9.5	5.5	2.9	-1.8	9.4	8.8*	10.8*	8.3	1.44	9.5
Econoviews International Inc.	1.0	8.2	9.1	11.6	1.2	13.0	-1.3	8.5	10.2	11.0	8.3	1.70	10.6H
Chamber of Commerce of U.S.	0.9	9.5	10.6	10.4	-1.6	5.8	1.2	9.8	9.0	10.7	8.3	1.70	9.6
Pennzoil Co.	0.9	9.4	10.5	10.6	5.7	6.5	1.4	9.8	9.3	10.8	8.2	1.65	9.8
Monsanto Co.	0.9	9.3	10.3	10.7	3.5	5.5	0.7	9.9	9.6	11.5	8.2	1.45	9.7
Bankers Trust	0.7	9.0	9.7	11.1	2.7	1.4	-0.6	7.9	N/A	N/A	7.7	1.49	9.7
Wayne Hummer & Co.	0.7	8.1	8.9	10.4	8.9	7.9	2.9	9.1	8.4	10.1	7.8	1.51	9.8
Brown Bros. Harriman & Co.	0.6	9.1	9.8	10.6	2.0	3.1	1.5	9.1	N/A	N/A	8.1	1.65	9.7
Philadelphia National Bank	0.5	8.9	9.5	9.3	-1.2	5.0	1.7	9.5	8.7	10.8	8.5	1.40	9.4

Table 9.1 Sample of Comparisons from the *Blue Chip Economic Indicators*, September 10, 1980, p. 2. *continued*

Bank of America	0.4	9.5	10.1	10.4	-3.8	3.6	0.1	10.0	N/A	N/A	8.4	1.64	9.6
Chase Econometric	0.3	9.0	9.4	8.7	-0.9	5.7	1.5	10.5	9.2	11.7	8.7	1.47	9.2
Security Pacific Bank	0.2	9.7	9.8	9.8	-8.8	3.7	-2.1	10.0	9.5	11.3	8.4	1.50	10.0
American Express Company	0.1	8.9	9.1	10.1	-5.5	1.0	-0.8	9.4	10.5	11.5	8.5	1.50	9.5
Shearson, Loeb, Rhoades, Inc.	0.1	8.9	9.0	8.0	-4.9	3.4	1.0	8.0	8.0	10.5	8.7	1.54	9.2
Goldman, Sachs Co.	0.0	9.5	9.5	8.4	4.2	3.5	1.6	9.6	N/A	N/A	8.9	1.48	9.8
Arthur D. Little	0.0	8.7	8.7	8.5	5.0	0.0	0.5	9.5	7.0L	9.5	8.5	1.30	9.5
Manufacturers Hanover	0.0	8.5	8.5	8.0	-4.0	0.5	0.8	9.5	8.8	11.8	8.5	1.70	9.5
Siff, Oakley, Marks Inc.	0.0	8.4	8.4	9.8	2.3	7.0	0.8	9.3	8.8	10.3	8.6	1.30	9.6
Prudential Life	-0.3	9.3	9.0	9.8	-6.2	2.8	-0.2	8.5	N/A	N/A	8.6	1.60	9.5
W. R. Grace	-0.5	10.0	9.5	9.6	10.0	2.9	-3.0	11.5	9.0	10.5	9.4	1.50	9.5
Dean Witter Reynolds	-0.7	9.3	8.6	9.0	-7.8	3.8	-1.3	8.4	8.4*	10.9	9.0	1.30	9.1
Business Economics Inc.	-1.0	8.5	7.4	9.0	-5.0	3.0	3.5	9.5	9.0	9.0L	8.6	1.40	10.3
A. G. Becker	-1.0	8.3	7.1L	10.0	-2.0	0.0	-4.0L	8.0	7.5	9.5	8.9	1.30	10.4
Sindlinger & Co. Inc.	-1.8L	10.7H	8.3	7.3L	-10.4L	-2.4L	-3.2	16.5H	17.8H	15.7H	9.9H	1.10L	9.9
1981 Consensus This Month	0.9	8.9	9.9	10.0	4.2	4.5	1.0	9.6	9.0	11.0	8.2	1.50	9.8
Last Month	0.8	8.7	9.6	9.7	2.8	4.2	0.6	9.2	8.9	10.5	8.3	1.50	9.7

H = Highest Forecast   L = Lowest Forecast   N/A = Not available

a Unadjusted (book).
b Department of Commerce total-current dollars.
c Prime commercial paper 4–6 months, week ended July 23, 9.9%.
d Corporate Aaa bonds, week ended July 23, 11.7%.
e Includes consumer imports of 2.1 million or 21% of estimated sales.
* Minor adjustments have been made to adapt to the above definitions.

Source: Copyright 1980, Capitol Publications, Inc.

Figure 9.2 Sample of Highlights from the *Blue Chip Economic Indicators*, September 10, 1980, p. 6.

COLOR TV SETS JUMP TO 11.2 MILLION

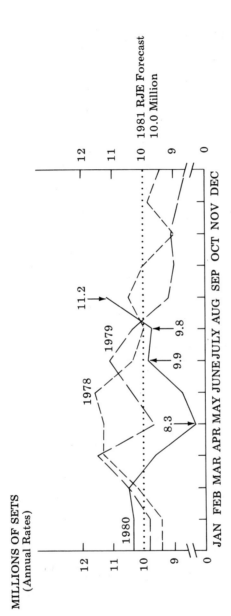

MILLIONS OF SETS
(Annual Rates)

1981 RJE Forecast
10.0 Million

11.2

1979

1978

9.9

9.8

8.3

1980

JAN FEB MAR APR MAY JUNE JULY AUG SEP OCT NOV DEC

Sales — Annual Rates	
	Millions of Sets
Year To Date	
1980	9.9
1979	10.4
% Change--5%	

Sources
Factory and distributor TV sales to retailers and other accounts reported by the Electronics Industries Association. Monthly seasonally adjusted annual rates and 1980 forecast by Eggert Economic Enterprises, Inc. Figures include imports of 1.3 million units in 1980, or about 14% of sales, and 1.4 million units in 1981, or about 14% of sales.

continued

Figure 9.2 Sample of Highlights from the *Blue Chip Economic Indicators*, September 10, 1980, p. 6. *continued*

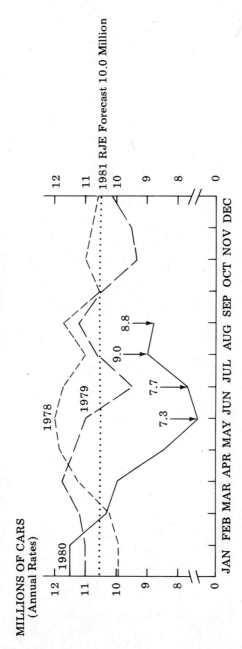

1980 AUTO SALES MAINTAIN STRONGER PACE

MILLIONS OF CARS
(Annual Rates)

1981 RJE Forecast 10.0 Million

JAN FEB MAR APR MAY JUN JUL AUG SEP OCT NOV DEC

Sources:
Basic data from the Motor Vehicle Manufacturers Association, excluding small buses. Monthly seasonally adjusted annual rate reported by Ford Motor Company. 1980 Forecast by Eggert Economic Enterprises, Inc. Figures include imports estimated at 2.5 million units in 1980, or about 27% of sales, and 2.2 million units in 1981, or about 21% of sales.

Sales — Annual Rates	
Year To Date	Millions of Autos
1980	9.1
1979	11.0
% Change–17%	

Table 9.2 Sample of Principal Indicators

Series title	Timing classification[3]	Unit of measure	Basic data[1] — Average 1978	Average 1979	1st Q 1980	2d Q 1980	3d Q 1980	Sept. 1980	Oct. 1980	Nov. 1980	Percent change — Sept. to Oct. 1980	Oct. to Nov. 1980	1st Q to 2d Q 1980	2d Q to 3d Q 1980	Series number
I. CYCLICAL INDICATORS															
A. Composite Indexes															
910. Twelve leading indicators	L,L,L	1967=100	141.8	140.1	133.3	124.0	131.2	135.0	136.0	137.6	0.7	1.2	-7.0	5.8	910
920. Four coincident indicators	C,C,C	do	140.1	145.1	145.0	138.4	137.3	138.7	140.0	141.2	0.9	0.9	-4.6	-0.8	920
930. Six lagging indicators	Lg,Lg,Lg	do	143.1	166.4	182.9	182.4	162.7	163.8	168.3	180.2	2.7	7.1	-0.3	-10.8	930
Leading Indicator Subgroups:															
913. Marginal employment adjustments	L,L,L	do	98.1	96.8	95.7	89.4	92.9	94.0	94.9	95.2	1.0	0.3	-6.6	3.9	913
914. Capital investment commitments	L,L,L	do	115.7	113.5	109.7	103.9	107.5	109.2	106.8	108.3	-2.2	1.4	-5.3	3.5	914
915. Inventory investment and purchasing	L,L,L	do	106.2	105.9	102.2	98.4	99.7	101.5	103.3	103.2	1.8	-0.1	-3.7	1.3	915
916. Profitability	L,L,L	do	93.2	91.7	90.5	89.1	NA	NA	NA	NA	NA	NA	-1.5	NA	916
917. Money and financial flows	L,L,L	do	149.0	145.5	137.1	129.2	135.9	138.3	139.6	139.6	0.9	0.	-5.8	5.2	917
B. Cyclical Indicators by Economic Process															
B1. Employment and Unemployment															
Marginal Employment Adjustments:															
*1. Average workweek, prod. workers, mfg.[2]	L,L,L	Hours	40.4	40.2	40.1	39.4	39.3	39.6	39.4	39.7	0.	0.3	-1.7	-0.3	1
21. Avg. weekly overtime, prod. workers, mfg.[2]	L,C,L	do	3.6	3.3	3.1	2.7	2.6	2.7	2.8	2.9	0.1	0.1	-0.4	-0.1	21
2. Accession rate, per 100 employees, mfg.[2]	L,L,L	Percent	4.1	4.0	3.8	3.1	3.6	3.8	3.9	3.6	0.1	-0.3	-0.7	0.5	2
5. Avg. weekly initial claims (inverted[4])	L,C,L	Thousands	339	381	406	607	513	501	439	399	12.4	9.1	-49.5	15.5	5
*3. Layoff rate, per 100 employ., mfg. (inv.[4])[2]	L,L,L	Percent	0.9	1.1	1.4	3.1	1.7	1.5	1.4	1.2	0.1	0.2	-1.7	1.4	3
4. Quit rate, per 100 employees, mfg.[2]	L,Lg,U	do	2.1	2.0	1.9	1.4	1.3	1.3	1.3	1.4	0.	0.1	-0.5	-0.1	4
Job Vacancies:															
60. Ratio, help-wanted advertising to persons unemployed[2]	L,Lg,U	Ratio	0.738	0.786	0.699	0.446	0.442	0.464	0.472	0.503	0.008	0.031	-0.253	-0.004	60
46. Help-wanted advertising	L,Lg,U	1967=100	149	158	150	116	119	122	127	134	4.1	5.5	-22.7	2.6	46
Comprehensive Employment:															
48. Employee hours in nonagri. establishments	U,C,C	A.r., bil. hrs.	164.56	169.89	171.97	169.39	168.38	169.07	169.86	169.61	0.5	-0.1	-1.5	-0.6	48
42. Persons engaged in nonagri. activities	U,C,C	Thousands	91,031	93,648	94,486	93,622	93,777	93,765	93,851	94,054	0.1	0.2	-0.9	0.2	42
*41. Employees on nonagri. payrolls	C,C,C	do	86,697	89,886	91,120	90,489	90,131	90,384	90,612	90,880	0.3	0.3	-0.7	-0.4	41
40. Employees in mfg., mining, construction	L,C,U	do	25,585	26,504	26,605	25,763	25,317	25,476	25,613	25,766	0.5	0.6	-3.2	-1.7	40
90. Ratio, civilian employment to total population of working age[2]	U,Lg,U	Percent	58.59	59.25	59.17	58.41	58.27	58.28	58.19	58.25	-0.09	0.06	-0.76	-0.14	90
Comprehensive Unemployment:															
37. Total unemployed (inverted[4])	L,Lg,U	Thousands	6,047	5,963	6,390	7,808	8,018	7,827	8,005	7,924	-2.3	1.0	-22.2	-2.7	37
43. Unemployment rate, total (inverted[4])[2]	L,Lg,U	Percent	6.0	5.8	6.1	7.5	7.6	7.5	7.6	7.5	-0.1	0.1	-1.4	-0.1	43

Table 9.2 Sample of Principal Indicators *continued*

Indicator	Unit	Class														No.
45. Avg. weekly insured unemploy. rate (inv.[4])[2]	...do....	L,Lg,U	3.2	3.2	3.0	3.2	4.2	4.4	4.4	4.1	3.8	0.3	0.3	-1.0	-0.2	45
*91. Avg. duration of unemployment (inverted[4])[2]	Weeks	Lg,Lg,Lg	11.9	10.7	10.8	10.7	11.2	12.4	13.1	13.3	13.6	-1.5	-2.3	-4.7	-10.7	91
44. Unemploy. rate, 15 weeks and over (inv.[4])[2]	Percent	Lg,Lg,Lg	1.4	1.3	1.2	1.3	1.6	2.0	2.2	2.2	2.2	0.	0.	-0.3	-0.4	44

B2. Production/Income

Comprehensive Output and Income:

Indicator	Unit	Class														No.
50. GNP in 1972 dollars	A.r., bil. dol.	C,C,C	1436.9	1483.0	1501.9	1463.3	1471.9	1208.6	1214.6	1218.2	...	0.5	0.3	-2.6	0.6	50
52. Personal income in 1972 dollars	...do....	C,C,C	1155.1	1197.4	1207.6	1194.8	1207.6	1036.9	1044.1	1048.3	...	0.7	0.3	-1.1	1.1	52
*51. Pers. income less transfer pay, 1972 dollars	...do....	C,C,C	1005.3	1043.8	1050.5	1036.2	1035.6	...	...	...	...	0.7	0.4	-1.4	-0.1	51
53. Wages and salaries in mining, mfg., and construction, 1972 dollars	...do....	C,C,C	244.3	247.2	238.8	228.2	226.2	228.0	229.3	230.6	...	0.6	0.6	-4.4	-0.9	53

Industrial Production:

Indicator	Unit	Class														No.
*47. Industrial production, total	1967=100	C,C,C	146.1	152.5	152.5	144.6	142.0	143.9	146.5	148.5	...	1.8	1.4	-5.2	-1.8	47
73. Industrial production, durable mfrs.	...do....	C,C,C	139.7	146.4	144.1	133.9	129.8	131.7	135.3	137.8	...	2.7	1.8	-7.1	-3.1	73
74. Industrial production, nondurable mfrs.	...do....	C,L,L	156.9	164.0	165.5	158.3	157.1	159.8	161.4	162.7	...	1.0	0.8	-4.4	-0.8	74
49. Value of goods output, 1972 dollars	A.r., Bil. dol.	C,C,C	655.9	674.5	682.1	658.1	657.5	...	...	...	...	...	...	-3.5	-0.1	49

Capacity Utilization:

Indicator	Unit	Class														No.
82. Capacity utilization rate, mfg., FRB[2]	Percent	L,C,U	84.4	85.6	83.4	77.9	75.7	...	...	...	...	...	...	-5.5	-2.2	82
83. Capacity utilization rate, mfg., BEA[2]	...do....		84	82	80	76	76	...	...	...	...	...	...	-4	0	83
84. Capacity utilization rate, materials, FRB[2]	...do....	L,C,U	85.6	87.4	85.5	78.7	74.9	...	...	...	...	...	...	-6.8	-3.8	84

B3. Consumption, Trade, Orders, and Deliveries

Orders and Deliveries:

Indicator	Unit	Class														No.
6. New orders, durable goods	Bil. dol.	L,L,L	70.19	77.20	80.01	68.73	75.14	78.96	80.69	81.46	...	2.2	1.0	-14.1	9.3	6
7. New orders, durable goods, 1972 dollars	...do....	L,L,L	41.48	41.40	39.61	33.71	36.10	37.82	38.23	38.31	...	1.1	0.2	-14.9	7.1	7
*8. New orders, cons. goods and mtls., 1972 dol.	...do....	L,L,L	37.16	36.46	35.21	29.45	32.26	33.26	35.10	34.24	...	5.5	-2.5	-16.4	9.5	8
25. Chg. in unfilled orders, durable goods[2]	...do....	L,L,L	3.68	3.26	2.33	-1.50	1.41	2.39	1.19	1.29	...	-1.20	0.10	-3.83	2.91	25
96. Mfrs.' unfilled orders, durable goods[5]	Bil. dol., EOP	L,Lg,U	228.82	267.88	274.88	270.38	274.62	274.62	275.81	277.10	...	0.4	0.5	-1.6	1.6	96
32. Vendor performance[2] ⑪	Percent	L,L,L	64	63	45	33	35	39	44	45	...	5	1	-12	2	32

Consumption and Trade:

Indicator	Unit	Class														No.
56. Manufacturing and trade sales	Bil. dol.	C,C,C	254.26	288.28	309.65	293.99	310.16	318.32	325.52	NA	NA	2.3	NA	-5.1	5.5	56
*57. Manufacturing and trade sales, 1972 dollars	...do....	C,C,C	156.32	159.82	158.76	148.54	152.07	155.85	156.06	NA	NA	0.1	NA	-6.4	2.4	57
75. Industrial production, consumer goods	1967=100	C,L,C	149.1	150.8	148.3	143.3	142.9	144.1	146.4	147.6	...	1.6	0.8	-3.4	-0.3	75
54. Sales of retail stores	Mil. dol.	C,L,U	66,741	73,837	77,997	75,200	79,048	80,087	80,519	81,826	...	0.5	1.6	-3.6	5.1	54
59. Sales of retail stores, 1972 dollars	...do....	U,L,U	44,314	44,800	44,344	41,777	43,000	43,011	42,989	43,248	...	-0.1	0.6	-5.8	2.9	59
55. Personal consumption expend., autos	A.r., bil. dol.	L,C,C	63.4	65.3	71.6	50.7	58.7	67.8	73.7	75.0	...	1.8	2.3	-29.2	15.8	55
58. Index of consumer sentiment ⑪	IQ 1966=100	L,L,L	79.4	66.0	63.5	54.4	67.8	73.7	75.0	76.7	...	...	2.3	-14.3	24.6	58

B4. Fixed Capital Investment

Formation of Business Enterprises:

Indicator	Unit	Class														No.
*12. Net business formation	1967=100	L,L,L	132.9	131.7	128.9	117.7	117.9	120.6	117.6	NA	NA	-2.5	NA	-8.7	0.2	12
13. New business incorporations	Number	L,L,L	39,996	43,714	43,882	41,394	44,604	46,488	NA	NA	NA	NA	NA	-5.7	7.8	13

Table 9.2 Sample of Principal Indicators *continued*

Series title	Unit of measure	Basic data[1]										Percent change			Series number
		Average			2d Q 1979	3d Q 1979	4th Q 1979	1st Q 1980	2d Q 1980	3d Q 1980		4th Q to 1st Q 1980	1st Q to 2d Q 1980	2d Q to 3d Q 1980	
		1977	1978	1979											

II. OTHER IMPORTANT ECONOMIC MEASURES—Con.
E2. Goods and Services Movements Except Transfers Under Military Grants

Series title	Unit	1977	1978	1979	2d Q 1979	3d Q 1979	4th Q 1979	1st Q 1980	2d Q 1980	3d Q 1980	4th→1st Q 1980	1st→2d Q 1980	2d→3d Q 1980	Series number
618. Merchandise exports	Mil. dol.	30,204	35,514	45,514	42,815	47,198	50,237	54,708	54,710	56,288	8.9	0.	2.9	618
620. Merchandise imports	do.	37,922	43,953	52,881	50,885	54,258	59,462	65,558	62,215	59,116	10.3	-5.1	-5.0	620
622. Merchandise trade balance[2]	do.	-7,718	-8,440	-7,367	-8,070	-7,060	-9,225	-10,850	-7,505	-2,828	-1,625	3,345	4,677	622
651. Income on U.S. investments abroad	do.	8,147	10,743	16,492	15,250	18,050	18,407	20,846	16,641	19,113	13.3	-20.2	14.9	651
652. Income on foreign investment in the U.S.	do.	3,650	5,518	8,365	7,980	8,731	9,524	10,752	10,508	10,646	12.9	-2.3	-1.3	652
668. Exports of goods and services	do.	46,177	55,260	71,627	67,763	74,773	78,305	85,647	81,892	80,403	9.4	-4.4	5.5	668
669. Imports of goods and services[2]	do.	48,543	57,560	70,408	67,873	72,267	78,555	86,445	82,997	80,026	10.0	-4.0	-3.6	669
667. Balance on goods and services[2]	do.	-2,366	-2,301	1,220	-110	2,506	-250	-798	-1,105	6,377	-548	-307	7,482	667

A. National Income and Product
A1. GNP and Personal Income

Series title	Unit	1977	1978	1979	2d Q 1979	3d Q 1979	4th Q 1979	1st Q 1980	2d Q 1980	3d Q 1980	4th→1st Q 1980	1st→2d Q 1980	2d→3d Q 1980	Series number
50. GNP in 1972 dollars	A.r., bil. dol.	1371.7	1436.9	1483.0	1473.4	1488.2	1490.6	1501.9	1463.3	1471.9	0.8	-2.6	0.6	50
200. GNP in current dollars	do.	1918.0	2156.1	2413.9	2374.6	2441.1	2496.3	2571.7	2564.8	2637.3	3.0	-0.3	2.8	200
213. Final sales, 1972 dollars	do.	1359.3	1423.0	1472.9	1455.0	1480.6	1491.3	1502.8	1462.0	1476.9	0.8	-2.7	1.0	213
224. Disposable personal income, current dollars	do.	1311.5	1462.9	1641.7	1612.8	1663.8	1710.1	1765.1	1784.1	1840.6	3.2	1.1	3.2	224
225. Disposable personal income, 1972 dollars	do.	939.8	981.2	1011.5	1006.9	1015.7	1017.7	1020.1	1007.3	1017.6	0.2	-1.3	1.0	225
217. Per capita GNP in 1972 dollars	A.r., dollars.	6,180	6,568	6,721	6,687	6,737	6,731	6,767	6,578	6,597	0.5	-2.8	0.3	217
227. Per capita disposable pers. income, 1972 dol.	do.	4,332	4,485	4,585	4,570	4,598	4,596	4,596	4,528	4,561	0.	-1.5	0.7	227

A2. Personal Consumption Expenditures

Series title	Unit	1977	1978	1979	2d Q 1979	3d Q 1979	4th Q 1979	1st Q 1980	2d Q 1980	3d Q 1980	4th→1st Q 1980	1st→2d Q 1980	2d→3d Q 1980	Series number
231. Total, 1972 dollars	A.r., bil. dol.	863.9	904.8	930.9	922.8	933.4	941.6	943.4	919.9	930.8	0.2	-2.6	1.3	231
233. Durable goods, 1972 dollars	do.	138.4	146.3	146.6	144.2	146.7	146.0	145.4	126.2	132.6	-0.4	-13.2	5.1	233
238. Nondurable goods, 1972 dollars	do.	334.0	345.7	354.6	350.6	355.4	361.3	361.5	356.6	354.9	0.1	-1.4	-0.5	238
239. Services, 1972 dollars	do.	391.5	412.8	429.6	428.0	431.3	434.3	436.5	436.5	443.3	0.5	0.	1.6	239
230. Total, current dollars	do.	1205.5	1348.7	1510.9	1478.0	1529.1	1582.3	1631.0	1626.8	1682.2	3.1	-0.3	3.4	230
232. Durable goods, current dollars	do.	178.8	199.3	212.3	207.4	213.3	216.1	220.9	194.4	208.8	2.2	-12.0	7.4	232
236. Nondurable goods, current dollars	do.	497.0	529.8	602.2	586.4	611.5	639.2	661.1	664.1	674.2	3.4	0.5	1.5	236
237. Services, current dollars	do.	547.7	619.6	696.3	684.2	704.3	727.0	749.0	768.4	799.2	3.0	2.6	4.0	237

A3. Gross Private Domestic Investment

Series title	Unit	1977	1978	1979	2d Q 1979	3d Q 1979	4th Q 1979	1st Q 1980	2d Q 1980	3d Q 1980	4th→1st Q 1980	1st→2d Q 1980	2d→3d Q 1980	Series number
241. Total, 1972 dollars	do.	213.5	229.7	232.6	238.7	232.6	221.5	218.3	200.5	195.3	-1.4	-8.2	-2.6	241
243. Total fixed investment, 1972 dollars	do.	201.2	215.8	222.5	220.4	225.0	222.2	219.2	199.2	200.2	-1.4	-9.1	0.5	243
30. Change in business inventories, 1972 dol.[2]	do.	12.3	14.0	10.2	18.4	7.6	-0.7	-0.9	1.3	-5.0	-0.2	2.2	-6.3	30
240. Total, current dollars	do.	322.3	375.3	415.8	423.2	421.7	410.0	415.6	390.9	377.1	1.4	-5.9	-3.5	240
242. Total fixed investment, current dollars	do.	301.3	353.2	398.3	390.1	408.3	410.8	413.1	383.5	393.2	0.6	-7.2	-2.5	242
245. Chg. in bus. inventories, current dol.[2]	do.	21.0	22.2	17.5	33.1	13.3	-0.8	2.5	7.4	-16.0	3.3	4.9	-23.4	245

Table 9.2 Sample of Principal Indicators *continued*

A4. Government Purchases of Goods and Services

Series	Units													No.
261. Total, 1972 dollars	do....	272.3	277.8	281.8	280.3	281.1	285.3	290.1	291.9	288.2	1.7	0.6	-1.3	261
263. Federal Government, 1972 dollars	do....	100.7	99.8	101.7	100.8	99.9	103.1	107.6	110.7	106.9	4.4	2.9	-3.4	263
267. State and local governments, 1972 dollars	do....	171.6	178.0	180.1	179.4	181.2	182.2	182.5	181.3	181.7	0.2	-0.7	0.2	267
260. Total, current dollars	do....	394.5	432.6	473.8	465.1	475.4	496.4	516.8	530.0	533.5	4.1	2.6	0.7	260
262. Federal Government, current dollars	do....	143.9	153.4	167.9	163.6	165.1	178.1	190.0	198.7	194.9	6.7	4.6	-1.9	262
266. State and local governments, current dollars	do....	250.6	279.2	305.9	301.6	310.4	318.3	326.8	331.3	338.6	2.7	1.4	2.2	266

A5. Foreign Trade

Series	Units													No.
256. Exports of goods and services, 1972 dollars	do....	113.2	127.5	146.9	140.5	151.3	154.8	165.9	160.5	160.5	7.2	-3.3	0.	256
257. Imports of goods and services, 1972 dollars	do....	91.3	103.0	109.2	108.8	110.2	112.6	115.8	108.9	102.8	2.8	-6.0	-5.6	257
255. Net exports of goods and serv., 1972 dol.[2]	do....	21.9	24.6	37.7	31.6	41.1	42.2	50.1	51.7	57.6	7.9	1.6	5.9	255
252. Exports of goods and services, current dol.	do....	183.3	219.8	281.3	266.8	293.1	306.3	337.3	333.3	342.4	10.1	-1.2	2.7	252
253. Imports of goods and services, current dol.	do....	187.5	220.4	267.9	258.6	275.2	298.7	329.1	316.2	297.9	10.2	-3.9	-5.8	253
250. Net exports of goods and serv., current dol.[2]	do....	-4.2	-0.6	13.4	8.2	17.9	7.6	8.2	17.1	44.5	0.6	8.9	27.4	250

A6. National Income and its Components

Series	Units													No.
220. National income	do....	1546.5	1745.4	1963.3	1932.0	1986.2	2031.2	2088.5	2070.0	2122.4	2.8	-0.9	2.5	220
280. Compensation of employees	do....	1152.3	1299.7	1460.9	1438.9	1476.7	1518.1	1558.0	1569.0	1597.4	2.6	0.7	1.8	280
282. Proprietors' income with IVA and CCA	do....	103.5	117.1	131.6	129.4	132.9	136.3	133.7	124.9	129.7	-1.9	-6.6	3.8	282
286. Corporate profits with IVA and CCA	do....	164.7	185.5	196.8	196.6	199.5	189.4	200.2	169.3	177.9	5.7	-15.4	5.1	286
284. Rental income of persons with CCA	do....	25.1	27.4	30.5	30.1	30.3	31.0	31.2	31.5	32.0	0.6	1.0	1.6	284
288. Net interest	do....	100.9	115.8	143.4	136.9	146.8	156.5	165.4	175.3	185.3	5.7	6.0	5.7	288

A7. Saving

Series	Units													No.
290. Gross saving (private and govt.)	do....	304.0	355.2	412.0	416.2	422.3	402.0	404.6	394.5	402.0	0.6	-2.5	1.9	290
295. Business saving	do....	230.7	279.1	312.7	310.3	320.5	315.7	326.7	325.8	334.6	3.5	-0.3	2.7	295
292. Personal saving	do....	72.9	74.9	84.7	90.9	89.3	80.7	84.8	108.5	109.8	5.1	27.9	1.2	292
298. Government surplus or deficit[2]	do....	-17.1	1.3	13.4	13.9	11.3	4.4	-8.1	-41.0	-44.0	-12.5	-32.9	-3.0	298
293. Personal saving rate[2]	Percent	5.6	5.2	5.2	5.6	5.4	4.7	4.9	6.2	6.1	0.2	1.3	-0.1	293

NOTE: Series are seasonally adjusted except for those indicated by (U) which appear to contain no seasonal movement. Series indicated by an asterisk (*) are included in the major composite indexes. For complete series titles (including composition of the composite indexes) and sources, see "Titles and Sources of Series" at the back of BCD. NA = not available. a = anticipated. EOP = end of period. A.r. = annual rate. S/A = seasonally adjusted (used for special emphasis). IVA = inventory valuation adjustment. CCA = capital consumption adjustment. NIA = national income accounts.

[1] For a few series, data shown here have been rounded to fewer digits than those shown elsewhere in BCD. Annual figures published by the source agencies are used if available.
[2] Differences rather than percent changes are shown for this series.
[3] The three-part timing code indicates the timing classification of the series at peaks, at troughs, and at all turns. L = leading. C = roughly coincident. Lg = lagging. U = unclassified.
[4] Inverted series. Since this series tends to move counter to movements in general business activity, signs of the changes are reversed.
[5] End-of-period series. The annual figures (and quarterly figures for monthly series) are the last figures for the period.
[6] This series is a weighted 4-term moving average (with weights 1, 2, 2, 1) placed at the terminal month of the span.

Source: Business Conditions Digest, U.S. Government Printing Office, December 1980, pp. 6 and 9.

Figure 9.3 Comparison of Selected Indices and Their Reference Series

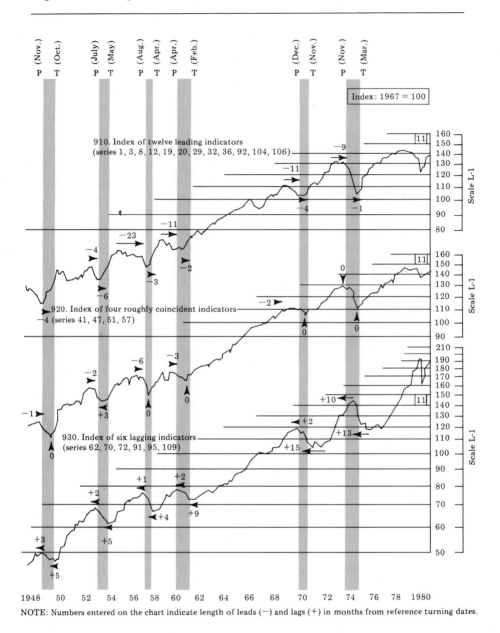

NOTE: Numbers entered on the chart indicate length of leads (−) and lags (+) in months from reference turning dates.

Source: Business Conditions Digest, U.S. Government Printing Office, December 1980, p. 10.

task. Multivariate correlation and regression are two powerful tools that are particularly suited for accomplishing this objective. When these tools are used for this purpose, the procedure is termed *econometric model building.*[2]

To be sure, econometric model building is no simple, straightforward task. Several problems need to be solved before reasonable solutions can be formulated. The two major problems involve (1) determining appropriate lag periods, and (2) dealing with multicolinearity. Each of these is discussed below.

— 11/20/89

Lag Periods

As mentioned above, the appropriate indicators and the appropriate lag-period lengths to use are situationally dependent. Logic is useful in selecting which indicators to consider initially. Reported construction contracts awarded for commercial and industrial buildings, for example, is a logical indicator of sales of concrete reinforcing rods. Disposable income, interest rates, and the unemployment level are logical indicators for consumer durable sales.

Logic can also be of value in assessing the appropriate lag length to use. For example, one might expect that concrete reinforcing rod sales would follow construction contracts awarded for commercial and industrial buildings by about six months, because it would take, on average, about that long to progress to that stage of construction. But perhaps seven months, eight months, or some other lag is more appropriate. Certainly, experience in the construction industry helps in making such estimates.

In fact, an underlying strong association can actually be concealed by comparing indicators and sales at the wrong intervals. Consider the hypothetical sales and indicator values presented in Table 9.3. If sales at period t are correlated and regressed against the indicator at $t = x$, $r^2 = 0.428$. Thus, x_t is a fair coincident indicator of y_t.

Whether or not x is a good *leading* indicator is another question, one which we can answer by lagging the time periods. A lag of one means that we compare the values of y_t with those of x_{t-1}. Thus, we enter the observation pairs

---

2. This book only touches on econometric analysis. For an excellent comprehensive examination, see J. Johnston, *Econometric Methods*, 2nd ed. (New York: McGraw-Hill Book Company, 1972).

	x	y
	60	17
	55	13
	.	.
	.	.
	.	.
	50	14

into the regression and correlation equations (see Chapter 4). With a lag of one period, $r^2 = 0.0207$. This means, of course, that we would not want to use x_t for forecast y_{t+1}.

This finding does not mean, however, that the indicator x is useless in forecasting y. A lag of two, three, or more periods might indicate a strong association. Table 9.4 summarizes the results for lag = 0 through lag = 3 for the example.

Notice that a very strong association exists at a lag of two periods. Conversely, a lag of three periods shows the two variables as being essentially uncorrelated. Logic is also of value in assessing the number of lags to be examined. If an indicator is believed to reflect a condition causing future sales to fluctuate, then the analyst should have some informed presumption as to the approximate lag. Only those lags in the

Table 9.3 Hypothetical Sales and Indicator Values, an Illustration of Lag Periods

Time t	Sales y	Indicator x	Time t	Sales y	Indicator x
1	50	17	11	55	10
2	60	13	12	50	12
3	55	12	13	35	18
4	45	17	14	40	15
5	50	14	15	60	12
6	55	12	16	50	14
7	45	15	17	40	20
8	40	18	18	45	15
9	50	17	19	65	14
10	60	15	20	50	17

Table 9.4 Correlation and Regression Results for Hypothetical Example Using Various Lag Periods

Number of Lag Periods	r^2	a	b	n	Adjusted r^2
0	0.4280	79.923	-2.015	20	0.396
1	0.0207	43.339	0.452	19	0
2	0.9125	7.009	2.871	18	0.907
3	0.0003	48.328	0.054	17	0

range somewhere near this number need be examined. For the example, if x appears to be a logical indicator of y in two periods, we would then use the regression equation and x_{19} to forecast states for $t = 21$, or

$$\text{Forecast } y_{21} = 7.009 + (2.871)(14) = 47$$

Also worth noting in Table 9.4 is that the number, n, of historical observations used in the analysis is reduced by each additional lag. There is not a problem when numerous observations are available, but when relatively few exist, the statistical measurements do become affected by longer lags. This being the case, it is best to use adjusted r^2, which takes n into account, as a criterion in selecting the appropriate lag length (see Chapter 4).

In practical situations, what complicates the analysis of lag periods is that many independent variables are often needed to develop a good predictive model, and it may be that each indicator has a different optimal lag length. Thus, each variable should be independently evaluated for its best lag length. Fortunately, a growing number of good regression programs exist that enable an analyst to lag a variable at the touch of a button.

Multicolinearity

Multivariate regression analysis assumes that the predictor variables are independent of each other (see Chapter 4). When using economic indicators in a forecasting regression model, however, it is all too common for this assumption to be violated. Indeed, economic indicators are often highly related to one another. For instance, disposable income is strongly related to GNP, interest rates are related to the money supply, and so on.

When the predictor variables exhibit substantially high correlations among themselves, the condition is termed *multicolinearity*. The effects of multicolinearity are as follows:[3]

1. The precision of estimating the coefficients of the regression equation may be dramatically reduced.
2. The ability to estimate the separate effects of each predictor variable may become impossible.
3. Predictor variables may be dropped incorrectly because of high standard errors.

Table 9.5 contains illustrative data, including data for the time period, sales, the interest rate, and the money supply. Note that a correlation matrix appears at the bottom of the table. This matrix displays all the bivariate correlations between all pairs of variables in the table. Such a matrix is relatively easy to obtain, as most regression computer software packages contain features to display these correlations automatically.

Notice that all the variables correlate very highly with sales. It would be tempting, therefore, to build a forecasting model with all the variables included. But also notice that all the other variables are very highly correlated with each other! This means that there exists excessive multi-colinearity, and, as a corollary, using all the variables in a regression model would lead to very questionable results.

When employing multivariate regression in forecasting, one frequently faces the dilemma of needing a large number of variables to achieve predictive accuracy. Yet, their intercorrelations often become larger as more predictors are added to the model. The germane question here is, "How much multicolinearity can be allowed without materially affecting the results?"

Unfortunately, there is no simple answer to this question because what constitutes "serious" multicolinearity is unclear.[4] Some researchers have adopted rules of thumb, such as, any pair of predictor variables must not correlate more than 0.9; if so, one of the pairs is to be discarded.

Such a rule can be extended, of course, to the examinations of multiple correlations between each predictor and all other predictors. As a rule, one would want to guard against a condition wherein any of the multiple correlations are greater than the multiple correlation of the forecast variable with the predictor set.

Another test for multicolinearity provided for in many of the better regression programs is an examination of the determinant.[5] A signal of

3. Johnston, *Econometric Methods*.
4. Paul E. Green and Donald S. Tull, *Research for Marketing Decisions*, 4th ed. (Englewood Cliffs, N.J.: Prentice-Hall, 1978), p. 333.
5. The determinant of a square matrix is a single number representing the sum of alternately signed products of matrix elements. In the simplest case, a 2 X 2

Table 9.5 Example of Multicolinearity

ROW	TIME	SALES	INTER	MONEY
* 1 *	1.00000	25.00000	15.00000	37.49999
* 2 *	2.00000	27.00000	14.70000	36.80000
* 3 *	3.00000	26.00000	14.80000	37.00000
* 4 *	4.00000	28.00000	14.60000	36.49999
* 5 *	5.00000	30.00000	14.40000	36.00000
* 6 *	6.00000	29.00000	14.60000	36.39999
* 7 *	7.00000	30.00000	14.40000	36.00000
* 8 *	8.00000	32.00000	14.20000	35.49999
* 9 *	9.00000	31.00000	14.50000	36.30000
* 10 *	10.00000	34.00000	14.20000	35.39999
* 11 *	11.00000	33.00000	14.20000	35.49999
* 12 *	12.00000	34.00000	14.00000	35.00000
* 13 *	13.00000	36.00000	13.80000	34.49999
* 14 *	14.00000	35.00000	14.00000	35.00000
* 15 *	15.00000	38.00000	13.70000	34.20000
* 16 *	16.00000	40.00000	13.60000	34.00000
* 17 *	17.00000	39.00000	13.80000	34.49999
* 18 *	18.00000	42.00000	13.50000	33.70000
* 19 *	19.00000	43.00000	13.40000	33.49999
* 20 *	20.00000	45.00000	13.20000	33.10000

```
> CORR
CONSECUTIVE COL(S) ? Y
FIRST COL, LAST COL= 1,4
 DECIMALS = 3
```

	TIME	SALES	INTER	MONEY
TIME	1.000			
SALES	0.981	1.000		
INTER	-0.970	-0.988	1.000	
MONEY	-0.971	-0.988	0.999	1.000

extreme multicolinearity is where the value of the determinant approaches zero. Unfortunately, it is not certain what a reasonable value of the determinant should be. Further research is needed to develop better guidelines. The existing programs, therefore, are not exact in pinpointing multicolinearity. But in general, an analyst can reasonably assume that multicolinearity is not an acute problem if the program being used has such checks and there is no indication of a problem.

When severe multicolinearity is detected, an analyst has one of four choices to make: (1) ignore it, (2) delete one or more of the offending predictors, (3) transform the predictors into a new set of predictors, and (4) use cross validation.

You may be surprised to learn that ignoring multicolinearity may not be as risky as it sounds. There may be strong enough effects in the predictor variables, despite the multicolinearity, that the estimation coefficients remain stable. Further, the multicolinearity may exist only within a subset of the predictor variables which does not account for much of the variance anyway. These may be tested by ignoring some of the observations, about 20% or so, and rerunning the regression. If the coefficients remain reasonably stable, one is probably safe in ignoring any multicolinearity.

A simple procedure to follow when multicolinearity is "severe" is to drop one or more of the predictors that are the major offenders. As a practical matter, one would choose to retain those variables that have the most logical causal link with the forecast variable. Returning to Table 9.5 to illustrate, the analyst, assuming that sales logically depend on interest rates, would drop all the other predictors and simply regress sales on the interest rates. This would be done, of course, only when there is substantial belief in the logic of the causal relationship between the two variables.

As a third solution, the original set of predictors could also be transformed to a new set of mutually uncorrelated linear composites. Principal components and factor analysis are two techniques that can

matrix, the determinant is computed as

$$|A| = \begin{vmatrix} a_{11} & a_{12} \\ a_{21} & a_{22} \end{vmatrix}$$

$$= a_{11}a_{22} - a_{12}a_{21}$$

If the determinant $A = 0$, the matrix is termed singular, which is the case with perfect multicolinearity.

accomplish this task.[6,7] These techniques are beyond the intended scope of this book and, consequently, are not discussed. Further, these techniques are seldom used in forecasting, probably because of the difficulty in understanding the meaning of the linear composites.

Perhaps the best and safest way to cope with multicolinearity, as well as a variety of related problems in multiple regression, is to use *cross validation* which assesses whether or not the regression equation holds up beyond the data on which its parameters are based. Here the analyst uses only part of the data to build the model, say the first two-thirds or three-quarters. The coefficients of this model are then used with the predictors of the last part of the data to forecast sales. The coefficient of determination (r^2) between the forecasts and the actuals is calculated. This r^2 is then compared with the original r^2, the one associated with the model, to assess the degree of "shrinkage."

No shrinkage, of course, would signal the presence of a very stable model, one that is not hampered by violated assumptions. In contrast, extreme shrinkage—where r^2 falls to zero—signals that the model is totally unreliable and should not be used to forecast into the future.

Another measure is to compare the mean squared error (MSE) of the initial model and that related to the model's forecasts with the remaining data. Now, however, a very substantial increase in the MSE signals an unreliable model that should not be used to forecast.

In general, neither of the abovementioned extremes is found. Although some analysts feel that no more than 10 to 20% is tolerable, there are no rigid guidelines to follow when assessing how much shrinkage is acceptable. The question is best answered by judgment. (More will be said about cross validation and stability in Chapter 10.)

Relative Importance of Predictors

With almost every applied multivariate-regression problem, there is a natural tendency for an analyst to want to rank the predictors, such as economic indicators, in the order of their importance when accounting for variation in the behavior of the forecast variable. This can be a sensible thing to do if the predictor variables are uncorrelated, as it sheds insight into the causal effects of each. Ranking can be accomplished by comparing the squared B(STD. V) values, termed *beta weights*, of the regression (see footnote 10 of Chapter 4).[8]

6. See Harold Hotelling, "Analysis of a Complex of Statistical Variables into Principal Components," *Journal of Educational Psychology*, 24 (1933), 417-44, 498-520.
7. See H. F. Kaiser, "The Varimax Criterion for Analytic Rotation in Factor Analysis," *Psychometrika*, 23 (1958), 187-200.
8. In fact, if the predictors are uncorrelated, squared simple correlations and squared betas will be equal and, obviously, rank the variables the same way. Such occasions are rare, however, because seldom are the predictors uncorrelated.

However, in almost every case, the predictor variables are correlated, at least to some extent. When this is the case, such a ranking should be avoided. There is simply no unambiguous way of measuring the relative importance of predictor variables when they are correlated.[9]

Breakdown Method

Some forecasting models involve the use of one or more indicators to forecast industry sales as an initial step. In turn, industry sales are then subdivided into various components, such as companies, product types, individual products, and so on.

To illustrate, the head of forecasting at Estée Lauder might discover that the cosmetic industry's sales have a personal income elasticity of 0.05, calculated as follows:

$$E_{PI} = \frac{\frac{\Delta S}{S}}{\frac{\Delta PI}{PI}} \qquad (9.1)$$

where $\quad E_{PI}$ = personal income elasticity of sales
ΔS = change in industry sales
ΔPI = change in personal income
S = industry sales
PI = national personal income

This would indicate that for every $100 increase in personal income, industry sales may be expected to rise by $5.

If industry sales this past year were $20 billion, personal income was $880 billion, and personal income is forecast to rise to $950 billion, the forecast of industry sales is

$$0.05(\$950 - 880) + \$20 = \$23.5 \text{ billion}$$

The next step is to break this forecast down to the company level. If the company's market share stabilized at about 16.5% over the past several years, for example, the forecast would be (0.165)($23.5 billion) = $3.88 billion. Still further breakdowns could be made.

The breakdown method has an advantage in its simplicity. But it is not always accurate because its focus on the number of indicators and their influence is limited. More complex procedures, like regression, will

9. R. L. Gorsuch, "Data Analysis of Correlated Independent Variables," *Multivariate Behavioral Research*, 8 (January 1973), 89–107.

seldom result in less accurate forecasts, given that the same variables are measured. And they will almost always yield more accurate results because of their mathematical precision and ability to handle multiple predictors. Further, the wide availability of computer software and high-speed computers have made the more advanced methods relatively simple to use as well.

OTHER METHODS

There are many other indirect methods that have been employed in forecasting. Of them, replacement cycle and input-output analysis appear to merit brief discussion.

Replacement Cycle

For some durable goods producers, forecasts should reflect customer replacement cycles. This cycle refers to a pattern of sales fluctuations that is brought about by large groups of customers replacing existing products with new ones. An example of this is in the trucking industry. The average life of a large trailer is about ten years, after which it is replaced. Another example is in the computer industry, for many computer users replace their hardware in response to the development of a new generation of equipment.

Replacement cycles may be operative for a number of reasons. One is that a product or product type may become technically obsolete. A new product or product variation that satisfies consumers' needs better than the old has come into being. When this happens on a recurring basis, a cycle is in existence. The airline industry illustrates this phenomenon. Beginning in the 1950s, producers of airplanes embarked on a recurring product improvement campaign, just when jet airliners were perfected for commercial airlines. Later, larger and more reliable aircraft were made available, replacing many of the older models. Shortly thereafter, short-range jets were produced which could fly short- and intermediate-length distances on an economical basis. Then, jumbo jets appeared. Still later, more fuel-efficient planes were developed, and again a large replacement cycle occurred. Each of these innovations generated a cycle of replacement.

Another reason for replacement cycles is that durables tend to wear out over time, to the point where they are no longer worth repairing. The above example of the trucking industry is a case in point. Another is home refrigerators, which tend to work efficiently for only about 15 years.

Still another reason for these cycles is style obsolescence. Consumers tend to replace their wardrobes when a new fashion trend emerges and may purchase a new automobile when the old one appears "old-fashioned."

Forecasting replacement cycles may or may not present a problem, depending upon the situation. If the replacements occur rather regularly, such that the waves of replacement are periodic, time-series techniques, such as decomposition, can easily handle the situation.

A problem, however, is that replacement cycles are sometimes aperiodic. The energy embargo of 1973–1974, to illustrate, caused a tremendous shift in the historical replacement cycle for automobiles. The deep recession of 1980–1982, coupled with the more than doubling in energy prices and interest rates, caused yet another substantial shift in the replacement cycles for many products from automobiles to home construction. Such aperiodic cycles are not easily forecast. Of course, regression methods can be useful in this regard, providing that the "right" indicators are utilized.

Similarly, major technological breakthroughs can have a dramatic impact on replacement cycles. The aperiodic pattern of airplane and computer generations are illustrations. Firms who are very adept in technical research, such as Texas Instruments, Eastman Kodak, and Envirotech, Inc., often alter the normal cyclical patterns with dramatic innovations.

Experience suggests that such aperiodic cycles are not easily forecast in a formal modeling sense. Regression methods can be useful, as was indicated earlier. So can well-conceived surveys of buyer intentions. But generally, good, sound business judgment is needed in these situations. For this reason, managers obviously should keep abreast of major economic, technical, and buyer behavior shifts. There are numerous good sources of insights, including the *Wall Street Journal*, *Forbes*, *Business Week*, *Barrons*, and *Fortune*.

Input-Output Analysis

Input-output analysis is another indirect method. The technique has received only limited attention by business forecasters, but it may become more widely used in the future. To date, its major utilization has been by those who formulate macro forecasts.

Input-output analysis is an accounting, a sort of map, of the entire economy. The analysis focuses on industry sales by setting forth data in a table depicting each industry as a row and a column. Each industry's row indicates its sales to firms in that industry, to other industries, and to other sections of the economy, such as governmental units and foreign firms. Some tables give the dollar volume or percent of total sales of the industry to the other sectors. The table most applicable to business sales forecasting presents indices representing expected increases in sales of the industry in question as a result of an increase in sales of other purchasing industries. The tables that have been prepared to date

Table 9.6 Hypothetical Input-Output

	Lumber and Wood Products	Household Furniture	Paper and Allied Products	Plastics and Synthetic Materials
Lumber and wood products	1.00	0.08	0.06	0.001
Household furniture	0.002	1.00	0.001	0.002
Paper and allied products	0.04	0.002	1.00	0.001
Plastics and synthetic materials	0.003	0.008	0.002	1.00

depict a large number of industries. The example presented here uses only a small number for purposes of illustration.

Table 9.6 is an abridged hypothetical input-output table involving only four industries. The coefficients reflect the impact of a dollar increase in sales in each industry on the expected sales of the industries in row 1. For instance, a one-dollar increase in sales of paper and allied products (column 3) is expected to produce a six-cent increase in sales of lumber and wood products. Thus, it indicates to firms in the lumber and wood products industry the impact of changes in sales in the paper and allied product industry. Similar conclusions can be drawn from data in the various other rows.

Input-output tables can shed considerable light on the functioning of the overall economy. For example, if falling interest rates are expected to stimulate upcoming sales of heavy equipment, the impact on even distantly related industries such as textile manufacturing can be estimated. Further, changes in the input-output tables from year to year depict emerging interrelationships among components of the economy. This information is also useful in forecasting.

Input-output analysis will probably come into increasing use as technical problems are resolved and needed data come into existence. These potential future developments may serve to enhance considerably the usefulness of future business sales forecasting.

SUMMARY

This chapter has discussed the indirect approach to forecasting, in which estimates are derived from economic measures normally separate from company internal records. We began with a discussion of economic indicators. There are numerous sources of such indicators, some who publish and disseminate their results widely and others made available through commercial sources.

Usually, these indicators are termed leading, lagging, or coincident. These categorizations typically reflect whether the indicators make their moves ahead, behind, or at the same time as the overall economy. As such, they may not register in the same status for different industries or companies. That is, for each case an analyst must determine which indicators are most appropriate to use and for what purpose.

Regression analysis is ideally suited to the task of forecasting with economic indicators. The process is termed econometric model building. Multivariate regression and correlation methods, in addition to logic, can help identify which economic indicators to use. But there are some problems that may pose obstacles to effective forecast implementation.

The first difficulty is in identifying the optimum lag-period length to use for leading indicators. Correlation helps here. The procedure is to first estimate, by logic, how far ahead a particular indicator should lead the forecast variable. Then the period lengths, or lags, are varied to see if a better coefficient of determination, r^2, can be found. It is generally best to use adjusted r^2 for this purpose because typically there are losses in the number of paired comparisons with each lag because of limited historical data. The appropriate lag period to use should be determined for each indicator. Fortunately, regression packages, which have the ability to lag variables, are becoming increasingly common.

The second difficulty is from multicolinearity. This is a condition where the predictor variables are highly intercorrelated, which is a violation of a regression assumption. Generally, intercorrelated predictor variables are common among economic indicators. There are several options available when excessive multicolinearity is detected. The first is to ignore it. The second is to drop one or more of the violators. A third is to transform the predictors to a new set of mutually uncorrelated linear composites.

Probably the best way to cope with the situation, along with other regression problems, is to cross validate the model. This is accomplished by building the model on the first two-thirds or three-fourths of the data and then using it to forecast the remaining sales. If the r^2's compare relatively well, then the model's coefficients may be considered to be reasonable.

We next looked at the breakdown method of using economic indicators. This procedure employs an indicator to forecast industry sales and then breaks this figure down into its components, such as company sales and so on. Seldom will this method yield more accurate results than the more formal methods, however.

Next, we briefly considered two other methods. Analyzing replacement cycles was the first. If replacement cycles are periodic, they can be handled easily with other techniques, such as decomposition. But if they are not, which is often the case with severe economic interruptions like a major technological breakthrough, estimating the replacement cycle becomes more difficult.

Finally, we considered input-output analysis, which requires accounting for all major interactions within an economy. This technique has not received widespread attention by business forecasters, but it might in the future as better data sources are made available.

DISCUSSION QUESTIONS

1. Examine two sources of indicators, such as the *Business Conditions Digest*. Compare and contrast them.
2. Which specific indicators appear to be logical lead indicators for sales of the following products?

a. Automobiles
b. Copper
c. Coffee mugs
d. Wheat
e. Computers
f. Textbooks

g. Women's clothing
h. Money market mutual funds
i. Hotel rooms
j. Passenger air travel
k. Heavy machinery
l. Pleasure motorboats

3. Forecast sales for $t = 21$ for the following:

t	Indicator	Unit Sales	t	Indicator	Unit Sales
1	49.8	30.5	11	53.6	30.6
2	56.7	31.2	12	47.8	33.7
3	45.0	29.9	13	41.5	29.3
4	48.7	34.6	14	53.1	28.2
5	61.2	32.4	15	60.0	34.1
6	59.6	36.6	16	50.0	31.9
7	47.6	29.1	17	42.0	26.3
8	51.8	31.3	18	56.8	34.9
9	45.6	39.5	19	43.5	39.0
10	43.8	38.6	20	51.2	32.5

4. Forecast sales for $t = 17$ for the following:

t	Indicator	Sales	t	Indicator	Sales
1	40.0	57.3	9	52.1	69.4
2	41.3	55.0	10	51.3	74.7
3	38.7	58.0	11	52.9	78.0
4	44.6	61.6	12	54.3	76.5
5	45.8	58.2	13	53.7	79.4
6	47.8	66.9	14	55.2	80.9
7	46.3	69.3	15	57.3	80.4
8	49.8	70.9	16	57.4	82.4

5. Forecast sales for $t = 21$ for the following:

	Indicators				Indicators		
t	1	2	Sales	t	1	2	Sales
1	30.0	55.9	35.1	11	35.6	57.4	43.0
2	33.1	61.9	36.0	12	36.1	54.8	45.8
3	36.8	56.8	44.4	13	32.7	59.6	45.8
4	35.2	56.9	49.1	14	36.8	65.1	43.4
5	34.7	58.0	45.9	15	37.9	55.9	46.8
6	35.6	59.8	45.3	16	34.3	55.2	51.6
7	36.6	54.8	45.9	17	32.7	53.1	45.1
8	34.5	62.4	47.3	18	32.5	56.2	44.0
9	37.8	53.6	44.6	19	34.5	58.3	43.1
10	32.6	57.9	49.0	20	35.0	57.1	44.9

6. Suppose a third variable were available in question 5, as follows:

	Indicator		Indicator
t	3	t	3
1	41.1	11	39.5
2	40.1	12	39.1
3	40.0	13	40.1
4	39.4	14	39.0
5	39.5	15	38.6
6	39.3	16	39.7
7	39.0	17	40.2
8	39.6	18	40.2
9	38.6	19	39.7
10	40.2	20	39.5

Now forecast sales for $t = 21$.

7. Locate economic indicators for your area and use them to forecast your area's retail sales. If they are not available, use national information and build a model to forecast new housing starts.

8. What, if any, unique problems are encountered with replacement cycles? How can they be handled?

9. Locate an input-output chart and examine it for the electronics industry. Summarize your findings.
10. Describe the breakdown method of using economic indicators. Assess its merits. Try to use the method for question 7.

RECOMMENDED READINGS

Blue Chip Economic Indicators. Washington, D.C.: Capital Publications. Monthly.
Business Conditions Digest. Washington, D.C.: U.S. Government Printing Office. Monthly.
Draper, N. R., and H. Smith. *Applied Regression Analysis.* New York: John Wiley, 1966.
Gorsuch, R. L. "Data Analysis of Correlated Independent Variables." *Multivariate Behavioral Research*, 8 (January 1973), 89–107.
Green, P. E., and D. S. Tull. *Research for Marketing Decisions.* 4th ed. Englewood Cliffs, N.J.: Prentice-Hall, 1978.
Hotelling, H. "Analysis of a Complex of Statistical Variables into Principal Components." *Journal of Educational Psychology*, 24 (1933), 417–444, 498–520.
Johnston, J. *Econometric Methods.* 2nd ed. New York: McGraw-Hill Book Company, 1972
Kaiser, H. F. "The Varimax Criterion for Analytic Rotation in Factor Analysis." *Psychometrika*, 23 (1958), 187–200.
Research. Princeton, N.J. Annual.
Moore, G. H. "The Analysis of Economic Indicators." *Scientific American*, January 1975, pp. 17–23.
Neter, J., and W. Wasserman. *Applied Linear Statistical Methods.* Homewood, Ill.: Richard D. Irwin, 1974.

CASE 9: LAMAR'S DEPARTMENT STORE

Lamar's Department Store is the largest independently owned department store in a Washington city of approximately 70,000 population. It is located in a modern suburban shopping center and stocks a full line of both hard and soft goods. The store serves middle- and upper-income consumers with offerings that are superior to those stocked by discounters and most other mass merchandisers. It is a full-service store with a large sales staff and numerous services, such as delivery, gift wrapping, and liberal credit terms. Lamar's advertises on local radio stations and in the city's major newspaper. The firm's major competitors are two other department stores in the city and various specialty shops. Generally, Lamar's prices exceed those of its rivals.

Management has used various sales forecasting methods in the past. Decomposition time series has been attempted and rejected, because of an inability to predict major turning points in sales. Management has also tried subjective judgment and found that, although this is superior to time series, it still does not generate acceptable levels of accuracy. These shortcomings have led management to consider multiple regression for estimating future levels of sales.

There are some independent variables, for which data is available, that might be expected to be good indicators of future sales. One of these is total dollars spent on advertising by the store. The other is the number of special promotions (short-term price reductions in one department). These data are given in the following table.

Store Sales (in Tens of Thousands of Dollars)	Ad Expenditures (in Thousands of Dollars)	Number of Special Promotions
$23	$10	7
12	2	3
15	4	2
17	6	4
23	8	6
22	7	5
10	4	3
14	6	3
20	7	4
19	6	3

no effect on sales

1. Do you believe that multiple regression should be used by Lamar's? Why or why not?
2. Are the assumptions of regression met by this firm?
3. What forecasting methods, other than decomposition time series, judgment, and multiple regression, might be useful to Lamar's?

no relationship between advertising and sales.

use some other variable other than sales to come up with a relationship for regression.

① assessment
② correlation
③ surveys

Chapter 10
Assessment and Implementation

11/27/89

INTRODUCTION

This chapter is concerned with the assessment and implementation stages of forecasting. *Assessment* refers to the process of examining the forecast as well as the methods used to derive it in order to test their validity. In turn, *implementation* involves taking steps to ensure that the forecast is effectively communicated to others, understood by them, and acted on.

Beginning analysts are likely to underestimate the significance of these steps, operating under the misconception that technical considerations will determine the usefulness of the forecast to management. This is indeed a misconception. The best technical forecast, if it is assessed or implemented improperly, may be of no value or even may be deleterious to managerial decision making.[1]

ASSESSMENT

The assessment process involves a rigorous examination of both the methods employed to derive the forecast and the forecast level itself. As to the former, the methodology is subjected to tests in order to provide some indication of the validity of the forecast. Should methodological weaknesses be discovered, the forecast may be disregarded entirely or may be treated with much less confidence. Another virtue of assessing methodology is that it provides a guide for future analysis. That is, methods found to be effective at present can be used again, whereas those that are not valid can be disregarded or revised.

In addition to methodological assessment, the forecast level itself should be examined. The objective here is to discern whether or not it seems to be reasonable in light of past experience and present and anticipated future developments. If, for instance, the five-year forecast

---

1. See Michael L. Ray, "Measurement and Marketing Research—Is the Flirtation Going to Lead to Romance?" *Journal of Marketing Research* (February 1978), 1-5.

is for a steady decline in company sales, yet consumer demand and rival sales are anticipated to remain strong, a red-flag signal of possible weakness in the forecast is in evidence. Thus, failure to assess the forecast correctly can result in very misleading conclusions.

When examining the forecast level, the analysts should receive inputs from managers as to just how precise the forecasts should be. It may be that management wants very accurate figures, perhaps for budgeting purposes. Should this be the case, the analysts must be very critical in their assessments of forecast levels. The opposite situation occurs, that is, critical assessments are not so important, when only appropriate forecasts are necessary, as when managers are deciding whether or not to introduce a new product.

In short, assessment is a vital forecasting function, the importance of which the novice is unlikely to recognize. The following sections describe many of the various kinds of assessments that can be conducted.

Sometimes, it is useful for someone other than the analyst to perform the assessment. An outside objective viewpoint is free from the biases that are likely to exist, when one is evaluating one's own work. If outside assessment is not practical, because of time or cost constraints or lack of qualified personnel, the analyst should attempt to conduct this work from the perspective of an outsider who is objective and disinterested in the forecast outcome.

The assessment process is facilitated by plotting historical and forecast sales on a graph and then visually comparing the two sets thus plotted. Variations between historical and forecast sales are readily discovered through this visual aid.

Data Validity   11/27 – make sure you have the right information

If the data employed in generating the forecast were in error, the forecast will most likely be also. For instance, if surveys were used to determine buying plans of consumers, numerous sources of data contamination are present. These include inadequate sample size, insufficiently trained interviewers, and poorly phrased questions. If secondary sources were employed, the analyst should take steps to ensure that these were reliable and that they were used correctly. In one forecast of the water needs of a western state, for instance, a typist added one digit to a series of value-of-shipment figures contained in the *Agricultural Almanac*. This resulted in a forecast that was much too large to be realistic.

In addition to examining raw data gathered through research or secondary sources, the analyst should scrutinize processed data, that which has been subjected to arithmetic manipulation in the forecasting process. It is possible, of course, that the analyst has made an error in multiplication or division or that the computer program contained errors. Such mistakes are often difficult to uncover, yet their effect on the validity of the forecast can be devastating. The analyst should search diligently for such mistakes.

Forecasting-Method Validity

Another possible weakness in a forecast is that the method employed may not be realistic. Each forecasting method requires that certain assumptions be made. Linear regression, for instance, requires that the relationship between independent and dependent variables be linear in form. This may not be the case in a concrete application of the linear regression model, however. Consider the case of the R. L. Steed Corporation, a producer of outdoor furniture, which has employed this method for a number of years. The analyst has used industry sales as the independent variable. Figure 10.1 indicates, however, that the

Figure 10.1 R. L. Steed Corporation Sales

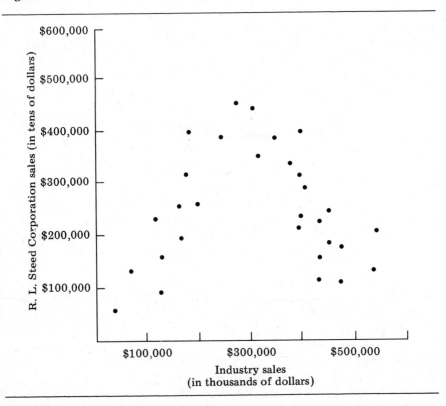

relationship is clearly not linear. Rather, the figure suggests a curvilinear relationship. It appears that the analyst should consider curvilinear regression, growth curves, or some other method of forecasting.

The Steed example illustrates the importance of examining the model's assumptions. A useful assessment technique is to review carefully *all* assumptions relating to the methods used. In the instance of the Steed forecast, a mathematical assumption was not realized. Another kind of assumption is that relating to the substance of the method itself. If the variables and the relationships between the variables that the model embodies are not realistic, the method is likely to be in error.

The Nubarr Corporation, a producer of ball bearings, employs time series as a forecasting tool. In the past, this method has contributed forecasts that corresponded closely to actual sales levels, but the 1982 forecast was much too high in comparison to actual sales. This was caused, in part, by drastic changes undertaken by the Nubarr marketing department. These included price decreases and enlargement of the sales force by 20%. A time-series forecast does not account for such variables. It assumes that sales are a function of the passage of time, rather than such factors as changes in price, the size of the sales force, advertising, and competition.

It is sometimes possible to assess a method's validity by comparing its forecasts with those derived from a similar class of model. If the two forecasts do not differ by much, there may be considerable evidence of validity. For example, the outcome of a survey could be compared with information from a panel.[2]

Substance Errors

Very often, forecasts based on surveys contain substance errors. Here analysts have failed to choose the proper variable for study. They may, for instance, ask consumers for their future buying plans for a product such as used lawn mowers. Many consumers, however, are incapable of correctly predicting their buying power for relatively inexpensive durable goods such as this and will not be able to provide valid responses. Thus, the variable "future buying plans" simply will not be predictive of future sales patterns. If a forecast was based on variables like the replacement cycle or leading series, it might be much more accurate. In short, analysts are well advised to take extreme care in determining the variables that are to be examined to form the basis for the forecast. If past experience or logic suggests that they will be insufficient, others should be sought.

2. Yoram Wind and David Lerner, "On the Measurement of Purchase Data: Surveys Versus Purchase Diaries," *Journal of Marketing Research*, 16 (February 1979), 39–47.

Causal Validity

Closely related to substance validity is *causal* validity. A method incorporating this characteristic uses independent variables exerting a causal influence on sales. It is difficult for analysts to prove a cause-and-effect relationship. However, the absence of causal relationships does not prevent analysts from making forecasts. They use variables that allow them to predict changes in sales, even though they do not necessarily cause these changes. In time series, for instance, the independent variable is time; in leading series, it is some economic indicator.

In the context of causal validity, a good method uses variables that might be *expected* to exert a causal influence on sales. A necessary but not sufficient condition of a causal relationship is high correlation and a lead-lag pattern; another is logical relationship, as when it is expected that sales of air conditioners and room fans will rise as temperatures rise. Evidence of causal influence is apparent if a variable is highly correlated with sales, leads sales movements, and is logically related to sales. The analyst looks for these phenomena in testing for causal validity.

An extreme example would be a small steel mill located near some of the larger and more powerful firms in the industry. Its products are all standard and do not differ substantially from those of rivals. It has a very small promotion budget and offers prices identical to those of the market leader. The correlation between industry and firm sales is 0.99, and industry sales fluctuations tend to lead that of the company by one month. Logically, the company sales forecaster uses regression analysis, with industry sales as the dependent variable, to predict company sales. Under the artificial conditions set forth in the foregoing, a high degree of causal validity is evident.

To sum up the foregoing discussion, in concrete situations, the analyst can test for causal validity by looking for:

1. Correlation between dependent and independent variables
2. Existence of a lead-lag relationship
3. Existence of a logical causal relationship

Ability to Predict

Another useful test of a forecast method is to measure its ability to produce accurate forecasts. One means of determining this is to make the forecast, using past and current data, and to compare this with actual sales levels as they transpire. After a succession of periods where "real" forecasts are compared with "real" actuals, management can assess how well the approach is performing.

Another means of assessing a model's ability to predict is to cross validate the model. (As discussed in Chapter 9, this involves building the model on the first part of a data set and then seeing how well it forecasts the last part.) Adamson Systems Corporation, to illustrate, has experienced the following sales levels over the past 15 years.

Year	Sales (in Thousands of Dollars)
1968	36,700
1969	35,100
1970	34,300
1971	35,400
1972	37,500
1973	39,400
1974	47,800
1975	49,900
1976	46,400
1977	53,700
1978	59,200
1979	63,400
1980	68,500
1981	77,600
1982	79,300

The fact that a positive linear trend exists should be apparent. This means that double exponential smoothing and regression (sales regressed on time) are two model candidates to forecast sales for the example.

Table 10.1 compares the ability of double exponential smoothing and regression to forecast sales for 1979 through 1982 with models based on data for 1968 through 1978. The computer program of Appendix 3.B was used to generate the exponentially smoothed forecasts, and a standard regression program was used for the other.

Notice that double exponential smoothing is more stable than the regression model. This is indicated by the smaller mean squared error. In fact, the square root of the MSE is $4,662, which is 60.4% smaller than that for the regression model ($\sqrt{13.877 \times 10^7} = \$11.780$). Thus, Thus, exponential smoothing has greater ability to predict and is the better forecasting model choice.

Once the appropriate model is chosen after cross validation, it is typical to rerun the model using all the data before forecasting with

Table 10.1 Adamson Systems Corporation, Comparison of Cross-Validated Forecasting Models

Year	t	Actual	Regression Model		Double Exponential-Smoothing Model	
			Forecast[a]	Squared Error	Forecast[b]	Squared Error
1979	12	$63,400	$57,536	$34,386E[c] 06	62,406	98,804E 04
1980	13	68,500	59,923	73,565E 06	66,314	47,786E 05
1981	14	77,600	62,309	23,381E 07	70,222	54,435E 06
1982	15	79,300	64,695	21,331E 07	74,130	26,729E 06
Mean				13,877E 07		21,733E 06

[a] Regression against time, t, based on 1968 through 1978; $r^2 = 0.85$, $a = 28,900$, $b = 2386.36$.
[b] Based on results of optimal weighting program, with least-squares initializations (Appendix 3.B); optimal $\alpha = 0.5591$, MSE at optimal (for first 11 periods) = $14.62E 06$; each subsequent forecast increments by $3,908.
[c] Read 34.386×10^6

the future. This enables the coefficients to be updated with as much current information as possible in case shifts in historical relationships occurred.

Flexibility

must be continually updated — not set in stone — reviewed and revised when new data obtained

Analysts should also assess the flexibility and ease of use of a forecasting method. This refers to the ease by which the method can be updated as new data or new information altering the assumptions underlying the method are made available. Examples of extremely flexible methods are some computer simulations that model the sales behavior of the firm. Flexibility exists when new input data are fed into the model or when information is transmitted to the computer program specifying the nature of the model. The method is enhanced when continuous information flows are automatically fed into the computer. Firms using management information systems, which provide for such flows, are in a position to generate sales forecasts that have been adjusted in light of the latest available data.

Exponential smoothing methods are also very flexible and easy to use in this regard. Once an appropriate model is found, subsequent forecasts can readily be made using new information as it emerges without having to reanalyze all the history completely. This is especially beneficial in cases where a large number of forecasts are needed, such as at the individual product level in a large multiproduct, multimarket company like IBM.

Other forecasting methods are not as flexible and easy to use. They usually require a complete re-evaluation every time a new forecast is being made. The difficulty of custom building a model to fit the data may impose a severe constraint on the use of such methods.

Forecast Level Reasonableness

An important segment of the validity-assessment process is to examine the forecasts generated by a given method in light of their reasonableness or believability. The analyst must ask whether such a forecast is believable in light of available evidence concerning the company and its environment.

One very effective method of determining reasonableness is to compare historical sales data with the forecast. Assume that a survey forecast has been conducted, the 1983 forecast level is $36,500, and historical sales are as specified in Table 10.2 and depicted in Figure 10.2.

When compared to past sales data, the forecast appears to be unreasonably low. The sales levels from 1976 to 1983 all surpass the estimate

Table 10.2 Historical Sales Data

Year	Sales (in Thousands of Dollars)
1969	22,200
1970	28,400
1971	29,200
1972	26,400
1973	30,260
1974	31,200
1975	37,400
1976	38,390
1977	40,620
1978	52,900
1979	41,600
1980	39,200
1981	46,600
1982	49,200

Figure 10.2 Historical and Forecast Sales

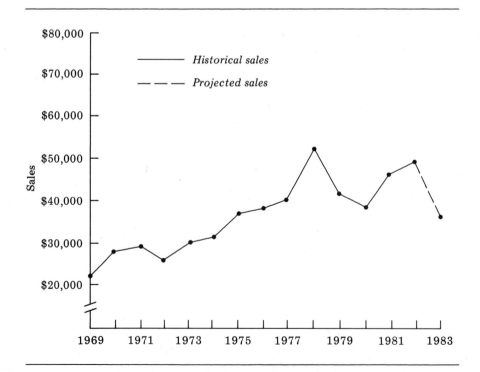

for 1983. Furthermore, the trend of the historical data is definitely upward. These comparisons should suggest to the analyst that further assessment of the forecast and its methodology is in order.

The analyst should seek out reasons for a serious future decline in company sales. Possible reasons are rigorous price competition by rivals, an expected downturn in the economy, probable decreases in industry sales, or deterioration in the quality of the firm's product. An examination of these factors may lend credibility to the forecast. They may indicate that a severe sales decline is indeed imminent, or they may indicate that the forecast is likely to be seriously incorrect.

Of particular importance in testing the reasonableness of a forecast is an examination of the present and future marketing activities of the enterprise. Changes in these can exert a strong impact on future sales and render the sales forecast invalid. Consider the experience of the North American Industries Corporation, a producer of small electric motors used in household appliances. North American's sales for the past ten years are given in the following table and also, along with the 1983 forecast, in Figure 10.3.

Year	Sales (in Dollars)
1973	11,450,000
1974	13,320,000
1975	9,402,000
1976	10,316,000
1977	9,406,000
1978	10,590,000
1979	10,780,000
1980	12,316,000
1981	14,408,000
1982	16,906,000

A time-series forecasting method produces a projected $18,100,000 in sales for 1983. In 1982 North American added four salespeople to its staff (an increase of 20%) and enlarged its trade magazine advertising budget by 34%. These moves resulted in sizable sales increases in 1982, which should continue to be significant in 1983 and succeeding years. The analyst should recognize these and similar nonrecurring sales volume influences in judging the reasonableness of a forecast.

Figure 10.3 North American Industries Corporation Historical and Forecast Sales

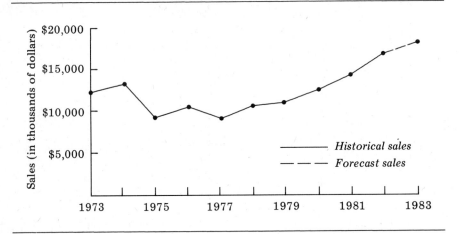

Reliability

Another desirable attribute of a forecasting method is reliability. To measure this, we have used mean squared error, which is the most widely used but not the only measure of reliability.

Another measure sometimes used is the mean percentage error. This involves calculating the mean of all the error percentages. This measure, sometimes called bias, provides an indication of whether or not the model is consistent in over- or underprediction. Table 10.3 provides an illustration. For the example, the forecasts are 8.4% below the actual values on average. Still another measure is the mean absolute percent error, also illustrated in Table 10.3. This measure ignores sign.

Emphasis was placed on mean squared error (MSE) in this text because large errors are given more importance in the calculation than are small ones.[3] In addition, it is useful to look at the mean percent error. Characteristics of a good model are both a small MSE and a small mean percent error. These conditions signal a small variance and little consistency in under- or overpredicting.

Another technique that can be employed to evaluate the reliability of a forecast is to compare it with a forecast generated by another method the analyst feels to be valid. This process is illustrated by the experience of the Northwest Continental Company, a producer of tires. The Northwest Continental analyst employed the company's historical data to forecast 1983 sales.

3. Some analysts use total error, the summation of the error column. For example, see Stephen McNees, "An Evaluation of Economic Forecasts," *New England Economic Review* (November-December 1975).

Table 10.3 Comparison of Error Measures

t	Actual	Forecast	Error	Percent Error	Absolute Error	Percent Absolute Error	Squared Error
1	9	8	1	11%	1	11%	1
2	10	9	1	10	1	10	1
3	9	10	-1	-11	1	11	1
4	11	11	0	0	0	0	0
5	12	11	1	8	1	8	1
6	11	9	2	18	2	18	4
7	10	7	3	30	3	30	9
8	9	8	1	11	1	11	1
9	10	8	2	20	2	20	4
10	8	9	-1	-13	1	13	1
Sum			9	84%	13	132%	23
Mean			0.9	8.4%	1.3	13.2%	2.3

The Northwest Continental analyst combined company sales figures with industry sales data to produce a breakdown-method forecast using linear regression as the statistical tool. The regression equation produced a 1983 Northwest Continental sales forecast of $62,950,000. The historical data and forecast appear in Figure 10.4. The Northwest Continental analyst feels that the forecast may be high enough to be unrealistic, and decides to compare the forecast with those derived from other methods.

The analyst first subjects the data in Table 10.4 to time-series projection. A linear trend analysis produces a 1983 forecast of $59,200,000, substantially below that generated by the regression analysis. The analyst decides that the disparity between the two estimates warrants further investigation, and contacts the marketing research department for estimates of the share of market captured by Northwest Continental. The share of market data appear in Table 10.5. Figure 10.5 depicts these in graphic form.

The share of market series is steadily increasing, especially in the last three years. This suggests that the estimate produced by the regression analysis may not be inordinately high; in fact, it may be more realistic than that produced by the trend analysis.

To check further the reasonableness of the forecast, the analyst contacts a random sample of 20 salespeople by telephone. Each salesperson is asked for an estimate of the expected percentage change in sales in his or her territory between 1982 and 1983. The arithmetic mean of these is 10.4%. This statistic tends to support the regression-derived forecast, since it suggests an increase of over 10%.

Figure 10.4 Northwest Continental Sales

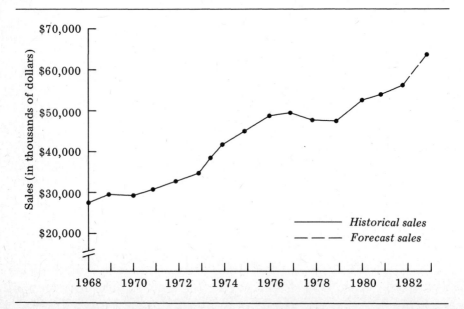

Table 10.4 Northwest Continental Sales

Year	Sales (in Thousands of Dollars)
1968	27,600
1969	29,450
1970	29,300
1971	30,400
1972	32,700
1973	34,800
1974	41,900
1975	44,650
1976	48,600
1977	49,200
1978	47,900
1979	47,600
1980	51,400
1981	53,700
1982	56,900

Table 10.5 Northwest Continental Share of Market

Year	Share of Market (% of Industry Sales)
1967	3.3
1968	3.4
1969	3.6
1970	3.5
1971	3.7
1972	3.7
1973	3.7
1974	3.9
1975	3.9
1976	4.1
1977	4.2
1978	4.2
1979	4.3
1980	4.4
1981	4.7
1982	4.9

Figure 10.5 Northwest Continental Share of Market

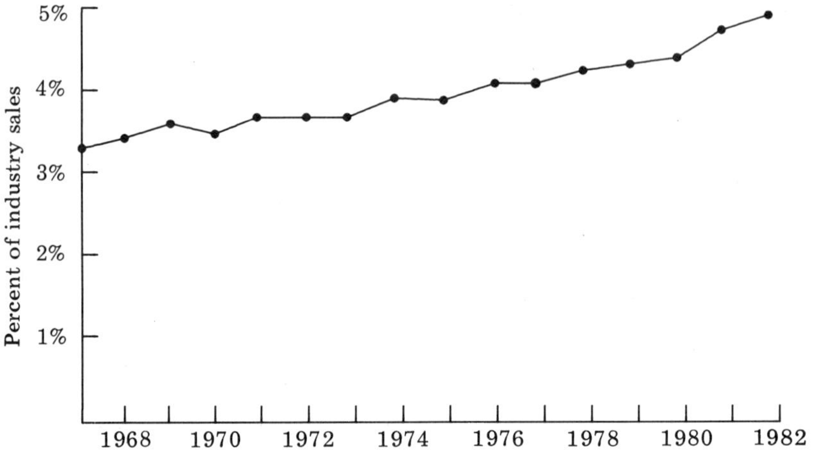

Finally, the analyst submits the forecast and a brief review of the forecasting method to several executives for their reaction to its reasonableness. These executives include representatives of general management, production, finance, sales, and advertising. The group in the main agrees with the forecast. One dissenter, however, an executive from the finance department, feels that the forecast is too high in light of past experience. The sales manager feels it is too low in light of planned increases in marketing expenditures for 1983. The remaining executive reviewers feel that the forecast is realistic, and the analyst concurs.

Some firms' forecasting procedures depart slightly from that given in the foregoing. Rather than using only one method, and then employing others to assess the reasonableness and reliability of the first, they construct two or more estimates, each derived from a different method. The resulting multiple forecasts are then compared, and any differences are reconciled. Reconciliation involves adopting the median, mode, mean, or weighted mean of all the forecasts used.

The Smith and Ferguson Corporation uses three methods in forecasting annual sales of its office furniture line:

1. Time-series analysis
2. Regression-leading series analysis
3. Survey of executive opinion

Table 10.6 presents the historical sales data employed in formulating the 1983 sales forecast. Figure 10.6 depicts the data in graphic form.

Table 10.7 sets forth the forecast level of sales derived from each of the three methods. Figures for some years are not presented, since particular methods were used during some years but not in others.

Table 10.6 Sales, Smith and Ferguson Corporation Office Furniture

Year	Sales (in Thousands of Dollars)
1966	4,300
1967	6,700
1968	8,900
1969	8,700
1970	8,600
1971	8,400
1972	9,200
1973	9,100
1974	10,700
1975	11,700
1976	14,200
1977	15,000
1978	15,100
1979	15,000
1980	15,300
1981	15,500
1982	15,800

Figure 10.6 Sales, Smith and Ferguson Corporation Office Furniture

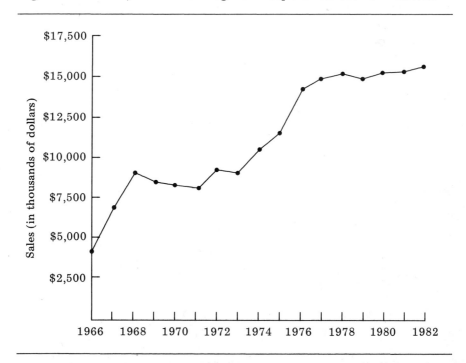

Table 10.7 Smith and Ferguson, Forecasts Produced by the Three Methods

	Sales (in Thousands of Dollars)		
Year	Time Series	Regression	Executive Opinion
1966	4,100		
1967	5,600		
1968	7,900		
1969	8,400		
1970	8,700		8,500
1971	8,900		8,000
1972	8,900		9,500
1973	9,200	10,100	9,400
1974	10,500	11,200	10,800
1975	11,200	9,400	11,700
1976	12,700	15,700	15,800
1977	12,900	17,900	15,300
1978	13,500	18,700	16,400
1979	14,200	17,100	15,900
1980	14,900	16,200	15,900
1981	15,200	14,900	15,800
1982	15,400	13,900	16,200
1983	16,500	16,100	16,900

The next step is to use multivariate regression, with actual sales being the dependent variable. A computer program, which checks for excessive autocorrelation, reveals that there is not a problem in this regard. Only data for 1973 through 1982 were used since forecasts from all three methods are available for these years. The multiple adjusted $r^2 = 0.98$. Table 10.8 presents the equation's coefficients.

Table 10.8 Smith and Ferguson, Multivariate Regression Output

```
> COEF

VARIABLE   B(STD.V)      B        STD.ERROR(B)     T
TIMSER      0.3845    4.3007E-01   1.7069E-01    2.520
REGR        0.0615    4.4112E-02   8.7473E-02    0.504
EXOPIN      0.5783    5.2053E-01   2.0294E-01    2.565
CONSTANT    0         6.7977E 01   7.3834E 02    0.092
```

The regression equation provides a means of combining the separate forecasts.[4] (Note: The data were entered into the program in thousands of dollars, so the constant must be interpreted in thousands.)

For the example, the combined forecast for 1983, therefore, is calculated as follows:

$$\text{Forecast sales} = \$16,500,000(0.430) + \$16,100,000(0.044)$$
$$+ \$16,900,000(0.521) + \$68,000$$
$$= \$16,676,300$$

This technique has produced a forecast that has inputs from three methods. The relative accuracy of each method has been reflected through its adjusted coefficient. The result is a forecast that is expected to be reasonably valid.

Our discussion of how to assess the reasonableness and reliability of a forecast has emphasized examination of the forecast level itself. The assessment process must, of course, include evaluation of the forecasting methods employed, as covered in the previous section. In the foregoing example, the analyst should examine the validity of the three methods employed in an attempt to discover weaknesses in data, methodology, and the like. Weaknesses in methodology of one of the methods might lead the analyst to place less credence in its output. If past sales data do not conform to a linear pattern, the linear trend-extension estimate would be suspect, for instance.

Review of Forecast Environment

Finally, the environment should be reviewed periodically to learn if significant changes having a major bearing on the forecast level should be expected. As examples:

1. Larger or smaller promotional programs may be planned by the firm or by its competitors.
2. The company or its competitors may change prices.
3. New competition, perhaps a foreign firm, may be entering or leaving the picture.
4. The firm or its competitors may have evolved a new level of technology.

Such changes in the environment may have a dramatic impact on sales, and judgment should be used to revise the level of the forecast accordingly. Analysts should work closely with management in identifying

---

4. The β coefficients are used instead of the beta weights. Any consistent bias is recognized and adjusted for by adding back the constant.

any such anticipated environmental changes as well as assessing the impact. This periodic review and revision, if necessary, is critical to the development of reasonable forecasts.

IMPLEMENTATION OF FORECAST

Once a forecast has been completed and assessed, it is implemented by transmittal to the proper executives for transformation into budgets and other control and planning tools, such as production schedules. Implementation requires convincing these executives that the forecast is likely to be sufficiently accurate that they should act on it.[5]

Transmission to Executives

In most companies, a firm policy has been established as to which executives are to receive the forecast. Executives obtain the forecast for review and scrutinize the figures presented to them by the analysts. Following this, they decide whether or not, in their opinion, they are adequate.

In the Salisbury Smelter Corporation, the analysts are required to submit copies of the annual forecast to the vice presidents of production, marketing, and finance. Each of these employs assistants who evaluate the reasonableness of the forecast data and convey the results of this evaluation to their superior. Should consideration of adjustments be required, in the opinion of the executives, the forecast is rerouted, along with comments about these considerations, to the analyst. Figure 10.7 depicts this process in graphic form.

In some cases, the analyst is not a member of the firm but is an outside consultant. In these cases, efficient practice dictates that specific procedures be determined in the consulting contract, as to whom the forecast is to be submitted and the process for review. It is assumed that the consultant will submit the forecast to high-level executives so that they can evaluate the forecast's validity and disseminate it to the proper people.

Ensuring that the Forecast Is Used

The analysts should try to ensure that forecasts are used by management for decision-making purposes. This requires convincing executives that

5. See Charles Gross and Robin Peterson, "Some Human Problems in Industrial Sales Forecasting: 'Users' versus 'Doers'—The Human Factor in Technical Dilemmas," *Industrial Marketing Management*, 7 (December 1978), pp. 367–368. Also see: Charles W. Gross and Thomas W. Knowles, "How to Cope With Realities or Why Forecasts Go Awry," *The Journal of Business Forecasting: Methods and Systems*, 1 (Spring 1982), pp. 6–10.

Figure 10.7 Salisbury Smelter Corporation Sales Forecast Routing Scheme

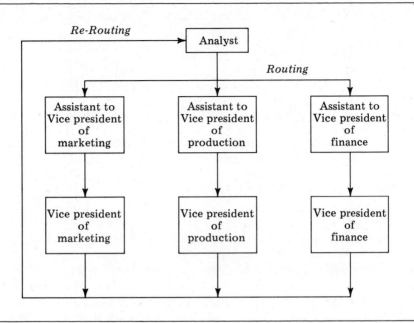

the estimates are valid, and it involves follow-up to determine if the forecasts were actually implemented.

Where possible, the analysts should present forecasts in both written and verbal form to promote understanding of and trust in the methodology employed. These reports should include careful explanation of assumptions and limitations of the methodology, techniques employed to gather base data, and steps performed in the assessment process.

An effective written report format consists of

1. The forecast figure or figures
2. Historical sales levels for years prior to the forecast
3. The methodology involved
4. Assumptions underlying the methodology
5. Limitations of the methodology
6. A description of the assessment process

This format provides a sequence whereby executive readers see at first glance the information that is probably of prime interest, namely, the forecast. The executives can examine the pattern of past sales in order to compare these with the estimated future level. Following this, they can pursue the description of the methodology, assumptions, limitations, and assessment, should they have unanswered questions. This format enables the executives to pursue details of the forecast to the extent desired without incurring undue reading time resulting from inability to locate pertinent materials without first reading unwanted details.

Generally, experience has indicated that certain procedures are useful in ensuring that the forecast is used:[6]

1. Frequent interaction between analysts and executives
2. Harmonious relations between analysts and executives
3. Effective communication between executives and analysts
4. Mutual trust among executives and analysts
5. Top management commitment to the forecasting function

In order to improve company utilization of forecasts, steps should be taken to ensure that these procedures are followed.

Follow-up

An important forecasting function is the follow-up. Here, the analysts maintain a continuous monitoring of sales in comparison to forecast figures. Differences between the two suggest the need for re-examination of forecast methods and assumptions. This allows the analysts to sense the need for changes in methods and to act accordingly. Effective follow-up is a prerequisite to accurate forecasting in today's changing world, where methods that were once reliable are no longer so. Companies such as Shell Oil, International Harvester, and the American Tobacco Company have recently experienced profound changes in their environments, for instance; as a consequence, they cannot safely depend upon forecasting methods that were used in the past.

Other Uses

The uses of forecasts were outlined in Chapter 1, so only a brief treatment is presented here. Long-run forecasts are used as an aid in decisions regarding long-run financing and in developing capital-expenditure budgets. Annual forecasts are employed for a variety of short-run planning and control activities.

A possible use of the sales forecast is for allocations of resources according to expected sales. Marketing and sales managers base sales quotas for various products, sales districts, types of retailers, and salespeople on sales forecasts. This assumes, of course, that the sales forecast has been subdivided in a manner permitting these allocations. Factors other than the forecast, such as the degree of competition, geographic

6. Ibid.

proximity of customers, and annual volume of purchases from various customers, are used in preparing quotas, but the sales forecast is still the basic determinant.

In the case of determining quotas of salespeople, a common procedure is to allocate the sales forecast to the various sales territories. The basis of allocation may be last year's sales. Thus, a salesperson who generated 1% of the firm's sales last year is expected to produce 1% of the sales forecast for next year. A more refined process involves separate forecasts for each territory, based on territorial trend analyses, estimates of salespeople, or surveys. Thus, in the foregoing case, trend analysis may indicate that the percent of company sales generated by the salesperson is declining, and that person can be expected to contribute only ½% of next year's sales.

A manufacturer of electronic equipment for industrial use subdivides expected sales by territory in the following manner. First, the percent of total sales generated by each salesperson is projected to the forecast year. This percentage, when multiplied by forecast total sales, yields a basic forecast for the territory. This figure is reviewed by the salesperson involved, the district sales manager, and the sales manager. Written reports of these reviews are forwarded to the analyst. The latter evaluates their worth and adjusts expected territorial sales accordingly. Executives of the firm report that the process has yielded reliable estimates in past periods.

Sales allocations by territory are useful in assigning other resources to these territories. Retail chains such as Sears, Roebuck, and Company, for instance, allocate retail units to areas with expanding sales. Manufacturers devote more advertising, promotion, and distribution funds to areas that are estimated to grow in the future. In sum, allocation of the sales forecast helps executives develop well-conceived allocation plans and tactics.

The annual sales forecast can also be used to adjust the level of operations for the coming year. If the forecast is for a decline in sales, management may decide to begin plans to reduce the future scale of operations as did the Chrysler Corporation in the late 1970s and early 1980s. This may include personnel layoffs, plant shutdowns, and reduced expenditures for categories like inventory and supplies. If an increase in sales is expected, expansion plans should be developed. The role of the forecast is to point out future sales changes in advance of their occurrence so that management may anticipate them.

The sales forecast is useful to the advertising department. This department is responsible for developing an advertising program for the coming year. Expected decreases in sales may require fewer expenditures for advertising. Or company policy may dictate increases in advertising expenditures under these conditions to prevent sales declines.

Brand managers employ the sales forecast as an index of which products have a promising future and which do not. Those products and brands that are expected to experience severely declining sales may be relegated to the over-the-hill category and de-emphasized in future promotion and distribution plans. Promising products and brands may be allocated increased volumes of time and funds so that their promise to the company can be fulfilled.

The financial executives of the firm can employ the sales forecast to develop annual financial plans. The sales forecast is the springboard for estimating the cash flow position of the concern. Cash flow, in turn, indicates when funds should be acquired, as through borrowing, and the extent of these needs.

Production personnel employ the sales forecast as a means of generating the production schedule. Forecasts of sales by month, in conjunction with company inventory policies, allow management to determine optimal production schedules. Sales forecasts used to determine the production schedule may have to be revised from time to time throughout the year, when experience indicates that prior forecasts may be invalid. The production schedule is useful for determining seasonal needs for parts, raw materials, and personnel.

Sales forecast data are used in producing the various budgets for the firm. The particular nature of these varies from one company to another, but basically they indicate the amounts of revenue that will be forthcoming to various divisions or departments. In addition, the budgets contain estimates of expenses for various functions undertaken by the concern.

SUMMARY

This chapter has been concerned with the assessment and implementation of sales forecasts, the importance of which is likely to be underestimated by beginning analysts. Assessment involves an examination of the reasonableness of the forecast level and the validity of the methods used to derive it. Implementation refers to the process of ensuring that management effectively uses the forecast.

A useful forecast method should have the following characteristics:

1. Data validity: are the data accurate?
2. Forecasting method validity: is the method realistic?
3. Lack of substance errors: is the proper variable examined?
4. Causal validity: do independent variables studied exert a causal influence on sales?
5. Predictive ability: can the forecast method accurately predict future sales?
6. Flexibility: can the method used be updated as changes in the firm's environment transpire?
7. Reliability: does the method produce the same results over more than one application?

A forecast, before it is implemented, should be assessed for its reasonableness. Various tests of reasonableness are possible. These include:

1. Comparison of the forecast figure with historical sales: do the two differ considerably?
2. Consideration of factors that might alter the forecast level, such as the marketing plans of the company.
3. Employment of alternate methods as checks on the forecast: do other forecasting techniques produce similar output figures?
4. Examination of the methodology validity.

An effective assessment process often requires a combination of two or more of these tests.

After assessment, the forecast is implemented by transmittal to the proper executives for transformation into budgets and planning tools. Implementation also requires convincing executives that the forecast is likely to be accurate and that they should act upon it. There are a number of procedures that are useful in ensuring that the forecast is used. The forecaster should be able to present the forecast in a manner that enhances its acceptance and to engage in follow-up activities that increase its chances of being acted upon. As a prerequisite to these activities, the analyst should be well informed about the uses of the forecast within the firm, including allocating resources, setting sales quotas, adjusting the level of production, setting advertising budgets, deciding which brands and products are most likely to be profitable, generating cash flow plans, and producing budgets. Further, implementation includes the follow-up, which consists of continuous monitoring of sales in comparison to forecast figures.

DISCUSSION QUESTIONS

1. Past sales of Barlow's, Ltd., a producer of briar pipes, are as follows:

Year	Sales (in Thousands of Dollars)
1973	11,140
1974	12,160
1975	13,940
1976	12,050
1977	11,300
1978	10,500
1979	13,400
1980	13,500
1981	14,300
1982	15,900

The Barlow's analyst uses linear regression against time to produce annual and five-year sales forecasts. The forecast for 1983, for instance, is $14,781,000, and for 1984 is $15,138,000. Evaluate this method. Can you propose effective means of assessment? Should other methods be used in conjunction with or to replace this method?

2. The analyst for the Abex Systems Corporation, a producer of microwave ovens, forecasts annual sales of ovens to consumers through a survey of buyer intentions. This involves telephone surveys of a nationally stratified sample of 2,000 women each year. Members of the sample are asked the following questions:

a. Do you currently own a microwave oven?
b. If yes, do you plan to replace it within the next year?
c. If no, do you plan to purchase one during the next year?
d. If you plan to purchase one, what brand will you choose?

The results of the survey are extrapolated to the population of potential buyers, and a forecast is constructed. Evaluate the methodology.

3. Historical sales for the Compton, Brooks, and Hale Corporation, a book publisher, are as follows:

Year	Sales (in Thousands of Dollars)
1967	26,050
1968	27,100
1969	28,300
1970	29,600
1971	30,800
1972	32,050
1973	33,200
1974	34,500
1975	35,800
1976	37,020
1977	38,600
1978	39,800
1979	41,000
1980	42,500
1981	43,900
1982	45,200

a. Which techniques are good candidates for forecasting sales? Why?
b. Compare the various techniques by cross validating them. Which would you use?

4. The Allied Chemical Corporation's sales of Midol, a pain reliever, is as follows:

Quarter	Sales (in $100 Thousands)	Quarter	Sales (in $100 Thousands)
1977: 1	68.3	1980: 1	155.0
2	68.0	2	147.0
3	60.5	3	125.0
4	59.2	4	116.8
1978: 1	98.1	1981: 1	188.0
2	94.0	2	170.0
3	84.8	3	150.0
4	77.4	4	129.0
1979: 1	125.8	1982: 1	207.0
2	121.3	2	203.5
3	104.0	3	165.6
4	96.0	4	154.8

   a. Which techniques are good candidates for forecasting sales? Why?
   b. Evaluate the various techniques by cross validating them.
5. The Southeastern Metal Products Company has used several forecasting methods. The following are historical comparisons:

Time	Actual Sales (in $000s)	Management Judgment	Decomposition	Winters's Model
1	9,085	8,600	8,950	8,800
2	10,753	12,416	11,100	10,850
3	11,892	13,510	11,953	10,605
4	11,317	11,852	11,210	11,450
5	14,801	15,106	15,050	14,600
6	10,652	11,200	10,820	10,920
7	9,814	10,100	9,600	9,975
8	14,688	15,200	15,010	14,850
9	15,500	15,900	15,350	15,450
10	15,602	16,100	15,650	16,025
11	14,326	14,800	14,400	14,875
12		15,800	15,350	15,450

     a. Combine the separate forecasts into one best estimate for period 12.

     b. Assess the combining procedure and the equation. What are the interpretations?

6. What is meant by the term *assessment*?

7. Explain each of the following, and indicate why it is of concern to the forecaster.

     a. Data validity

     b. Forecasting method validity

     c. Substance errors

     d. Causal validity

     e. Flexibility

     f. Forecasting method reliability

     g. Forecast level reasonableness

8. What steps are involved in implementing the forecast? Indicate the duties of the analyst in regard to implementation.

9. What steps should analysts take to ensure that the forecast is used?

10. Explain what is meant by the follow-up of the forecast.

11. Briefly outline the uses of the forecast by operating executives.

12. How can analysts determine the "reasonableness" of a forecasting method?

13. What is an effective format for a formal written forecast?

14. Explain how executives can utilize forecasting figures for allocating company resources.

RECOMMENDED READINGS

Ackoff, Russell L., and Maurice W. Sasieni. *Fundamentals of Operations Research.* New York: John Wiley and Sons, 1968, Chaper 1.

Adler, Lee. "Phasing Research into the Marketing Plan." *Harvard Business Review*, 38 (May–June 1960), 113–122.

Bunn, Derek W. "The Synthesis of Predictive Models in Marketing Research." *Journal of Marketing Research*, 16 (May 1979), 280–283.

Crawford, C. Merle. "Marketing Research and the New Product Failure Rate." *Journal of Marketing*, 41 (April 1977), 51–61.

Ferber, Robert, William J. Hawkes, Jr., and Manuel D. Plotkin. "How Reliable Are National Retail Sales Estimates?" *Journal of Marketing*, 40 (October 1976), 13–22.

Gandz, Jeffrey, and Thomas W. Whipple. "Making Marketing Research Accountable." *Journal of Marketing Research*, 14 (May 1977), 202–207.

Godet, M. *The Crisis in Forecasting and the Emergence of the Prospective Approach.* New York: Pergamon Press, 1979.

Gross, Charles W., and Thomas W. Knowles. "How to Cope With Realities Or Why Forecasts Go Awry." *The Journal of Business Forecasting: Methods and Systems*, 1 (Spring 1982), 6–10.

Gross, Charles W., and Robin T. Peterson. "Some Human Problems in Industrial Sales Forecasting: 'Users' versus 'Doers'—The Human Factor in Technical Dilemmas." *Industrial Marketing Management*, 7 (December 1978), 367–368.

"High Technology, Wave of the Future or a Market Flash in the Pan?" *Business Week*, November 10, 1980, pp. 86–97.

Labrecque, David P. "A Response Rate Experiment Using Mail Questionnaires." *Journal of Marketing*, 42 (October 1978), 82–83.

Mahajan, Vijay, and Manoj Agarwal. "Single Purchase Growth Models: A Review and Extension." *1976 Proceedings, American Marketing Association, Educators' Conference*. Chicago: American Marketing Association, 1977, pp. 234–239.

Moriarty, Mark, and Gerald Salaman. "Estimation and Forecast Performance of a Multivariate Time Series Model of Sales." *Journal of Marketing Research*, 17 (November 1980), 558–564.

Mosteller, Frederick, and John W. Tukey. *Data Analysis and Regression*. Reading, Mass.: Addison-Wesley Publishing Co., 1977, Chapter 14.

Myers, John G., Stephan A. Greyser, and William F. Massey. "The Effectiveness of Marketing's R&D for Marketing Management: An Assessment." *Journal of Marketing*, 43 (January 1979), 17–29.

Nerlove, M., D. M. Grether, and J. L. Carvalo. *Analysis of Time Series: A Synthesis*. New York: Academic Press, 1979, Chapter 11.

Sharma, Subhash, and Vijay Mahajan. "Early Warning Indicators of Business Failure." *Journal of Marketing*, 44 (Fall 1980), 80–89.

Pruden, Henry D. "The Kendratieff Wave." *Journal of Marketing*, 42 (April 1978), 63–70.

Woods, D. M. "Improving Estimates That Involve Uncertainty." *Harvard Business Review*, 44 (July–August 1966), 91.

CASE 10: ZURICH CHEMICAL CORPORATION

Zurich Chemical Corporation was the seventh largest worldwide producer of petroloids as of March 1982. Petroloids are substances formed from synthesizing organic hydrocarbons into families of unique materials. There are three major categories: oils; petro-rubbers; and foams, adhesives, and sealants (FAS).

Petro-oils are used as engine additives, lubricants, defoamers, water repellants, rust preventives, hydraulic oils, and so on. Zurich makes about 2,800 different petro-oils in all and holds about 12% of the world market. Generally, relatively few large customers account for the vast majority of the petroloid market. These customers are typically large producers who use petro-oils in the production of their own end products.

Zurich has a 6% worldwide penetration into the petro-rubbers market. These items are sold to molders for the manufacture of rigid and flexible rubber materials. Most of the molders are relatively small independent businesses who sell their output to a wide variety of manufacturers, usually under contract. There are a wide variety of potential applications for petro-rubbers. Therefore, Zurich works closely with end users as well as molders in developing new methods and uses.

Materials in the FAS category are sold to both consumer markets and industrial users. These materials vary in consistency from liquid to stiff paste, and can be applied by spraying, caulking, brushing, dripping, or pouring to form a seal. Zurich has a 4% worldwide market share of FAS and handles about 1,800 different items in the product line.

Nearly every basic manufacturing industry uses petroloids in one form or another, and there is widespread use by consumers. About 65% of Zurich's products are made from stock, and the rest are made to order. Products are marketed through a company sales force of 125, and there is an extensive distribution network involving 500 distributorships operating in 725 locations and employing about 4,500 salespeople.

Management of Zurich was disappointed with last year's results. Over-all sales were up 15%, as Dr. Harold Browne, the company's economic consultant, had predicted, but costs were up even more. Because man-ufacturing anticipated an overall increase of 15%, as Dr. Browne had suggested, a large increase in the production of petro-oils was scheduled. However, sales of these items actually fell by 10%, resulting in large ending inventories and excessive carrying costs. The problem was especially acute in North America.

In contrast, inventories of FAS were almost depleted during the year. Production increased at 18%, and sales increased 22%. Further, Zurich's market share of FAS fell from 6 to 4% during the year.

1. What basic mistakes is Zurich making?
2. What can be done about them?
3. What are the organizational changes that Zurich should make?

Chapter 11
Epilogue

This brief epilogue provides some qualitative opinions regarding the current and future status of forecasting in firms. Essentially, it provides perspective to the text's discussion.

FORECASTING IS AN ONGOING PROCESS

Previous chapters may have given the impression to some readers that forecasting is an activity that takes place at only periodic intervals, such as once a year, and ceases entirely between these intervals. To the contrary, both short- and long-term forecasts are continually being made, evaluated, and revised. As new products are considered or are adopted, their sales potential is assessed. Changes in the environment and internal structure of the firm are likely to be continual. Events such as price alterations by competitors, strikes by labor unions, and changes in the advertising strategy of the firm occur from time to time. Many of these phenomena are of sufficient significance to warrant alterations in existing sales forecasts. Forecasting, then, is not a one-time and static activity. It is a continuing process that merits constant attention.

The practices of the Webster Corporation, a large catalogue mail-order distributor of general merchandise, exemplifies the ongoing nature of forecasting. Each year a leading series forecast of sales for the upcoming year is compiled by the analysts. This is forwarded to the vice presidents of finance, marketing, and production for review. Normally, these three rely on staff assistants and line subordinates to suggest possible needed changes in forecast levels. Suggested changes are conveyed to the analysts who are responsible for determining their worth and, where needed, generating a revised forecast.

Another responsibility of the analysts is to compare actual with forecast sales for each quarter. When the departures between the two are significant, in their judgment, the annual forecast is revised to reflect the new circumstances. Figure 11.1 illustrates this process. The figure depicts actual sales for the first three quarters and forecast sales for each quarter in the year. Sales in the third quarter were substantially below the forecast levels. Consumer research indicates that this is the result of decline in consumer discretionary income.

Figure 11.1 Forecast and Actual Sales, Webster Corporation

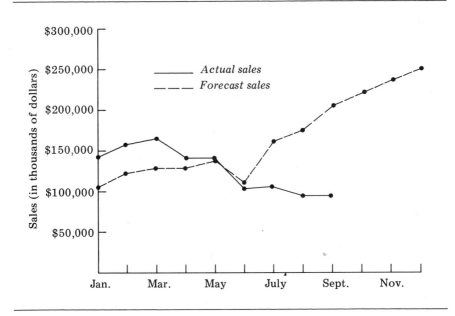

The factors outlined in the foregoing lead the analysts to revise their initial forecast for the fourth quarter to a lower level, one that is compatible with the decline in income. This comparison and subsequent change process is a vital one. If it is not conducted or if it is accomplished in a slipshod manner, forecast levels may be very much in error. In short, if forecasting is not treated as an ongoing process, its results may be most undesirable to managers.

FORECASTING IS ESSENTIAL

Chapter 1 described executives' need for forecasting. That topic is mentioned again at this point to emphasize and enlarge upon it. It is difficult and in some cases impossible for a firm to develop and implement effective plans in the absence of well-conceived sales forecasts that provide managers with the means for planning, organizing, and controlling all the resources at their disposal. In the absence of forecasts, these activities must be based on mere hunch and guesswork. The dynamic and uncertain nature of the business world dictates that sales forecasts be the springboard for virtually all major decisions made by management.

Despite the great need for forecasting, many firms do not avail themselves of the more useful techniques. This is especially true in the case of smaller enterprises. In a study conducted by the authors, it was found that numerous small business firms do not take advantage of most of the more refined sales forecasting techniques available.

The study involved telephone interviews with managers and owners of selected small business firms involved in the manufacturing, wholesaling, retailing, and service industries. It revealed that the respondent firms tended to rely on simple and often nonscientific sales forecasting methods. These included intuition and subjective judgment, subjective trend estimates, and perusal of estimates of national and regional economic activities reported in business and news magazines and newsletter services. The respondents were not aware of the existence or nature of the various statistical and survey techniques available. Some managers and owners of small firms could benefit tremendously by using more sophisticated techniques.

FORECASTING IN THE FUTURE

Any discipline or managerial function can be expected to change over time, and forecasting is no exception. Alterations in the methodology and uses of forecasting can be expected to increase and will take the form of more sophisticated techniques and their increased employment by management.

More Sophisticated Techniques

The passage of time should witness advances in the quality of forecasting technology. Among the forces contributing to the elevation of the art are new developments in the social sciences, mathematics, research techniques, and data processing. Progress to date has been considerable, as witnessed by analysts who use innovations in simulation, brand-share models, and survey techniques.

A survey of the literature suggests that sensitivity analysis—a refined feature of model building—is being widely adopted by analysts today. This technique was not frequently employed a decade ago. Sensitivity analysis involves manipulating a mathematical model and observing the effect on the dependent variable. If the effect is small, analysts need not concern themselves with attempting to develop more precise estimates of the magnitude of that variable. If the effect is substantial, attempts to improve preciseness may be in order.

A very simplified example of sensitivity analysis can be performed through manipulation of a simple model.

$$Y = 20A + 7.2B + 0.10C$$

where Y = the annual sales forecast
         A = advertising expenditures by the firm
         B = personal selling expenditures of the firm
         C = research and developing expenditures of the firm

Over the last fiscal year, a firm spent $11,500,000 on advertising, $12,600,000 on personal selling, and $650,000 on research and development. This information, when combined with that in the function, indicates that advertising expenditures account for much of the variation in sales. Next in order of importance are personal selling and research and development expenditures. The latter is relatively insignificant in helping forecast future sales; the focus of the analyst should be on A and B.

Increasing use of sensitivity analysis is only one indicator of advance in methodology. Virtually every phase of the forecasting process can be expected to become more sophisticated in upcoming years.

Increased Use of Forecasting by Management

It is likely that managements of the future will use forecasting to a larger extent than is the case now. Part of the impetus for this development will evolve from increasing educational levels of executives. Larger numbers of managers have college degrees, many of them in business administration. These better educated managers are likely to give more importance to forecasting as a planning and control tool than did their predecessors. The modern manager is more likely to have the training required to understand the methodology and even to construct forecast models.

The increased pace of change is a second force that will contribute to increased employment of forecasting. More and more products are displaying shorter life cycles, and industry sales change abruptly, producing rapid and significant fluctuations in company sales. These forces of change make it necessary for managers to be in possession of methods that will signal what is expected to take place in the future. No longer are managers able to sit back and assume that their sales will more or less automatically grow at a pace of 5% annually. They must continually monitor sales levels and be prepared to respond to change.

In the future, cost pressures on management are expected to be a continuing reality. These take the form of increments in wages, power rates, interest rates, and costs of raw materials, supplies, parts, and equipment. These cost advances put pressures on management to produce effective plans and controls. In turn, as this text has repeatedly documented, plans and controls are dependent on the sales forecast.

Increases in the intensity of competition can be expected to generate increments in forecasting use. Rivalry among both foreign and domestic firms is increasing, especially in industries like packaged foods, automobiles, and computers. As competition steps up, managers are forced to use effective forecasting processes to compete with rivals who are enhancing their own forecasting abilities.

Advancing inability to predict the future behavior of the consumer through simplistic methods that were effective in the past tends to induce further use and sophistication in sales forecasting. Increasing consumer education and discretionary income tend to render consumers less brand-loyal and more inclined to attempt new forms of behavior, including purchase and use of previously unknown products. Consumers are tending to become more fickle and more difficult to predict, despite considerable advances in the quality of consumer behavior research and theory.

Finally, the increasing sophistication of methods should help produce more use of forecasting. As methodology improves and becomes more accurate and precise, managers can be expected to rely on forecasting more than they did in the past. Better tools are likely to yield wider use.

Index